CROWN INSIDERS' GUIDE™ TO NEW YORK CITY & STATE

Also in the series:

CROWN INSIDERS' GUIDE™ TO NEW YORK CITY & STATE

Patricia and Lester Brooks

Crown Publishers, Inc.
New York

Copyright © 1988 by Crown Publishers, Inc.

Published by Crown Publishers, Inc., 225 Park Avenue South, New York, New York 10003 and represented in Canada by the Canadian MANDA Group.

CROWN and CROWN INSIDERS' GUIDE are trademarks of Crown Publishers, Inc.

Manufactured in the United States of America

Library of Congress Cataloging in Publication Data

Brooks, Patricia
    Crown insiders' guide to New York City and State
    Patricia and Lester Brooks
        p.   cm.
    Includes index.
    1. New York (State)—Description and travel—1981—Guidebooks. I. Brooks, Lester. II. Title. III. Title: Insiders' guide to New York City and State.
F117. 3. B76   1988
917. 47'0443—dc19   87–31858
ISBN 0-517-56861-6

10 9 8 7 6 5 4 3 2 1

First Edition

CONTENTS

NEW YORK INSIDE OUT

NEW YORK STATE'S REGIONS

LIST OF MAPS

EDITORS' NOTE

New York State is a lot more than the Big Apple, it's the Big Surprise! Not everyone in Gotham or outside the state knows of the magnificence of the Adirondacks, the beauty of the Catskills, the glories of the Hudson Valley, or the awesome wonder of the Thousand Islands. For too long, the utter gorgeousness of the state has been eclipsed by the glitter of the city.

"I Love New York" was, and is, a wildly popular slogan, copied by tourist promoters around the world. But though it was a state slogan, would-be visitors everywhere confused it with the Big Apple's appeal. And why not? City and state bear the same name, let them bear the same tourist fate. Still, only a fraction of visitors to the city ever explore beyond its boundaries. They are missing a lot.

Some say New York City isn't "typical" of America (a few want to write it out of the country altogether). They are wrong, for what would the United States be without the energy, determination, glitter, and brass that the Big Apple represents? But for those who want something other than these high-speed attributes, a look at the rest of New York State will be rewarding.

In upstate New York, you'll find the rural ambience of the Midwest, the peaceful towns of New England, some wonders as impressive as the Far West (Niagara Falls, for one), and some things bigger than they have in Texas (buildings in New York City for one example, Adirondack State Park for another . . . it's bigger even than Wyoming's Yellowstone National Park!). On Long Island, you'll find fishing villages reminiscent of Maine, electronics firms evocative of California's Silicon Valley, and the best beaches in America.

New York State, in fact, is much like mainstream America, with all its virtues and faults. The closer you get to The City, though, the more you'll notice differences—differences in attitude, scale, and perceptions. You have to shift into high gear to enjoy the Big Apple.

This doesn't mean you have to become hyperactive, just that you have to widen the lens of your mind a bit more, the better to take everything in. If you can retain your inner peace while the city spins and whirls around you, so much the better, but do be alert. Watch for the wonderfully wacky life-styles paraded on the city streets, but don't stare . . . that's not polite, even here. Keep your ears open for all the sounds, of the street vendors and foreign-language babble as well as the gut-wrenching fire engine klaxons. And don't forget to look up, for the details of tall buildings and church spires, and behind, for an angle you might otherwise have missed.

The old horror stories about New York City's indifference to those in trouble may seem true at first, as you watch the poor street people, many of them evicted from mental homes, wander and importune. Even worse will be the occasional toppled drunk, ignored by those with noses keen enough to tell what ails the fallen figure. But if you have ever fainted in a public place, or seen someone else stricken or falter, and noted the immediate response of several persons eager to help, you'll feel much better about the city and your fellow human beings.

New York, state and city, make up a pretty big microcosm of America. You won't find a better cross section of the country anywhere, so I recommend both as places to have a good time, learn a little (or a lot, it's up to you), and savor some thrills you'll never forget.

THE CROWN INSIDERS' GUIDE™ SERIES

Knowing New York State inside out isn't enough, by itself, to make a good travel guide. A good writer has to get inside his subject, yet keep the perspective right. The best authors learn to think like the people they portray. At the same time, they can't be chameleons, all things to all readers. In this series the authors try to show the reader what each place looks like from the viewpoint of a trained observer, someone who knows the ground thoroughly but isn't blinded by tradition, connections, or misplaced loyalties. Our Insiders, in short, have to be Outsiders for the very reason that natives of the place have too many obligations, too much cultural baggage of their own, too little knowledge of what readers want.

You'll learn from a Crown Insiders' guide the perils and pitfalls of travel, items that most travel books ignore. We'll make it a point to highlight the good things too, calling attention to special finds, such as the best egg cream in New York City, where you can get free information, make reservations, buy guidebooks, or place phone calls.

THE AUTHORS

The Crown Insiders' guide authors have all lived in the areas they write about. The coauthors of this book on New York State, Patricia and Lester Brooks, are veteran travel writers who now live in Connecticut, but who formerly lived in New York for several years. They spend more than one-third of each year traveling and reporting on various destinations (including New York) for *Bon Appétit, Family Circle, Harper's Bazaar, House Beautiful, McCall's, Modern Bride,* the *New York Times, Travel & Leisure, Travel-Holiday, Vogue,* and many other publications. Between them, they are the authors of 21 books, including *The Crown Insiders' Guide™ to Britain.* In their travels, they combine their interests in food and wine, Pat as restaurant and food critic for the Connecticut section of the *New York Times,* Les as a beverage writer and member of the Sommelier Society of America.

The authors wish to thank the following friends and associates—New York explorers, residents, and enthusiasts, all—for their invaluable help, counsel, and encouragement:

Jane Abrams, Teddy Abueva, Marguerite Allen, Maureen and Dick Baxter, Jackie Berg, Sue Buyer, Barbara Caren, Amanda Cushman, Pat Estess, Trudy Goldberg, Mark Gompertz, Tommy Hardy, Don Hutter, Ruth Layton, Coleman Lollar, Alice Lowenthal, Cornelia and Mark McCain, Nancy Mitchell, Carmela Peters, Stephen A. Pisni, Marian Reiner, Morris Simoncelli, and Nancy Walworth, among scores of others who contributed advice, suggestions, and ideas.

Thanks also to Stephen Apesos and various members of the New York State Commerce Department's Division of Tourism for their help, patience, and responsiveness in dealing with our endless barrage of questions.

THE INSIDERS' RATING SYSTEM

The authors and the editors jointly award 1, 2, 3, 4, or 5 crowns to hotels, restaurants, and such places as museums, monuments, churches, landmark buildings, and other sights or sites that seem important to them. Here is our interpretation of the awards:

Hotels and Restaurants

♛♛♛♛♛ Best in the state
♛♛♛♛ Outstanding
♛♛♛ Excellent
♛♛ Very Good
♛ Recommended

Sights and Sites

♛♛♛♛♛ Once-in-a-lifetime
♛♛♛♛ A "must see"
♛♛♛ Worth a considerable detour
♛♛ Important
♛ Interesting

BECOME AN INSIDER

Nobody's perfect, and though our Insiders have tried to include everything worthwhile, omit the tourist traps, and maintain up-to-date prices and other information, the ever-changing aspects of travel ensure that something in this book will change between the time we wrote about it and the time you read or visit. Let us know, by writing to the authors and/or the editor at Crown Insiders' Guides, Crown Publishers, Inc., 225 Park Avenue South, New York, New York 10003. We'll be grateful for corrections, suggestions for new listings, or any comments you care to make.

NEW YORK STATE

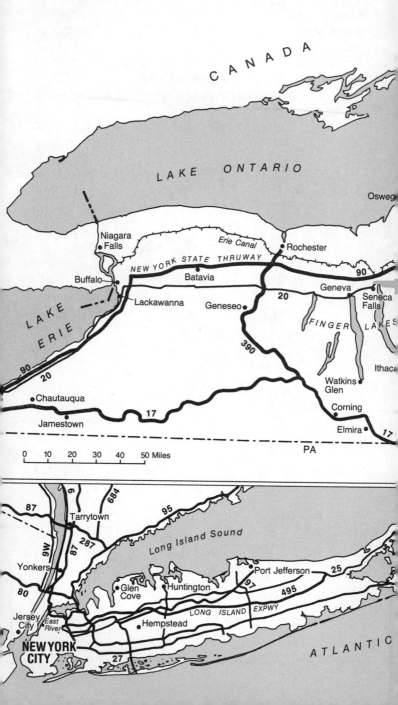

CANADA

LAKE ONTARIO

Osweg

Niagara
Falls

Erie Canal

Rochester

NEW YORK STATE THRUWAY

90

Buffalo

Batavia

Geneva

LAKE

Lackawanna

Geneseo

20

Seneca
Falls

ERIE

FINGER LAKES

390

90

20

Watkins
Glen

Ithaca

Chautauqua

17

Corning

Jamestown

390

Elmira

17

0 10 20 30 40 50 Miles

PA

87

6

684

95

Tarrytown

9W

87 287

Long Island Sound

Yonkers

Port Jefferson

25

80

Glen
Cove

Huntington

97

495

Jersey
City

East
River

Hempstead

LONG ISLAND EXPWY

NEW YORK
CITY

27

ATLANTIC

BEFORE YOU GO

WHY YOU SHOULD VISIT NEW YORK STATE NOW

Whether you're planning your first or your twenty-first trip to New York, you can be sure of one thing: it won't be the same. It never is.

It won't be the same as it was on your last trip, or as it will be on your next. If ever there was a place where *change* is inexorable and quick, New York is it!

In New York City, today's hit musical will be superseded tomorrow; the hottest restaurant in town will be topped by another—or a "new taste sensation" or fad food; a Picasso retrospective will be upstaged by a new exhibition of Minimalists; the "in" disco today will be passé by Christmas. Last month's new young discovery (in fashion, art, music, whatever) is replaced by a newer one today. The only question is "Who will it be tomorrow?" Andy Warhol had it right: In the future, "everyone will be famous for fifteen minutes." In New York, a quarter of an hour is a long time.

That's what makes New York such an exciting place to visit. A rundown area of ten years ago becomes rejuvenated into a new center for arts and shopping. New buildings continue to sprout, new plays open, new shops and stores proliferate, new talents are discovered. And for the visitor there's the thrill and adventure of making these and other discoveries every day and minute of your stay. New York's dynamic is palpable. It's where the world comes to put forth its best—and you're part of the audience that can enjoy it.

You don't have to go to England to see the latest London hit plays; they're already on Broadway. You don't need to fly to Paris for the latest fashions and French couturier labels; they're all along Fifth Avenue in their own shops. The latest haircut, the newest (and oldest) books, the latest art—name it, it's in New York.

In the more spacious areas of the state, change may be less frenetic, but it's happening all the same. Whether it's converting the land from crops to vineyards (as in the Finger Lakes) or resorts (the Catskills), building new museums, renovating decayed factories into fashionable shopping malls (as in Rochester), or reclaiming historic waterfronts (like Buffalo's) and landmark buildings (Schenectady's Proctor Theater), the New York dynamic is constantly at work.

In a state where the land and waters predominate, the changes are those of the seasons—and those too, all four of them, are compelling enough for your imminent enjoyment. If you visited the Hudson Valley one spring, come in the fall this time around. You'll find its changes—like those in the Adirondacks and the Cooperstown area, or the beautiful gardens of Old Westbury, Long Island—as showy and spontaneous as nature itself.

At the same time, New York offers visitors a reassuring renewal of links with the past. You can visit the places where history was made—along the Hudson, Fort Ticonderoga, Albany, and Saratoga—and see the houses of past presidents (Theodore and Franklin Roosevelt, Martin Van Buren, Millard Fillmore). As one of the original thirteen states, New York has history and a panoply of past events to rival any of the others. These will remain.

Nowhere else do the revered old and the funky new exist in such creative harmony.

No question about it, New York challenges each visitor. The range of sensations is so vast that no one visits without experiencing something singular, innovative, unprecedented. No wonder a visit to New York is memorable.

If you're considering costs, remember that you may save by coming to New York now. Yes, it can be expensive (we have some tips to cut your costs), but the trend of costs is inevitably upward: It won't get any cheaper next year, so there's no reason to wait.

Come see it now, before it changes so that you wouldn't recognize it! Then come again. And again.

New York gets to be a habit. And think of it: all the things that make New York so special—its blend of old and new, luxurious and free, foreign and familiar—are accessible. You don't have to learn the language, you can read the street signs and speak the tongue. And, oh yes, the natives are friendly.

HISTORY IN A HURRY

Key Events in New York's Past

1524	Giovanni Verrazano explores the New York bay and coast.
1609	Henry Hudson explores coast, sails up Hudson River to Albany area.
1613–14	Adriaen Block explores Long Island Sound, maps Manhattan.
1625–26	First permanent settlement in lower Manhattan. Dutch buy island from Indians for $24 worth of beads, baubles, and blankets.
1636	Dutch buy Brooklyn land from Indians.
1639	Jonas Bronck buys part of Bronx from Indians.
1643	First of intermittent Indian uprisings.
1647	Peter Stuyvesant is governor.
1664	Dutch surrender Nieuw Amsterdam to the British, who rename it New York.
1673	Dutch recapture New York without a fight, rename it New Orange.
1674	Westminster Treaty returns New York to British.
1693	First bridge across Harlem River joins Manhattan to Bronx.
1713	First Staten Island ferry.
1735	John Peter Zenger acquitted of libel, establishing freedom of the press.
1754	King's College (now Columbia University) founded.
1763	French-Indian War ends, giving British control of North America.
1776	Colonies declare their independence. British win Battle of Long Island, occupy Brooklyn and Manhattan.
1777	British General Burgoyne surrenders after Battle of Saratoga, and France decides to support Americans.
1783	Revolutionary War ends, Britain recognizes United States, capital is established in New York City.

1789	Constitution ratified, Washington inaugurated at Federal Hall, New York.
1790	Capital is moved to Philadelphia.
1792	Embryonic New York Stock Exchange formed.
1797	Albany named state capital. Manhattan Company formed to bring water to New York City.
1801	Brooklyn Navy Yard established.
1807	Robert Fulton's steamboat *Clermont* paddles up Hudson.
1812–14	War with Britain.
1820	New York City population reaches 123,700, making it the nation's largest city.
1825	Erie Canal gives access to American Midwest through Great Lakes.
1837	Financial panic. Martin Van Buren becomes first U.S. President from New York State.
1846	Irish flee potato famine, emigrate to New York.
1848	First women's rights convention, Seneca Falls. Germans flee revolutions in central Europe, arrive in New York.
1851	*New York Daily Times* first published.
1854	Young Men's Christian Association has its first meeting, Buffalo.
1857	Financial panic.
1861–65	Civil War.
1861	Vassar College, Poughkeepsie, chartered—first college for women in U.S.
1863	Draft riots paralyze New York City for three days.
1870–83	Brooklyn Bridge built by J. A. Roebling. Equitable Life building erected—first building with passenger elevators.
1871	Grand Central railroad depot inaugurated. Tammany Hall Boss Tweed arrested.
1880	Metropolitan Museum of Art opens in Central Park.
1882	Thomas Edison's electric plant opens.
1883	Brooklyn Bridge and Metropolitan Opera open.
1884	Buffalo's Grover Cleveland elected President (reelected 1892).
1886	Statue of Liberty opens to the public.
1890	First Madison Square Garden opens.
1891	Carnegie Hall inaugurated (Tchaikovsky conducting); New York Botanical Garden opens.
1898	Boroughs of New York join in single municipal government, with city population of 3.4 million.
1904	IRT subway begins operation.
1908	Subway links Brooklyn and Manhattan; Hudson Tube from Manhattan to New Jersey. "Ashcan School" art exhibit.
1909	Pennsylvania Railroad completes Penn Station.

1910	National Association for the Advancement of Colored People established in New York City.
1911	Triangle Shirtwaist Company fire; 145 die. National Urban League established in New York City.
1912	Movies are made at Biograph studios, 14th Street, Manhattan: Lillian Gish, Mary Pickford star in D. W. Griffith productions.
1913	Present Grand Central Terminal opens. Armory Show of avant-garde art. Flatiron Building is New York's first "skyscraper." Woolworth Building completed.
1917–18	U.S. enters World War I.
1921	Port of New York Authority formed by New York and New Jersey.
1926	Bank clerk Arthur Schomburg sells collection to New York Public Library, first archive of black historical books, documents.
1927	New York City parade celebrates Lindbergh's transatlantic flight. First "talkie," Al Jolson in *The Jazz Singer*, shown in New York City. Holland Tunnel links New Jersey and New York City.
1928	Franklin D. Roosevelt elected governor of New York (reelected, 1930); former New York governor Al Smith defeated in presidential election.
1929	Stock market "Lays an Egg," says *Variety*. Bank closings, Great Depression follow market crash. Museum of Modern Art opens; Chrysler Building completed.
1930	"Hooverville" shantytown in Central Park.
1931	Empire State Building (102 stories) completed. Municipal airport opens. Waldorf-Astoria Hotel inaugurated. George Washington Bridge links New Jersey and Manhattan.
1933	Franklin D. Roosevelt inaugurated as President. Fiorello La Guardia elected mayor of New York City.
1937	Joe Louis wins heavyweight boxing title.
1938	First jazz concert at Carnegie Hall; Benny Goodman conducts.
1939	New York World's Fair. La Guardia Airport opens. Rockefeller Center's initial phase completed. RCA Building is heart of American radio broadcasting.
1940	Queens-Midtown tunnel links Manhattan and Queens.
1941–45	World War II.
1942	New York International Airport (now John F. Kennedy Airport) opens.

1946	United Nations headquarters established in New York.
1952	Lever House, first glass-walled skyscraper, completed.
1956	Brooklyn's Ebbets Field converted to housing; Dodgers move to Los Angeles.
1959	Frank Lloyd Wright–designed Guggenheim Museum opens.
1962	Lincoln Center's first building, Philharmonic Hall, opens.
1964	Verrazano Bridge links Staten Island to Brooklyn; New York World's Fair 1964–65; race riots in Brooklyn and Harlem.
1965	Entire Northeast blacked out in power failure (Nov. 9–10).
1966	Marcel Breuer's Whitney Museum completed.
1969	New York Mets win their first World Series.
1973	World Trade Center towers completed.
1975	New York City escapes bankruptcy through austerity program and federal bailout.
1976	"Tall Ships" sail up Hudson in Bicentennial celebration.
1977	New York City power blackout for full day (July 13)
1980	Census shows whites represent 51.9 percent of New York City population, blacks and Hispanics 48.1 percent. Total population of 7,071,639 New Yorkers, by borough: Brooklyn, 2,230,936; Queens, 1,891,325; Manhattan, 1,428,285; Bronx, 1,168,972; Staten Island, 352,121.
1981	New York City now solvent.
1986	Rededication of Statue of Liberty on her one hundredth anniversary.
1986–87	New York Mets and New York Giants win World Series and Super Bowl, respectively.

HOW MUCH WILL IT COST?

As the saying goes, "one person's luxury is another's necessity." That makes it difficult to predict accurately what expenses might be from one individual to another. Yet there are some valid observations to be made.

1. New York City can be extremely expensive. As the locals like to joke, "When you come to visit, bring money." Organizations that measure business travel costs internationally rank New York City among the most expensive cities in the world. However, you don't need an expense account to have an enjoyable visit.

Food and lodging are the high-ticket items, and you can economize on both of these (especially food) by wise choices from our restaurant and hotel lists (even without resorting to fast-food outlets, group tour hotels, and bed-and-breakfast places), and by taking advantage of hotel discounts and special offers.

2. Cities, towns, and most rural areas outside the Big Apple are extremely reasonable in their prices, and in many instances are real bargains. You receive exceptional value for your money.

3. How to economize: Pay careful attention to package deals, off-season and weekend rates, discounts for association members or senior citizens, savings on an extra bed in a room; book a room that has cooking facilities; eat your major meal at lunchtime (when prices are lower) and select the *prix fixe* meal at a restaurant. These are easy, sure-fire (and painless) ways to save.

Here are some specific figures, taken from the hotels and restaurants we list, to help you estimate your possible costs per person, per day:

	Deluxe	*Moderate*	*Inexpensive*
Hotel			
(half of double room			
Price			
New York City	$115–163	$70–93	$39–43
New York State	58–66	38–50	30–37
Restaurant			
(lunch and dinner w/o drinks)			
New York City	$47–80	$28–40	$10–24
New York State	29–36	20–27	10–19
DAILY TOTALS PER PERSON			
New York City	$162–243	$98–133	$49–67
New York State	87–102	$58–77	40–56

In your reckoning, don't lose sight of the largesse that New York spreads before you. In addition to the delights of nature and of experiencing unforgettable cityscapes and the ever-exotic human parade, the menu of free concerts, theatricals, impromptu performances, and festivals is enormous. The parks, atriums, churches, libraries, commercial art galleries, shops, boutiques, and store displays are free. (Most museums, however, *request* a "suggested" contribution, which one usually feels compelled to "donate.") By carefully scanning the listings of events, concerts, and exhibitions in the newspapers and magazines, you can indulge that passion for Mozart, mums, or Matisse at minimal cost.

With the help of this book, you can enjoy a New York trip that will give you an emotional high, for a total outlay that may be surprisingly low.

THE BEST TIME TO GO

New York City

The records claim that New York City is hottest in August and coldest in January, and has the most rain in August, November, and March (in that order).

However, New York weather can be full of surprises. You may find yourself sweltering in June or September, chilled to the bone in December and February, and deluged in July or December as well. Remember that humidity makes the temperature feel hotter or colder, as the case may be. There can be an icy "wind tunnel effect" when breezes whip down the high-rise canyons of the city—even in midsummer.

Generally, the best, most temperate weather can be expected in April and May and September through November. And you can figure that, on average, one out of every three days will have some precipitation. (New York City has more rain than London!)

But always expect the unexpected, weather-wise. In summer, the buildings that have soaked up heat all day radiate it back all night. Almost every place is air-conditioned (some overdo it, so a light wrap, jacket, or sweater is advisable), even buses and some subways and taxis. In winter, the problem is just the opposite: stores, theaters, restaurants, hotels, and apartments are generally overheated and as dry as the Sahara.

In planning a visit, it's best not to worry about the

weather; just be prepared for it to change.

The time to visit depends on what you want to do. Cultural events go on year-round. But for theater premieres, special exhibition openings at museums, and opera and ballet, fall, winter, and spring bring an endless cascade of events.

INSIDERS' TIPS

Some other festival days when it's fun to be in New York:

- Chinese New Year, Chinatown, end of January or early February. Gala banquets at Chinatown restaurants (there are firecrackers in the streets, however, and the noise is scary).

- Easter Day Parade, Fifth Avenue from 49th to 59th streets, 11:00 A.M. Everybody, from the Mayor down and up, takes a walk.

- Ninth Avenue International Food Festival, Ninth Avenue between 37th and 57th streets, about May 20. Blocks of international food stands, plus street music, entertainment, ethnic baubles and buyables.

- TAMA Fair, Third Avenue between 14th and 34th streets, first Sunday after Labor Day. Open-air street booths of collectibles, antiques, and arts and crafts.

- Feast of San Gennaro, Mulberry Street, Little Italy, second week of September. Wall-to-wall people enjoying pizzas, sausages, other street foods, dancing, entertainment, music, parades, and a religious procession. This is the granddaddy of the outdoor festivals.

- New York City Marathon, Staten Island to Central Park, November. A major sports event, both for those who run and for those who only stand and wait and watch and cheer the runners on.

- Macy's Thanksgiving Day Parade, down Central Park West and Broadway from 81st to 34th streets, 12 noon, Thanksgiving Day. A kiddies' delight, with imaginative floats, gigantic Disney characters. (For an unusual treat, visit the "great blowup" the night before, when the floats are inflated next to the American Museum of Natural History, Central Park West at 79th Street.)

The Christmas season is wonderful in Manhattan. Store-window displays positively sparkle. Twinkling holiday lights and decorated trees are everywhere. Magic is truly in the air. You feel it especially at Rockefeller Center, standing beneath the giant Christmas tree in the Plaza.

PERILS & PITFALLS

St. Patrick's Day Parade, Fifth Avenue from 44th to 86th streets, 12 noon, March 17. This used to be fun, with the green stripe down the middle of Fifth Avenue, and everybody Irish for the day, especially in bars named O'Neil's or McSorley's. But it has degenerated into an excuse for underaged kids (many from the suburbs) to get drunk, obstreperous, and sick.

Yet summer can also be a delightful time to visit. That's when the natives depart on holiday, and the city, especially on weekends, seems, if not deserted, at least quieter. Too, there are loads of outdoor happenings: Summerstage at the Central Park Bandshell, Metropolitan Opera in the Parks, "Lincoln Center Out Of Doors," street fairs, the Washington Square Outdoor Art Show, and many more. The most celebratory happening of all is the Harbor Festival on July 4 in lower Manhattan, when the tall ships sail up the harbor and almost everybody is in a euphoric holiday spirit. It's the city at its friendliest and most relaxed.

New York State

Outside New York City, the weather tends to be cooler, no matter what the season. *The* favorite season for travel is fall, when the days are sunny and crisp, and the foliage throughout the state is, to put it mildly, glorious.

Spring along the Hudson (and elsewhere) is almost as beautiful as fall (and there's less traffic), as the dogwood, fruit trees, and lilacs burst into bloom. In fact, spring and summer almost everywhere in the state are welcoming times, both in weather and in things to do.

INSIDERS' TIPS

New Yorkers like foliage-viewing, too. To avoid the miles-long caravans of slow-moving cars on mountain roads, plan your foliage-viewing jaunt for midweek. It'll be easier to get inn and restaurant reservations then, too.

If you're an outdoor sports buff, winter also has its charms, especially in the ski areas of the Catskills, Buffalo-Rochester, and the North Country. The snow-glazed landscape is incredibly beautiful. Indoor sports find plenty to do in museum-hopping shopping, and antique-hunting.

PERILS & PITFALLS

Be forewarned, though, that in winter many historic houses throughout the state (except New York City) have shortened, limited schedules. Some are closed altogether. That's why we've included phone numbers in our listings. Always check ahead.

HOW TO GO

In planning a trip to New York City and/or State, it's best to pinpoint what you most want to do and the actual time you have in which to do it. Both city and state are so vast, with so many things to see, do, and explore, you need to establish your priorities clearly.

You may decide, especially if it's a first trip, to take a package tour, in which case you'll have to choose the type that most coincides with your interests. Be sure to check the alumni association of your college and your leading local museums for their special tour offerings. (See Package Tours, page 16.)

If you choose to go on your own, there are plenty of aids to help you custom-design your own trip. This book will help in your decision-making. Visit your local library for other references and recent magazine articles about New York (see the *Reader's Guide to Periodical Literature* for specific article titles). Talk to friends, listen to their advice and tips. You may want to consult a travel agent to locate the best deals on airfare and accommodations and make reservations (the agent's fee is paid by the carrier and/or hotels).

You will find racks of brochures and maps in local convention and visitors' bureaus, chambers of commerce, and automobile club offices. Your travel agent also will have literature. There's even a number you can call for a "Dial-a-Trip" recording through which you can request maps and routings from the American Automobile Association office in Manhattan: (212) 734-9232.

New York City and New York State tourist offices are extremely well organized and helpful, with the latest information about what's happening and how you can enjoy it and masses of brochures available on request.

If you have a specific interest (Egyptian archaeology or music for string quartets, for instance) you may find special study tours or seminars offered in your subject. You'll want to call or write one of the agenices in Useful Addresses and Telephone Numbers, page 61, for help in finding out who, where, and when.

INSIDERS' TIPS

One request to the New York State Division of Tourism can bring you the following items free: quarterly "Events" listing; highway and tourism map; parks and outdoor activity guide; brochures on tour packages, New York City tour packages, skiing and winter sports. Also, be sure to request a free "I Love NY Great Vacation Savers," an extraordinary book of 500 coupons good for reduced rates, rentals, fares in parks, museums, theaters, restaurants, hotels, and attractions from one end of the state to the other.)

WHAT TO PACK

You'll find that it's better to be savvy than chic while traveling in New York—both city and state.

In Manhattan, where much walking and standing is

unavoidable if not essential, you'll want to have comfortable, casual clothing and shoes for sightseeing, museum-going, strolling, and shopping.

An all-purpose wardrobe for a week, with at least one dress-up occasion, should include the following:

- For women: A lightweight wool suit and several skirt-and-blouse combinations, with a sweater or jacket for "layering" on days that begin cool and warm up later, then cool down at night. Cottons in summer; lightweight woolens the rest of the year; silk dress or suit for dress-up evenings.
- For men: A suit, slacks, and knit sports shirts, with a sweater, blazer, or windbreaker for sightseeing, a dress shirt or two and a tie for dress up occasions. Cottons in summer, woolens the rest of the year.
- Firm, comfortable, all-weather walking or jogging shoes (yes, even elegant little old ladies wear tennis shoes on Fifth Avenue these days), which you can alternate with dress shoes (carried in a tote bag) when necessary.
- A serviceable raincoat and rain hat (or warmer, heavier gear in winter). Umbrellas have short lives when subjected to the unpredictable, heavy gusts of wind that are common here.

PERILS & PITFALLS

New Yorkers caution visitors to leave valuable jewelry at home; wear showy jewelry under your coat or keep it in your handbag until you've reached your destination. All it does is call attention to you and make you a "mark" for potential pickpockets or worse.

HINTS ON YOUR HEALTH

New York State is a healthful place to visit. Its climate is temperate, its topography is attractive and benign, hazards are within the "reasonable" range, pollution is down, and attention to health-sustaining or -promoting elements is above average.

In a state this big, with its large, active population

and diversity of urban/rural, sophisticated/rustic, high-tech/natural settings, there can be hazards. You can easily sunburn on the state's beaches in summer, or get caught in a snowstorm in the Niagara area (or anywhere else, for that matter), or be hit by a once-in-a-lifetime hurricane, for instance.

Pollution is a never-ending problem, but the air in the country is salubrious (though acid rain continues to afflict upstate forests and lakes). Even in the cities, the air is remarkably improved over a decade ago, and you will find it far superior to that in counterpart cities abroad. Drinking water is pure and dependable.

INSIDERS' TIPS

New York City's tap water was examined and found to be superior in purity to almost all the highly touted, expensive bottled waters on the market.

Generally, you will find that health facilities and care are excellent, if you need them. Your medications and replacement glasses or appliances are readily found at city pharmacies, or optometrists or orthopedic specialty stores. You will be able to stay within your dietary restrictions by communicating with restaurants beforehand or checking menus carefully.

If a health problem arises during your visit, be assured that some of the world's best medical institutions and facilities, as well as health specialists, are a phone call away. (See emergency listings in our Insiders' Information sections for telephone numbers of hospitals, ambulances, doctors, dentists, etc.)

TRAVEL FOR THE HANDICAPPED

In New York City, most street intersections have ramps for wheelchair access and some city buses are equipped to lift wheelchairs aboard. Major department stores and office buildings have elevators that make wheelchair access possible.

There is a Mayor's Office of the Handicapped (52 Chambers Street, Room 206, tel. 566-0972), which has information about programs and events available to people with disabilities. The Junior League of the City of New York (130 East 80th Street, 10021, tel. 288-6220) publishes *Access New York City,* a free guide to 400 of Manhattan's major public buildings that are accessible to the handicapped. It includes department stores, hotels, transportation terminals, museums, and more.

Other sources of information are the New York Society for the Deaf (344 East 14th Street, 10003, tel. 673-6500) and the New York Association for the Blind (111 East 59th Street, 10022, tel. 355-2200).

Some museums offer special tours for deaf, blind, and handicapped persons, and several theaters have installed infrared systems to aid hearing-impaired patrons. A list of special tour operators for handicapped persons in Manhattan is available from the Society for the Advancement of Travel for the Handicapped (26 Court Street, Brooklyn, NY 11242, tel. [718] 858-5483).

The book *Access to the World,* by Louise Weiss, published by Henry Holt and Company, carries valuable travel information for handicapped persons.

GETTING TO NEW YORK

PACKAGE TOURS

We usually think of package tours for foreign travel, rarely for domestic U.S. trips. Yet there *are* times and reasons when a package tour in the United States makes sense. Often it's the *price.* A group of people touring together get better prices on hotels, restaurants, and attractions.

Then there's the companionship that a tour offers. Though many people enjoy travel with family and/or friends, it takes a true loner to savor a trip all by himself. A group tour provides company when needed, but free time for branching out on one's own if desired. Many tours today build in such flexibility.

Finally, there's the question of security. Many people, especially the older or very young (or parents of the young), welcome the security that group travel provides. For those of us who have lived in and know New York City well, it is as familiar, comfortable, and safe as Oshkosh. But for the first-time visitor, full of disaster images from movies and the news, the city *can* seem an overpowering, even frightening place. Traveling with a group provides the security of numbers and the savvy of a tour leader who knows where to go and when.

Package tours to New York City usually run from one to five days. Cost often depends on the category of accommodations you opt for; the more expensive the hotel you choose, the higher the tour tariff.

For instance, Mainstream Tours' five-night "Theatre Trio" costs from $443 to $786 per person in a double, depending on which of eighteen hotels you choose. Included are accommodations; orchestra tickets to three Broadway shows or two shows and a supper club dinner or dinner cruise; cocktails at the Waldorf-

Astoria, or a Lincoln Center or Radio City Music Hall tour.

INSIDERS' TIPS

Crime in New York City is somewhat exaggerated by fiction and the media. The city's crime rate (including burglary, larceny, car theft, rape, robbery, assault, and murder) puts it in fourteenth place among major American cities. It ranks better than such usually considered "safe" cities as Seattle (third), Boston (fourth), Denver (fifth), San Antonio (sixth), Memphis (tenth), Houston (eleventh), and Jacksonville (thirteenth). As in any large city, one should be alert at all times on the street.

In addition to numerous theater tours, there are shopping tours—like Inside New York's two-night "Fashion Inside New York," with visits to better designers' showrooms (tel. [212] 861-0709); food tours—such as Firstours' two-night "Gourmet Delight," with dinner at a top restaurant and a Broadway or dinner show; art tours—like Small Journeys Inc.'s two-night "Art—Alive in New York," with a guided gallery tour of SoHo, Greenwich Village, the East Village, and 57th Street, plus museum and "city lights" evening tours (tel. [212] 889-7676). An unusual tour is Guide Service of New York's two-night "New York Melting Pot," which takes you to the city's ethnic communities—Greek Astoria, Little India, Chinatown, Harlem, the Polish East Village, Little Italy, Little Ukraine, Hassidic Williamsburg, and El Barrio (tel. [212] 408-3332).

Many New York City hotels have their own tour packages that include special hotel rates, and often some sightseeing and theater options. Because of the huge number of hotels, competition is fierce, and the wise shopper can find some excellent values in such packages. Most are weekend packages, for that's when hotels have more vacancies. If you're considering a splurge, such a package often gives you accommodations at a super-deluxe hotel for half its normal cost.

For example, a "Bed and Breakfast Weekend" package at the Vista International costs $79 per person per night and includes room, full breakfast, free parking, two tours (Heritage Trail Walking Tour and South

Street Seaport Walking Tour), full use of the hotel's fitness center, and a free shuttle bus to midtown. The one-night "Essex Weekend Package" for two provides deluxe accommodations, dinner at Devereux's restaurant, and breakfast or Sunday brunch for $249. Even the luxurious Plaza offers a "Westin Plaza Weekend" with 50 percent off regular room rates.

INSIDERS' TIPS

For a very helpful booklet, "New York City Tour Package Directory," write to the New York Convention & Visitors Bureau, 2 Columbus Circle, New York, NY 10019. It describes hundreds of current packages available.

Many packages within New York State are provided by specific hotels. For instance, there's one from Geneva on the Lake, a deluxe resort hotel: a four-day "Four-Star Gourmet Getaway" tour that includes visits to Rochester and Elmira, winery tours, and a stay at the Finger Lakes resort, which costs approximately $285 per person. Another offering, a three-day "Capital Circuit" tour, from $138 (depending on accommodation chosen), is available from The Saratoga Circuit, Inc.

Some package tours of New York State include other eastern destinations as well. For instance, a budget-priced six-day $288 Cosmos "Niagara Falls and Washington, D.C." tour begins in New York City, goes by coach to Corning, the Finger Lakes, Niagara Falls, then south through Pennsylvania to Washington, ending up back in New York City on the final day. A 14-day Saga Holidays tour, called "USA: The East," costs from $1,319 to $1,549, depending on which of 36 major gateway cities you depart from, and includes three days in New York City, one in Binghamton, two in Niagara Falls, the rest in seven other Eastern cities.

The following is a list of addresses of major tour operators featuring a number of New York City and State options (area code 212 unless otherwise stated):

■ American Express Destination Services, 65 Broadway, Mezzanine Level, New York 10006. Tel. 493-6558 or (800) USA AMEX.

- Amtrak National Railroad Passenger Corp., 250 W. 34th St., 1 Penn Plaza, Suite 1425, New York 10119. Tel. 560-7158.
- Around Town Inc., 240 E. 27th St., New York 10016. Tel. 532-6877. Specializes in custom-designed tours for adults, children, groups. Multilingual guides and drivers make anything possible.
- Cosmos Tours, 95–25 Queens Blvd., Rego Park, New York 11374. Tel. (800) 221-0090.
- Firstours, 1633 Broadway, New York 10019. Tel. 582-7800, U.S.A.; outside the state, (800) 223-6493; in New York State, (800) 522-1891.
- Gray Line New York Tours, Inc., 254 W. 54th St., New York 10019. Tel. 397-2620 or (800) 437-0051.
- Mainstream Tours, 690 Market St., San Francisco, CA 94104. Tel. (415) 391-9070 or (800) 227-4000.
- Saga International Holidays, Ltd., 120 Boylston St., Boston, MA 02116. Tel. (800) 343-0273.
- The Saratoga Circuit, Inc., 417 Broadway, Saratoga Springs, NY 12866. Tel. (518) 587-3656.
- Yankee Holidays, 20 Spring St., Saugus, MA 01906. Tel. (617) 231-2884 or (800) 225-2550. In Canada, tel. (800) 255-2560.

BY AIR

There are modern airports at key New York State cities, and there's a web of scheduled airline flights to service them.

New York City, perhaps the world's premier flight destination and certainly one of its busiest air *entrepôts*, is served by three major commercial airports: John F. Kennedy International Airport (tel. [718] 656-4520) and La Guardia Airport (tel. [718] 476-5000) on Long Island, and Newark International Airport (tel. [201] 961-2000) across the river in New Jersey.

Because New York is such a travel magnet, you will find many flights there from all parts of the nation. From many cities there are multiple daily departures and highly competitive, bargain-priced flights. It pays to check the travel pages of your local newspaper, or to contact the airlines directly or through your travel agent.

Buffalo, Albany, Rochester, and Niagara Falls are also major air destinations. They are served by the larger domestic carriers and have first-class, modern airports with excellent local transportation, hotel, and restaurant facilities.

Estimating the cost of air transport to New York is not easy. The complexity of fares offered and the multitude of qualifiers and disclaimers involved are enough to melt your computer's memory. For illustration, recent "super-saver" fares from Los Angeles and San Francisco to New York have been as low as $238 round trip (weekdays, over Saturday night, booked 7 days ahead). At this writing, regular coach fare from the 2 California cities is $458 round trip, *the same as first-class fare* (if booked 7 days in advance). Business-class fare is $680, and regular first class is $1,020.

A money-saving alternative is to book a round-trip package that includes round-trip air fare and hotel accommodations as part of the "tour." Ads for these are found in the Sunday travel pages of major newspapers.

At this time, the following domestic airlines serve New York City: American, tel. (800) 557-7386; Continental, tel. (800) 525-0280; Delta, tel. (800) 221-1212; Eastern, tel. (800) 327-8376; Midway, tel. (800) 621-5757; New York Air, tel. (800) 221-9300; Northwest, tel. (800) 225-2525; Pan Am, tel. (800) 221-1111; Piedmont, tel. (800) 251-5720; TWA, tel. (800) 221-2000; United, tel. (800) 241-6522; USAir, tel. (800) 428-4322. From Canada, Air Canada, tel. (800) 422-6232 or (800) 930-8363.

To reach more remote areas of New York State: Adirondack Flying Service, Allegheny Commuter (USAir), Catskill Airways, Empire, Mall, Northeastern, Pilgrim, and Tri-Lakes Flying Service.

SHIPS AND CRUISES

Yes, it is possible to arrive in New York by ship.

The last of the great transatlantic liners, the *Queen*

Elizabeth 2, or *QE2,* still makes the journey to and from Europe to New York City. The schedule is about every 11 days (the trip takes 5 days each way) except in winter, when the *QE2* shifts to Caribbean runs. Other Atlantic arrivals in New York are cruise ships.

Still other travelers take ships to New York State:

Long Island is reached by ferries from Bridgeport (seasonal) and New London, Connecticut, and from Block Island, Rhode Island (seasonal).

Lake Champlain towns are reached by ferries from Vermont; Cape Vincent is reached by a St. Lawrence River ferry from Wolfe Island, Ontario; Buffalo and Rochester are reached by Lake Erie and Lake Ontario steamers and cruise boats on a regular basis.

And citizens of Staten Island regularly take a ship to reach the borough of Manhattan via one of the best-publicized "sea" voyages extant, the Staten Island Ferry. It runs night and day, throughout the year, at a bargain 25¢ per passenger trip.

Perhaps of more interest to New York visitors are the cruises that depart from New York City. There are Hudson Day Line excursions to West Point and Bear Mountain during summer. There are luncheon and dinner cruises of New York harbor by World Yacht Enterprises.

Scores of luxury cruise ships start and/or end their excursions in New York City. Among them are the Chandris Fantasy Cruises' "Overnights to Nowhere," and trips to the Bahamas and Mexico; the *Bermuda Star* to that island; Cunard's and Home Lines' ships to the Caribbean; Royal Viking's voyages through the Panama Canal to Mexico and California and via the St. Lawrence River to Montreal and Quebec.

Similarly, there are ships that depart from Buffalo for Lake Erie cruises and from Rochester for Lake Ontario pleasure circuits from spring through fall.

BY TRAIN

The days when most people arrived in New York by "rail" are past.

Trains have yielded pride of place to autos, buses, and airliners. Still, modern Amtrak, Conrail, and Metro-North trains roll along the rails once reserved for the mightiest of the Pennsylvania, New York Central, and New Haven lines. They arrive in New York City's Pennsylvania Station, a relatively new, well-lighted, and reasonably comfortable facility (Amtrak tel. [212] 736-4545), or Grand Central Terminal (tel. [212] 532-4900), which still looks spacious and grand, but has minimal seating and facilities for travelers and has become a haven for indigents.

PERILS & PITFALLS

New York City commuters caution against using the restrooms in Grand Central in off-peak hours because of the derelicts you might find there. Wait for the train or go next door to the Grand Hyatt Hotel or through the tunnel that connects Grand Central to the Hotel Roosevelt. The same warning applies to Penn Station. Use the Penta Hotel, across Seventh Avenue.

Both stations are in midtown Manhattan. Penn Station is at 33rd Street and Seventh Avenue, and gets heavy use by commuters from Long Island (it's the terminus for the Long Island Railroad) and Amtrak. Grand Central Terminal, whose commuters ebb and flow from Westchester and Connecticut, is on Park Avenue between 42nd and 45th streets. It is more convenient to major hotels.

Via Amtrak you can reach many of the state's major cities, including Rochester, Buffalo, Utica, Syracuse, and Albany. Metro-North serves communities along the east bank of the Hudson River.

For schedule and fare information, contact the following:

- Amtrak Penn Station, 32nd St. and Seventh Ave. 10001, tel. (212) 736-4545; Grand Central Terminal, 42nd St. and Lexington Ave. 10017, tel. (212) 736-4545.
- Long Island Railroad (at Penn Station), tel. (718) 739-4200.

- Metro-North Commuter Railroad, 347 Madison Ave. 10017, tel. (212) 340-2144.

BY CAR

Most visitors driving to New York State will arrive via these major highways:

- From Canada: I-190 along the Niagara Frontier; I-81 and the St. Lawrence River bridges near Johnstown and Cornwall; highways from Quebec, especially I-87.
- From Vermont: ferries across Lake Champlain at Plattsburgh, Fort Ticonderoga, Crown Point, Essex, Port Kent, and Rouses Point, New York, and many roads south of Lake George.
- From Massachusetts: I-90 from West Stockbridge and U.S. 20 west of Pittsfield.
- From Connecticut: I-84 near Brewster, New York; I-684 near Armonk, New York; and the Merritt/ Hutchinson River Parkway and I-95 (the New England Thruway), which follows the Long Island Sound coastline.
- From New Jersey: U.S. 9W; the Palisades Parkway along the Hudson River; the Garden State Parkway; and NJ-17, which intersects I-87. Routes into New York City are NJ-440 from Perth Amboy to Staten Island and I-278 from Elizabeth to Staten Island; the New Jersey Turnpike Extension from Jersey City to lower Manhattan (Canal Street) via the Holland Tunnel; Weehawken to midtown Manhattan (39th Street) via the Lincoln Tunnel; Fort Lee to upper Manhattan (178th–179th streets) via the George Washington Bridge.
- From Pennsylvania: I-84 at Port Jervis; I-81 south of Binghamton; U.S. 220, north of Athens, Pennsylvania; U.S. 219 north of Bradford, Pennsylvania; and I-90 along the shore of Lake Erie.
- Ferries connect Bridgeport, Connecticut, to Port Jefferson, Long Island (seasonal), and New London, Connecticut, to Orient Point, Long Island (advance reservations required).

ARRIVING IN NEW YORK

A LITTLE GEOGRAPHY

Although New York City is world-famous, and Manhattan's attributes are widely known, the state is less well understood.

It is a great triangle of fertile and productive land (49,576 square miles), bordered by two vast lakes (Ontario and Erie), a mighty river (the St. Lawrence), a friendly neighboring country (Canada) and 5 states (New Jersey, Pennsylvania, Vermont, Massachusetts, and Connecticut), with a magnificent harbor and seacoast on the Atlantic Ocean.

It was so strategically located that most of Britain's battles with France in North America were fought in the New York colony. Fully one-third of the battles of the Revolution took place in New York, and after victory, New York City was the first capital of the fledgling United States.

Its waters made the state. Through Nieuw Amsterdam/New York City, its Atlantic access brought millions of immigrants from 1624 onward. Its Hudson River–Lake George–Lake Champlain route and St. Lawrence River frontage provided easy water highways to Canada.

The famed Erie Canal, completed in 1825, made it possible to ship goods (from New York City via the Hudson River, Albany, Rochester, and Buffalo) from the corners of the earth to America's heartland bordering the Great Lakes. With access to these markets, New York City quickly outdistanced all rival American ports. Meanwhile, the nation milled its grain at Rochester, which became known as the "Flour City," and Buffalo grew mighty as a manufacturing center because of its strategic location at the Erie Canal's terminus.

The railroad era widened the scope and quickened the pace of trade and manufacturing in New York State, while New York City became the nation's largest metropolitan area and preeminent American financial center. In the 20th century the city took the crown as cultural center, and after World War II, few would contest its claim to the title of world financial *and* cultural capital.

Geography was, if not the key to New York's destiny, a major factor in it.

GETTING TO THE CITY FROM THE AIRPORT

New York City

Your airport-to-Manhattan options:

Taxi. This is the fastest and most convenient way to get to the city, but will cost more than $25 for the trip from JFK, $35 from Newark, and over $18 from La Guardia.

PERILS & PITFALLS

Perennial complaints about taxi drivers center on these outrageous abuses, which are not common, but you should know about them: (1) overcharging strangers unmercifully (a $400 charge from airport to Manhattan); (2) charging for each person in the cab (the meter amount pays for the *ride,* regardless of how many are riding); (3) leaving the meter off, then haggling with customers after the trip; (4) purposely failing to turn the meter back to zero before starting a trip (so that you pay for the last fare plus your own). Unlicensed "gypsy" cabs may try any of the above scams, and you will have no recourse and little if any insurance protection in case of accident. Be alert. And look for the yellow, *licensed* taxis.

The meter amount is the total fare for everyone in the cab. All bridge and tunnel fees are extra. All day Sunday and from 8 P.M. to 6 A.M. other days there is a surcharge of 50¢ (per person). Also, there is a charge of 50¢ if you have a large trunk (not a suitcase) that requires two people to manage it. If the destination is outside New York City limits, the fare is double the meter reading, plus tolls, or the total agreed upon before start-up. *Do not pay in advance.*

Taxi dispatchers in uniform are at some official taxi stands at the three airports during rush hours. Queue up. At Newark Airport there are "Share & Save" booths on the arrivals level in Terminals A and B, or call (201) 961-2047.

Have $5, $10, and/or $20 bills ready to pay the driver (some of them refuse to change larger bills).

Expect to tip 15 percent.

PERILS & PITFALLS

Do not let anyone take your bags "to hail a cab for you." You may never see them again—or you may have set yourself up for a heavy ($10) unnecessary tip.

Buses. *From La Guardia and JFK Airports:* Carey Express Buses ($6 LGA, $8 JFK) to Grand Central Terminal (Park Avenue & 42nd St.), 6 A.M.–midnight; Olympia Airport Express ($5) to World Trade Center, via Brooklyn LIRR Terminal, 9 A.M.–9 P.M. (from 11 A.M. at JFK).

From Newark Airport: Olympia Airport Express ($5) to World Trade Center and Grand Central Terminal, 5 A.M. to 1 A.M. Transport of New Jersey buses ($5) run to Port Authority Bus Terminal at 41st Street and Eighth Avenue, 5:45 A.M.–12:30 A.M. (reduced service on weekends).

An Abbey minibus (tel. [201] 961-2535) operates to certain midtown Manhattan hotels every half hour during key portions of the day. $12.

Airlink air-conditioned minibuses ($3) go from Newark Airport to downtown Newark, for transfer to rail or bus to Manhattan's Penn Station, at 32nd Street and Seventh Avenue, 6 A.M.–9 P.M. PATH trains run from Penn Station, Newark, to West Side Manhattan stops between 34th Street and the World Trade Center. (For information, call [201] 963-2588 or [212] 466-7649).

There are private bus companies (often called "limousines") that serve suburban areas in and around

the airports. A desk with dispatchers or direct telephones is in each terminal.

Rental cars. The major car-rental companies have
counters at the airports, but unless your business or
physical condition requires it, forgo the cares, expense,
and hazards of operating a car in Manhattan.

Helicopter. New York Helicopter and Island
Helicopter hop from 34th Street and East 60th Street
heliports to all three airports; tel. (718) 895-1626. Fare
$58.

The JFK Express (a.k.a. "The Train to the Plane").
This subway-bus combination starts from JFK Airport
via bus (catch it at the blue signposts) to the subway,
which makes 8 stops and terminates at West 57th
Street. Fare $6.50. No porters are available. Operates
from 5 A.M. to midnight. Traveling time is about an hour
and a half.

Albany, Buffalo, Niagara Falls, Rochester

Compared with the complexities of traveling into Manhattan, the trip from airport to downtown in these four
cities is a piece of cake.

Major hotels in some cities provide free shuttle service from airport to hotel and back. (Rochester's
Strathallan sends a posh antique limo to pick up and
deliver guests, for instance.)

In Albany, the usual Red taxi fare is about $10.
There's also a limousine that charges $4.90 per person.
The city bus from the airport costs 60¢.

In Buffalo, the taxi fare to downtown is about $11.

In Niagara Falls, the taxi fare ranges from $20 to
$28, and the Airporter bus charges $8 to drop you at
your hotel.

In Rochester, the Cardinal Cab taxi fare is $10 and
the RTS city bus from airport to city center is 70¢.

TIPPING

Most services are more expensive in New York City, and
tipping is (if merited at all) a form of payment for

services. It may not work out that way, depending on
peer pressure and your resistance to intimidation.
However, here are typical circumstances when tipping
generally occurs and something is expected:

	Amount in NYC	*Amount in NY State*
Hotel bellman	50¢ per bag, $1 min.	50¢ per bag, $1 max.
doorman	$1	50¢
room service	15%*	10%*
restroom attendant	50¢–$1	50¢
maid service in room	$1 per day per person, from 2nd day onward	
shoeshine attendant	$1–$1.50	75¢–$1
Barber	15%–20%	10%–15%
Hair stylist	15%–20%	10%–15%
Manicurist	10%	10%
Theater usher	0	0
Outdoor sports event usher (sweeping seats)	50¢	50¢
Resort pool attendant	$1 per day	50¢ per day
Resort locker attendant	$1 per day; $2.50 per wk.	50¢ per day
Resort golf caddy	$1–$2 per bag or 15% of greens fees (18 holes)	$1 per bag
Restaurant waiter	15%–20%*	10%–15%*
captain	5%*	0–5%*
maitre d'	$5 or $10†	$5†
wine steward	$5 or $10†	$5†
coat check	$1	50¢
cocktail waiter	15%*	10%–15%*
Counter (fast food eatery)	10%–15%	10%
Taxi	15%	10%

*If not added to the bill.
†If warranted for extra personal service and attention.

INSIDERS' TIPS

In New York City restaurants the tax is 8¼ percent, so
doubling it is a quick way to estimate a very acceptable
tip in most circumstances.

THE INSIDERS' NEW YORK

WHERE TO STAY

Just name your ideal place to stay and you can be sure New York has it—whether it's an Adirondack Indian wikiup, a Victorian Gothic Revival inn, a millionaire's mansion, or a 21st-century high-tech hotel suite. The range of lodgings available is extraordinarily broad—and so are the prices.

INSIDERS' TIPS

A directory listing more than 200 Big Apple hotel and tour packages is available free from the New York Convention & Visitors Bureau, Inc., 2 Columbus Circle, New York, NY 10019. The offerings range from $32 per person per night upward.

Highest prices, as you'd expect, are in New York City. Here, with hosts of hotels (a total of 100,000 rooms) to choose among, you'll find a surprising spectrum, from legendary movie star-and-mogul palatial penthouse suites to the YMCA.

PERILS & PITFALLS

Noise is an ever-present problem in New York City. To escape it, book into a hotel with soundproof (double-glazed) windows or choose a room above the tenth floor. (Noise generally diminishes the higher you go.)

In New York City, expect these additions to your hotel bill:

- $2 per room per night city occupancy tax
- 8.25 percent New York State tax
- 5 percent New York City tax

There are big, brassy hotels geared for business travelers and tour groups; small, discreet European-style hotels that cater to a guest's every wish; landmark hotels that wear their past glories like living legends. A recent development in New York is the upscale B&B—bed and breakfast in a private home. Brooklyn brownstones, with spacious guest rooms furnished with antiques, are a prime example.

INSIDERS' TIPS

B&B accommodations range in price from $35 per night, double, upward for rooms, $65 and up for a complete fix-your-own meals apartment. A central booking agency is City Lights Bed & Breakfast, Ltd, P.O. Box 20355 Cherokee Station, New York, NY 10028, tel. (212) 737-7049 or 877-3235.

Outside the city, the circle of choices widens greatly. You can be at a posh beach resort in the Hamptons, a cottage on Lake George, or a fishing camp in the Adirondacks. You may prefer the something-going-on-every-minute gargantuan resorts of the Catskills, or a historic country inn in Leatherstocking country near Cooperstown, or a restored way station on the Erie Canal.

In all New York cities you'll find familiar national hotel and motel chains, offering the standards you have learned to expect from others in the chain. But we suggest that you look also for smaller, more personal hostelries, village inns, family-owned hotels, even B&Bs with distinctive character. And for that occasional splurge, there are some highly personalized former mansions-turned-inns.

For budget-watching or family travel, New York State's vast network of state parks makes camping a pleasure, even for those of us who aren't camping enthusiasts.

INSIDERS' TIPS

Fridays, Saturdays, and Sundays, rates at even the best hotels plummet, sometimes more than 50 percent. Many hotels give discounts to members of various organizations—motor clubs, retired persons, business and professional societies. It never hurts to ask.

There is no overall government or industry review service that examines and rates places to stay in New York. The automobile clubs review and rate some, but by no means all.

PERILS & PITFALLS

Beware telephone charges! Here is the schedule for a ♛ ♛ ♛ ♛ hotel on Central Park South:

- 75¢ per local, third party, information, or credit card call, 800#, 900#, 950#, or collect call;
- All long-distance calls charged at standard AT&T operator-assisted rate plus 40 percent;
- For calls not completed, charge will be made *as if completed* if telephone is allowed to ring more than 36 seconds for local, 48 seconds for domestic long distance, or 60 seconds for international long distance.

Our ratings and listings are not encyclopedic; we have cited those hotels and inns we think offer special quality. Charm, furnishings, service, historic associations, a hospitable staff—any or all of these are part of the ambiance and are important to a visitor's enjoyment of a place. So are cleanliness, good housekeeping, firm mattresses, strong reading lights at bedside, rooms that are warm in winter and cool in summer, and quiet during the night.

We should state what will very likely seem obvious as you read the Insiders' Listings of hotels: all things being equal, we prefer the charm of a country or village inn or small hotel to the impersonality of a motel or large city hotel. So now you know our biases.

WHERE TO EAT

New York City

If you tried to eat your way from A to Z through the restaurants listed in the Yellow Pages of the New York City telephone directory, you would be like Sisyphus rolling the stone uphill, only to have it roll down again as you neared the top. That's because there are always so many new restaurants opening, you'd never catch up.

When it comes to food, whatever you crave, New

York City has it. That old term "melting pot" doesn't just mean a wide and deep mix of ethnic groups. It means their foods as well.

So whether you want baba ganooj or bouillabaise, you'll find it here. Seviche, sushi, saganaki, pita, pasteles, papadums, flan, frikadeller, or Florentines, take your choice—somewhere in Manhattan these and other ethnic specialties are being chopped, kneaded, rolled, beaten, shaped, steamed, broiled, boiled, oiled, or prepared in their own authentic and inimitable ways.

From Argentina and Afghanistan to Zambia and Zamboanga, Morocco to Madrid, Brazil to Bangkok, there are more ethnic and national cuisines to be found in New York than there are member nations of the UN.

Of course you'll find all the more familiar cuisines as well: more French (*haute,* provincial, and *nouvelle*), Italian (northern, Neapolitan, Genoese, Sicilian), and German than you can shake a fork at.

INSIDERS' TIPS

At New York's better restaurants, jackets are *de rigueur* for men. When in doubt, ask when you make your reservations. (Reservations are a must at most of the city's better places, and must often be made days or sometimes weeks ahead.)

There are two telephone services that advise on restaurants without charge to callers:

Dial & Dine, tel. 226-3388.

Restaurant Hot Line, for East Side restaurants above 59th Street, tel. 838-6644; below 59th Street, tel. 838-7020; West Side above 59th Street, tel. 838-6883; below 59th Street, tel. 838-7430.

You can book tables through these services without cost to you, *but* keep in mind when weighing their suggestions that Hot Line receives a commission if you dine at certain restaurants it recommends, and that Dial & Dine is supported by restaurants who pay a monthly subscription fee.

The maitre d' usually deserves a tip only if he performs heroically (such as finding you a table when there are none).

INSIDERS' TIPS

If you want to try one of the celebrated temples of *haute cuisine,* but shudder at what the tab might be, go for lunch. It won't be cheap, but it will be cheaper. For example, Le Bernardin's *prix fixe* lunch is $35 per person, dinner $60.

If the wine steward or sommelier opens and pours, no tip is necessary. If he goes to elaborate trouble on your behalf, 10 percent of the price of the wine will generously compensate him for his toil. The usual upstate tip is 5 to 10 percent.

You'll enjoy sampling the latest food trends: Last year Cajun; this year Southwestern American; next year who knows? And of course, there is plenty of comfortingly familiar dining: The steak houses, seafood and clam parlors, mom-and-pop luncheonettes, fast-food chains (noodle and sushi as well as burger), and dairy bars.

There are restaurants where people go to be seen, super-stylish places where the menu is secondary to the milieu. There are neighborhood hangouts, and since Gotham's neighborhoods include the theater district, the garment district, and artists' quarters such "locals" often attract some of the big names in these fields as their regular clientele.

In short, New York has something for every palate—and pocketbook.

PERILS & PITFALLS

When your waiter reels off today's specials, *do not* hesitate to ask their prices. It's not gauche; if you're not told automatically or given the information in writing, you're being pressured and you should resist. If you don't, you can be certain of expensive surprises when you read the bill.

It isn't just the diversity of restaurants (though their listings in the Yellow Pages take up almost 50 single-spaced, small-type pages). There are food stores, markets, entire neighborhoods where you can buy Indian and Middle Eastern foods, Oriental items, Jewish,

Hungarian, Russian, English, or Italian specialties. Certain stores specialize in a single item: chocolate, paprika, coffee, yogurt, cookies, even falafel.

Could a fanatical foodie ask for anything more?

INSIDERS' TIPS

Visitors who complain about the high cost of dining out in New York haven't been going to the ethnic restaurants. This can be the best—and often the most interesting—way to stretch your food dollars *and* enjoy the New York experience of discovering a new, exotic cuisine prepared by the people who know it best.

New York State

Outside Manhattan, the restaurant scene becomes more traditional.

You'll find many excellent French, Italian, American, and seafood restaurants around the state. In the cities, such as Albany, Buffalo, Rochester, Schenectady, and Syracuse, you'll also find Manhattan's trendiness creeping in—but slowly. Look for an occasional Japanese, Vietnamese, or Indian restaurant, but there are still relatively few of them.

PERILS & PITFALLS

Many of the Chinese eateries you will discover on your trip through the state cater to what they perceive as American taste. Be forewarned: if you are used to the Chinese food of Vancouver, Manhattan, San Francisco, Los Angeles, or Chicago (not to mention the "real fare" of mainland China, Taiwan, or Hong Kong), you may be disappointed.

FOOD AND DRINK

Food

Food in New York City, as the preceding section indicates, is virtually encyclopedic. If you can't find a specific food item here, it's doubtful that it's available anywhere in the United States. That's not New York hype, it's merely a fact.

The variety is astonishing. In seafood, you'll find everything from Dover sole flown in fresh from England to mahi-mahi direct from Hawaii; cockles, whelks, sea urchins, and Spanish *angulas,* to say nothing of all the familiar oysters, lobster, shrimp, and crabs you'd expect in a port city.

Wonderful breads representing many nationalities can be found, ranging from Jewish challah to Irish soda bread, Polish rye, Indian papadums, to the best, crustiest French and Italian breads imaginable. And of course there are bagels, once a New York standby but now available all over the country.

Sandwiches weren't invented in New York, but when you've tried a genuine New York deli hot pastrami on rye, or a Reuben, with its multiple layers of corned beef, you'll think they were. And while you're at it, sample the delicious kosher pickles at any delicatessen. Or maybe a bagel with cream cheese and lox (smoked salmon) or novie (Nova Scotia salmon).

INSIDERS' TIPS

For the New York deli experience, here are some of the favorites:

- Barney Greengrass, 541 Amsterdam Ave, tel. 724-4707.
- Carnegie Delicatessen, 854 Seventh Ave., tel. 757-2245.
- Kaplan's at the Delmonico, 59 East 59th St., tel 755-5959.
- Katz's Delicatessen, 205 East Houston St., tel. 254-2246.
- Second Avenue Deli, 156 Second Ave., tel. 677-0606.
- Zabar's Deli & Gourmet Foods, 2245 Broadway, tel. 787-2000.

Natural foods, fresh-grown fruits and vegetables, are at their most tempting in the displays of the city's many Korean produce markets: all kinds of wild mushrooms, unusual herbs like fresh coriander, sorrel, and fresh ginger, greens such as arugula, bok choy, mâche, and radicchio, Philippine mangos, New Zealand kiwis, persimmons, and pomegranates. Imported delicacies can be found in ethnic neighborhood enclaves all over the city, and in fancy food markets and the food sections of some of the big department stores (notably Bloomingdale's and Macy's).

Then there's the street food in New York. Vendors now hawk everything from Greek souvlaki and gyros to Dove Bars and vast displays of dried nuts, apricots, prunes, and shiny fresh apples and oranges. The hot chestnut and soft pretzel vendors, with their charcoal carts outside concert halls or wherever an event is taking place, are a ubiquitous presence in city life.

Good food in rich variety isn't confined to New York City. New York is an agricultural state, and you'll find fresh produce and high-quality meats everywhere. Local farmers' markets, such as the Broadway Market in Buffalo and New York City's Greenmarkets, sell farm-fresh fruits and vegetables, meats, cheeses, homemade apple or apricot or prune butter, and baked goods. New York is a big cheese-producing state; you'll have many a chance to sample the indigenous sharp cheddar, Cuba, and goat cheese, among many others.

As you travel through the state, notice the numerous apple orchards. If it's the season, you'll find many "pick your own" roadside signs. Northern Spy, Jonathan, Empire, McIntosh, and Cortland are among the diverse types you can try.

In your peregrinations, you'll want to sample local specialties. There are many. Buffalo, for instance, is home of the popular spicy Buffalo chicken wings. It's also home to the *kümmelweck,* a unique soft roll with salt and caraway seeds baked on top, used to make roast-beef sandwiches.

In Rochester, look for Boss sauce, brushed on barbecued chicken, and Zab's hot dogs, served with a very spicy hot sauce. Abbott's frozen custard is also a local product—rich and creamy, unlike any facsimile, Rochesterites insist.

Flavorful, fresh, varied, and plentiful—that's food in New York!

Wine

Cheers! There's reason aplenty to cheer about New York's wines. They are a major pleasure. The state is second only to California in quantity produced, but is second to none in quality of many of its wines (take that, Napa Valley!). Many New York State wines win prizes at prestigious international wine tastings.

Now before you think, "Aha, there's that local chauvinism again—if it's from New York it's bigger, better, tastier, whatever," let us explain.

In the past, New York's wines were known as being excessively sweet, with a foxiness that wasn't always pleasing. If you're old enough to remember New York wines of the 1950s, you may question our judgment (and perhaps our sanity) in touting the local grape. New York was best known for Concord, Catawba, and Niagara table wines, which it has produced for a century and a half. (Concord has been the archetypal grape flavor in America, used in jellies, juices, and sodas.)

But times have changed—and so has the state's wine industry. New York produces attractive sparkling wines and serviceable table wines made from French-American hybrid grapes. But now it also grows viniferas, the best wine grapes of Europe. And this has made all the difference.

The state now has 71 wineries that produce about 30 million gallons of wine with gross sales of some $150 million per year. (Less than half of the state's 186,000 tons of grapes each year are used for wine.) The wineries operate in four regions: Lake Erie, Finger Lakes, Hudson River, and Long Island districts.

(We suggest winery visits in the itineraries in this book and list addresses of many open-to-view wineries in the Insiders' Information sections. Most wineries welcome visitors and offer free tastings. Some charge a nominal fee.)

So, if you like wine at all, be the first kid on your block to "discover" the *new* New York wines. These are the types you will find:

■ Native American (generally fruity, sweet, or semi-sweet; either table or sparkling; from *Vitis labrusca*

grapes): Concord, Catawba, Niagara, Delaware grapes.
- French-American hybrids (table, dessert, and sparkling wines, usually dry or semisweet, the major factor in the New York wine industry): Baco Noir, Seyval Blanc, Aurora, De Chaunac, Marechal Foch, Ravat grapes.
- European (classic wines from European vines; dry table and sparkling wines; from *Vitis vinifera* grapes): Chardonnay, Johannisberg Riesling, Gewurtztraminer, Sauvignon Blanc, Cabernet Sauvignon, Pinot Noir, and Merlot.

INSIDERS' TIPS

We suggest that you go with New York State white wines, especially the Johannisberg Riesling, Gewurtztraminer, Chardonnay, and brut "champagne." For a very special treat, try one of the remarkable dessert wines—late-harvest Ravat, Ravat Vignoles, and so-called ice wine (the best of these compare favorably with Sauternes).

Beer

Beer is a beverage of choice with many New Yorkers, as a quick scan of the many local pubs and taverns will affirm. But, as has happened elsewhere, in other beer-proud communities, many of New York's old breweries have gone out of business, victims of the "bigger is better" school of brewing. Thus, most of the beer available throughout the state is of the familiar, nationally distributed types (which shall be nameless here).

There is a bright note, however. The 1978 law permitting home brewing has led to an upsurge of microbreweries, which are attempting to produce beer in the old-fashioned way (with long aging times, more hops and malt). You'll find one of these breweries in New York City: the Manhattan Brewing Company, which produces seven English-style ales. You can sample their products in their own taprooms or elsewhere in the city at select places with large beer lists. (See Insiders' Information for addresses.)

As of this writing, there are only three other independent regional breweries in New York State: F. X. Matt in Utica, which produces Utica Club, Saranac 1888, and Maximus Super; the Genesee Brewery in Rochester, with its 12 Horses ale and Genesee beer and ale; and the Neuman Brewery in Albany, producer of Albany Amber.

There are, however, more and more pubs and bars, and even better restaurants, with expanding beer lists that include small brewery offerings as well as many imported beers. So don't settle for the national "Lite." Ask for the New York alternatives.

HOW TO GET AROUND

New York City

The limousine halted at the curb, and the impeccably coiffed matron in furs and pearls alighted. The chauffeur then carried a nattily dressed young man from the car into the expensive restaurant. "What a pity that one so young and handsome can't walk," clucked a sympathetic sidewalk observer. "Don't be absurd!" snapped the matron. "Of course he can walk, but thank God he doesn't have to!"

For those of us who are not that wealthy, getting around New York City is done on foot or by bus, taxi, subway, car, or combinations of the above. Each has its advantages and hazards.

Walking. Seeing and enjoying the city—its fabulous window displays, garrulous vendors, vivid street traffic, and passersby—is best done by walking the streets and byways. The midtown avenues (from 34th to 86th streets) boast some of the finest and most famous shops and stores in the world, as well as the people who frequent them. But New York pavements can be tiring, and unless you have the legs of a goat, walking should be done in moderation, to conserve your strength for the *real* challenges—shopping, museum- and gallery-hopping, and discoing the night away.

Above 10th Street, the grid pattern makes navigation relatively easy: streets run east to west and are numbered consecutively from south to north; avenues run from north to south and start on the East Side with First and proceed west (with Lexington between Third and what would be Fourth if it were not named Park, and Madison squeezed between Park and Fifth). Almost all of them are one-way streets; the odd numbers usually go west, even numbers east.

Fifth Avenue is the dividing line between the East Side and the West Side, where address numbering starts, so 1 East 42nd Street is at the northeast corner of Fifth, and 210 East 42nd is just past Third on the way to Second Avenue. Numbers to the west also start numbering at Fifth, which may be confusing when you are above 59th Street, because numbers must begin west of Central Park, which borders Fifth Avenue's west side.

Below 10th Street, the farther south you go, the more labyrinthine the streets are; it's their heritage from Colonial days. Plan your itinerary to conserve your energy, using wheels (bus, taxi, subway) to transport you *to* a specific area, and then savor the fun of walking around it. With a city map to pinpoint your destination(s), your hotel concierge will start you in the right direction.

PERILS & PITFALLS

Walking is a favorite New York habit, but do it as New Yorkers do: be alert and avoid eye contact on the street. This averts any possible confrontation with crazies or worse. If anyone tries to stop you for a handout, keep right on walking; don't let yourself be drawn into conversation. Also, avoid walking on deserted streets and at night.

Bus. For distances, use the buses if you have time. They are usually clean, well-lighted, air-conditioned, and comfortable—but slow, painfully so during peak rush hours. The fare is $1, and you must have it in *exact* change (*not* a dollar bill) or tokens (your hotel cashier and some banks should have them), as the drivers handle no cash and cannot change bills.

INSIDERS' TIPS

Have your change handy in a pocket. Never bring your wallet out to count money on the street. Many New Yorkers carry no cash in their billfolds.

Buses run 24 hours a day (reduced schedule at night), stop on demand about every two blocks, and run north on First, Third, Madison, Avenue of the Americas, Eighth (which becomes Central Park West), and Tenth (which becomes Amsterdam) avenues. They run south on Second, Lexington, Park (south of 42nd Street), Fifth, Seventh, Columbus, Ninth, West End, and Eleventh avenues and Broadway (like a bar sinister across the city from northwest to southeast). There are several crosstown streets with buses; the major ones are 14th, 23rd, 34th, 42nd, 57th, 72nd, 79th, 86th, and 96th streets. You can get a free transfer for all intersecting bus routes; just ask for one as you board the bus and pay your fare.

INSIDERS' TIPS

For advice on how to get from where you are to where you want to be by bus, call Transit Authority Information, (718) 330-1234. The best time to call is after 7:30 P.M.

Cabs. There are supposed to be about 12,000 licensed taxis in New York (there were 29,000 operating in 1929)—but try to find one when you desperately need it—especially during rainstorms, rush hours, and after the theater!

Licensed cabs for hire are yellow, have their roof numbers lighted, and can be flagged down in the street. Look for them also in taxi lines at major hotels. All licensed cabs are metered, prominently display the driver's photo and registry number, and carry insurance. Unlicensed ("gypsy" cabs) may or may not have meters or insurance and are strictly last-resort, no-other-recourse options. (A recent survey found that many gypsy-cab drivers were relatively new to the city and had trouble recognizing and/or reaching specified addresses, even though they had passed taxi driver licensing tests.)

PERILS & PITFALLS

According to the city laws, (1) a driver may not refuse to take you anywhere in the city unless his off-duty sign is posted and his roof light is off; (2) he may ask your destination only after you sit down; (3) he may take no more than 4 passengers in a standard cab and 5 in a Checker cab; (4) you may bring along a pet if it is well-behaved and not unduly large; (5) if you tell him to, the driver must stop smoking, open or close the window, and stop to pick up or drop off passengers as you direct. If he fails to obey any of the above regulations, you may report these infractions (or fare arguments) to the Taxi and Limousine Commission, tel. 869-4237. You'll need the cab's number (rooftop sign) and driver's license (number and name) on the dashboard.

Subway. Fortunately or not, there is no relationship between the train letter or number and the quality of transportation in New York's subways. Many, if not most, are grungy and graffiti-saturated. They are definitely not for stylish travel, but they are quick and usually dependable and whisk you to the far reaches of the city faster and cheaper than any other ground transportation. *However*, if you are a stranger to New York and its subway system, you are probably better off staying above ground.

INSIDERS' TIPS

There are lost-and-founds for items left in taxis (tel. 869-4513); buses (tel. 690-9638), and subways (tel. [718] 625-6200).

Subways carry more than 3.5 million passengers during their 24-hour-a-day service, and are jammed during rush hours and nearly empty during the reduced schedule, late night hours. To ride them, you need a token to put in the turnstile slot. Tokens are sold for $1 each at booths in major stations and also at some banks and hotel cashier's desks. Don't try to use any old tokens you have lying around. The only ones that work are brass with a silvery disc in the center.

Which way is up? Only trains marked 7, S, or L (old LL) run basic east-west routes. All the others run north-south in Manhattan at least, but once they leave the island, they meander in all directions.

Pick up a free subway map at token booths. Each token is $1, good for any distance or time inside the system. For 24-hour information, call (718) 330-1234.

Some old signs remain from the days when there were three separate systems running the subways. If you see them, this key might help:

Old IRT system: 1, 2, 3, 4, 5, 6, 7, and Shuttle.

Old IND system: A, B, D, E, F, G, K.

Old BMT system: J, L, M, N, QB, R.

For a single fare, you can ride from the northernmost Bronx to the easternmost part of Queens—or spend all day riding around the system, if you wish. (One man did cover all 704 miles in 22 hours.)

PERILS & PITFALLS

According to the thirteenth survey by the Straphangers' Campaign consumer advocacy organization, the best subway trains and performance were on #7 line; the worst were on the B line. Billions are being spent for improvements due to be completed in 1991.

Driving. Operating a car in the city involves several major hazards (in addition to other vehicles and jaywalking pedestrians): potholes (for which there is no useful game plan) and parking in such a way that the car will be intact (i.e., not stripped of its parts when you return.

PERILS & PITFALLS

Subway veterans stay close to the token booths (where possible) until trains arrive; never stand near the tracks while waiting for the train; avoid riding in empty cars or the last car if it is nearly empty (if necessary, stay close to the conductor or transit policeman); enter and exit via the best-lighted, most trafficked stairways; avoid subway usage altogether after 10 P.M.; and never, ever use the subway restrooms.

Parking. This is safest at garages. (Whatever the garage rate, it's cheaper than possible parking fines and risks of vandalism on the street.) Garages with the lowest rates are west of Eighth Avenue or downtown (below 14th Street). Intermediate in price are the garages at Lincoln Center (West 65th Street at Amsterdam-Columbus avenues) and at the Metropolitan Museum of Art (Fifth Avenue at 81st Street). Convenient commercial garages include one on 54th Street between Fifth Avenue and Avenue of the Americas, and the Hippodrome, Avenue of the Americas at 44th Street.

INSIDERS' TIPS

It is possible to park on the street on upper Park Avenue (above 60th Street) from 6 P.M. Friday to 8 A.M. Monday, and on the east side of Fifth Avenue (above 90th Street) with relative confidence that the police will not ticket or tow your car away for parking violation overnight. You can also park on many east-west streets on alternate days during certain hours. Look for the signs, usually at each end of the block.

Street Address Key

The nearest cross street on any avenue is found by using this system: Cancel the number's last digit, divide by 2, then add or subtract (as specified) the key number given below. Example: 350 Park Avenue: Cancel last figure (0), divide by 2, add key number (35). Result: 52nd Street.

Avenue	*Key Number*
A, B, C, D	Add 3
First	Add 3
Second	Add 3
Third	Add 10
Fifth up to 200	Add 13
201–400	Add 16
401–600	Add 18
601–775	Add 20
776–1286	Cancel last digit, do not divide by 2, but subtract 18
1287–1500	Add 45
2000+	Add 24
Ave. of the Americas, formerly Sixth	Subtract 12
Seventh, to 110th St.	Add 12
Seventh, above 110th St.	Add 20
Eighth	Add 10
Ninth	Add 13
Tenth	Add 14
Audubon	Add 165
Amsterdam	Add 60
Broadway (23rd–192nd Sts.)	Subtract 30
Columbus	Add 60
Lenox	Add 110
Lexington	Add 22
Madison	Add 26
Park	Add 35
Park Ave. South, formerly Fourth Ave.	Add 8
West End Ave.	Add 60
Central Park West	Divide by 10, then add 60
Riverside Drive	Divide by 10, then add 72

To find crosstown addresses:

The numbers go up 100 each block to the west or east of Fifth Avenue. Thus, Fifth Avenue to Avenue of the Americas = 1–100; Avenue of the Americas to Seventh Avenue = 101–200; Seventh Avenue to Eighth Avenue = 201–300; etc. The same is true to the east of Fifth Avenue, if you ignore the "intrusion" of Madison and Lexington avenues: i.e., Fifth to Park = 1–100; Park to Third = 101–200; etc.

New York State

If you are trying to bite off a chunk of this large state at one time, the auto is *the* way to do it. The combination of interstate and state highways and even the back roads that lace the state are excellent and well-marked. Gas stations are plentiful, and gas costs less now than a few years ago (and even less the farther away from New York City you go).

If you are concentrating on a specific area of the state, you'll save time by flying to the major city, then renting a car to drive around. Among the pleasures of this beautiful and lushly foliated state are the discoveries along many of the back roads. A car makes such exploration easy.

Even within the larger cities (except New York City), driving is relatively easy and problem-free, once you get the hang of locations. If you prefer to park your car at your hotel and rely on local taxis or buses, it is convenient to do so in such cities as Albany, Binghamton, Rochester, Syracuse, or Buffalo (which has an attractive new, but short, subway system).

SHOPPING

New York City

Shopping is to New Yorkers as oil is to Texans or corn to Iowans. It is ingrained, a way of life, or, as one friend of ours put it, "Shops are us."

For the visitor, the reason quickly becomes apparent: no matter where you live or visit in Manhattan, shops surround you. Big, fancy, sleek shops, especially on Fifth and Madison avenues; clever little one-of-a-kind boutiques, found on upper Madison Avenue and also in Greenwich Village, in SoHo, and on the Upper West Side. Department stores, bargain discount stores, neighborhood mom-and-pop shops—they're everywhere in New York.

What are the best buys? Clothes, for sure. After all, the Garment District is in New York. Couturier and big-name label clothes are at their most diverse in the city, as are the "knockoffs" of such stylish clothes. But mass-produced clothing is another big, big value in New York, and because of the competition, you won't find better buys anywhere.

Art, antiques, and adornments (jewelry, baubles, personal accessories) all can be found in endless variations in galleries and specialty shops all over town. You'll see irresistible *objets* you can't live without (though before you saw them, you may never have known you needed them).

New York has been the great world *entrepôt* for nearly a century. You'll find in Manhattan every conceivable kind of merchandise made by the hand of man. Especially alluring are goods from exotic lands—Indian fabrics, South American leatherwork and African carvings, electronic marvels from Hong Kong, Taiwan, Korea, and Japan. From France, Italy, and other European countries come great fabrics, high-fashion clothes and accessories, and succulent table delicacies, often in dazzling packages.

New York is a publishing capital—and also a center of reading. No wonder there are so many bookstores featuring such a diversity of reading matter, old, new, rare, and blue.

There are also the permanent flea markets: the shops of Canal Street and those of the Lower East Side (Orchard and Delancey streets), where goods spill out into the street and shopping is like running an obstacle course. There are the delights of shopping in China (Chinatown), in Greece (Astoria), in Lebanon (Brooklyn), in India (6th Street, Manhattan) and other ethnic centers.

New York Style

Outside New York City, the countryside hums, buzzes, clangs, and whirs with craftsmen producing handmade pottery, woodwork, jewelry, handwoven rugs, clothing, wall hangings, and fabrics. Such handwork can be seen not only in Elbert Hubbard's old Roycrofter enclave in East Aurora, but in small towns along the Hudson, the Adirondack lakes, and in all the larger cities as well.

Upstate, a favorite mode is factory outlet shopping. You'll find them in enormous malls in the Albany area, Schenectady, Utica, Rochester, Buffalo, and Niagara Falls. Flea markets are popular too, and who knows, you may find a lamp base that is a twin to one you have, or a picture frame just perfect for your aunt's portrait.

PERILS & PITFALLS

New York's diversity can cause some shopping inconvenience. The shops of many Jewish and Seventh-Day Adventist merchants are closed on Saturdays but open on Sundays.

Antiques is a magic word throughout New York, and the byways are veined with tiny shops that yield unexpected treasures, often at surprisingly modest prices. Antiquers find rural New York's concentrations of antiques shops in the central and far western parts of the state to be a happy hunting ground.

NIGHTLIFE

New York City

New York City at night can be nonstop. The only problem you face (other than having sufficient money) is choosing among the many things to see or do. Theater—Broadway, Off-Broadway, and Off-Off-Broadway—beckons. So do dance, concerts, comedy clubs, revues, nightclubs, cabarets, jazz clubs, and piano bars.

INSIDERS' TIPS

Coupons for discount tickets and cut-rate tickets are available. See Insiders' Information, page 218, for details.

Broadway has long been a nighttime (and matinee) magnet to visitors. But although prices soar, so do the choices. Many of the liveliest, most unusual, experimental, and offbeat productions can be found off Broadway these days. You'll find professional groups staging plays, workshops, and readings in churches, lofts, warehouses, and hotels all over town. Check the

New York Times, The New Yorker, or *New York* magazine for current offerings.

PERILS & PITFALLS

The Broadway—Times Square area ain't what it used to be. It's not only tacky, but it can be downright dangerous late at night. If you attend the theater or a nightclub in the area, by all means taxi back to your hotel. Don't walk the long, dark cross-streets from Broadway to Fifth Avenue at a late hour. It's an open invitation to trouble. Stick with the crowds near the theater or on Broadway until you can flag down a cab.

Music is another New York mania, so pervasive that it alone makes choosing difficult. Whether it's the New York Philharmonic performing at Lincoln Center, the Metropolitan Opera at full volume, chamber music on a river barge, or Gilbert and Sullivan in Central Park, there's always some first-rate music playing somewhere in the city.

Summer in Manhattan is especially fruitful, as entertainment spills outdoors. Much of it's free, like the Philharmonic, Metropolitan Opera, or Shakespeare in Central Park, the Washington Square Festival, and the Naumburg Orchestra concerts at Damrosch Park, as well as myriad events during Lincoln Center Out of Doors.

INSIDERS' TIPS

Some of New York City's best restaurants offer "loss leaders," special pre-theater dinner specials. The Four Seasons, for instance, offers a *prix fixe* menu that's remarkably reasonable for the quality.

If it's mainstream jazz you fancy, Art Blakey and the Jazz Messengers may be at Sweet Basil and Mel Lewis and orchestra at the Village Vanguard. In the cabarets you will find Bobby Short, the doyen of cabaret troubadors, at his favorite stomping grounds, the Cafe Carlyle. At other venues you may find Anita Ellis, Jon Hendricks, or comics such as Bob Nelson. For other tastes there are discos, nightclubs, jazz clubs, rock groups, "big name" powerhouse bands (Woody Herman, "Glenn Miller") in concert, and, for contrast, tinkly piano bars.

If you want to dance the night away, Sounds of Brazil (S.O.B.'s) is but one of the places that beckons.

If you want something racier, Manhattan has it too, in spades: topless bars and shows, porno, S&M, and gay films—all in the 40s west of Times Square.

PERILS & PITFALLS

Expect a doorman at "in" discos, lounges, and popular watering holes. If the doorman views your costume and appearance as consonant with the "image" of the place, you are (for a fee) allowed in. If you don't measure up to his "customer profile" and can't supply the proper incantation or owner/partner reference, skip along elsewhere; no hard feelings, but you've had it, kid.

New York State

Manhattan hasn't cornered the culture market. Albany, Buffalo, Rochester, Schenectady, Syracuse, and even smaller cities and towns have their share of professional theater, active music programs, and nighttime goings-on.

Jazz and cabaret thrive in Rochester's Yuk Yuk's Komedy Kabaret, Jazzberry's Music Hall, and Lloyd's, to name a few. In Buffalo, it's Upstairs at the Tralf (Tralfamadore) for a 7-nights-a-week variety diet that runs from comedy to international stars of folk, rock, bluegrass, and jazz.

Summer is especially bountiful, bringing delightful theatricals (revivals and recent Broadway hits) on the "straw hat circuit"—the theaters that blossom from Memorial Day to Labor Day, usually located near major cities, in resort and popular vacation areas (such as the Westbury, Long Island, Music Fair). All over the state you'll find festivals, fairs, and special celebratory events. (Among the finest: Artpark at Lewiston; Chautauqua Institution; Saratoga Performing Arts Center; Pepsico Summerfare at Purchase, Caramoor at Katonah.)

PAMPERING THE BODY BEAUTIFUL

New York City

When it comes to the pursuit of health and beauty, New York takes second place to no other city.

Some of the world's most famous beauty specialists operate in Manhattan. Here is a mere sampling: *For your body:* Elizabeth Arden, 691 Fifth Avenue at 54th–55th streets, tel. 486-7900; Pilates Studio for Body Conditioning, 29 West 56th Street, tel. 974-9511. *For your hair:* Vidal Sassoon (for men and women), 767 Fifth Avenue, tel. 535-9200; Monsieur Marc, 22 East 65th Street, tel. 861-0700 (a Nancy Reagan favorite). *For your skin:* Christine Valmy Skin Care salons, 153 West 57th Street, tel. 581-9488, and 1 Rockefeller Plaza, tel. 315-4141.

For personal service: Rosalinda, 22 East 66th Street, tel. 737-2788, for both men and women, specializes in manicures and pedicures, waxing and wining (free glass), massages and facials, to a Bach beat.

If you want walk-in *facial make-over* suggestions on the spot, visit the cosmetics section at Bloomingdale's, Bonwit's, and other department stores. If the cosmeticians don't satisfy you, check the Yellow Pages again, under "Physicians and Surgeons, Plastic Surgery."

For shaping up, there are scores of health clubs and gymnasiums in New York's major cities (see the Yellow Pages). Many are on hotel premises, and as a hotel guest you're eligible to use the facilities. They're equipped with the latest self-torture instruments to burn away fat and upgrade muscle tone.

If you want to maintain your condition by jogging or bicycling, most hotels can suggest routes and bike rentals close by.

PERILS & PITFALLS

Before heading out on a jog, ask the concierge for safe routes and safe hours and *follow his advice.* Don't think you can do Central Park alone or after dark, for instance.

INSIDERS' TIPS

Health clubs in Manhattan: Body Basic, 145 East 47th Street, tel. 751-2260; New York Health & Racquet Club, 132 East 45th Street, tel. 924-4600, 110 West 56th Street, tel. 541-7200, and 39 Whitehall Street, tel. 269-9800; One to One Fitness Center, 220 East 86th Street, tel. 737-2016.

New York State

The spa experience can be an enjoyable part of a visit to New York. Most famous, perhaps, is the traditional, state-owned Roosevelt Baths at Saratoga Springs. There's also the New Age Health Farm of Neversink in the Catskills, as well as several spas-within-hotels.

YOU AND YOUR MACHINES

No surprises here. Electric current is the same 120 AC you're accustomed to elsewhere in the United States.

If you are staying at a luxury, super deluxe, or deluxe hotel, you will find the room equipped with a color TV, probably equipped to play cable or in-hotel movies along with the usual selection of programs. Most such rooms are equipped with small clock radios, many with programmable alarms. Hair dryers are frequently standard equipment, and irons usually are available on request.

PERILS & PITFALLS

One note of caution: stow your own prized gadgets (cameras, portable computer, calculators) in a locked suitcase or a closet or dresser when you leave your hotel room. This is a recommended safeguard against a possible theft by someone cruising the hallway, ready to duck in and swipe any loose valuables that are visible, while the maid who is cleaning the room has the door open and her back turned.

If you bring your own tape- or disc-player "boom box," plug it in without qualms (except for complaints from the next room). And if you are in search of any electronic or photographic item, New York's discount stores have the best prices (See Where to Shop, page 195).

TELEPHONE, TELEGRAPH, AND MAIL

Telephones in New York State are part of the Nynex system. Local coin phone calls are 25¢. You will find that airports, bus stations, and some hotels now have alternate telephones that accept your MCI, AT&T, or Sprint charge numbers or cards.

New York City area codes are 212 for Manhattan and the Bronx, 718 for Queens, Brooklyn, and Staten Island. The tariff is 25¢ in or between these areas, but if you call from 212 to 718 or vice versa, you must dial 1 before the area code.

There are six other area codes in New York State, from 516 for Long Island and 914 for Westchester to 716 for the Buffalo-Niagara region.

Telegrams and mailgrams can be sent from your hotel room by telephoning Western Union at (800) 325-6000 and charging the message to your home telephone.

Mail is collected several times a day at busy places such as major office buildings, airports, and train and bus stations. You can leave mail at hotel desks and streetcorner mailboxes or post offices. (In Manhattan, the main post office is a grand McKim, Mead & White edifice of 1913 that covers two blocks between 31st and 33rd streets on Eighth Avenue.)

BUSINESS HOURS

Yes, business hours for *business* are pretty much the same in New York City and State as elsewhere in the country.

However, there are some other hours that you may want to keep in mind.

Many businesses, banks, schools, museums, and other public places shut down on major holidays (Thanksgiving, Christmas, New Year's) and often the federal holidays, as well as some religious holidays (Good Friday and Rosh Hashana).

Museums and special exhibitions generally do not open before 10 A.M., usually close at 5 P.M., and are often closed Mondays.

Theaters—(Broadway, Off-Broadway, and Off-Off-Broadway)—usually have Wednesday matinees at 2 P.M. Broadway theaters also have Saturday matinees at 2 P.M. The other theaters sometimes have Sunday, not Saturday, matinees, often at 3 P.M. Evenings, curtain time is usually 8 P.M. Many theaters are closed on Monday.

Restaurants—good ones—are mobbed at lunchtime, with 1 P.M. the peak time. If you want to try your luck without a reservation, arrive at 11:30 A.M. or after 2 P.M. In the evening, some restaurants serve pretheater dinners beginning about 6 P.M. (it's much easier to get a table at this hour), but the most popular dining time is from 8 to 9:30 P.M.

Galleries and boutiques seldom open before 10 A.M. (in SoHo, noon), and may be open Sunday, closed Monday.

Cabarets and nightspots begin to warm up after 11 or 12 P.M. and may continue until the adrenaline plays out.

Resorts. In these areas seasonal rules often apply. During the "mud season" (much of April) the Catskills seem closed down, especially during the week. Mountain and lake areas, popular amusements, and tourist attractions extend their hours and operating schedules during the height of their seasons. That means summer, fall, and, in ski areas, much of the winter.

STUDYING IN NEW YORK

New York is the world's primary clearinghouse and key transaction point for information—economic, social, you name it—and as such, it is a major educational hub.

The state has hundreds of academic institutions, many of them venerable, prestigious, and immense in enrollment. It also has highly focused commercial in-

stitutions that teach specific subjects—especially the
hottest ones of the moment (computer programming,
word processing, Cajun cooking). Additionally, there
are seminars, one-day institutes, and special educational sessions (some of them perennial, many of them
one-time-only) by the hundreds.

Are there courses of study in subjects that interest
you? Undoubtedly, you can be sure. Your problem,
however, is to find such courses at the time you can or
will be on the scene, and of the length your visit allows.
This will require digging on your part, using the help of
your local librarian for referral to schools or institutions
offering the courses in the city you plan to visit. Not to
be overlooked are the Yellow Pages (under "Schools").

Some suggestions on other sources:

Check academic institutions. Some offer short-term
courses, all-day institutes, or seminars. Write or telephone the continuing-education or general-studies division of the college or university you believe may have
the courses that interest you, and ask for information.
Among the possibilities:

- City University of New York Continuing Education,
  48 East 26th St., 10010. Tel. 725-7172.
- Columbia University School of General Studies,
  116th St. and Broadway, 10027. Tel. 280-3786.
- New School for Social Research, 66 West 12th St.,
  10011. Tel. 741-5600.
- New York University School of Continuing Education,
  25 West 4th St., 10012. Tel. 598-3591.
- Pace University, 1 Pace Plaza, 10005. Tel 488-1200.

Try specialized schools in your area of interest.
These (and hundreds of others) focus on specific areas
of instruction:

- Art Students League of New York, 215 West 57th St.,
  10019. Tel. 247-4510.
- New York Institute of Dietetics, 154 West 14th St.,
  10011. Tel. 675-6655.
- Parsons School of Design, 66 Fifth Ave., 10011. Tel.
  741-8900.
- Pratt Institute, 295 Lafayette St., 10005. Tel. 925-
  8481.

- School of Visual Arts, 209 East 23rd St., 10011. Tel. 683-0600.
- Stuyvesant Adult Center, 225 East 23rd St., 10010. Tel. 254-2890

Don't overlook cultural institutions that offer short courses in cooking, languages, history, music, culture, and so on. These are representative:

- Asia Society, 725 Park Ave., 10021. Tel. 288-6400.
- China Institute in America, 125 East 65th St., 10021. Tel. 744-8181.
- French Institute/Alliance Française, 22 East 60th St., 10022. Tel. 355-6100.
- Japan House, 333 East 47th St., 10017. Tel. 832-1155.
- Metropolitan Museum of Art, 82nd St. at Fifth Ave., 10028. Tel. 879-5500.
- Spanish Institute, 684 Park Ave., 10028. Tel. 628-0420.

SPORTS IN NEW YORK

New York City is the nation's number-one center for contests, whether it's pitting individuals or teams against one another.

The major site for many events is Madison Square Garden, 4 Pennsylvania Plaza, Seventh Avenue and 32nd Street (212) 564-4400.

Here are the major teams and sports, and their venues:

Baseball
- New York Mets, Shea Stadium, tel. (718) 507-TIXX.
- New York Yankees, Yankee Stadium, tel. 293-6000.

Basketball
- New York Knicks, Madison Square Garden, tel. 564-4400.

Football
- New York Jets, Giants Stadium, tel. (201) 421-6600.
- New York Giants, Giants Stadium, tel. (201) 935-8222.

Hockey
- New York Rangers, Madison Square Garden, tel. 564-4400.
- New York Islanders, Nassau Coliseum, tel. (516) 587-9222.

Horse Racing
- Aqueduct, Ozone Park, Queens, tel. (718) 641-4700.
- Belmont Park, Belmont, Queens, tel. (718) 641-4700.
- Meadowlands, NJ, tel. (201) 935-8500.
- Roosevelt Raceway, Westbury, tel. (516) 222-2000.
- Yonkers Raceway, Yonkers, tel. (914) 968-4200.

Soccer
- Cosmos, Giants Stadium, tel. (201) 265-8600.

Tennis
- U.S. Open, USTA National Tennis Center, tel. (718) 271-5100.
- Davis Cup Matches, USTA National Tennis Center, tel. (718) 271-5100.
- Tournament of Champions, West Side Tennis Club, tel. (718) 268-2300.

Buffalo and Rochester both have professional sports teams. You'll find them mentioned in Insiders' Information for the West, at the end of the last chapter in this book.

INSIDERS' TIPS

If you're a jock at heart, these two Manhattan restaurants might interest you (just remember, food is secondary): Rusty's, 1271 Third Avenue at 73rd Street (owner Rusty Staub is a former Met, now a Mets announcer); 17 Murray Street, same address, downtown, West Side (Ron Darling, Mets pitcher, is part owner).

TRAVELING WITH CHILDREN

New York City and State offer an unequaled menu of attractions with enough pizzazz and variety to appeal both to youngsters and their parents.

In the state's parks you'll find superb beaches, pounding surf (on Long Island), serene forest glades, mountain aeries, or lakefronts jumping with water sports—the choices are yours. (Information and maps are available, see Useful Addresses and Telephone Numbers, page 61.)

There are places where history comes alive, such as Cooperstown, with its Baseball Museum and Hall of Fame; Forts Stanwix, Niagara, and Ticonderoga; the homes of Washington Irving and Presidents Franklin D. and Theodore Roosevelt. Also, the *Intrepid* Sea-Air-Space Museum on that heroic World War II aircraft carrier. And there's every American's favorite lady, the Statue of Liberty.

There are awesome places, such as Niagara Falls; Rhinebeck Aerodrome, when vintage planes are roaring overhead; Manhattan viewed from bridges, boats, or observation decks; and a visit to the State Capitol in Albany or the New York Stock Exchange on Wall Street.

Other sure-fire kid- and parent-pleasers are the Bronx Zoo; Indian, African and dinosaur exhibits at New York City's American Museum of Natural History and Buffalo's Museum of Science; the Metropolitan Museum's New Guinea sculpture and medieval armor departments; and Albany's New York Museum. There are children's museums in Manhattan, Staten Island, Brooklyn, and Utica; children's zoos in Manhattan's Central Park and in Syracuse.

There are living events, including parades, celebrations, and festivals, outdoor and summer theater, opera and concerts, old steam train and barge and boat trips and on-the-spot action at the circus and the South Street Seaport. Historic villages bring the past to life—like the Genesee County Museum near Rochester, Museum Village of Orange County near the Catskills, Erie Canal Village in Rome, and the Shaker village at Old Chatham. For a brief entertainment, call the recorded Children's Story telephone line in New York City at 976-3636.

One thing's certain—your problem will not be *finding* things to interest the youngster, but sorting out which ones you have the time to enjoy.

INSIDERS' TIPS

If you need a baby-sitter, try the Gilbert Child Care Agency, 206 East 81st Street, tel. 302-3200 (hourly rate per child, with a 4-hour minimum and transportation extra); and Barnard College child-care service, tel. 280-2035 (hourly rate plus taxi fare).

READING MATTER AND OTHER MEDIA

For entertainment information about New York City—who or what is playing where and when—your best bets are the following:

- *The New Yorker* magazine's weekly "Goings on About Town" listings include succinct comments on theater, concerts, movies, art exhibitions, sports, and other treats.
- *New York* magazine features a thorough weekly listing, called "Cue," of theater, music, dance, movies, art, nightlife (cabaret, comedy, pop and jazz, discos, hotel and piano bars), sports events, and radio and TV highlights.
- *The New York Times* Friday "Weekend" section reviews the latest plays and films, and prints a "weekend movie clock" that lists interesting films. It also has an avalanche of theater, movie, art museum, and gallery ads, plus an "events and openings" schedule that includes concerts, recitals, opera, and dance. The section also carries at least one major restaurant review and a "dining out guide" with brief notes about eateries. The daily TV page lists all the programs plus major radio concerts, talk and sports programs.

INSIDERS' TIPS

Look for the Friday *Times* "Availability of Theater Tickets" report for accurate information about current shows.

- The *New York Times*'s Sunday "Arts & Entertainment" section carries ads, previews, and reviews of new plays, operas, concerts, dance, and movies. Its "The Guide" section is a comprehensive listing of what's going on in the city. It details TV programs and radio concerts for the week, lists theater openings and previews, "Performance Art," spectacles and comedians, and new, "recommended" and revival films, opera and concerts, jazz, pop/folk/rock, dance performances, and art and photography exhibitions in galleries and museums.

■ The *Village Voice* is the liberal weekly newspaper that pulls no punches and prides itself on reviewing the newest, most outrageous or courageous offerings from Broadway to Off-Broadway. This is the paper to check if you want to know what's going on in SoHo, TriBeCa, and Greenwich Village.

For really funky news, look for *City Paper* or *Details*, in the Village and East Village, especially.

■ *New York Newsday*'s daily edition gives complete TV listings and reviews new theater and movies. Its weekend edition spells out current movie and theater offerings and the TV schedule.

■ *Where* magazine is distributed free at hotel desks.

■ *Art Now/New York Gallery Guide* lists current art exhibitions of the month, with maps of commercial gallery and museum locations. Copies are free at art galleries and showrooms.

INSIDERS' TIPS

For advice, counsel, free literature, and maps, as well as notices of new plays, musicals, attractions, *and* discount coupons to some of them, call the New York Convention & Visitors Bureau, 2 Columbus Circle, tel. 397-8222.

For more information, be sure to check the TV in your hotel room. Many hotels now have a cable TV service that carries one channel featuring news of current theater, museum, concert, and other attractions.

VHF television channels in New York City are 2 (CBS), 4 (NBC), 5 (WNEW), 7 (ABC), 9 (WOR), 11 (WPIX), and 13 (technically, Newark, New Jersey, is metropolitan New York's Public Broadcasting System station, WNET). The city itself owns Channel 31 (WNYC). Look for local news between 4:30 and 6 and at 11 P.M.

For classical music on radio, try WNCN at 104.3 FM, WNYC at 93.9 FM, and WQXR at 1560 AM and 96.3 FM. WCBS-FM, 101, plays golden oldies, and rock may be heard on Z100, K-ROCK, and WNEW-FM, 102.7.

All-news, round-the-clock radio stations are WCBS at 880 AM and WINS at 1010 AM.

USEFUL ADDRESSES AND TELEPHONE NUMBERS

Travel Information

- For information and publications, contact New York State Tourism, Department of Commerce, 1 Commerce Plaza, Albany 12245 (tel. [800] 225-5697 from out of state, or [518] 474-4116 in New York State): "Outdoors" and camping guide; tourism map, "Skiing and Winter Sports"; discount coupon book; seasonal events (arts, cultural, sports) listing. Dial toll-free (800) 637-8800 for a free coupon book and the rest of an I Love NY Great Vacations Kit. New York Convention & Visitors Bureau, 2 Columbus Circle, New York 10019. Tel. (212) 397-8222. For literature: "NYC Tour Package Directory," "NYC Visitors Guide and Map," calendar of events, etc.

- State Parks & Historic Sites, Office of Parks and Recreation, Albany 12238, for hunting, fishing, boating, canal-boating, and bicycling info, and schedule of park events, skiing, and skating in parks.

- Department of Agriculture & Markets, Albany 12235, for leaflets about "Grown in NY State, U-Pick Farm List," New York State wineries and wine tours, dates of agricultural fairs.

- Albany County Convention & Visitors Bureau, 52 South Pearl St., 12207. Tel. (518) 434-1217 or (800) 622-8464.

- Greater Buffalo Chamber of Commerce, 107 Delaware Ave., 14202. Tel. (716) 852-7100.

- Rochester Convention & Visitors Bureau, 120 East Main St., 14604. Tel. (716) 546-3070.

LEAVING NEW YORK

GETTING TO THE AIRPORT

From New York City

To La Guardia and Kennedy International airports. Express motor coach (Carey Transportation or Olympia Express Bus) from certain hotels and AirTransCenter at Port Authority Bus Terminal, Eighth Avenue at 42nd Street entrance; every 30 minutes from 7:15 A.M. to 10:15 P.M. (to La Guardia), Carey $6, Olympia $5; and 7:15 A.M. to 11:15 P.M. (to JFK) Carey $8. Tel. 564-8484. Also from Grand Central Terminal. From World Trade Center and Brooklyn LIRR Terminal, Olympia charges only $5.

Helicopter service from East 34th Street Heliport (at East River) to TWA International Terminal every 40 minutes from about 7 A.M. to 7 P.M. Flight time, 10 minutes. Fare, $58, one way. Tel. (718) 895-1626 for information.

Taxis, licensed and metered. Fare, about $25 to JFK, about $18 to La Guardia.

To JFK International Airport. Subway/bus "Train to the Plane" from 8 subway stations via B and F trains: Borough Hall (Brooklyn), Broadway-Nassau St., Chambers St. (World Trade Center), West 4th St., 34th St., 42nd St., 50th St. (Rockefeller Center), and 57th St. in Manhattan. Departs every 20 minutes from 5 A.M. to midnight, connects with air-conditioned bus marked "JFK Express Shuttle." Combined fare, $6.50. Running time, 1 hour and 20 minutes. Tel. (718) 330-1234.

PERILS & PITFALLS

No sweat. The "Train to the Plane" may be right for you *if* you have only light hand luggage. There is no porter service available, and you have to descend and climb subway stairs, board and disembark from a bus.

To Newark International Airport. Express motor coach (New Jersey Transit) from AirTransCenter, Port Authority Bus Terminal, 42nd St. and Eighth Ave., runs every 15 minutes from 5:45 A.M. to 1:15 A.M., fare $5. Tel. 564-8484.

Taxi service, at about $35.

Other bus services: Mini Bus Service, tel. (718) 361-9092; Greyhound, tel. (201) 642-8205.

To Albany Airport. Albany Airport Limousine Service, tel. (518) 463-4455, fare $4.90 per person. Public transit bus 60¢; tel. (518) 482-9191.

To Rochester Airport. Cardinal Cab, tel. 424-4475, fare $10 per person. Public transit bus 70¢; tel. 288-1700.

To Greater Buffalo International Airport. Taxis, fare about $11, tel. (716) 852-4000.

To Niagara Falls Airport. Taxi, fare about $20–$28, tel. (716) 633-1473 or 633-8294. Airporter buses, from hotels directly to airport, $8 per person.

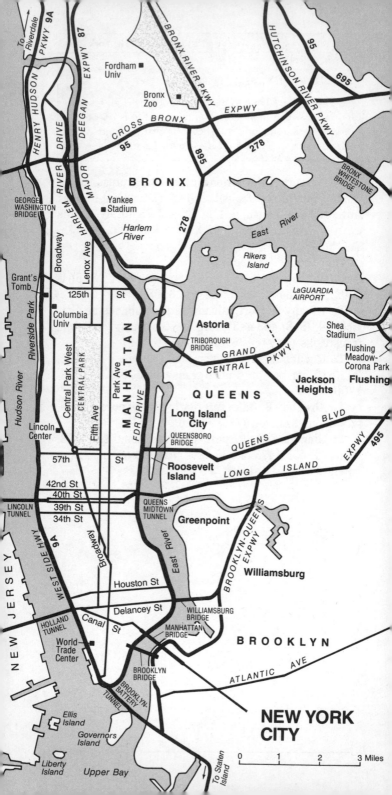

NEW YORK CITY

0　　1　　2　　3 Miles

NEW YORK CITY

NEW YORK CITY IN A HURRY

> ### ONE-DAY ITINERARY
>
> Empire State Building, Rockefeller Center, St. Patrick's Cathedral, Museum of Modern Art, Grand Central Terminal, United Nations, Times Square.

What to see with limited time in New York? That's like leading a toddler to a candy store and saying, "Choose only one item, and you have just one minute to do it."

Consider this and subsequent chapters on things to see in New York as *guidelines.* Your own special interests should dictate whether you gorge yourself on New York's rich art diet to the exclusion of other sights, have an orgy of theatergoing or shopping, or spend all your free time exploring the city's historic or literary sights. *Chacun a son goût.* The choices are yours.

For the first-time visitor, we'd suggest beginning your first day in the center of the city, seeing sights unique to New York, that are part of Manhattan's cultural excitement.

Another possibility you might consider is an "overlightly" city view. This means a half-day bus tour and/or (depending on the clarity of the weather) a boat-trip circuit of Manhattan.

Two reliable bus tour companies are
- Carey Gray Line, which offers 15 different tours, ranging from 2 hours to all day. Call them at 397-2620 for fares, schedules, itineraries, departure times and points.
- Short Line Tours/American Sightseeing International, 166 West 46th St., tel. 354-4740.

A boat cruise around Manhatten shows you the Statue of Liberty, the skyline from four points of the compass, bridges, buildings, and many sights at water level. Circle Line boats depart frequently (every 45 minutes from mid-June until September 1 from 9:30 A.M. to 5 P.M., less often from March to mid-June and from September through November). A trip takes 3 hours and covers some 35 miles, departing from Pier 83 on the Hudson River (at the foot of West 43rd Street). The fare is $12 for adults, $6 for children 12 and under.

New York is called the Empire State, so it's only fitting that one of the city's most famous landmarks is called the Empire State Building, at 350 Fifth Avenue, between 33rd and 34th streets. Our suggestion is to visit it, of course, and then head uptown to other important and impressive sights.

The 102-story Empire State Building♛ ♛ ♛ ♛, a marvel of engineering in its time, was completed within two years and opened in 1931. This was during the Depression, when office space went begging, so for years the vast structure was dubbed the Empty State Building. The story goes that the owners paid their taxes solely on the fees charged sightseers who flocked to the observation decks. The building is on the site where two hotels, the Waldorf and the Astoria, originally were.

For decades—until Chicago's Sears Tower and New York's World Trade Center surpassed it in recent times—the Empire State Building was the world's tallest structure (originally 1,250 feet high—before TV antennas were added). It certainly dominated Manhattan. It still does. At night, when the top 30 stories are lighted (from twilight to midnight), the Empire State Building is like a beacon visible for miles around the city. The only times you won't see it are cloudy and foggy nights, and also during the spring and fall migratory bird season, when the lights are turned off because the flocks might get confused by the light and fly into the building. (Who says New York doesn't have a heart?) The last—and only—time a movable object flew into the Empire State Building was in 1945 when a U.S. bomber crashed into the 78th and 79th floors. The building sways in the wind, as it was designed to do, but it remains sturdy and steadfast, a tribute to the engineering skill of its builders.

You'll want to buy a ticket to the Observation Tower (open from 9:30 A.M. to midnight), and head upward, not by the King Kong method, but via an express elevator that whizzes you to the 80th floor within a minute. You then transfer to another elevator to the 86th-floor Observatory, an open platform with a protective wall.

On a clear day, it seems that you can see forever. In fact, the view reaches 50 miles in every direction. And your overview, or pigeon perspective, of New York is exhilarating. The excitement intensifies if you take another elevator to the glass-enclosed, circular, 102nd-floor Observatory, where views can extend 80 miles.

PERILS & PITFALLS

Mist, haze, smog, or rain can reduce visibility. Ask about the current visibility *before* buying your ticket. If it's bad, save the visit for a later time or for evening, when you won't see 50 miles, but you'll have a view of New York lit up. Some say the best time is when lights begin to go on at dusk. Pure magic.

When you return to earth, move uptown to the Rockefeller Center area, either afoot (it's 14 short blocks) or by walking over to Madison Avenue to hail a taxi or take a bus. (Fifth Avenue is one way going downtown or south, Madison is one way uptown or north.)

If you walk uptown along Fifth Avenue, you'll pass the New York Public Library♕ ♕ ♕, between 40th and 42nd streets. No danger of missing it. The massive, elongated 1911 building, guarded by two imperious marble lions (the work of E. C. Potter), spreads over two full blocks and is one of Gotham's many architectural gems. Built in the Beaux Arts style of white Vermont marble, with Corinthian entrance columns and superb neoclassical detailing, the library is a delight inside and out.

You approach it by climbing a set of broad stairs on Fifth Avenue (a popular reviewing stand to assay the passing parade and also to eat a bring-your-own lunch). Inside is a collection of books and manuscripts so vast it makes the library the second-largest research library in the United States (surpassed only by the Library of Congress in Washington, D.C.).

INSIDERS' TIPS

Be comfortable during your sightseeing and museum-going. Although New York can be America's dressiest, most stylish city at night, by day it is as casual as you want it to be. If you want to blend in like a native, don't give a second thought to wearing sneakers. You'll see prim-looking executives "dressed for success" from the ankles up, with tote bag in hand for quick shoe-changes at lunch or tea time.

For the visitor with the time and inclination, the library has a splendid original print collection, and there's always a changing exhibit in the Print Gallery. One of many treasured documents the library owns is a draft of the Declaration of Independence in Jefferson's hand. It and many other rare documents and books are on display from time to time.

Between the library and Avenue of the Americas is Bryant Park, which was the site of the first world's fair held in the United States, back in 1853–54. Today the park's arching shade trees, sculpture, fountain, and inviting open areas provide the setting for free summer concerts. There is also a TKTS (tickets) sales booth (for dance and Lincoln Center events) in the park.

PERILS & PITFALLS

Druggies, pushers, and derelicts sometimes use the park to "score," so unless there's a special event, such as an exhibit, a free concert, or a rally, with crowds on hand, tourists are advised to be extremely careful there.

On the southwest corner of 43rd Street, notice a small, glass-walled jewelbox of a building, Manufacturers Hanover Trust Co. ♛ It doesn't look remarkable today, but back in 1954 when "Manny-Hanny" hired Skidmore, Owings & Merrill to design it, it seemed revolutionary (and certainly profligate in its conspicuously minimal use of the air rights), especially for such a bastion of conservatism as a bank.

In retrospect, it was the prototype for the "open" (rather than "fortress") bank. (See how the massive vault door is a focal point, visible from all areas, inside as well as out.) It gave tremendous impetus to the move to sleek, finely detailed, glass-and-steel skyscrapers that soon mushroomed all over the city.

PERILS & PITFALLS

All along Fifth Avenue and certain side streets, you'll see sidewalk vendors with wares displayed on the ground (the better to scoop it up if the cops approach)— anything from nuts and dried fruits to umbrellas, imitation designer watches, leather belts, bags, blacksnake whips, and windup toys, all at knock-down bargain prices. Some New Yorkers swear by the value, but we say inspect carefully and *caveat emptor*.

And watch out for the "three-card monte" dodge, a playing-card variation of the old shell game, usually set up on a makeshift "table" of cardboard boxes. Believe it or not, this hoary, no-win swindle still works on gullible rubes, including some New Yorkers.

At West 47th Street you have reached "Diamond Row." This one long block between Fifth Avenue and Avenue of the Americas is the center of New York's wholesale and retail diamond and jewelry district. It is studded with shops, such as the Diamond Center of America, International Jewelers Exchange, and National Jewelers Exchange, plus a multitude of upstairs shops and booths. Many of these are manned by Orthodox Jews in side curls, black hats, and long frock coats. An estimated 80 percent of the United States' wholesale diamond business is conducted on this block, sometimes right on the sidewalk, often in a babel of foreign languages.

Rockefeller Center ♛ ♛ ♛ ♛ ♛ begins at Fifth Avenue and West 48th Street and extends north to 51st and west past Avenue of the Americas, covering some 22 acres in all. Most of the 19 structures date back to before World War II (1931–40), when John D. Rockefeller, Jr., decided to build a commercial center on land largely owned by Columbia University.

The result has been called the most beautifully designed urban complex of the 20th century. The original buildings complement each other. There are well-planned open spaces, pedestrian and vehicular thoroughfares, and a large subway station, plus a labyrinth of underground concourse passageways that interconnect the buildings and have shops and eateries. One short street carved out of a block between Fifth Avenue and Avenue of the Americas cuts a swath from West 48th to West 50th. It is actually a private thoroughfare, and to preserve its private status, it is closed one day a year.

Rockefeller Center may not be the navel of New York's universe, but judging by the crowds of camera-toting tourists, it is obviously one of the places many visitors head first. It is certainly a focus and a handy starting point for a walking romp through the city's culture canyons.

"Rock Center" is lively any time of year. Of course, during the Christmas holidays, everyone, local *and* out-of-towner, comes here to see the enormous (usually 65 to 90 feet tall) fir tree that's become a symbol of New York at Christmastime.

PERILS & PITFALLS

Many of the shops and restaurants in the complex are geared to the tourist trade, with prices often reaching ozone heights.

Yet Rock Center has something to offer in any season. Mostly it's a sense of the rush and flow of New York life. It has been estimated that in the course of a business day there are more people in Rockefeller Center than in the entire state of Alaska. Some 65,000 work in the Center's buildings.

Tourists come to try the restaurants (34 in Center buildings), watch the skaters in the open-air ice-skating rink (or put on the blades themselves), shop in the concourse and ground-floor stores (200 shops and ser-

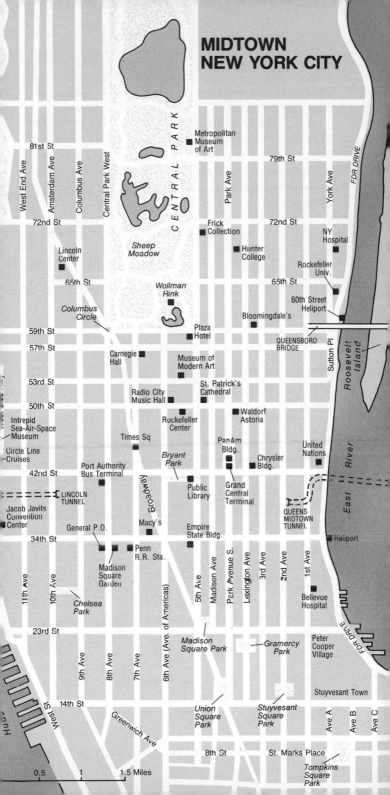

MIDTOWN NEW YORK CITY

CENTRAL PARK

Metropolitan Museum of Art

Sheep Meadow

Wollman Rink

Columbus Circle

Lincoln Center

Frick Collection

Hunter College

NY Hospital

Rockefeller Univ.

60th Street Heliport

Bloomingdale's

Plaza Hotel

QUEENSBORO BRIDGE

Carnegie Hall

Museum of Modern Art

St. Patrick's Cathedral

Roosevelt Island

Radio City Music Hall

Rockefeller Center

Waldorf Astoria

Intrepid Sea-Air-Space Museum

Circle Line Cruises

Times Sq

Bryant Park

Pan Am Bldg.

Chrysler Bldg.

United Nations

Port Authority Bus Terminal

Public Library

Grand Central Terminal

East River

LINCOLN TUNNEL

QUEENS MIDTOWN TUNNEL

Jacob Javits Convention Center

Macy's

General P.O.

Empire State Bldg.

Heliport

Penn R.R. Sta.

Madison Square Garden

Chelsea Park

Bellevue Hospital

Madison Square Park

Gramercy Park

Peter Cooper Village

Union Square Park

Stuyvesant Square Park

Stuyvesant Town

St. Marks Place

Tompkins Square Park

81st St
79th St
72nd St
72nd St
65th St
65th St
59th St
57th St
53rd St
50th St
42nd St
34th St
23rd St
14th St
8th St

West End Ave
Amsterdam Ave
Columbus Ave
Central Park West
Park Ave
York Ave
FDR DRIVE
Sutton Pl
Broadway
5th Ave
Madison Ave
Park Avenue S.
Lexington Ave
3rd Ave
2nd Ave
1st Ave
FDR DRIVE
Ave A
Ave B
Ave C
11th Ave
10th Ave
9th Ave
8th Ave
7th Ave
6th Ave (Ave. of Americas)
Greenwich Ave
West St
Hudson

0.5   1   1.5 Miles

vices in all), enjoy a drink in the outdoor café or the Rainbow Room atop the RCA Building, or see a Rockettes extravaganza in Radio City Music Hall.

You might want to take a one-hour guided tour of Rockefeller Center (which includes a tour of Radio City Music Hall and the Observation Roof of the RCA Building). If so, buy your ticket at the Guided Tour office on the ground floor of the RCA Building, then wait right there for the next tour to form. Tours leave every 30 minutes, from 9:30 A.M. to 4:45 P.M.

If you want to explore the area on your own, begin at the Channel Gardens or Promenade, an oasis between the French (number 610) and English (number 620) buildings, which face Fifth Avenue. Both have brightly re-gilded bas-reliefs on their Fifth Avenue façades. The gardens are really a series of formal pools bordered by flowerbeds that change with the season (from pre-Easter lilies to autumn chrysanthemums).

INSIDERS' TIPS

On Fifth Avenue near Rock Center, you'll find people offering free tickets to TV shows—usually game shows or previews of new programs. Another source of free TV tickets is the Information Center, New York Convention & Visitors Bureau, 2 Columbus Circle. You can also secure tickets at the TV companies: NBC at 30 Rockefeller Plaza; CBS at 51 West 52nd Street, and ABC at 1330 Avenue of the Americas. Go as early as possible for choice tickets. But if you want tickets for "Saturday Night Live" or "Late Night with David Letterman," you'll have to write months in advance to NBC, Rockefeller Center, 10020.

At the far end of the garden area, steps lead down, below street level, to the Lower Plaza, ringed by a parade of national flags (all of those in the United Nations) that flutter here. This lower level is where you'll find the outdoor café in summer, the ice-skating rink in winter.

Marking the far edge of the Lower Plaza is a gilded sculpture of Prometheus stealing the gods' fire for mankind (the 1934 work of sculptor Paul Manship). Towering above the Plaza is the 70-story RCA Building, a slender, well-proportioned slab that rises 850 feet from street level. In this are the National Broadcasting Company offices and studios. Be sure to have a look at the murals in the lobby, the work of Catalan artist Jose Maria Sert. These replaced earlier murals by the Marxist Mexican painter Diego Rivera. When Rivera refused to modify a panel glorifying Lenin, Rockefeller ordered the murals removed.

INSIDERS' TIPS

Up on the 65th floor is the Rainbow Room restaurant, where you can have a drink, do your Fred Astaire-and-Ginger Rogers twirl, and enjoy some fine wide-angle views as well. Just keep in mind it's the views, not the food, you're there for.

The most renowned building in Rockefeller Center is Radio City Music Hall, whose façade and interiors represent a triumph of the art deco style. It is difficult to imagine today in the affluent 1980s what this building meant to Depression-era moviegoers.

The Grand Foyer with its enormous, shimmering crystal chandeliers, the sweeping Grand Staircase, thick-piled art deco carpet, ornate rest rooms (which, in their heyday, were hung with pictures by top-flight painters), and the massive, 5,882-seat theater, all wrapped themselves around the awed visitors, enclosing them, for the length of the program, in a luxurious make-believe world. In addition to first-run movies, spectators watched a live show, featuring the famous Rockettes, precision dancers whose lock-step high kicks made them famous all over the world.

The sense of grandeur was revived at Radio City Music Hall in 1979, when the art deco furnishings were restored. There are usually two performances daily of a live 90-minute show during the regular season from spring to Labor Day, and many specials throughout the year. The Rockettes are back, too, in a Christmas Spectacular, which runs from mid-November to early January. Phone 757-3100 for ticket information and show schedules.

A good luncheon choice in this area is Raga 🦅🦅, an Indian restaurant at 57 West 48th Street. Its waiters don't hassle you to promote drink sales or to hasten your departure. The tables are so well-spaced that privacy is a given. Prices are moderate, considering Raga's location. It has a generous luncheon buffet and "happy hour" canapés.

At the Trans-Lux Experience Theater in the lower plaza of the McGraw-Hill Building, practically across the street at 1221 Avenue of the Americas, there's an hourly multimedia show called "The New York Experience" 🦅🦅 that gives a wonderful sense of the zest and character of New York. You'll experience flashbacks of old New York, fog enveloping the East River, lightning striking the Empire State Building, and much, much more (tel. 869-0345).

INSIDERS' TIPS

Discount tickets for the show are available at the New York Convention & Visitors Bureau.

As you walk, notice some other Rock Center art and amenities. There's a whale-like sculpture in the McGraw-Hill Building's sunken entrance plaza, and the Time-Life Building sports a popular fountain on its serpentine-paved patio. In the Fifth Avenue courtyard of the International Building is a monumental bronze sculpture by Lee Lawrie of Atlas struggling under the weight of the world.

Cross Fifth Avenue to another beloved New York building, St. Patrick's Cathedral 🦅🦅, at 50th Street. The Gothic Revival structure echoes Catholic cathedrals of Europe, but in fact it was started in 1879 and completed in 1906. Fittingly, in light of the large Irish population of New York, it was named in honor of the patron saint of Ireland.

Its architectural model was the cathedral at Cologne, Germany. Highlights of the 331-foot-high edifice are the Gothic-style stained-glass windows (45 of the more than 70 windows were made in Chartres and Nantes, France). In the nave, note the cross-ribbed Gothic arches, the Dutch-made Stations of the Cross, the bronze sculpted doors, and the Lady Chapel behind the altar.

Catholics will want to see the shrine of St. Elizabeth Ann Seton (the first American-born saint, canonized in 1975) on the right side of the nave, and the shrine of St. John Neumann (the first American-born male saint, canonized 1977) on the left side of the nave by the confessionals.

What gives St. Pat's, as it is affectionately called, its special aura are the fashionable weddings and many historic events, notably funerals, celebrated here. Americans old enough to remember Robert Kennedy's assassination in 1968 will recall seeing his televised funeral Mass in St. Patrick's, with his brother Edward's moving eulogy.

Behind St. Patrick's, in the next block, 451–455 Madison (50th–51st streets), is the Helmsley Palace Hotel, a modern tower added to remarkable 19th-century houses that form a U around a central court-yard. These magnificent brownstone mansions, the work of McKim, Mead & White in 1884, were modeled after Rome's Italian Renaissance Palazzo della Cancelleria and were built for Henry Villard, publisher of the *New York Post.*

Later, one section became the home of Whitelaw Roid, publisher of the *New York Tribune,* and another section was bought by Random House. Through all the metamorphoses, the complex was known as the Villard Houses. In their latest reincarnation (before they became part of the hotel), some of the houses were owned by the Roman Catholic Archdiocese of New York. The interiors have been preserved and artfully absorbed into the hotel.

From St. Patrick's, enjoy the two-block saunter up fashionable Fifth Avenue to 53rd Street. On the north-west corner is the Gothic Revival Episcopal Church of St. Thomas, notable for its façade festooned with sta-tues of saints and delicate tracery and, inside, a beautiful reredos over the altar. St. Thomas is well known for its music and many concerts.

Half a block up West 53rd Street is a "church" of another kind: the foremost temple of modern culture, the Museum of Modern Art ♛ ♛ ♛ ♛ ♛, known locally as MOMA, at 11 West 53rd Street.

MOMA's 100,000 paintings, sculptures, drawings, prints, architectural models, original designs, and photographs are considered the most comprehensive modern art collection in the world. To all this add some 8,000 films, videos, and a research library of 80,000 books and periodicals. MOMA is the essential archive and treasury of the modern movements in the arts, beginning with 1885.

MOMA's original 1939 building was designed by Edward Durrell Stone and Philip L. Goodwin. There were subsequent additions in 1951 and 1964 by Philip Johnson. The most recent expansion, in 1984, was by Cesar Pelli, who created a major four-story, glassed-in Garden Hall overlooking the Abby Aldrich Rockefeller Sculpture Garden, and a new West Wing.

INSIDERS' TIPS

Gallery talks on the MOMA collection, given by art experts, are free (with museum admission) twice daily (except Wednesday) at 12:30 and 3 P.M. and Thursday evenings at 5:30 and 7 P.M. Film showings in MOMA's two theaters are included in the museum admission (tel. 708-9400 for schedule).

Exhibitions of major importance in the art world are part of MOMA's steady appeal to local and visiting museum-goers. But if this is your first visit, you'll want to savor and enjoy MOMA's remarkable permanent collection, only a fraction of which is visible at any given time.

You'll find the painting and sculpture collections on the second and third floors of the expanded museum. The collections have been arranged chronologically, so that by following a suggested route (delineated for you), you will have a good *précis* of the history of modern painting and sculpture as they developed.

Among the hundreds of artworks, you might look especially for the galleries devoted solely to works by Matisse and Picasso, as well as Matisse's *The Swimming Pool* and Monet's *Water Lilies*, each in its own special room. A special fillip of the Garden Hall is its panoramic overview of the massive sculptures by Rodin, Picasso, Maillol, and others, framed by weeping beech and birch trees, set among reflecting pools and fountains.

MOMA is open Thursdays until 8:40 P.M.; between 5 P.M. and closing, you pay what you wish.

If it's lunchtime, you can have a quick, cafeteria-style lunch at MOMA's Garden Café, which opens to the tranquil Sculpture Garden. Once you've chosen your salad or sandwich, find a table in the Sculpture Garden and enjoy the outdoors (weather permitting).

You may prefer a more ambitious lunch, which is easy to arrange in this part of the city, because so many restaurants are within easy walking distance east, west, north, or south. Among the handy good ones are Siam♛♛ or Shezan♛♛. (See Insiders' Information for New York City, page 181.)

INSIDERS' TIPS

Safe and clean public rest rooms are difficult to find in New York. In midtown try department stores such as Lord & Taylor, Saks Fifth Avenue, Henri Bendel, or Tiffany (mezzanine); hotels such as Omni Berkshire Place, Drake Swissôtel, Helmsley Palace, New York Hilton, Waldorf-Astoria, or Wyndham. Other possibilities are Trump Tower (ground floor) and IBM Gallery (basement).

Diagonally down West 53rd Street from MOMA is the American Craft Museum♛♛, now lodged in three soaring, spacious floors of a rejuvenated old brownstone building at 40 West 53rd. This handsome museum is devoted to special changing exhibitions, often showing the most avant-garde work in pottery, glass, wood, weaving, silver, paper, and any other handcraft you can imagine (tel. 869-9422). Admission is free from 5 to 8 P.M. Tuesdays. If it's midafternoon, you might consider a stop at Omni Berkshire Place Hotel, 21 East 52nd Street. In the rear of the lobby is an airy atrium, which seems designed for a rest stop. There's usually relaxing live harp music as teatime melts into the cocktail hour.

Continue north up Fifth Avenue to 57th Street. As you walk, you'll be tempted by many fine shops, for along Fifth and on 57th Street between Seventh Avenue to the west and 3rd Avenue to the east, you'll find some of the great names in merchandising and some of the world's best stores: Tiffany, Henri Bendel, Bergdorf Goodman, and Van Cleef & Arpels, among dozens of others.

PERILS & PITFALLS

Beware the electronics and linen goods stores along Fifth Avenue with big "Going out of Business" signs splashed across their front windows. Most of them have been going out of business for 40 years. No bargains here.

Long considered "art gallery row" (though SoHo and TriBeCa are recent contenders for the title), 57th Street still boasts many prestigious, internationally established galleries. Among them are the Kennedy Galleries, Hammer, Terry Dintenfass, Allan Frumkin, Marlborough, and Betty Parsons.

One block north, at 58th Street, you'll come to Grand Army Plaza, known simply as the Plaza, a bustling beehive of traffic highlighted by clusters of horse-drawn carriages, whose drivers will be happy to give you a ride.

INSIDERS' TIPS

Carriages are licensed by the Taxi Commission. Their rates are $17 for the first half hour plus $5 each quarter-hour thereafter, for up to 4 people.

The Plaza was designed like a European square as a "people place." Among its adornments are the Pulitzer Fountain with its beautiful bronze nude and, at the north end, a bronze sculpture of General William Tecumseh Sherman of Civil War fame. The statue was sculpted by Augustus Saint-Gaudens for the Paris Exposition of 1900, and brought to the present site in 1903.

That makes the Sherman sculpture the Plaza's oldest resident. Next came the Plaza Hotel, the most conspicuous landmark of the area, located to the west. Frank Lloyd Wright made the venerable hotel his New York headquarters. Generations of matrons have graced its elegant Palm Court, where afternoon tea has been raised to an art form. (Alas, the Tiffany glass roof is long gone.)

The Plaza was the 1907 work of Henry Hardenbergh, the architect who also designed the famed Dakota apartment house (where John Lennon and scores of other celebrities have lived). *New York Times* architectural critic Paul Goldberger considers the Edwardian Plaza "the greatest hotel building in New York." Not only does it have elegance and grace, but the site is choice, facing—and with superlative views of—Central Park.

While you're in the neighborhood, have a look at several of New York's newer monuments. On Fifth Avenue between 56th and 57th streets is Trump Tower♛♛, a dark glass tower with a glitzy interior of pink marble punctuated by gleaming brass in a soaring atrium. The building is a residential and office mixture, but the atrium is lined with exclusive shops (Harry Winston, Asprey, Plantree, Albert Nipon, Abercrombie & Fitch), and there's a stunning, five-story, lighted "water wall" to focus your attention.

INSIDERS' TIPS

On the Trump Tower atrium's fifth level is Terrace Five restaurant, which serves soups, salads, and sandwiches out on the open garden terrace overlooking the street and city. It's also open for light meals from 6 to 10 P.M. (the atrium shops and the DDL Bistro on the ground level keep regular business hours) via private elevator. Handy for pre-theater dining. Tel. 371-5030 to reserve.

From Trump Tower you can enter Bonwit Teller or the IBM Garden Plaza♛♛♛, an 11,000-square-foot, four-story glassed-in atrium, where you can sit, rest, read, and enjoy the huge stone tubs filled with azaleas and towering bamboo groves. A small kiosk sells snacks and beverages. It's a surprising oasis of peace and quiet at the center of one of New York's busiest areas.

INSIDERS' TIPS

In the IBM atrium, the New York Botanical Garden operates a small shop where you can buy its high-quality seeds, bulbs, books, etc. Open from 10 A.M. to 6 P.M. Monday through Saturday.

The IBM Garden Plaza leads into the Edward Larrabee Barnes–designed 43-story IBM Building, at 590 Madison Avenue (at 56th Street), where you can visit the downstairs IBM Gallery of Science and Art♥♥. There is usually a free art exhibit of considerable interest.

In the IBM lobby are two inconspicuous 10-foot-high gray columns, each with two computer screens, one above the other. (There are four such columns in the atrium as well.) These columns, which many people (including natives) pass without noticing, are called "New York Culture Guide," and they can be invaluable in helping you plan your New York visit.

Want to find what's going on in Brooklyn? Where you can see the work of Andy Warhol? What's the current lecture series at the Metropolitan? Is lunch available at Goethe House? What's the admission fee at the Cloisters?

By touching the screen with one finger, you can find information and minute details about 244 nonprofit cultural institutions (no restaurants, galleries, or theaters included). This databank includes museums, historic sites, zoos, exhibits, and botanical gardens in the city's five boroughs. It's packed with information that's roughly analagous to a 5,000-page illustrated guidebook.

Within a few seconds, the press of your finger can give you specific locations, hours, and descriptions of specific collections, even such details as whether the facility has a restaurant or gift shop. In short, it's an encyclopedia of valuable, *up-to-the-minute* information at your fingertips.

One block south of the IBM Building on Madison is another recent addition to the city's skyscraper scene, the AT&T Building at 550 Madison. Designed by Philip Johnson and John Burgee, it is one of the more controversial of the new buildings, mainly because of the traditional, antimodernist appearance of its cleft-triangle rooftop. "It looks like a gigantic Chippendale highboy," one passerby observed. But if you disregard the roof, the 110-foot-high arched stone arcaded entrance is immensely dramatic. Its block-long galleria with old-fashioned white cast-iron chairs is somewhat more human in scale.

Adjacent to the AT&T Building is the AT&T Info-Quest Center (fourth floor), which offers a free "hands-on" introduction to the Information Age, with technological exhibits and the chance for a poke-and-touch experience.

INSIDERS' TIPS

Another haven is Paley Park, between Fifth and Madison on East 53rd. It was donated by (and named for) William S. Paley, chairman of CBS. One of a number of "vest pocket" parks that now brighten the city, it offers a few trees and a delightful, cooling waterfall "wall" as a tiny oasis from city traffic.

Continue east on 53rd Street to the northwest corner of Park Avenue, where a teal green glass-and-steel structure dominates the landscape. This is Lever House ♛ ♛ ♛, one of the pioneer post–World War II high-rises in New York City, built by Skidmore, Owings & Merrill in 1952.

Controversial in its day, the 21-story tower, with its open courtyard and spaciousness, today seems timelessly elegant.

To admire the work of two other architects, you might walk north to 430 Park Avenue, at the southwest corner of East 56th. It's the Mercedes-Benz showroom, and the ramp was designed as part of the building by

Frank Lloyd Wright in 1955. More recent is the 1981 black glass-and-aluminum tower at 499 Park (between 58th and 59th streets), which I. M. Pei designed.

The 38-story Seagram Building♛♛♛♛, 375 Park Avenue (at East 52nd Street), is another post–World War II edifice (1958), also the object of scorn and derision in its day. The work of Mies van der Rohe and Philip Johnson, the beautifully proportioned bronze and glass tower, set back on a marble and granite plaza, is now a city landmark.

On warm days the plaza is filled with brown-baggers, office workers from nearby buildings, lunching, snacking, socializing, and enjoying the noonday sun. At Christmastime the space is a dazzle of Christmas trees and lights.

INSIDERS' TIPS

There is an attractive rest room in the 52nd Street ground-floor entrance to the Four Seasons Restaurant in the Seagram Building. The men's room is immediately to the right of the entrance door; the women's is to the left of the stairway. Note the large Picasso painting.

Between East 53rd and 54th streets on Lexington Avenue is a stunning modern complex—Citicorp Center♛♛♛. The 59-story aluminum and glass building, designed by Hugh Stubbins & Associates in 1977, is unique among recent buildings and clearly a landmark in midtown. Its arresting tower is truncated at a 45-degree angle. What seems to be a rock of granite nesting at one corner near the tower's base is in reality St. Peter's Lutheran Church.

The church inside is full of surprises. First, the interior is deceptively simple: altar, platform, lectern, and pews all are beautifully spare, designed in red oak, with roof and wall skylights providing quantities of light. Surprisingly, there is no sound from outside, despite the fact that the corner is such a pulsatingly busy, noisy one. Tucked even farther inside the church is the Erol Beker Chapel of the Good Shepherd designed all in white by sculptor Louise Nevelson.

INSIDERS' TIPS

Throughout the year there are often free noontime concerts in the Citicorp atrium. In fact, free concerts have become a New York institution—at Federal Hall, Trinity Church, St. Paul's Chapel, the World Trade Center, Central Park, and even in the subways. Pick up free brochures on "Atrium Concerts," "Big Apple Freebies," "Free Things To Do," and seasonal free events at the Information Center, New York Convention & Visitors Bureau, 2 Columbus Circle.

Citicorp's street-level interior is an airy, tree-filled atrium called The Market. A panoply of shops and restaurants on three levels makes this a lively daytime scene. There are café tables where you can lunch, snack, or simply relax.

If you walk down Park Avenue between 51st and 50th streets, you'll come to a Byzantine-style basilica in limestone and salmon-colored brick that may make you think you've dropped into Athens unannounced (except for the art deco tower). It's St. Bartholomew's Episcopal Church♛♛♛, a 1918 edifice. Its French Romanesque front portal was earlier (1902), the work of McKim, Mead & White. This was brought from an older St. Bart's. Note the low reliefs on the three bronze doors, the high-relief frieze of biblical scenes over the entrance doors, and the richly decorated interior.

St. Bart's has lately been at the center of a local maelstrom, because church officials want to allow a high-rise apartment house to be built on the property, the profits from which would help support the church. The city's Landmarks Commission has three times rejected the proposal. Preservationists are hopeful that this calm and quiet island can remain unchanged.

As you stroll down broad Park Avenue, with its central islands, your eyes will be drawn to the graceful building at the southern end. Until 1963, when the Pan Am Building was built behind it, the edifice in the foreground (the New York Central Building then, now called the Helmsley) formed part (with Grand Central Terminal) of a perfectly harmonious visual composition at this break in Park Avenue. The façade has been scrubbed and its Renaissance Italianate flourishes refurbished in gleaming gold.

The Pan Am Building behind it blocks the view of Grand Central Terminal ♛ ♛ ♛, a splendid Beaux Arts monument in its own right, with an imposing façade of triumphal arches surmounted by a sculptural group and a giant clock. (The statue in front of the clock, facing south on Park Avenue, is of Cornelius Vanderbilt.)

Preservationists still smolder over the Pan Am savaging of the skyline above the magnificent station. The building has graced this space since 1903 with an appropriately grand presence at the 42nd Street juncture with Park Avenue. Grand Central, a designated landmark, is on the National Register of Historic Places, which has saved the building itself from legal vandalism on several occasions. Be sure to enter Grand Central to see the cavernous and beautifully proportioned central concourse, whose 125-foot-high vaulted ceiling seems skylike, painted with the major constellations of the zodiac.

If exhaustion has set in, you might want a pick-me-up drink or a spot of tea in the greenhouse lounge of the "this is New York" brassy Grand Hyatt Hotel next to Grand Central Terminal. This superseded the old Commodore Hotel—named after "Commodore" Vanderbilt.

Fanciers of art deco style will want to savor the ornamented façades of two nearby structures. The Chrysler Building ♛ ♛ ♛ ♛, 405 Lexington Avenue, is across the street from Grand Central. Its 1,048-foot tower was designed by William Van Allen in 1930 and made it the world's tallest building—until the Empire State Building was completed weeks later.

INSIDERS' TIPS

For a "future that never arrived" dining experience, try the Automat at 200 East 42nd Street. This is the last survivor of the 1930s eateries where entrées, appetizers, and desserts displayed in glass-doored cubbyholes are released by a coin inserted in a slot, and savored in art deco surroundings.

It is embellished with automotive designs—most noticeably the (vastly enlarged) radiator caps of the 1929 Chrysler. Be sure to walk into the lobby for a peek at marble and steel art deco design at its zenith.

Across 42nd Street and east of Grand Central Station is the New York Daily News Building♕♕ at 220. It's an excellent art deco building, and you will want to see how the theme has been carried out inside the lobby, where there is a huge, rotating globe of the world.

Walk east on 42nd Street to United Nations Headquarters♕♕♕♕ at First Avenue between East 42nd and 48th streets.

The UN location is splendidly open, allowing the 39-story vertical glass box of the Secretariat Building to present a dramatic profile, 544 feet high, unencumbered by other buildings crowding in on it. Note the stunning Barbara Hepworth sculpture in a pool in front of it.

An $8.5-million grant from John D. Rockefeller, Jr., helped buy the 17-acre site facing the East River in the section known as Turtle Bay. (On this site eons ago, Paddy Corcoran, a notorious felon, and his "Rag Gang" hid out in the crags of "Corcoran's Roost." It later became a mishmash of slaughterhouses, breweries, slums, factories, and coal docks.)

INSIDERS' TIPS

For a romantic nighttime view of the UN, the East River, and Queens, try the cocktail lounge atop the Beekman Towers Hotel, First Avenue and East 49th Street. For a late-afternoon pick-me-up, try the lobby-lounge of the Algonquin Hotel, 59 West 44th Street. This was the locus of the famous "Algonquin Round Table" of the 1920s and 1930s, where Robert Benchley, Dorothy Parker, Franklin P. Adams, James Thurber, and other *New Yorker* writers lunched. It still attracts theater and literary lights.

French architect Henri Le Corbusier developed the original concept, and Wallace K. Harrison (of Rockefeller Center fame) created the major building, the Secretariat, and supervised the construction of all four (completed in 1952). He was aided by an international team of architects that included Oscar Niemeyer of Brazil, Sven Markelius of Sweden, Alvar Aalto of Finland, and nine others. The other buildings are the General Assembly Building, the Conference Building, and the Dag Hammarskjold Library (open only to UN staff members and delegations, or by special permission).

General Assembly meetings (regular sessions begin the third Tuesday of September) are on occasion open to the public. Admission is free, but tickets are on a first-come, first-served basis. It's best to check in advance (tel. 754-7713).

INSIDERS' TIPS

It isn't widely known, but the Delegates' Dining Room on the fourth floor of the General Assembly Building is open to the public (tel. 754-7625). The spacious room is attractive, less for the food (which is okay), than for the multilingual diplomatic scene and river views.

Also, check out the UN Craft Shop for unusual handicrafts from various of the 159 member nations. It, a souvenir shop, and the UN Post Office (where you can mail letters with UN stamps) are all in the basement.

There are regular 45-minute tours of the UN complex that provide insight into the workings of the UN. You listen to simultaneous interpretations of speeches in the six official UN languages (Arabic, Chinese, English, French, Russian, Spanish), and see the Security Council Chamber and works of art by Marc Chagall, Pablo Picasso, Henry Moore, Norman Rockwell, Fernand Leger, and others. The tours leave from the Visitors' Entrance of the General Assembly Building, First Avenue at 45th Street.

INSIDERS' TIPS

If you need relief, the Marriott Marquis Hotel (Broadway and 46th St.) may be helpful. It has rest rooms, telephones, and lounges on floors 2 through 8. Take the escalator.

At 37 West 44th Street is the unmistakable New York Yacht Club building, recognizable by its façade of three sailing vessels' sterns, complete with dolphins and waves. Dating from 1901, and designed by the architects of Grand Central Terminal, the Yacht Club is best known, perhaps, as the sponsor of many of the America's Cup sailing races, which its boats won from 1851 until 1984.

Times Square is named after the pie-wedge building where Seventh Avenue and Broadway intersect. Built by *New York Times* publisher Adolph Ochs in 1904, the building and new subway station beneath it gave the area its name. Its celebration on New Year's Eve, 1904, started the tradition of gathering in Times Square to watch the descent of the lighted ball (now an apple) signifying the waning of the old year and the birth of the new.

PERILS & PITFALLS

Have a look at Times Square—admittedly it's a "must see"—but don't linger. The area west of Broadway is at its all-time lowest, home to all kinds of sleaze, a gathering place for pimps, hookers, pickpockets, and worse. Hang on to your purse. Don't carry your wallet in your back pocket.

Though the *Times* sold the building to Allied Chemical and moved to its new building on West 43rd Street years ago, the name Times Square has stuck to "the crossroads of the world." To the north of the Allied Tower (the building's new name) is Duffy Square and the statues of Father Duffy, famous World War I chaplain, and George M. Cohan, the musical comedy author and star who wrote "Give My Regards to Broadway," among many hits.

INSIDERS' TIPS

If you want to experience what most tried-and-true New Yorkers believe to be the best hot dogs in America—Nathan's Famous—but don't have time to make the trip to the Original Nathan's at Coney Island, take heart: there are branches of Nathan's in Times Square, at 1482 and 1515 Broadway. Enjoy!

As you look at the signs of the "Great White Way," as Broadway at Times Square was called, you may be excused for wondering if you are in New York, Seoul, or Tokyo. The signs dominating Times Square currently advertise Coca-Cola, "42nd Street" (the musical), Panasonic, "La Cage aux Folles," Aiwa, Citizen Quartz Watches, JVC, Samsung Electronics, Olympus, Kodak, Bond Stores, and Toshiba.

INSIDERS' TIPS

For the shopping maven, New York's Upper East Side, from 50th to 80th streets, along Fifth, Madison, Park, and Lexington avenues, is the place where materialists' dreams are fulfilled. Here are located most, if not all, the big names of international merchandising. In addition, you'll find fascinating boutiques, small one-of-a-kind shops with many a rare or special item, exclusive hair stylists, furriers, art and antiques galleries, and florists. This is the elitist's New York; save time for browsing the area on foot.

NEW YORK CITY THE SECOND DAY

ONE-DAY ITINERARY

Battery Park, Castle Clinton, Statue of Liberty, Staten Island Ferry, Fraunces Tavern, Wall Street, Federal Hall, New York Stock Exchange, Trinity Church, World Trade Center, St. Paul's Chapel, Old City Hall, Woolworth Building, Chase Manhattan, Federal Reserve Bank, South Street Seaport, Brooklyn Bridge.

Let's start at Bowling Green ❦ ❦, easily reached by taxi or subway (IRT lines to Bowling Green station). It's a welcome divot of parkland at the foot of Broadway. Here the Dutch bought and sold cattle from 1638 to 1647. The fence you see was built in 1771 around a statue of King George III on horseback. Patriots celebrating the Declaration of Independence on July 4, 1776, toppled George and melted him and his horse for bullets. The fence was made of sterner stuff.

PERILS & PITFALLS

Flee for your life if you happen to be near the Bowling Green subway entrance from 4:30 to 5:30 P.M. when the Wall Street herds thunder into it to start their journeys home.

Just to the south of Bowling Green is a prize Beaux Arts building, the U.S. Custom House ♛♛♛ of 1907. Designed by Cass Gilbert, it has sculptures by Daniel Chester French (who did Washington, D.C.'s Lincoln in the Lincoln Memorial) representing Asia, America, Africa, and Europe; they're worth a close look. Its grand interior pavilion has a dome whose WPA murals were painted in the 1930s by Reginald Marsh. At present there is a proposal to move the Museum of the American Indian here from its cramped quarters at Audubon Terrace, West 155th Street at Broadway. The symbolism of the Indians taking over the site would have special irony, for this was where Peter Minuit bought Manhattan from the Algonquins in 1626, allegedly for $24 worth of trinkets and baubles.

South of the Custom House is Battery Park ♛♛, the southernmost extremity of Manhattan, at the very water's edge. It is a splendid, leafy, and welcoming place to get your bearings.

Walk through the park, noting the historic markers and sculptures along the way. (Did you catch that one of the three nudes on the park bench?) Confederate prisoners were kept here, at Castle Clinton, during the Civil War.

At the water's edge, look south across the harbor and you'll see Brooklyn's waterfront on your left. As your eyes sweep to the right, note the islands: Governors Island, with Fort Jay on it; then Liberty Island, with its famous statue; and Ellis Island, close to the Jersey City shore. Far out in the bay is Staten Island, and if the air is crystal clear, you may see the Verrazano-Narrows Bridge, which links Staten Island and Brooklyn. Its name commemorates the Florentine Giovanni da Verrazano's discovery of the harbor in 1524, when he was exploring for France's King

Francis I. (There's a 1909 bronze memorial to Verrazano in the park.)

This restless harbor is Upper New York Bay, one of the world's busiest, most industrial ports, administered by the Port Authority of New York and New Jersey.

It is sobering to note that if those early Dutch settlers had stood where you are, they would have been wet from shoe buckles to hatbands—in fact, they would have been underwater. Like much of Manhattan's rim, the Park is built on landfill that pushed outward the original island's shoreline.

When the Dutch were in charge, the water lapped at what is now Pearl Street. The shore was extended and Water Street became the shoreline. Later the land was built out to the present South Street. On the Hudson River side there were similar additions. The most recent is the huge Battery Park City development, built largely on fill from the World Trade Center excavations. (All of which tends to cast doubt on Will Rogers's pronouncement about land: "They ain't making no more of it.")

"The Battery's down," as the *On the Town* song states ("New York, New York, it's a helluva town"), at the present south tip of Manhattan. It takes its name from cannons that once stood where State Street now borders the Park. The artillery was along what was then the shoreline, and was intended to protect against invaders three centuries ago.

After the British attacked an American frigate in 1807, there was a feverish effort to build a better defense of New York. It culminated in South-west Battery, a fortress that never fired a shot in battle, situated on a pile of rock 200 feet out in the harbor. Today that fort, having gone through many transformations, is the low, circular stone structure close to the shore.

After its service as a federal fort it was turned over to the city in 1824 and rebuilt as Castle Garden. This was used for band concerts, scientific demonstrations, balloon ascensions, and receptions for famous visitors such as Lafayette, Andrew Jackson, and the Prince of Wales. It was here, after the structure was roofed over, that P. T. Barnum introduced Swedish songbird Jenny

**DOWNTOWN
NEW YORK CITY**

0   200 400 600 800 1000 Feet

Hudson River

East River

Brooklyn Bridge

Peck Slip
Beekman St
SOUTH
STREET
SEAPORT
Pier 17
FDR DRIVE
Schermerhorn Row
Maiden Lane
South St
Front St
Water St
Old Slip
Mill Lane
Coenties Alley
Coenties Slip
Hanover Sq
Hanover St
Pine St
Pearl St
Cedar St
Platt St
Cliff St
Gold St
William St
Ann St
Dutch St
Maiden Lane
Liberty Pl
Federal Hall
Nassau St
Wall St
Pl
Broad St
S. William St
Stone St
William St
Beaver St
Exchange
New St
Whitehall St
Battery Pl
Old Custom House
Bowling Green
Morris St
Bridge St
Pearl St
State St
Fraunces Tavern
Water St
Peter Minuit Plaza
BATTERY PARK
Castle Clinton
Staten Island Ferry
Governors Island Ferry
Downtown Heliport
Pearl St
Fulton St
John St
Church St
Dey St
Cortlandt St
Thames St
Trinity Church
Trinity Pl
Broadway
N.Y. Stock Exchange
St. Paul's Chapel
Vesey St
WORLD TRADE CENTER
Liberty St
Cedar St
Albany St
Carlisle St
Rector St
Greenwich St
Washington St
BROOKLYN-BATTERY TUN.
West St
BATTERY PARK CITY
Broadway

Statue of Liberty Ferry

Lind to American audiences in 1850. (More than 6,000 music lovers paid $3 or more to attend and cheered her "tempestuously.")

In 1855, Castle Garden became the depot for immigrants, and welcomed them until 1890, when it was superseded by Ellis Island in 1892. (The powerful bronze group, "The Immigrants," at the building's entrance, was sculpted by Luis Sanguino in 1981.) In 1896 the building was converted to an aquarium. The doors closed in 1941, when fish and tanks were transferred to the Coney Island aquarium.

Named Castle Clinton National Historic Monument in 1946, the former fortress is a National Park Service responsibility and now houses rest rooms, three small dioramas of the Battery's development, and an office for tourist literature. But its key feature is the ticket kiosk for the Circle Line Statue of Liberty ferries. You buy your ticket here and walk 300 feet to the point where you board the ferry.

The first building to the west at the shoreline is century-old Pier A, the harbor Fire Department station. To the east is the Staten Island Ferry building. Through it pour thousands of New Yorkers daily, en route to work in Manhattan and later on the way home to the city's least populous borough.

For the price of a telephone call (25¢) you can enjoy one of the world's exhilarating short "sea" trips, from Manhattan to Staten Island, passing Liberty Island, the Statue of Liberty, the U.S. Navy Yard at Bayonne, New Jersey, and a gallimaufry of watercraft, from pilot boats and tugs to tall ships, sleek liners, and even men-o'-war. If you stay aboard, your return passage is free.

The Statue of Liberty ♛ ♛ ♛ ♛ ♛ has the American Museum of Immigration in its base. Both of these are open daily except Christmas, from 9:15 A.M. to 5 P.M., with extended hours in summer and on weekends (tel. 732-1286 [recorded info] or 732-1236).

The Circle Line Statue of Liberty ferries (tel. 269-5755) leave every day on the hour, from 9 A.M. to 4 P.M., more often in summer. Fare, $3.25 for adults, $1.50 for children under 12.

The grand copper lady (152 feet tall), designed by

French sculptor Frederic Auguste Bartholdi and engineered by Gustave Eiffel, has stood here since 1886 and in her refurbished (with stainless steel structure) state beckons with even greater brilliance, thanks to new lighting. The experience of viewing New York Harbor from the crown is unforgettable, worthy of the praise heaped on it.

INSIDERS' TIPS

The ascent to the crown of the statue is some 12 stories and may require waiting up to three hours in line. To minimize the wait, avoid crowds by going early, on a weekday, when the kids are back in school, or on a day that starts out rainy but clears later.

Look north now, at the city. Beyond the park you will see towering office buildings, the newer ones of glass and metal in rectangular shapes, older ones of masonry with classical references. But completely out of scale in the middle of the scene you will see two 3-story brick buildings with white wooden trim, the last vestiges hereabouts of the Federal period.

Walk to these and you will find yourself at 8 State Street, built about 1800. It was lived in by the first native-born American to become a Roman Catholic saint (for launching parochial schooling in 1810 and establishing the Sisters of Charity). The adjoining chapel is named after her, the Shrine of St. Elizabeth Ann Seton, and its spare, gray and white interior is in keeping with the Federal period.

Walk east on State Street a few steps to Whitehall Street, and go one block north to Pearl Street (so called because of the oyster shells that carpeted it when it was the shore). A block east, at 54 Pearl (at Broad Street) is the Georgian brick Fraunces Tavern ♛♛, built in 1907 in the manner of the original "Queen's Head Tavern," which was owned by free black patriot Samuel Fraunces on this site.

Here, in 1783, Washington lived for ten days before becoming President. His farewell to his officers in the Tavern has been commemorated in the "Long Room" and museum ♛♛ of Revolutionary times (tel. 425-

1778) in the upper floors. The museum has a program of special exhibitions, events, and lectures throughout the year.

The restaurant on the ground floor is colorful and atmospheric, good for a restorative libation.

PERILS & PITFALLS

Think drink. The food, to put it politely, leaves something to be desired. At lunchtime the restaurant is a mob scene.

A short block farther northeast on Water Street is Coenties Slip. In Dutch days, the Stadt Huys, Manhattan's first city hall, stood here. It started out as a tavern in 1641, then served as jail, debtors' prison, courthouse, and public warehouse. In front of it at the river stood state-of-the-art correctional apparatus to punish violators of the moral code: a ducking stool, pillory and stocks, and (for the ultimate reproach) a gallows.

Return one block to Broad Street (which was a wide canal in Dutch days) and follow it north. In front of 40 Broad Street you will see in the sidewalk the message that on June 27, 1792, the "outdoor brokers" who used to do business at this site finally moved indoors. The brokers of this "curb market" adopted the name New York Stock Exchange.

A short distance north is Wall Street. It was here that Nieuw Amsterdam Governor Peter Stuyvesant built a palisade fence in 1653 to keep the English colonials out. When England took over in 1695, the "wall" was demolished, but the name lived on. There was a slave market here in 1709.

This intersection of Broad and Wall streets is "Power Corner," surrounded by the showcase main offices or headquarters (current or former) of many of the most powerful banks and corporations in the world.

Dominating the intersection physically is Federal Hall National Memorial ♛ ♛ ♛, a monumental marble Greek temple reminiscent of the Parthenon. This building was erected in 1862 as the nation's Subtreasury. It supersedes a previous U.S. Custom House that replaced the City Hall at this location.

The site is a significant one in the struggle for liberty. Here, editor Peter Zenger was tried in 1735 for his *New York Weekly Journal*'s "seditious libels" against the British government and Governor William Cosby. (Cosby had the paper confiscated and burned in Wall Street.) Acquitted because he printed the truth, Zenger's was a milestone victory in the free press/free speech battle.

Later, irate colonists met here as the Stamp Act Congress in 1765 to draft a "Declaration of Rights and Grievances" protesting taxation without representation. They followed up by boycotting British goods. The Declaration of Independence was read here on July 18, 1776, but its brave words did not prevent the British from using the building as their headquarters during most of the Revolutionary War.

After the American victory, the onetime City Hall was remodeled by Pierre L'Enfant and served as the U.S. Capitol, where Washington was inaugurated on April 30, 1789, as our first President. (His justifiably heroic figure, sculpted in bronze ♕ ♕ ♕ by J. Q. A. Ward in 1883, stands facing down Broad Street.) It was here, five months later, that the nation's first Congress adopted the Bill of Rights. (An exhibit and diorama on the second floor tell about this.)

Federal Hall is worth a brief visit, especially if there's a concert in the rotunda, which happens occasionally—usually at noon on Wednesdays. (See the bulletin board on the corner of the steps for information.) There is also a small exhibition of George Washington memorabilia (including his brown Connecticut homespun Inauguration suit) on display along with changing exhibits.

Next door to Federal Hall is the Seamen's Bank for Savings ♕, on the site of the old Assay Office (whose façade is now preserved as the exterior of the American wing of the Metropolitan Museum of Art).

Following the gaze of Washington's statue to the southeast corner of Wall and Broad streets, you will see number 23, "the House of Morgan," headquarters of

J. P. Morgan & Company. Now Morgan Guaranty Trust Company, the building bears the pockmarks of September 16, 1920, when a wagonload of explosives detonated at high noon, blowing to bits one horse and 33 people (injuring 400 others). The incident was blamed on anarchists who had aimed this "statement" at Morgan as the world's arch-capitalist. An explosives company, illegally transporting dynamite on a prohibited street, was also blamed.

The skyscraper at 40 Wall Street ♔♔♔ (with the lantern top) was the headquarters of the Manhattan Company, an enterprise started by Aaron Burr in 1799, initially to bring clean water to the city. (The building's recent owners were Ferdinand and Imelda Marcos.) Burr wrote the charter so that it permitted various pursuits, and he began a bank under its aegis. It competed, of course, with Hamilton's Bank of New York (founded in 1784) and exacerbated their antagonisms.

The Manhattan Company's water system of pine-log pipes (which are still turned up in excavations in downtown Manhattan) was made irrelevant by the Croton Water System in 1842, but its Bank of the Manhattan Company thrived and merged into today's Chase Manhattan Bank.

The skyscraper across Nassau Street from Federal Hall at 16 Wall Street is the Bankers Trust building, easily identified by its ziggurat pyramid top.

Be sure to turn and look back up Wall Street for one of the impressive and enduring sights of the city: A vista ♔♔♔♔♔ down a valley of skyscrapers that frames Trinity Church where Wall Street meets Broadway. (Wall Street's curbs are lined with tree boxes.)

Just across Wall Street from Federal Hall, at 8 Broad Street, is that premier bastion of capitalism, the New York Stock Exchange ♔♔♔, whose marble façade is in the form of a Roman temple. Tradition has it that in 1792, 24 merchants and auctioneers gathered under a "buttonwood tree" where 70 Wall Street is now, and drew up the trading agreement that became the NYSE. Their earliest indoor trading occurred at the Tontine Coffee House (long gone) at 82 Wall Street.

The Exchange is open to visitors every business day from 10 A.M. to 4 P.M. The visitors' gallery includes exhibits, narration, and views of the floor where 3,000 frantic traders are to be seen in fascinating, if arcane, action that has titanic impact on the financial circumstances of millions of people. The visitors' entrance is at 20 Broad Street (tel. 623-5167).

A block west, where Wall Street meets Broadway, is Trinity Church ♛♛♛, whose steeple points heavenward like a stone finger of stern rectitude (apparently disregarded by many of the fast-track denizens of the area). The original Trinity Church on this site (this is the third, dating from 1846) was built in 1698 and burned in 1776. Trinity's splendid bronze doors are by Richard Morris Hunt.

The church has a small museum and a schedule of first-rate free Tuesday noontime concerts. It is open daily to minister to its frenetic, financially fixated flock.

Trinity Churchyard ♛♛ dates from 1681. In this green and serene burial ground are interred Robert Fulton, Albert Gallatin, and Alexander Hamilton, among many others. In a small frame schoolhouse in the churchyard, King's College opened its doors in 1754. It changed its name to Columbia University—after the unpleasantness with King George III—and later moved uptown.

Just a block west and a few doors away at 78 Trinity Place is another scene of contained bedlam, the American Stock Exchange ♛♛. It also offers an opportunity to see the frenzy of a trading floor in action and a guided tour (free). The visitors' gallery is open Monday through Friday from 10 A.M. to 4 P.M. (tel. 306-1642).

Nearby on Trinity Place is the 16-acre World Trade Center complex ♛♛♛ (information tel. 466-4170), from which sprout six buildings, including the twin 110-story towers by architect Minoru Yamasaki. The complex includes the Vista International Hotel at 3 World Trade Center, the Commodities Exchange (visitors' gallery, ninth floor, 4 WTC, tel. 938-2025; free), and the U.S. Customs House in 6 WTC. There are six levels belowground, with parking for 2,000 cars, the Port Authority Trans-Hudson (PATH) railroad, access to NYC subways, and storage.

Some 50,000 people work in the World Trade Center, and 80,000 more visit or do business with its 1,200 companies, services, organizations, and 22 or more restaurants and cafés. (This is a convenient point to break for lunch. See suggestions below and in Where to Eat listings.)

INSIDERS' TIPS

Broadway show tickets at half-price are available at a TKTS sales booth on the mezzanine (plaza level—reached by escalator from the concourse level) at 2 World Trade Center. Tickets are sold on the performance day only, and there's seldom a waiting line (tel. 354-5800).

A branch of the New York Convention & Visitors Bureau in the same building also has discount admission coupons to some theaters, plus maps, literature, information on events (tel. 397-8222).

Within the World Trade Center is an 8-acre concourse of shops, stores, restaurants, and services billed as the city's largest indoor mall.

INSIDERS' TIPS

Attention art lovers—on the open-air 5-acre plaza you will find a fountain and sculptures by leading contemporary artists: *Ideogram* by James Rosati, a granite pyramid by Masayuki Nagare, a bronze globe centerpiece by Fritz Koenig, and, at the corner of Church and Vesey, a stabile by Alexander Calder. Indoors at 1 World Trade Center is Louise Nevelson's wall sculpture on the mezzanine, and at 2 World Trade Center's mezzanine is a 35-foot-long tapestry by Joan Miro.

The Concourse seethes with people flowing from/to transportation (subways, PATH trains), shops, department stores, banks, and the six buildings. Hungry? In one area is a group of fast-food stations. You choose what you wish and carry it to a table. There are two other informal eateries, The Corner and Eat & Drink, for soups, sandwiches, and deli specialties.

Outdoors on the Plaza in moderate weather you will see salesgirls, stockbrokers, and lawyers lunching alfresco and enjoying free Wednesday concerts from July through September.

You'll thrill to 360-degree views ♛ ♛ ♛ ♛ that encompass northern New Jersey, Staten Island, the Statue of Liberty, the Brooklyn Bridge, Long Island, and all of Manhattan from the glass-enclosed Observation Deck on 2 World Trade Center's 107th floor. (You'll also note a major limitation of architect Yamasaki's design: panoramic views are impossible because vertical ribbing cuts the scene into narrow vertical portions.) If weather permits, you might take in the scene from the 110th-floor Rooftop Promenade, open from 9:30 A.M. to 9:30 P.M. (tel. 466-7377); admission is $2.95 for adults, $1.50 for children.

If you look west from any of the World Trade Center buildings, you will see the new structures of Battery Park City ♛ ♛ ♛ on a wide flatland between West Street and the Hudson River. One-third of that landfill came from beneath the World Trade Center.

Battery Park City's 92 acres are due for completion in the 1990s, but many buildings are already in use and $4.5 million has been spent on its art program to lure tenants and visitors.

Among the sculpture and landscapes is a vast "Winter Garden" at the self-styled World Financial Center (which includes headquarters buildings for heavyweights such as American Express, Dow Jones, and Merrill Lynch). There are 18,000 square feet of exotic plants enclosed under an arched glass roof. You can reach it via a bridge from the U.S. Custom House at 6 World Trade Center, concourse level. The developers promise a schedule of performing arts in the 3½-acre adjoining plaza, which was designed by architect Cesar Pelli. (Check with the Convention & Visitors Bureau before you traipse all the way down here.)

Now turn your attention to the east, follow Fulton Street (named after Robert Fulton, the steamboat inventor) to Broadway. Here on the left is St. Paul's

Chapel ♛ ♛ ♛ ♛, the only Colonial church (1766) surviving in Manhattan. Built of local stone as a branch of Trinity Church, it was patterned after London's St. Martin-in-the-Fields.

The sedate interior has a barrel-vaulted sky-blue ceiling, gray and white marble checkerboard floor, and delicate crystal chandeliers above the severe, ivory-painted pews. Delicately fluted Corinthian columns conceal sturdy oak tree trunks that bear the weight of the roof. Look for George Washington's pew (along the left wall), where he worshiped regularly. He led guests here after his inauguration to pray together. Now a plain, painted wood enclosure, the pew was originally canopied and richly furnished.

On the Broadway porch (the rear of the church) is a monument to Major General Richard Montgomery, who was killed in the assault on Quebec in 1775. His remains were brought here in 1818. The church is open daily from 8 A.M. to 4 P.M. and regularly presents an ambitious series of prize-winning free noontime concerts on Monday and Thursday.

If you look north from St. Paul's corner of Fulton and Broadway, you will see the beautiful 1811 City Hall ♛ ♛ ♛ in the center of City Hall Park. (Looming behind it in the distance is the Municipal Building, a remarkably successful 1914 civic skyscraper by McKim, Mead & White.) This, one of the rare gems of municipal construction, was the result of a collaboration between a Scot (John McComb) and a Frenchman (Joseph Mangin) whose designs won a competition.

The red brick and gray stone Romanesque buildings across Park Row from City Hall Park are the sole remnants of what was once Newspaper Row. Here the hottest, most successful competitors—the *Globe*, *Times*, and *Herald*—were located before they migrated uptown.

If you have the time and there is no demonstration or protest in progress (many of them are directed at City Hall), enter and see where Lincoln and Grant lay in state, then visit the gallery of portraits of leading Americans through the ages.

INSIDERS' TIPS

Park Row and Nassau Street have traditionally been low-priced shopping areas. Park Row has become a cluster of electronic discount stores featuring name brands.

Closer at hand at 233 Broadway is the "Cathedral of Commerce" completed in 1913 for Frank Woolworth, the dime-store king, who paid $13.5 million for it.

For 17 years the tallest structure on earth, the Woolworth Tower ♛ ♛ ♛ is still one of the modern world's great and graceful buildings. This delicate Gothic skyscraper, replete with gargoyles, flying buttresses and finials soars 60 stories. Be sure to see its uniquely rich Gothic lobby, with bronze coffered ceilings, marble walls and floors, and brilliant gold mosaic barrel-vaulting. In the balconies are murals of Queen Commerce and Queen Labor facing one another across the ornate lobby. Look for amusing corbel caricatures, which include architect Cass Gilbert (holding a model of the building) and Frank Woolworth (counting the coins that made him wealthy).

For contrast, walk south on Broadway. The massive Ionic columns at 195 mark the entrance to what was American Telephone & Telegraph's head office ♛ ♛ until it moved to Madison Avenue. Continuing south on the west side of Broadway, you come to the all-black Merrill Lynch office tower ♛ ♛ between Cortlandt and Liberty streets. With its tinted glass windows and recessed bays, it looks like a gigantic rectangular metal-working file.

Across the street, at 140 Broadway, is Marine Midland Bank's black tower ♛ ♛ ♛, with Isamu Noguchi's perforated, inflated red cube *en pointe* in the travertine plaza before it.

At 55 Liberty Street you will see an impressive 1901 Beaux Arts marble "palace"—the New York State Chamber of Commerce ♛ ♛.

Where Liberty Street intersects Nassau Street, looming on the right is the plaza and 813-foot, 65-story aluminum and glass tower of the Chase Manhattan Bank ♛♛♛. It was completed just 47 years after the Woolworth Building.

INSIDERS' TIPS

Art note: Chase Manhattan's plaza features an incongruous black-and-white plastic sculpture, "Trees," by Jean Dubuffet, and a sunken fountain-pool with rocks by Isamu Noguchi. Where Liberty intersects Maiden Lane is Louise Nevelson Plaza, with a cluster of seven of her huge steel sculptures.

The Chase building (by Skidmore, Owings & Merrill) was a deliberate act of conspicuous commitment to stem the 1950s exodus from the financial district by major companies. The effort (with a concerted rejuvenation of the area by many companies in addition to Chase) was remarkably successful, as the proliferation of plazas, new buildings, and renovations—including the World Trade Center, Battery Park City, and South Street Seaport—clearly demonstrates.

For yet another contrast in aesthetic viewpoints, look at Chase's neighbor to the north across Liberty Street. This noble, 14-story Florentine *palazzo* is the home of the Federal Reserve Bank of New York ♛♛♛♛. Built in 1924, it is said to take its inspiration from the Strozzi palace in Florence. With Italianate wrought-iron lanterns flanking its rusticated stone entrance, it conveys the sober solidity and strength you would want to protect the hoard of gold (estimated at a value of $14 billion in 1981) in its interior. Here, 80 feet below street level, major noncommunist countries have rooms in which their gold reserves are kept—and moved from "country" to "country" as the balance of payments dictates, without ever leaving the building!

Just beyond the Fed to the east, Liberty Street merges with Maiden Lane, which bears this name because in the 17th century it was a stream where young girls did laundry. A block north of the Fed, at 44 John Street, is the austere, dignified 1841 Methodist Church ♛♛, with historical artifacts and displays commemorating the first Methodist church in the United

States (built here in 1768). Its simple Georgian interior is worth a visit.

INSIDERS' TIPS

If you want to see more of the shiny gold stuff than exists anywhere but under King Fahd's bed (more even than in Fort Knox), take a free Federal Reserve tour. You must make reservations at least a week ahead (tel. 720-6130). The one-hour tour visits the gold vault and the machine cash-counting section Monday through Friday at 10 and 11 A.M. and 1 and 2 P.M.

This area in the 1840s was the newspaper and publishing district, where Edgar Allan Poe eked out a precarious existence writing for *The Sunday Times and Weekly Newspaper, The Sun,* and *The Mirror* (which published "The Raven"). He lived with his tubercular child-wife in a $7-a-week, third-floor boardinghouse room at Cedar and Greenwich streets. For a time they lived 4 blocks to the north at 4 Ann Street, around the corner from Barnum's Museum. In that era the city streets were littered with garbage, and the cleanup was left to the random urges of itinerant pigs who occasionally nipped unwary pedestrians.

Continue along Maiden Lane to South Street (remember, the original shoreline was at Pearl Street) and walk north. You will soon see 127 John Street ♛♛♛, a unique, happy-go-lucky 1969 building. Its east face bears what may be the world's largest digital clock, and its lobby is brightened by neon and an entry that looks like the business end of a gigantic vacuum cleaner. Around the building are brightly painted seats, and on the north side is a sun deck.

From these streets you will glimpse one of the city's outstanding beauties: The Brooklyn Bridge ♛♛♛♛. This elegant and practical delight is a poem in stone and steel, with its Gothic-arched granite piers and gossamer webs of steel cables. It has drawn praise ever since its completion in 1883. The original toll was 1¢ for pedestrians. (Confidence men charged gullible travelers exorbitant fees and "sold" the bridge to others.) It is crossed by thousands of cars daily, and many people walk the exhilarating span from Brooklyn homes to Wall Street offices (no tolls now).

INSIDERS' TIPS

If the weather permits, stroll across Brooklyn Bridge for soul-stirring views of Manhattan *and* Brooklyn from the bridge. Then treat yourself to a slice of pizza (the best in New York, some say) at Fascatto's on Henry Street in Brooklyn Heights

---

At what was 255–257 Pearl Street, Thomas Edison installed the nation's first plant to generate electricity for his new incandescent lighting in 1881. He picked "the worst dilapidated street there was" to buy cheap property for the plant. He wound up paying $65,000 for one-quarter of the land he thought he would need—so he was compelled to build "upward in the air where real estate was cheap." He purposely put the plant here to convince the "money men" that his incandescent lighting system was practical so they would invest in its development.

INSIDERS' TIPS

If you enjoy *trompe l'oeil,* 2 blocks north of Fulton on Water Street is Consolidated Edison's power station at Peck Slip, between South and Front streets. Its entire side has a prize-winning, brilliantly disorienting mural by artist Richard Haas of the Brooklyn Bridge and the buildings approaching it. Looming in the background is the real bridge.

Just prior to the American Revolution, this was an area of quiet, fashionable residences; by the 1820s it had become thoroughly commercial. By midcentury it was a tough waterfront where merchants, warehouses, cheap hotels, and saloons elbowed one another.

For instance, the Joseph Rose house of 1771, once at 273 Water Street, started as a family home in a desirable neighborhood. It became a boardinghouse, then a hotel with shops on the ground floor. After midcentury, a notorious buccaneer named Kit Burns made it his headquarters and built an amphitheater inside to stage dog and rat fights. He took up the midday slack by holding noontime prayer meetings in the hall. Reverend William Boole bought the building in 1870 and converted it to a home to redeem prostitutes.

At Fulton and Water streets, the cobblestones underfoot announce that you have arrived at the entrance to the South Street Seaport 🏆 🏆 🏆 🏆. This 11-block historic district includes three piers with a collection of antique ships, authentic, meticulously restored and preserved 19th-century landmark buildings, a museum, a theater, and other attractions. (It was restored by the Rouse Company, which did similar work on Faneuil Hall Market in Boston and HarborPlace in Baltimore.)

This adult play-space offers a hint of the "Street of Ships," which the street actually was during the sailing era. The Seaport is always lively, sports a menu of concerts and events to appeal to a wide range of visitors, and has become a gathering place for singles on evenings and weekends. No cars are allowed, so the walking and dawdling (which you may have thought were impossible in New York) are unhurried. Friday evening is the Great Yuppie Unwinding, and is a fascinating sociological study. There's entertainment, food and drink aplenty. Bring money. Nothing comes cheap.

Look down Fulton Street toward the East River and you'll see a row of 1811 merchant warehouses and countinghouses on your right. Peter Schermerhorn built them on "water lots"—artificially created by landfill 600 feet into the East River. His family's ships had been important in the packet boat run to Charleston, South Carolina, in the 18th century. This row of buildings gives you a good idea of the type of architecture that once prevailed here—except that these have been scrubbed and gussied up as part of the Seaport project.

Facing the Schermerhorn block on your left is (first) the Seaport Museum block of renovated buildings, some of which date from 1797. Beyond them is Fulton Market, a 1980s creation that conveys no sense at all of the untidy, tumultuous old market that once thrived on this spot. (For the real thing, cross South Street to the active, operating Fulton Fish Market.)

Straight ahead, beyond South Street, are the Seaport's 3 piers: Piers 15 and 16 hold the antique ships, and Pier 17 has a new, 3-story, glass-and-steel, Victorian-style pavilion with more than 100 shops, fast fooderies, restaurants, and outdoor promenades.

INSIDERS' TIPS

For the best views of the Brooklyn Bridge, the East River, the Statue of Liberty, and downtown Manhattan, try the skylighted Promenade (top) Floor, the verandas at Pier 17 (free), or the highly popular *Liberty Cafe* or *Fluties* (second floor) *Oyster Bar & Restaurant* (both on Pier 17). Vistas are 180 degrees and exhilarating; you can see three bridges from the north, water traffic from all sides.

The history of this venerable seaport is a long one. In 1822, Fulton Market opened its doors here and over the years became the nation's best known seafood wholesale center, the Fulton Fish Market. By 1825, South Street was one of the busiest parts of a busy New York. The street's water side was crowded with the prows of packet boats, schooners, and clipper ships shouldering one another. The traffic was both local (the Fulton Ferry to Brooklyn) and international, and it boomed during the age of sail.

Slowly, as steam replaced sails, South Street declined because the larger, heavier ships required deepwater piers such as those in the Hudson River. By the 1950s, the Fulton Fish Market was the only flourishing element in a backwater of decrepit and decayed buildings. A South Street Seaport Museum committee was formed, and by 1979 federal, state, and city funding made the $351 million development possible.

The entire area, including Piers 16 and 17, is open to strollers. It is a festive delight at any season, what with mimes and musicians, hawkers and mountebanks, concerts and theatricals attracting 1 million visitors a year. In spring there's an "All That Jazz" Festival, in autumn a Pumpkin Festival, and in December a "singing Christmas Tree."

A Seaport tour really begins at the Pilot House on Pier 16. That's where you get tickets (adults $4, children under twelve $2, seniors $3) for the guided walking tour (50 minutes, hourly from 10 A.M. to 5 P.M. daily). This includes the ships and the Seaport Gallery at 215 Water Street. (It doesn't include *The Seaport Experience*, a multiscreen feature about seafaring and the area, which is shown in the Trans-Lux Seaport Theater at 210 Front Street, tel. 608-6696.)

INSIDERS' TIPS

The daily schedule of films, craft demonstrations, lectures, and special tours is posted on the "Special Programs" signboards throughout the Seaport.

Main Seaport features are these:
- The Visitors' Center, 14 Fulton Street.
- The South Street Seaport Museum ♛♛, 207 Front Street (tel. 669-9411), has historical exhibits and information about current and future events.
- Bowne & Co., Stationers ♛, at 211 Water Street, is a typical mid-19th-century print shop. This building dates from 1836 (restored 1974), and there are demonstrations of printing.
- Pier 17, at Water Street and the East River, is a huge waterfront shopping, drinking, and dining pavilion.

The ship collection includes these vessels:
- *Maj. Gen. William Hart* ♛ (1925), a ferry that originally ran between Queens and the Bronx.
- *Lettie G. Howard* ♛ (1893), a 2-masted fishing schooner.
- *Ambrose Lightship* ♛♛ (1908), formerly a floating lighthouse at the Ambrose Channel entrance to New York's port.
- *Wavertree* ♛ (1885), a steel-hulled, 3-masted vessel built in Southampton, England, in clipper ship layout. (She sailed for years from Dundee, Scotland, was damaged by a 1910 hurricane, and languished in the Falklands until restored.)
- *Peking* ♛♛♛ (1911), a 4-masted, steel-hulled bark—the second largest sailing ship still afloat—sailed the route from Valparaiso to Europe.

For visitors who want a short voyage, the Seaport's century-old sailing schooner *Pioneer* makes trips into the harbor daily. Fares for the 2-hour sail: adults $16, seniors $13, children 12 and under $11 (tel. 669-9416). There's also a paddlewheel steamer that makes a 1½-hour excursion around the harbor 4 times a day (tel. 964-9082).

If hunger assails you at this point, you have literally scores of eating choices in the Seaport complex. The Fulton Market building's ground floor is jammed with market stalls and vendors of fresh cheese, meats, and right-off-the-farm produce. There's Roebling's New York Bar & Grille on the second floor; the third floor has dozens of small food and delicacy shops selling everything from hot cookies, kebabs, and pasta to papadums, tapas, and tacos, plus American regional specialties.

At Pier 17 on the Promenade level, the fast-food places include Jerry's Sub Shop, La Familia Italian fare, Diner Dogs, Jack's Deli, Wok & Roll, Yorkville Burgers, Minter's Ice Cream Kitchen, and Coffee Experience, plus Bergin's Wine Bar. The *modus operandi* here is to buy your foods of choice, tote them to a table (inside or out), and dine while surveying the East River traffic, Brooklyn Bridge, and the financial district.

One of the popular watering holes hereabouts is Caroline's, a restaurant with comedy and live music, on the ground floor at Pier 17.

While you're in the area, you may want to have dinner at Sweets Restaurant♛, 2 Fulton Street (tel. 344-9189), a link with the area's past. It opened in 1842 and has always served fresh fish and seafood direct from the Fulton Fish Market. Its renovated quarters evoke little of the oldtime Sweets, but the kitchen turns out acceptable simple dishes.

PERILS & PITFALLS

If curiosity should seize you and cause you to think of eating at Sloppie Louie's, 92 South Street (tel. 509-9694), just remember, the name refers not to the house-keeping but the food. You've been warned.

A THIRD DAY IN NEW YORK CITY

ONE-DAY ITINERARY

Includes some or all of these museums: Frick, Asia Society, Metropolitan, Guggenheim, Cooper-Hewitt, Jewish, City of New York, El Barrio, Natural History. Also: Central Park and Lincoln Center.

Although it requires lots of stamina to spend an entire day museuming, a number of New York's great museums are close to one another along Fifth Avenue—an area dubbed Museum Mile—making a walk from one to the next relatively easy (assuming temperate weather and comfortable shoes).

On the assumption that you have the interest *and* perseverance to spend a full day at museums, we're laying out a third day in this upper stretch of Manhattan, aware that it really includes more than the human eye and mind can absorb in such a concentrated time.

INSIDERS' TIPS

A helpful brochure, called "Museum Mile," a guide to 10 cultural institutions along the "Mile," with their hours and fees listed, is available free from the Office of Museum Mile (tel. 722-1313). An annual Museum Mile Festival is held on an early June weeknight from 6 to 9 P.M. on Fifth Avenue between 82nd and 104th streets. The street is closed to motor traffic, and is a carnival of jazz, string quartets, clowns, folk musicians. Most of the 10 museums on the route are free at this time, with special exhibits. For specifics, tel. 722-1313.

Loosely defined, Museum Mile stretches from the Metropolitan Museum of Art to El Museo del Barrio, but we're extending the parameters to include the Frick Collection on 70th Street, and a detour one block east to Madison Avenue to see the Whitney Museum of American Art as well. We also suggest crossing Central Park to still another world-class New York museum, the American Museum of Natural History, ending up at the fabulous Lincoln Center complex for dinner and an evening of theater, music, or dance.

You should, of course, pick and choose the museums of primary interest to you. There's no way you can see on a single day all of those included in this chapter without suffering from MEGO (My Eyes Glaze Over) as you stagger from room to room.

Start at the southern outpost of the Mile, the Frick Collection ♛ ♛ ♛ ♛, 1 East 70th Street at Fifth Avenue (tel. 288-0700). It is the legacy of coal baron Henry Clay Frick and is installed in his elegant mansion, which has a graceful, restful, glass-roofed Garden Court. His acquisitions were dazzling, and what makes this small museum such a gem is being able to view rare Old Master paintings in the kind of intimate, private home setting for which many were created. The furniture and accessories are works of art themselves.

Note especially Titian's *Portrait of a Man in a Red Cap*, Vermeer's *Officer and Laughing Girl*, Rembrandt's self-portrait, Goya's *Forge*, Hals's *Portrait of an Elderly Man*, Bellini's *Saint Francis*, and El Greco's *Purification of the Temple*. *Pieces de résistance* are the flowery French bonbons: the Fragonard and Boucher rooms. Quite astonishing is the number of major treasures in such a relatively small museum.

If you've a penchant for Oriental art, just 2 blocks east is the Asia Society ♛ ♛ ♛, 725 Park Avenue (tel. 288-6400). The small gallery in the society's handsome granite building (the work of architect Edward Larabee Barnes) almost always has a fascinating art exhibit from some Asian country, carefully chosen examples of a genre—a particular period in Chinese or Japanese brush paintings, perhaps, or a specific school of Indian miniatures.

INSIDERS' TIPS

The tiny Gallery Shop at the Asia Society manages to crowd a range of excellent Asian handicrafts into limited space. A good place for unusual, high-quality gifts.

Walk back now one block west to Madison and 5 blocks north to the Whitney Museum of American Art

♛ ♛ ♛ ♛, 975 Madison at East 75th Street (tel. 570-3676). You'll notice first the handsome contemporary building designed by the late Marcel Breuer. Enjoy it while you can; controversial plans are in the works to engulf it in a new addition by Michael Graves, which threatens to overwhelm the scale and impact of the strong lines of the Breuer building.

If you want to see the Whitney's permanent collection—and we recommend it as a syllabus of what's been happening in American art from colonial times to the present—you'll head for the third floor, where selections from the museum's 10,000 paintings, sculpture, and graphics are displayed.

But don't miss whatever the current exhibition is. Chances are it'll be provocative and daring. When Gertrude Vanderbilt Whitney launched the Whitney in a few Greenwich Village rooms in 1930, her goal was to give support to new artists. The Whitney continues to uphold this tradition of showing the innovative and experimental in modern American art. It isn't always great, but it's usually interesting.

INSIDERS' TIPS

The Whitney sponsors a special New American Filmmakers Series. You can see these or other films at the museum from September through June, as part of the regular admission.

Back you go, one block west to Fifth Avenue. Your first stop will be at the Metropolitan Museum of Art ♛ ♛ ♛ ♛ ♛, Fifth Avenue at 82nd Street (tel. 879-5500). In fact, if you had to limit your New York museum-going to a single one, this should be it. It is unquestionably one of the three or four most important art museums in the world. To miss it would be to miss the essence of cultural New York.

PERILS & PITFALLS

Weekends the Met is jammed; making your way from section to section can be slow, especially if there's a popular new exhibition. Weekdays are best for a visit.

What makes the Met so magnificent are the range of its collections—everything from ancient Egypt and Greece to medieval armor, from Roman art to 20th-century costumes—and the depth and richness in each category. There are some 20 separate departments, ranging over 50 centuries. All collections are good, but the scope and richness of the European painting collection are truly staggering. It would take years of visits to do it justice.

INSIDERS' TIPS

On weekdays, the Met offers free walking tours (about 15 a day) and Gallery Talks (2 or 3 a day). The schedule is available at the entrance desk.

In addition, like the city itself, the Met never stands still. In its many loan exhibitions, whether treasures from the Louvre, the Vatican, Nuremburg, India, or King Tut's tomb, there's always something new to see.

But, more remarkably, even the building keeps changing. New wings are added to house new collections. Just within the past decade the Met has added the American Wing; the Robert Lehman Collection of European works, especially the Italian Renaissance; the Sackler Wing, created to accommodate the Temple of Dendur, which was built by the Roman Emperor Caesar Augustus before the birth of Christ, dismantled in Egypt, and reassembled here; the Michael C. Rockefeller Wing, with its remarkable collection of African and Polynesian sculpture; the Astor Court and Douglas Dillon Galleries of Chinese Painting, with a moon gate, moon-viewing terrace and re-creation of a Ming Dynasty Scholar's garden.

The most recent additions are the spacious 2-story Lila Acheson Wallace Wing of 20th-century art; the Iris and B. Gerald Cantor Roof Garden with sculpture (on top of the Wallace Wing); and the new Japanese section, with 11 display areas that unfold with the subtlety of a Japanese fan, revealing rare works that date from 1,000 B.C. to the late 19th century. Note the modern "Water Stone" basalt sculpture-fountain by Isamu Noguchi.

METROPOLITAN MUSEUM OF ART

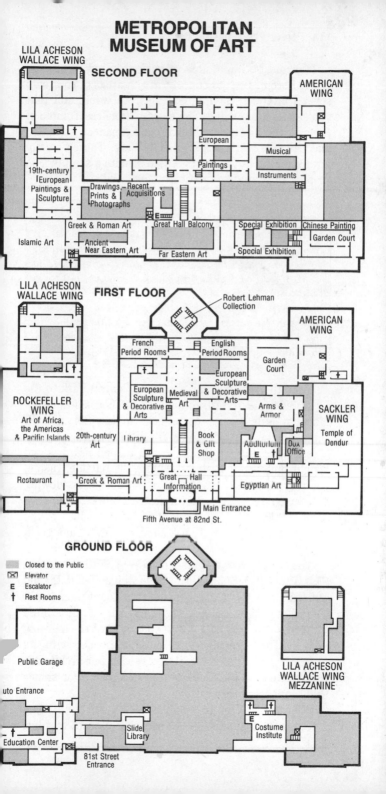

LILA ACHESON WALLACE WING

SECOND FLOOR

AMERICAN WING

European Paintings

Musical Instruments

19th-century European Paintings & Sculpture

Drawings, Prints & Photographs

Recent Acquisitions

Greek & Roman Art

Great Hall Balcony

Special Exhibition

Chinese Painting

Garden Court

Islamic Art

Ancient Near Eastern Art

Far Eastern Art

Special Exhibition

E

LILA ACHESON WALLACE WING

FIRST FLOOR

Robert Lehman Collection

AMERICAN WING

French Period Rooms

English Period Rooms

Garden Court

European Sculpture & Decorative Arts

Medieval Art

European Sculpture & Decorative Arts

Arms & Armor

SACKLER WING

Temple of Dondur

ROCKEFELLER WING
Art of Africa, the Americas & Pacific Islands

20th-century Art

Library

Book & Gift Shop

Auditorium

Box Office

E

Restaurant

Greek & Roman Art

Great Hall
Information

Egyptian Art

Main Entrance
Fifth Avenue at 82nd St.

GROUND FLOOR

Closed to the Public
⊠ Elevator
E Escalator
† Rest Rooms

Public Garage

Auto Entrance

Education Center

Slide Library

81st Street Entrance

Costume Institute

LILA ACHESON WALLACE WING MEZZANINE

It would be impossible to explore in any depth the riches herein. Best to concentrate on areas of your own special interest. Having said that, we would add that you should also include the solemn, timeless Temple of Dendur, the new, incredibly private Japanese galleries, and the Michael C. Rockefeller Wing. There's really nowhere else in the world where primitive sculpture is so brilliantly and dramatically displayed.

INSIDERS' TIPS

Most museums have gift shops these days, but the Met's is full of surprises: many bibelots, jewelry copies from its collection, rugs, books, and charming *chatchkas*. In short, it's a good place to pick up an unusual gift for a hard-to-please friend.

If spirits are flagging at this point, you might stop across the street for tea or lunch at the Stanhope or at the Boathouse Cafe in Central Park (see Insider's Information, Special Places, pages 193–194).

From the Met you can go across Central Park to the West Side and *its* attractions. But if you continue up Museum Mile, you'll come next to the Solomon R. Guggenheim Museum ♛♛♛, Fifth Avenue at 89th Street (tel. 360-3500). The spiral-shaped Frank Lloyd Wright building is distinctive from the outside. Inside, you may need sea legs as you round the spiral, viewing the museum's many colorful abstract works. There are some 5,000 paintings, sculptures, and graphics in the collection—only a fraction of them on view at any given time.

The Cooper-Hewitt Museum ♛♛♛, Fifth Avenue at 91st Street (tel. 860-6868), seems well suited to the old 1901 Andrew Carnegie mansion in which it finds itself. The museum is unique, the only one in the United States devoted to the history of decorative arts and design. The splendid neo-Georgian house, with its ornate ceilings, elaborate staircase, and fine architectural detailing, couldn't be a better backdrop for shows that emphasize decoration.

There are 12 to 16 exhibits each year, often using pieces from the museum's huge collection of textiles, furniture, ceramics, glass, wall coverings, rare books, and drawings, a collection spanning 3,000 years.

INSIDERS' TIPS

All the museums mentioned here are closed Mondays, except the American Museum of Natural History, which is open daily, and El Museo del Barrio, which is closed both Mondays and Tuesdays.

Next stop north on the "Mile" is the Jewish Museum ♛♛, at Fifth Avenue at 92nd Street (tel. 860-1888). Its well-mounted exhibits are geared to aspects of 4,000 years of Jewish history, and cover a wide swath, from coins, medals, and religious objects to modern paintings by Larry Rivers and others.

At this point you should decide whether to go west across Central Park to the American Museum of Natural History or continue north another 11 blocks to the Museum of the City of New York ♛♛♛, Fifth Avenue at 103rd Street (tel. 534-1672).

The City museum may sound dull, like a musty-dusty archive, but it's one of the liveliest places in town. You never know what you'll find. The exhibits—retailing the story of various aspects of New York's development—range from playful to informative, sparked by old costumes, posters, prints, photos, toys, and marvelous memorabilia. It's a delightful place to spend a rainy day. Kids love it too, and on weekends you'll often find puppet shows and/or concerts.

INSIDERS' TIPS

In spring and fall, the museum conducts Sunday Walking Tours that explore architectural treasures in various New York neighborhoods. For details, call the museum.

A final Fifth Avenue stop could be at El Museo del Barrio ♛, just a block farther north. This relatively new museum (1969) is devoted to exhibits relating to Puerto Rico and Latin America. Shows change often and might feature contemporary art or photography.

Your next stop, via taxi or bus (conserve those feet!)

is across Central Park to the American Museum of Natural History at 86th Street and Central Park West.

A word about Central Park ♛♛♛♛. This beautifully designed, 840-acre wooded landscape in the heart of New York was the work (in 1857) of Frederick Law Olmsted and Calvert Vaux. It extends east to west from Fifth Avenue to Central Park West (the equivalent of Eighth Avenue), and north to south from 110th Street to 59th Street.

INSIDERS' TIPS

There's a veritable cornucopia of cultural events all summer long in Central Park. Stop by the Information Center, New York Convention & Visitors Bureau, 2 Columbus Circle, for a brochure detailing all of the current ones.

It has evolved as a multi-use, open-air entertainment facility, with a lake (where you can rent rowboats), a children's zoo, a swimming pool, two ice-skating rinks, a Conservatory Garden, and paths through wooded, hilly, and natural terrain. In summer, there are concerts and free theater performances. You'll see joggers and cyclists, sunbathers perched on huge hillside boulders, toddlers sailing boats, office workers munching their brown-bag lunches, lovers enjoying a row, boys playing softball. In short, the park is well used by city inhabitants.

PERILS & PITFALLS

In daytime, Central Park is crowded and enjoyable. Even so, avoid off-the-beaten-track locales. Stay where the people are, and *above all* stay out of Central Park from dusk on, except during concerts and special events. Too many incidents have put this beautiful expanse of greenery off limits after dark.

The American Museum of Natural History ♛♛♛♛♛, Central Park West at 79th Street (tel. 769-5000) is one of the world's great museums, with something for every age group and interest. It's doubly enjoyable if you have a youngster in hand. There are so many "gee whiz" exhibits that make young eyes widen with amazement: the dinosaurs, the Hall of Ocean Life with its life-size model of a blue whale, the Northwest Coast Indian Hall and its fierce and eerie masks, Reptiles and Amphibians. A show-stopper is the African Mammals Gallery, where a herd of eight elephants seem to be staring you down. And there's the knockout Naturemax giant multiscreen film presentation. Too much to see at one time. Here, too, you must pick and choose.

But that's not all. Add the attached Hayden Planetarium, with its sky shows in the Guggenheim Space Theater, and the Halls of Minerals and Meteorites, and you'll have had quite a day of it!

INSIDERS' TIPS

The museum and planetarium have separate admissions, *but* if you visit the planetarium first, you can enter the museum without that extra fee. Don't ask us why. It just works that way.

South of the museum is Lincoln Center for the Performing Arts ♛ ♛ ♛ ♛ ♛, 64th Street and Broadway, a unique $185-million arts complex of 6 modern structures built around a travertine and black granite plaza.

INSIDERS' TIPS

Columbus Avenue from just below Lincoln Center up to the museum has become "Yuppieville," or the "Yupper West Side," replete with fashionable and sporty boutiques (see Where to Shop, page 200), sidewalk cafés, gourmet delis, and trendy eateries. Late afternoon is the perfect time to stroll the area, with time out, perhaps, for an aperitif somewhere along the route.

Lincoln Center was developed in stages, beginning in 1962. Philharmonic Hall (later renamed Avery Fisher Hall) was first, and the Juilliard School of Music and the small Alice Tully Hall (finished in 1969) were last.

Today more than 50 million people attend performances in Lincoln Center each year, more than

70,000 tour backstage at the State Theater and the Metropolitan Opera House, and 6 million or so simply revel in the delights of the plaza itself, perhaps for a stroll, a sip of espresso or Campari, a contemplative rest by the fountains or reflecting pools, a chance to admire the gigantic black Alexander Calder stabile and the two-part bronze sculpture by Henry Moore that seems to defy gravity and float in the serenity of the reflecting pool next to the Vivian Beaumont Theater.

If the weather is warm, there may be mimes, acrobats, magicians, dancers, and musicians by the dozen. This is the free part, the *entr'acte* between and before performances at the various theaters. There are also free performances of music and dance in Damrosch Park and on the plaza itself.

INSIDERS' TIPS

The Performing Arts Research Center of the New York Public Library at Lincoln Center (111 Amsterdam Avenue at 65th Street) has an outstanding record collection— some 400,000 records dating back to the earliest phonograph—in the Rodgers & Hammerstein Archives of Recorded Sound. You can listen to your favorite discs. You can also screen Broadway shows on film or video in the Billy Rose Theatre Collection and the Dance Collection.

As you face the complex from the steps where Columbus Avenue joins Broadway, the buildings are as follows, from left to right:

- New York State Theater, to the left on the south side, home of the New York City Ballet and New York City Opera. It is a Philip Johnson/Richard Foster–designed building, with slender paired columns and an elegant 4-story foyer with balconies at each level, sculptures by Elie Nadelman, and a decorative gold-leaf ceiling. (For information, tel. 870-5570.)
- Guggenheim Bandshell, in the rear, behind the New York State Theater, in Damrosch Park (where the Big Apple Circus performs free), for free outdoor productions by the Alvin Ailey Dance Theater, the Goldman Band, the Joffrey II Ballet, and more (tel. 755-4100).

- Metropolitan Opera House, next to the bandshell, directly in front of you, beyond the fountain. It's the home of the Metropolitan Opera and is the center-piece of the complex: a graceful 10-story building with elongated columns and arches and a glass façade. Its two mammoth, vibrant Marc Chagall murals are visible through the glass (tel. 362-6000).
- Vivian Beaumont Theater, recessed to the right of the Met, a small but comfortable theater for comedy and drama.
- Juilliard School of Music, to the right of the Vivian Beaumont, reached via a travertine bridge over 66th Street. Most Juilliard student concerts are free, but you need a ticket (tel. 874-7515 or 874-0465).
- Alice Tully Hall, where chamber music is king, is to the right of Juilliard, reached from Broadway (tel. 362-1900).
- Avery Fisher Hall, on your right, directly opposite the New York State Theater. This is the home of the New York Philharmonic, the Film Society of Lincoln Center, and the annual New York Film Festival. It's a Max Abramovitz building with a 44-column peristyle and foyer stabile by Richard Lippold (tel. 799-9595).

There are continuous daily tours of Lincoln Center (they're behind-the-scenes and fascinating) from 10 A.M. to 5 P.M. The tour desk is located on the Underground Concourse level (tel. 877-1800 for current price information).

INSIDERS' TIPS

Parking is easy at Lincoln Center. It has its own underground garage, entered from the north side (it's one way, going east) on West 65th Street.

NEW YORK CITY WITH PLENTY OF TIME

If you're fortunate enough to have unlimited time on your New York visit, or if you come frequently for short stays, there are many areas of interest that you can nibble on a bit at a time.

New York consists of clusters of neighborhoods, many of which are rich in history, literary associations, and touristic interest. Here are a few among the most intriguing to visitors.

Greenwich Village

One story is that the name goes back to 1664, when it was named Greenwich (*wich* is Saxon for village) by the British squadron commander Sir Peter Warren, who captured Nieuw Amsterdam. It had been an Algonquin Indian settlement, a Dutch tobacco plantation, and then a quiet, bucolic hamlet where emigrants from the frenzy of New York city life settled. In had no plan, as you will quickly discover on its wandering streets, which intersect at odd angles. They follow cattle and Indian paths and banks of long-paved-over streams.

For generations of Americans, Greenwich Village, or "the Village," has been a symbol of Bohemianism. That wasn't planned, either. In fact, in 1822, when a yellow fever epidemic hit New York City, everyone south of Cith Hall was evicted and many decamped to the Village. After the infection subsided, some survivors stayed, and by the 1850s Greenwich Village was a stylish area with many imposing mansions.

But the wealthy eventually moved uptown, the area declined, and near the end of the century a few artists and writers arrived, lured by cheap rents, among them the artists John LaFarge, Winslow Homer, and Augustus St. Gaudens, and the writers Mark Twain, O. Henry, and Henry James. By 1900 Greenwich Village was the American Bohemia, attracting waves of aspiring actors, writers, and artists.

The notion that all serious American artists, actors, musicians, and writers had to experience the Village became an *idée fixe* that waned only after World War II. In the 1940s and 1950s, the popular conception of the Village was an idealized Bohemia, pictured in the media as an amalgam of *My Sister Eileen* and *On the Town*. The Vietnam, civil rights, and Gay Rights demonstrations

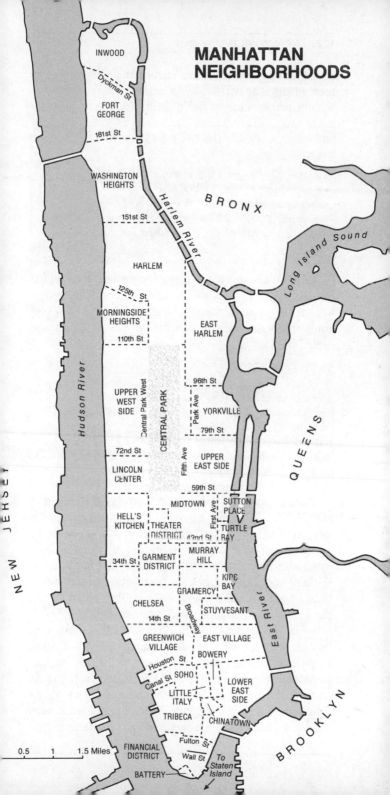

of the sixties and seventies stirred the Village, but by then, struggling artists couldn't afford Village rents and were heading south to SoHo. Still, the image persists.

INSIDERS' TIPS

The most deliriously mad time to be in the Village is October 31, night of the annual Halloween parade, when Villagers (and anyone else who wants to join in) create and wear some of the most *outré,* inventive, and humorous costumes imaginable. If you're anywhere in New York City that day, head fast for the Village. It's the *wildest!*

Many tours of the Village begin at Washington Square Park, but to see where some of the better-known artists and writers lived and worked, we suggest you begin your walk at Avenue of the Americas and 10th Street.

PERILS & PITFALLS

Street name dizziness: Avenue of the Americas is the official name, Sixth Avenue is what everybody calls it. St. Luke's Place is also called Leroy Street. Minetta Street runs into Minetta Lane. Greenwich Street and Greenwich Avenue are both important and completely separate thoroughfares.

On the corner is the splendid Victorian Gothic Jefferson Market Library. Originally (1877) a courthouse, jail, and market, this wonderfully ornate and turreted building won beauty prizes in its day. It was designed by Calvert Vaux (of Central Park fame) and Frederick C. Withers and was destined for destruction in the 1960s, until neighbors rallied to save it. At Christmastime the clock tower is festooned with colored lights.

Walk southwest on 10th Street. On the south side, on the door of old Engine Company 18, is a fresh fire-wagon mural, and next door at 138 is an old-fashioned Italian grocery, Pasta Villagio. On the north side of the street a few steps from Avenue of the Americas is tiny Patchin Place, one of only four remaining mews (originally stables and living quarters built around a secluded courtyard) in Manhattan. These small brick houses were built in 1848 as housing for waiters from the (then) fancy Brevoort Hotel. Later they were lived in by poets e.e. cummings and John Masefield, and journalist John Reed.

At Christopher Street, head southwest. You will pass a small park with a 1936 statue of Civil War General Philip Sheridan standing among its trees. (The general looks more like Mark Twain in costume than the hard-bitten nemesis of the South.) At the park, Christopher and Grove streets converge. You'll then come to Sheridan Square (where there is *no* statue of the general)—one of the most confusing intersections in the city.

INSIDERS' TIPS

Christopher Street was the main drag for homosexual Greenwich Villagers. The impetus for gay liberation centered in the Village, but the move "out of the closet" has been so successful that the once-compact gay community has dispersed widely. Centers of information for and about homosexuals are the gay bars and restaurants, such as Uncle Charlie's Downtown, 56 Greenwich Avenue (men's bar); Bonnie's, 82 West 3rd Street (women's bar); and publications· *Village Voice. Michael's Thing.*

This was *the* center of Bohemian Greenwich Village in the 1920s. Much earlier, in 1863, it was the site of vicious and bloody draft riots. Mobs dragged free blacks from their homes on Gay Street to protest drafting men into the Union Army during the Civil War. People who lived at 92 Grove braved the mob and saved the blacks from being lynched.

At the southwest corner, where Grove intersects Seventh Avenue South, the city's smallest chunk of private real estate can be seen. Look at the sidewalk in front of the Village Cigars store for a triangle marked by mosaic tiles. It reads "Property of the Hess estate which has never been dedicated for public purposes." Trespass if you dare.

Around the corner southwest on Grove, you will find 59 Grove Street, where Tom Paine died in 1809 and Marie's Crisis Restaurant later thrived. Though Marie, who is long gone, may have had her problems, the reference, as noted in the plaque by the door, is not to hers or to Paine's final days, but to his famous pamphlet "The Crisis." (When we last saw it, Marie's was in sad shape. It may have snapped back by the time you read this.)

Continue down Grove to Bedford Street. On the corner is the oldest house in the Village, the 1799 three-story Isaacs-Hendricks House, in the Federal style, with crescent-marked shutters and hand-hewn clapboard siding. Turn left on Bedford and look for number 75½, built in 1873, but much changed. The city's narrowest house (less than 10 feet wide), it was first a cobbler's shop, then a candy factory.

But that's not why it's famous. Actor John Barrymore lived here. So did poet Edna St. Vincent Millay (in 1923 and 1924) briefly with her husband before migrating to upstate New York. (Her "candle burns at both ends" abode was at 25 Charlton Street.)

Head south to number 86, Chumley's Restaurant♕, long a favorite hangout of journalists and writers. During Prohibition, it was so popular a speakeasy that it needed no sign, and it still has none. As you enter the dimly lighted taproom, note, as the rock music pounds, that the tables are heavily carved with patrons' initials, and if the Feds raid, you can easily exit through the back door, which leads around the corner to Barrow Street.

Back on Grove Street, between number 10 and number 12, is a touch of serenity—famous Grove Court, six 1850s Federal-style houses surrounding a garden, a refuge from urban tremors and traumas. Ironically, the court was a late-19th-century slum, once so abysmal it was known as "Pig's Alley." It was reclaimed in 1921 by individuals who bought and restored the buildings and garden. Grove Court is often painted, sketched, and photographed; it's said to be the setting for O. Henry's story "The Last Leaf."

Steps away, on Commerce Street at number 38, is the old Cherry Lane (the street's original name) Theater, a Village landmark. Once part of a brewery, it was one of the first Off-Broadway theaters, and in it many

Theater of the Absurd plays by Ionesco and Samuel Beckett premiered. Washington Irving lived at number 11 for a while.

When you reach Seventh Avenue, turn south to St. Luke's Place, another celebrated street. The whole block looks a bit like London's Chelsea, with 4-story brick façades and steps up to the first-floor entries and rear gardens. At number 6, New York Mayor (1926–1932) Jimmy Walker lived. Note the entrance lamps, traditional symbols of the mayor's residence.

Walker's high living during the Roaring Twenties (showgirls, speakeasies, sartorial splendor, and song—he had been a Tin Pan Alley songwriter—earned him the sobriquet "Beau James" before he resigned in the face of mounting scandal.

At 12 St. Luke's Place, playwright Sherwood Anderson lived in 1922. At number 14 you would have found poet Marianne Moore from 1918 to 1929. She worked part-time at the Hudson Park Library across the street. And novelist Theodore Dreiser lived at number 16 in 1922 and 1923 while working on *An American Tragedy*.

Reverse your steps to Seventh Avenue, zig a short block south past "Mexico Next to Texaco" (Mexican restaurant) to Carmine Street, and zag northeast two brief blocks to Father Demo Square (his parish was the Church of Our Lady of Pompeii on Carmine Street for 35 years). Mother Cabrini, America's first saint, often worshiped at this parish church. This is the heart of the old Italian neighborhood, as the signs and goodies on display will confirm.

Cross Avenue of the Americas to Minetta Lane (Minetta Street feeds into it). On these streets were many of the speakeasies that supplied the roar in the Roaring Twenties. Now there's the modern Minetta Lane Theatre and, at number 24, the La Boheme Restaurant (a bistro with pizza and pasta).

Continue east and turn up MacDougal Street, where, in good weather, sidewalk cafés blossom. You will find the Players Theatre, the Olive Tree Café and Comedy Cellar, Mamoun's Falafel, Café Reggio (at 119 MacDougal since 1927, with its ripe old oil paintings and smoke-darkened interior, still specializing in *cappuccino*). At the corner of MacDougal and Bleecker is Minetta Tavern at number 113, which has a veritable "rogues' gallery" of photos of Village denizens.

MacDougal's cafés launched diva Grace Moore and film stars Al Jolson and Norma Shearer. Much earlier, while living at number 132, Louisa May Alcott wrote *Little Women*. The petite Federal-style houses from numbers 127 to 131 were built in 1829 by Aaron Burr.

Across West 3rd Street you come to La Lanterna di Vittorio, another venerable *caffe* shop, with tiny marble tabletops, a fireplace, and opera music in the background. Next to it is the Provincetown Playhouse, where some of Eugene O'Neill's plays premiered, and where Paul Robeson played the lead in *The Emperor Jones.*

A few steps farther on, you arrive at the southwest corner of Washington Square (where MacDougal Street changes its name to Washington Square West). You'll see NYU's huge brick Law School on the site where John Sloan, William Glackens, Maurice Prendergast, and Ernest Lawson once painted.

In good weather the park is thronged with people enjoying themselves. Kids are all over the playground swings, constructions, and climbing rigs. Musicians and troubadors serenade and dancers, mimes, acrobats and jugglers perform. Many people are picnicking, some are kibbitzing off-the-wall orators, some are making drug transactions (though there are usually many policemen on duty). The Square's former attractiveness is disfigured by chain-link fence surrounding the children's section of swings and slides. Beware the occasional crazy, junkie, or derelict.

In the early days, this was a marshy area fed by Minetta Brook; Angolan blacks freed in 1644 by the Dutch farmed here. Later this was the city's potter's field. Washington Square yielded 10,000 skeletons when it was renovated a few years ago. It was also used for public executions—which were numerous. In 1824, for instance, when Lafayette was the city's guest of honor, 20 highwaymen were hanged in the park at the "hanging tree" at the northwest corner. A gala celebration! After it became a parade ground for the militia and a public park in 1828, the Square entered a fashionable mode.

PERILS & PITFALLS

Aggressive cyclists and skateboarders, young and old, are occasional menaces here and elsewhere in the Village. As a matter of fact, cyclists are a menace to pedestrians all over Manhattan. Be alert and give them plenty of room.

The Washington Arch was designed by Stanford White for the centennial parade marking Washington's inauguration as President. Originally built of wood for $2,700, its popularity spurred a drive to replace it with marble (for $178,000), which project was completed in 1895. The sculpture of Washington the soldier by Hermon MacNeil and Washington the civilian by A. Stirling Calder (father of Alexander) were added in 1918.

It was atop the arch that an abortive "revolution" took place in 1916. Fortified with quantities of drink, food, and arms (cap pistols), John Sloan and fellow artists took over the top of the arch and decorated it with lighted Japanese lanterns. To the accompaniment of volleys of cap-pistol fire, they read a manifesto declaring the "independence" of the "state of New Bohemia." The new state survived only until the gendarmes rounded up the exuberant revolutionaries.

Each holiday season, the area in front of the arch sports a huge decorated and lighted Christmas tree, with much caroling and occasional music.

New York University, founded by Albert Gallatin, Jefferson's Treasury Secretary, opened its doors on Washington Square in 1831, and, having taken over 75 percent of the property around it, now uses it as its "campus." On the southwest corner is the NYU Law School. At the corner of Washington Square South and Sullivan Street is a forbidding granite fortress, NYU's Kevorkian Center for Near Eastern Studies (designed by architects Philip Johnson and Richard Foster).

On the next corner is the ornate façade of Judson Memorial Church (locked), built in 1892 in Greco-

Romanesque style by McKim, Mead & White. In it is the Judson Poets' Theatre, an Off-Off-Broadway showcase for the works of Al Carmines in times past. The handsome contemporary building across the street is a Catholic Center for students and faculty.

At the corner of Washington Square South and La Guardia Place is Loeb Student Center. (On this spot was Marie Blanchard's rooming house, onetime home to Willa Cather, Stephen Crane, Theodore Dreiser, O. Henry, and Eugene O'Neill.)

At 70 Washington Square South is NYU's striking Bobst Research Library. Look inside to see how architects Johnson and Foster used Palladio's San Giorgio Maggiore piazza as inspiration in the *trompe l'oeil* gray, black, and white marble floor of the soaring 12-story atrium.

The north side of Washington Square is made up of 5-story brick town houses with Doric column–framed portals and black cast-iron fences. These date back to the 1830s and were built for wealthy burghers of that era.

This is Henry James country. The houses on Washington Square North, to the east of Fifth Avenue, are known as the "Old Row" ♔♔♔. James's *Washington Square* was written about his grandmother's house at number 18, which gave way in 1950 to an apartment house. James's friend, the novelist Edith Wharton, lived at number 7 in 1881.

The official residence of New York's mayors was number 8. The novelist John Dos Passos and artists Rockwell Kent and Edward Hopper once lived in various of these houses, which today are all owned by NYU and used for various university purposes.

On Washington Square West, the apartment building at number 29 was the New York City home of Mrs. Eleanor Roosevelt from 1942 to 1949.

If you walk from Washington Square up Fifth Avenue, the first tiny street on your right is cobblestoned Washington Mews (formerly Stable Alley). Here are tidy if uninspired rows of what once were the stables and carriage houses of the mansions on Washington Square North and West 8th Street, respectively. Columnist Walter Lippmann lived here, as did official city greeter Grover Whalen and Gertrude Vanderbilt Whitney, who launched the Whitney Museum of American Art.

INSIDERS' TIPS

If you are in the city in spring or fall, you may see the Washington Square Outdoor Art Exhibition, in which all available display space is literally covered with paintings, drawings, photographs, prints, and mixed-media efforts. The scene and participants are fascinating, even if the art is not.

The shows are held on 3 weekends each spring (usually the last 2 weekends in May, first weekend in June) and 3 in the fall (usually the first 3 weekends in September).

Far more attractive are the buildings in MacDougal Alley, which is blocked from Fifth Avenue by the 2 Fifth Avenue building. Walk west on 8th Street, considered by many to be Greenwich Village's "Main Street." The large New York Studio School on the south side of 8th Street was the original home of the Whitney Museum of American Art before it went uptown. The rest of 8th Street is chockablock with shops dedicated to selling to the NYU students and tourists, and is famous for its shoe stores.

INSIDERS' TIPS

For a glimpse of the luxury that was, when lower Fifth Avenue was rimmed by millionaires' mansions, stop in at the Salmagundi Club, 47 Fifth Avenue, now a private club for artists. It was built in 1854 for a coal baron named Irad Hawley. As it is open most afternoons, you may be able to peek at the baroque parlor.

When you reach MacDougal Street, turn left and walk a few steps south to see MacDougal Alley, a real charmer, with its window boxes and Old World ambiance (though it could stand a general paint-up and refurbishing).

For a hint of the passions that were generated in the 1960s, look at the Greek Revival houses on 11th Street west of Fifth Avenue. When you reach number 18 you will find a completely modern building unlike all the rest. This is the site of the March 1970 explosion that destroyed the old town house here, killing three of the Weathermen radicals who were making bombs in the basement. Eleven years later, Kathy Boudin, one who managed to escape after the blast and whose parents owned the building, was arrested during a bank robbery attempt.

To wind up your Greenwich Village tour at one of its historic and absolutely unvarnished venues, the White Horse Tavern ♛, cross Avenue of the Americas and proceed southwest on Christopher Street to Hudson, then turn and walk 3 blocks north. The venerable White Horse is at 567 Hudson Street.

It was for decades the favorite watering hole of longshoremen, and was the haunt of poet Dylan Thomas during his New York sojourns. He bragged that he had downed 18 whiskies at the White Horse just before he collapsed and was hauled away to St. Vincent's Hospital (at 11th Street and Greenwich Avenue), where he died of alcohol poisoning in November 1953. The White Horse has a room with Dylan Thomas memorabilia.

For a more upbeat finale to your Greenwich Village visit, try the old standby, the Blue Note at 135 West 3rd Street, where mainstream jazz has been thriving for decades. These days, Maynard Ferguson and High Voltage are featured.

Jazz has been created for nearly 40 years at the Village Vanguard, 178 Seventh Avenue South at 11th Street, a cramped basement hangout with tight-fitting tables and consistently top-quality mainstream jazz. Farther south, after Seventh Avenue South becomes Varick Street, it's the irresistible Sounds of Brazil at 204. If it isn't an all-encompassing samba night, S.O.B.'s may reverberate to jazz or blues.

A current "in" place where art types like to hang out is Café Orlin, 41 St. Marks Place, an extension of 8th Street, east of Third Avenue. This is really where the

East Village begins, where the punk rock scene is strong, and where part of the movie *Desperately Seeking Susan* was filmed.

The East Village

Several years ago, the Greenwich Village—or West Village—and SoHo action began to spill over into the East Village, as struggling artists looked for cheaper rents in not-yet-gentrified neighborhoods.

In fact, the area was first "discovered" in 1951 when Beat poet Allen Ginsberg sought cheap "digs" at 206 East 7th Street. His pal William Burroughs followed and Jack Kerouac spent time here, too.

Be sure to look in at St. Mark's-in-the-Bowery on East 10th Street, the oldest continuously used church in New York City. (Parts date from 1799.) Poetry readings and dance concerts are performed in the Georgian-style main sanctuary.

The East Village is still not overly Yuppified, but its many east-west streets now shelter tiny art galleries, secondhand clothing shops, and cheap eateries. Most such places are undercapitalized and are here today, gone by the time you read this book. But others will take their place, and the fun of poking around the East Village is making your own discoveries.

The East Village's not-always-friendly confines stretch from 14th Street south to Houston Street, east to Avenue D, west to Lafayette Street or a block farther to Broadway. By far the liveliest street scenes center on St. Marks Place, Astor Place, Lafayette Street, and along Second Avenue.

Theatre 80, at 80 St. Marks Place, offers a steady diet of rare, old, unusual, foreign, and seldom-seen movies. La Mama E.T.C., at 74A East 4th Street, is probably the most venerable of the live experimental theaters in the city. On Lafayette, two major Off-Broadway theaters confront each other across the street: the Public Theatre (with fascinating experimental plays, plus an excellent film series) and the

Astor Place Theatre. The latter is ensconced in one corner of one of the area's most illustrious buildings: Colonnade Row. Now 4 attached buildings with a row of 13 Greek Revival columns marching along the second-story level, it was originally 9 buildings, built in 1831 by Seth Geer and known as La Grange Terrace. In the mid-19th century this was considered the finest row of private dwellings in New York. Washington Irving once lived here, as did John Jacob Astor.

Astor's legacy is remembered in the well-restored Astor Place subway station a block away. The original terra-cotta interior tiles feature beavers—a reminder that Astor made his fortune in the fur trade, in an era when beaver hats were the rage.

Another building of note is across the street from the subway station: Cooper Union. When it was built in 1859, it was one of the first buildings designed with a wrought-iron framework. It remains the oldest building in the United States supported by rolled structural beams.

The East Village is the place to scout out unusual and inexpensive ethnic restaurants (see Insiders' Information). Check out East 6th Street, off Second Avenue, for a cluster of East Indian shops and restaurants. (You'll find the street by the scent of cumin, cilantro, and coriander that pervades it.)

Favorite discos are Saint, 105 Second Avenue (it has no sign), with one of the best sound-and-light systems around, and the Palladium, 126 East 14th Street, a one-time vaudeville hall, now a super state-of-the-art disco. Artistic types hang out at Café Orlin, 41 St. Mark's Place, and visiting Europeans head for the outdoor garden (in temperate weather) of the Cloister Café, 238 East 9th Street.

The East Village is full of surprises, as you'll discover on a leisurely ramble. But plan your stroll for late afternoon; that's when the area really gears up for the evening action.

INSIDERS' TIPS

For the best egg cream (a drink made of seltzer and chocolate syrup with milk or ice cream) in town, as well as out-of-town newspapers and a large selection of magazines, check out the Gem Spa, a corner soda fountain at Second Avenue and St. Marks Place. In the sixties, this was the place where radical newspapers were sold, and although it isn't as politically fashionable anymore, all types of people still meet there.

SoHo and TriBeCa

What is SoHo? The name was coined from "*So*uth of *Ho*uston Street," and refers to the 26 blocks bounded by Canal Street on the south, Avenue of the Americas on the west, and Lafayette Street on the east. Where Greenwich Village ends, SoHo begins on the south side of Houston.

SoHo began to develop as an artistic force in the late 1960s and now is definitely a world center, showcasing "what's happening" in the visual and performing arts. If you've seen the movie *After Hours,* you'll have a pretty good idea of the unpredictable wackiness of the SoHo scene (Though most of the film was shot in TriBeCa).

There are many reasons to visit SoHo: for the latest, funkiest, most outrageous, provocative painting and sculpture, exhibited at dozens of small-, medium-, and big-name galleries all along West Broadway and numerous cross streets; for avant-garde theater; for marvelous shopping at one-of-a-kind boutiques; and for happy dining at outdoor cafés, *intime* bistros, and trendy restaurants.

PERILS & PITFALLS

SoHo art galleries (and many shops and boutiques) are closed mornings and often all day Monday. On Saturdays and Sundays, especially in balmy weather, the sidewalks are jammed, as though all New York were on a SoHo stroll.

And then there's the cast-iron architecture. This is the place to see the world's greatest concentration of it. The Cast-Iron Historic District buildings date from 1850–80.

Historically, this area was transmogrified after the Revolution, from farmland to densely settled cityscape by 1825. On Broadway were the city's most fashionable emporia—Lord & Taylor, Tiffany's, Arnold Constable—elegant hotels, and popular theaters. And off Broadway in those years were casinos, dance halls, taverns, and bordellos.

By the Civil War years, the dynamism of entertainment, business, and residences had moved north to the 14th Street area. Textile, clothing, fur, and millinery manufacturers and shops took over the SoHo area, converting or replacing existing buildings with the then-new cast-iron edifices you still see today.

The beauty of cast-iron construction was that it could so well replicate classical forms at low cost. (It also allowed larger windows and more light.) The designs followed such masterpieces as the Sansovino Library in Venice, the Roman Colosseum, and French neo-Grecian and Renaissance examples. Architects and their clients ordered from catalogs the Corinthian columns, Empire cornices, Palladian doorways and window surrounds, and acanthus leaf and other embellishments. When they arrived at the site, they were simply riveted in place. Presto! Nearly instant façades, often of considerable beauty. The interiors above the showrooms, however, were where the "teeming masses" worked as sweatshop labor.

Labor laws and unions, restricted immigration, and economic pressures changed this and turned SoHo over the years into a wasteland of grungy warehouses, light manufacturing, and empty buildings. In the 1950s and 1960s, artists began to move in surreptitiously (it was zoned for business) to claim studio and living space. They formed cooperatives, bought buildings, and formed associations to bring about zoning changes. In the 1970s, SoHo and the art market boomed, and there hasn't been a slowdown since. SoHo has become the city's cultural supermarket.

But as SoHo has prospered, it has also gentrified, and the lesser-known artists have moved farther south to the area called TriBeCa (*Tri*angle *Be*low *Ca*nal), edging SoHo, bordered by Chinatown to the southeast.

For the intrepid walker, sturdy of shoe and foot, it is a pleasant stroll through the East Village and Greenwich Village, down to SoHo, and into TriBeCa. Each neighborhood melts into the next, and there's much to see, the human parade as much as the imaginative shops and galleries. If you're short of time or stamina, concentrate on SoHo, a far livelier scene than TriBeCa.

West Broadway is *the* action street in SoHo. As you turn south to stroll down it, you will note that buildings on the east side have retained their historic appearances and those across the street have been drastically altered. It's because the Historic District's western limit is in the middle of the street, so only the east side is protected.

On weekends and holidays, West Broadway from Houston to Canal streets is often impassable because of slow-moving stretch limos, Jags, and Mercedeses. Cruising Big Money art buyers, earnest *dinky* (Double-Income-No-Kids-Yet) couples, Connecticut and New Jersey suburbanites, foreign tourists, and resident artists all swarm the sidewalks.

East-west streets, such as Prince, Spring, Broome, and Grand, and north-south streets, such as Wooster, Greene, and Mercer, are almost as jammed, and every bit as interesting with clusters of galleries, boutiques, and eateries. Spring Street is particularly good for shopping.

Among SoHo's many galleries, there are a few super-influential trend-setters you should be sure to visit: O. K. Harris, Mary Boone, Sonnabend, and Leo Castelli. (See Insiders' Information, page 207, for addresses.)

Farther south on West Broadway, near Thomas Street, below Canal in TriBeCa, is Odeon, a Depression-era cafeteria (note the cafeteria sign) turned 1980s stylish bar (and restaurant) that is currently *the* hangout of the area's resident artists. Have a look at the Odeon building's 1869 façade; it looks like carved stone but is cast iron. Around the corner at 62 Thomas, you'll see one of the few cast-iron façades in a Gothic design.

As you walk through SoHo, and even TriBeCa, keep an eye peeled for the many diverse cast-iron façades. So well done are the casting and painting—with marbling and sandstone effects—that it often takes a magnet or a rap on a façade to verify its composition if the foundry mark is absent.

On both sides of Greene Street from Canal north, the façades are cast iron to the next corner (Grand Street) and also on the west side between Grand and Broome. Especially satisfying is 72 Greene Street, because of its graceful symmetry. Also on Greene, 139 is a Federal-style, 1824 brick house, one of the few originals left in SoHo. On Broome Street you will also see the Broome Street Dutch Reformed Church, secure in its Greek Revival building with white picket fence.

Walk east on Broome to Mercer (which was notorious for its "sporting houses"—brothels). At number 11 is something new: the Museum of Holography ♛, open Tuesday through Sunday, from noon to 6 P.M. (tel. 925-0581). In 3 galleries it exhibits amazing 3-D holograms, the "photos" taken with laser photography. You have to see (and walk around them) to believe them. The current exhibit is "European Display Holography."

Continue onward to Broadway. Look now at the splendid building on the northeast corner. This Venetian *palazzo* at 488 Broadway ♛ ♛ ♛, often called the "Parthenon of Cast-Iron Architecture in America," is a designated Landmark Building, listed in the National Register of Historic Places.

Built in 1857 for Eder Haughwout, one of the nation's leading chinaware retailers, this was an unprecedented 5 stories high because it had a steam elevator equipped with automatic safety devices—the first ever installed by Elisha Otis. The building looks much as it did then, even to the clock above the Broadway entrance. This is the oldest remaining cast-iron building, and one of the best.

A block south, at the northeast corner of Grand Street, 462–468 Broadway, is the building that once housed Brooks Brothers Store. The company supplied Union Army uniforms during the Civil War.

Chinatown

Chinatown begins at Canal Street. If you think you won't find it, just get out of the Canal Street IRT or BMT subway station and look around. You'll feel you're in Hong Kong, with the masses of Chinese milling past you, intent on their shopping errands. Some wear traditional clothes, many also speak in various Chinese dialects. Notice the public telephone booths here, with red Chinese temple roofs.

There's no special itinerary to follow in Chinatown, just go with the flow. Busiest streets are the narrow Mott, perpendicular to Canal, and Bayard and Pell, both of which branch off from Mott. All three streets were named after pre-Revolutionary residents of the area: Mott and Pell were both prosperous butchers, Bayard was the nephew of Peter Stuyvesant and mayor of New York in 1686. They'd never recognize the old place.

Just before turning from Canal Street south onto Mott, look in at 200 Canal Street, one of the most prosperous Chinese food markets in Chinatown, Kam Man. You'll see all the traditional Chinese delicacies, items such as glazed ducks, dried shark's fin, and tiger lily buds, as well as kitchenwares, casseroles, furniture.

On Mott Street, you'll pass the Eastern States Buddhist Temple of America, number 64, and the Chinese Museum, number 8, whose ground floor is an arcade of computer games, a "dancing chicken" (which will win a tic-tac-toe game with you), and a coin-gobbling "dragon." Upstairs, cases display costumes, calligraphy, and Chinese inventions and arts in dim surroundings.

Plan on lunch, dinner, or a *dim sum* brunch in one of Chinatown's many bustling, noisy, gregarious restaurants.

As you wander, you might sample a large, cookie-like lotus-seed "moon cake" at Lum Fong Bakery, 41 Mott Street at Pell (tel. 233-7447), which has a big pastry selection. Another treat is ice cream in exotic flavors (ginger, almond cookie, red bean, green tea, papaya, lichee, mango, coconut) at the Chinatown Ice Cream Factory, 65 Bayard Street.

PERILS & PITFALLS

Many Chinatown establishments, especially restaurants, do not accept credit cards. Take traveler's checks with you.

Little Italy

Wedged between Greenwich Village on the north, SoHo on the west, and Chinatown on the south is the ever-narrowing area called Little Italy, where immigrant Italians clustered for generations. (Actually, part of the old neighborhood to the northwest has been absorbed by the Village—and vice versa.)

If you follow Mulberry Street north of Canal on a balmy day, you'll get the spirit of the neighborhood. Languid Neapolitan love songs sidle out of the many sidewalk cafés between Canal and Hester. Maybe you'll sip a cappuccino at La Bella Ferrara Pastry Shop, just opposite the brick Church of the Most Precious Blood. Inside the church is the San Gennaro Shrine. It's San Gennaro who brings the street to vibrant, frenetic life in early September, when the entire city seems to become Italian to celebrate the saint's feast day with a 10-day, blocks-long eating-and-entertainment binge.

Another big 10-day celebration is Festa Italiana in mid-July, in honor of Our Lady of Pompeii, whose church is at 25 Carmine Street (between 6th and 7th streets) in Greenwich Village, which illustrates how much the two old neighborhoods have melded.

Gramercy Park Area

Gramercy Park, 1½ blocks east of Broadway, is a decidedly fashionable address, and reminds many of London squares.

The name may derive from the Dutch *Crommessie Fly* (Crooked-Little-Knife Stream). Samuel B. Ruggles bought the land, drained the marsh, and deeded the 1½-acre park (which is kept locked) to the 60 lot owners around it. (Residents of the brick town houses surrounding the park carry their own keys.) He named Lexington Avenue to the north and Irving Place (after his friend Washington Irving) to the south. The park's cast-iron fence went up in 1832. In the center you'll see a statue of Edwin Booth as Hamlet. The whole area is now Gramercy Park Historic District ♛ ♛.

On the west side, houses number 3 and 4 date from 1846, designed by Alexander Jackson Davis and festooned with cast-iron lace reminiscent of New Orleans's Vieux Carre. There are lanterns in front of number 4 because in 1844 it was the residence of Mayor James Harper, a founder of the publishing company that later became Harper & Row. Such lanterns designated the mayor's residence before Gracie Mansion became the official city home of the mayor.

On the south, number 19 is the Stuyvesant Fish house, bought by (and named for) the then-president of the Illinois Central Railroad in 1887. His wife, Mamie, was the doyenne of New York society (after Mrs. William Astor) and was famed for abbreviating dinners to fifty minutes—a radical reform from bouts of eating that typically lasted hours. Flamboyant public-relations specialist Ben Sonnenberg bought the house in 1931 and made it his home and reception center.

The big brownstone at number 15 was home to Samuel Tilden, governor of the state and would-be President (1876). He had an escape tunnel built to 19th Street for a quick exit (not a bad idea for a politician). Tilden's house now belongs to the National Arts Club. Actor Edwin Booth bought number 16 in 1886, and hired Stanford White to remodel it into a haven for fellow actors, the Players Club, which it still is today. Stanford White's own house was on the north side, just west of Lexington Avenue.

Just a few hops from the park is Theodore Roosevelt's birthplace, 28 East 20th Street, between Broadway and Park Avenue South—a brownstone town house built in the 1840s. Restored in 1923 and maintained by the National Park Service, its rooms are done in the period of T.R.'s childhood. The front bedroom (where he was born) has its original furniture and the nursery and open porch/gymnasium adjoin. It's an interesting stop for any student of history. There's also a 30-minute film about T.R. No admission charge.

A block south of the park, 19th Street between Irving Place and Third Avenue is lined with small 19th-century houses, in one of which the painter George Bellows lived in the 1930s. And on the corner of Irving Place and 18th Street (129 East 18th) is Pete's Tavern, an old-timer (from 1864) where O. Henry was a patron. (He lived at 55 Irving Place.) It's the setting he used in his story "The Lost Blend."

Chelsea

Chelsea extends from 14th to 28th streets, and from Fifth Avenue west to the Hudson River. Named after London's artistic area of Chelsea near the Thames, *our* Chelsea is an engaging art and ethnic mix, a neighborhood whose long-time Latino accent has been changing slowly into one of small boutiques, cafés, restaurants, and theaters.

The enduring anchor of the neighborhood is the Chelsea Hotel, at 222 West 23rd Street, a comfortable home away from home for artists and writers for many generations. Brass plaques on the front of the red brick building (listed in the National Registry of Historic Places) remind you that Arthur Miller lived in the hotel from 1962 to 1968 and wrote *After the Fall* and several other works here, and that Brendan Behan, O. Henry, James T. Farrell, Thomas Wolfe, and John Sloan also lived here. But our favorite plaque says, "Dylan Thomas lived here and from here sailed out to die." Note the seven splendid stories of black cast-iron balconies with their handsome sunflower motif along the façade, and be sure to step inside to see the art-decorated lobby, with works by Larry Rivers and others.

A plaque on a brick apartment house at 420 West 23rd Street identifies this as the site of the 1822 home of Clement Clarke Moore, who wrote "Visit from St. Nicholas" (" 'Twas the night before Christmas . . .").

Moore gave the land for St. Paul's Church, a sturdy Gothic structure around the block on West 22nd Street between Eighth and Ninth avenues.

INSIDERS' TIPS

If you'd like to take an organized walking tour of Chelsea, contact Chelsea Visiting Neighbors, 30 West 16th Street, for information.

While wandering Chelsea, don't miss its most sparkling current magnet: Barney's New York, at 17th Street and Seventh Avenue. Once a discount men's store, Barney's has metamorphosed into one of the most lustrous upscale department stores in the nation, featuring clothes by big-name American, European, and Japanese designers, as well as elegant housewares and decorative accessories.

INSIDERS' TIPS

For a pristine oasis on your peregrinations, descend the winding staircase to Barney's Le Cafe in the basement, for a light lunch or midafternoon beverage and dessert. The soft green, refreshingly cool, restful surroundings are almost a pick-me-up in themselves. Handsome rest rooms are down the hall.

At the lower end of Chelsea, the major landmark is Union Square, currently undergoing a major expansion of the park in the square's center, after years of decline, neglect, and worse. As many publishing houses have moved to this area, it has undergone a renewal and transformation—a typical tale in New York, where growth, decline, and renewal are part of the city cycle.

The best times to be in Union Square are Wednesday, Friday, and Saturday mornings, when the north side of the square is occupied by vendors in the Greenmarket farmers' market. This is the largest and liveliest of the city's 17 Greenmarkets, with some 60 farmervendors selling fresh fruit, vegetables, homemade jams, honey, cheeses, Finger Lakes wines, breads, and baked goods. (And you thought New York lacked the homey touch!) Farmers come from Long Island, Westchester,

Connecticut, New Jersey, and even from the Amish country of Pennsylvania.

While in Chelsea, note also the Joyce Theater, 175 Eighth Avenue, with some innovative offerings; the WPA Theatre on West 23rd Street between Tenth and Eleventh avenues; and the 23rd Street YMCA, known for its fine athletic facilities that include an indoor jogging track.

INSIDERS' TIPS

New York's new multimillion-dollar glass showcase for every conceivable type of convention and exhibition is the Jacob K. Javits Center at 36th Street and Eleventh Avenue.

Museums of Special Interest

If you are an aficionado of Spanish art, American Indian treasures, and/or coins as collectibles, the complex of museums at West 155th to 156th streets and Broadway is a destination you'll want to check out. No crowds to buck or lines to stand in. The area isn't chic, but the collections are exquisite and extraordinary.

In Beaux Arts limestone buildings built around a grandiose courtyard are the Hispanic Society of America ♛♛♛, the Museum of the American Indian ♛♛♛♛, the American Numismatic Society ♛♛, and others. The property was once the John James Audubon estate, so the complex is called Audubon Terrace. It was a Huntington family project: Archer Milton Huntington financed it, brother Charles Pratt Huntington designed most of the buildings, and his wife, Anna Hyatt Huntington, did the heroic bronze of *El Cid Campeador* that dominates the plaza.

The fate of the Museum of the American Indian (tel. 283-2420) is undecided. By the time you read this, it may be on its way to new quarters in the old Custom House at South Ferry, to space in the American Museum of Natural History, or to a building of its own in Washington, D.C. But for the moment it's here, all 3 floors of exhibits showing small portions of the greatest extant collection of priceless Indian masks, trade goods, clothing, tools, baskets, weapons, and weaving. Here are dioramas and artifacts of the major Indian tribes, with Sitting Bull's war club, Crazy Horse's bonnet, Tecumseh's tomahawk, and much more. The third floor has South American and Central American Indian items and changing exhibits.

The massive Hispanic Society of America building (at Broadway and 155th St.; tel. 926-2234) holds many surprises. Its interior is a strikingly authentic Spanish courtyard done in Plateresque style. On the mezzanine are outstanding paintings of the 14th and later centuries by many of Spain's finest artists, among them El Greco, Zurbaran, Ribera, Velazquez, and Goya. Hispano-Moresque tiles and mosaics are on display.

There are also 14 sunny canvases by Sorolla of street scenes in Spain's provinces, as well as outstanding sculptures, pottery, wrought iron, and textiles from pre-Roman times to the 19th century, and a treasure house of books, manuscripts, prints, and photographs.

The American Numismatic Society (at Broadway and 155th Street; tel. 234–3130) has one of the great coin and money collections, and displays part of its holdings at all times. You can examine specific coins, ask questions, and chat about money with a curator at the Public Inquiry Counter. (They won't authenticate or evaluate your coins, though.) You can also order a plaster cast (for $2) of that Greek *tetradrachm* (or other coins in the collection) you've always coveted but couldn't afford.

An absolute gem is the Pierpont Morgan Library ♛ ♛ ♛ ♛, 29 East 36th Street (tel. 685-0610), housed in a beautiful McKim, Mead & White *palazzo*, where the New York financier once lived. The library mounts dazzling small shows of prints, rare books, illuminated medieval manuscripts, master drawings, and historical documents—in truth, the very best of their kind.

In addition to special exhibitions, you'll see Morgan's private study (as he might have left it), Renaissance painting and sculpture, a Gutenberg Bible, and many splendid medieval gold and enamel *objets*. Almost everything is on a small scale, except the lavish interior, proving once and for all that small is beautiful.

At the New-York Historical Society ♛ ♛, Central

Park West at 77th Street (tel. 873-3400), you'll find more than 32 gallery areas devoted to an eclectic but fascinating collection of New Yorkiana, everything from original Audubon watercolors to ancient fire engines, from early silver to Tiffany lamps. In the library are more than 4 million manuscripts, photos, prints, music, and rare books. There are lectures and concerts from time to time. It's a treasure house of unexpected delights.

The Museum of Broadcasting ♛♛, 1 East 53rd Street (tel. 752-7684), has a huge collection of radio and television programs, spanning more than 60 years of broadcasting. Greatest fun for the visitor is being able to check out a radio or TV program from the past, take it to a booth, and enjoy it to your heart's content in the Broadcast Study Center.

In Harlem is the Schomburg Center for Research in Black Culture ♛♛, at 515 Lenox Avenue (tel. 862-4000), a new building showcasing the oldest and largest collection of photos, books, art, sculpture, and artifacts relating to the black experience.

Also uptown is the Studio Museum in Harlem ♛♛, 144 West 125th Street (tel. 864-4500; closed Monday and Tuesday). In a recently renovated 5-story building you'll find outstanding exhibits, concerts, lectures, films, and workshops about black Americans and their African heritage. (A recent show, "Harlem Renaissance Art," won critical acclaim.) There's also a terrific gift shop featuring excellent African handicrafts.

EXCURSIONS FROM NEW YORK CITY: THE BOROUGHS AND LONG ISLAND

This is a time for decisions. As you must have known when you came to New York City, regardless of how omnivorous you are, there are too many attractions here to be devoured, or even tasted or sampled, in a single visit (possibly even in a lifetime). Therefore, we set before you here some of the goodies we consider outstanding and let you decide which are of greatest appeal. Some places are dependent on season (do you *really* want to visit the zoo or gardens in the rain?), others on the amount of time required to reach them.

ONE-DAY ITINERARY

The Cloisters, Morris-Jumel Mansion, Dyckman House (Manhattan); Brooklyn Museum, Brooklyn Botanic Garden, New York Aquarium, Children's Museum (Brooklyn); Bronx Zoo, New York Botanical Garden (Bronx); Isamu Noguchi Museum, Little Athens (Queens); Staten Island Institute, Jacques Marchais Tibetan Museum, Richmondtown Restoration (Staten Island); and on Long Island, Old Bethpage Village, Sagamore Hill (Theodore Roosevelt's home), Planting Fields Arboretum (Oyster Bay); Old Westbury and Clark Garden; Sands Point Park, Cold Spring Harbor Whaling Museum; Stony Brook Museums; Jones Beach, Fire Island, the Hamptons, and Long Island wineries.

Manhattan

There are scores of Manhattan attractions (in addition to the ones mentioned in earlier chapters), but you should seriously consider these three:

The Cloisters ♛ ♛ ♛ ♛ ♛, Fort Tryon Park (tel. 923-3700), looms like a medieval monastery high above the Hudson River at the northern tip of Manhattan (reachable by the M4 Madison Avenue bus, which lets you off at the door). Visiting it is the next best thing to a trip to Europe. Actually, the tile-roofed granite building was completed in 1938, but was meticulously patterned after a 9th-century monastery in southern France. (Even the herb garden is true to manuscript illuminations of the period.)

The Cloisters owes its inspiration to sculptor and medievalist George Barnard, who spent years before World War I ferreting out and buying art, sculpture, and fragments of abandoned churches and monasteries in Italy and France. (He found a Romanesque wood torso of Christ in use as a scarecrow!)

John D. Rockefeller, Jr., gave the Metropolitan Museum of Art $600,000 to purchase the collection in

1925 and contributed the site to display it. Now the Cloisters represents the Metropolitan's medieval wing, displaying sculptures, paintings, stained-glass windows, and rare illuminated manuscripts in appropriate settings.

In fact, inside the Cloisters are elements of one Romanesque and three Gothic cloisters, and a 12th-century chapter house transported stone by stone from Spain and France and reassembled here. Other highlights include a Spanish Room, with a 15th-century Spanish ceiling and Flemish "Annunciation" altarpiece; the famous illuminated Book of Hours of the Duc de Berry, and the exceptional series of 6 "Unicorn Tapestries" depicting a medieval unicorn hunt.

INSIDERS' TIPS

"Greensleeves," anyone? Medieval music concerts are presented often. At Christmastime there are medieval songs, plantings, and Nativity displays. Call for ticket information (even if you can't get into the hall, you'll hear the music piped through the Cloisters).

For a taste of American history, visit the Morris-Jumel Mansion♛♛, Edgecombe Avenue at 160th Street (tel. 923-8008), Manhattan's oldest residence. Built about 1765 as a summer house by Colonel Roger Morris, this splendid Georgian mansion was Washington's New York headquarters for part of the Revolution. After the war, it became a roadside tavern. In 1810 the house was purchased by Stephen Jumel, who renovated it in Federal style and added the grand portico. Aaron Burr later married Jumel's widow, Eliza, in the front parlor (for her money), as you will learn in your visit.

Manhattan's only surviving farmhouse, Dyckman House♛♛, is at the corner of West 204th Street at Broadway (tel. 755-4100). Farmer William Dyckman rebuilt his house in 1783 after the British burned the original. Its gambrel roof, wide plank floors, stone and brick walls, and original furnishings give you an accurate picture of 18th-century life in what was then rural New York.

Brooklyn

The Dutch named this westernmost edge of Long Island "Breuckelen" when they settled it in 1646, displacing Canarsie Indians. The British renamed it "Brookland" when they took over. It became a bedroom community for Manhattan after Robert Fulton began regular steam ferry service in 1814. Some 20 years later, Brooklyn was the nation's third largest city. In 1883 the new Brooklyn Bridge accelerated the borough's growth, but it wasn't until 1898 that Brooklyn became part of metropolitan New York.

Like other New York boroughs, Brooklyn is one of shifting ethnic enclaves. Today, Puerto Ricans and Hassidic Jews are in the Williamsburg section, blacks and Hispanics in Bedford-Stuyvesant, Italians in Bensonhurst and Bay Ridge, and "Odessa on the Sea" is the Russian Jewish area near Coney Island. Arabs, Lebanese, Yemenis, and Syrians have made Atlantic Avenue perhaps the nation's largest concentration of Middle Easterners, but in 1900 this area was so heavily Scandinavian that the street was called "Swedish Broadway."

INSIDERS' TIPS

Fanciers of ethnic foods have a heyday by journeying for dinner to the area they favor. The Middle Eastern section on Atlantic Avenue is especially rich in restaurants, most of them bargain-priced. Antique collectors will find Atlantic Avenue and Coney Island Avenue fertile fields for browsing.

Brooklyn is justifiably famous for its homes (half of them built before 1860) and churches, notably in the gentrified sections of Brooklyn Heights (New York's first suburb), Park Slope, and Cobble Hill. The Degraw Mansion at 219 Clinton Street, the prize among Cobble Hill houses, was built in Greek Revival style for a merchant (Abraham Degraw) in 1844, then enlarged in 1891. It has been owned by only three families and remains true to its original designs. Cobble Hill's handsome 19th-century atmosphere has won its 22 blocks a Landmarks designation as the Cobble Hill Historic District.

From the Esplanade in Brooklyn Heights, above the Brooklyn-Queens Espressway, looking over Upper New York Bay, you'll have one of the great panoramic views ♛ ♛ ♛ ♛ of Manhattan.

The views are also splendid from the River Café, on a barge at the foot of the Brooklyn Bridge (see Insiders' Information, Where to Eat). And the sight of Manhattan from the Brooklyn Bridge itself ♛ ♛ ♛ ♛ ♛ is exhilarating, especially if you cross the bridge on foot.

The Brooklyn Bridge was designed by John Roebling (who died from an accident during its construction) and completed in 1883 by his son Washington Roebling from his sickbed, where he was suffering from "caisson disease" (nitrogen narcosis or bends), caused by surfacing from pressurized underwater chambers too rapidly.

At the time, the bridge's steel roadbed (an innovation) was the world's longest single span (1,595 feet) between its Gothic-arched granite piers (which were surprisingly pink when cleaned recently). The main suspension cables are more than 15 inches in diameter, and all metal is painted the original colors, mocha and white.

Brooklyn Heights, with its solid brownstone houses (ranging in style from Queen Anne to Greek Revival and high Victorian) and tree-lined avenues, has been home to many writers, including Walt Whitman, Herman Melville, Carson McCullers, W. H. Auden, Thomas Wolfe, Truman Capote, and Norman Mailer.

Other Brooklyn residents have included Jennie Jerome (mother of Winston Churchill), who was born here (at 197 Amity Street) in 1854. The antislavery fulminations of Henry Ward Beecher, the most influential cleric of his era, carried far and wide from his Plymouth Church pulpit in Orange Street. Mark Twain, Abraham Lincoln, John Greenleaf Whittier, Charles Dickens, and William Lloyd Garrison were among those who addressed Beecher's parishioners.

This, New York City's most populous borough, has several outstanding attractions. At the top of any list must be the Brooklyn Museum, Brooklyn Botanic Gar-

den, and New York City Aquarium. Also worthy of
notice by the visitor is the Brooklyn Academy of
Music ♛ ♛ ♛ (a.k.a. BAM), which has been a setting
for world-class concerts and entertainments for a century.

The entrance to Brooklyn's major cultural sites is
via the appropriately named Grand Army Plaza ♛ ♛ ♛,
a landscaped oval on Flatbush Avenue at the threshold
of Prospect Park. The park was the place (then called
Flatbush Pass) where Washington's forces were defeated by Lord Howe's superior British and Hessian
armies.

Dominating the Plaza is a triumphal Civil War Soldiers and Sailors Arch completed in 1892 by John Dun-
can, who later created Grant's Tomb. The arch has
vigorous sculpture groups of symbolic figures by Frederick MacMonnies, and a bas-relief of Lincoln by Thomas Eakins. Nearby is a memorial to John F. Kennedy.
All of this is prelude to the Park, designed by Olmsted
and Vaux (and considered by them to be better—though
smaller—than their Central Park).

INSIDERS' TIPS

Summer activities—called "Celebrate Brooklyn"—
abound in Brooklyn, especially frequent free concerts in
Prospect Park. They're rarely announced in advance—
it's just potluck.

Immediately to the north of the entrance is the
Brooklyn Public Library. Beyond it is the Brooklyn
Museum, and their neighbor to the south is the Brook-
lyn Botanic Garden.

The Brooklyn Museum ♛ ♛ ♛ ♛ ♛, 200 Eastern
Parkway at Washington Avenue (tel. [718] 638-5000),
is a neoclassical stone palace designed by McKim,
Mead & White in 1897, with some of the world's great
art treasures. The Museum's strong suits are a top-
rank Egyptian collection; European Impressionist and
American Hudson River school paintings; African, pre-
Columbian, and American Indian sections; and a world-
famous contemporary print collection. The fourth-floor
decorative arts section has interiors and furnishings

from the 17th century onward (including a Moorish-style room from John D. Rockefeller, Sr.'s 1885 Manhattan town house).

INSIDERS' TIPS

While most museums now have shops, the Brooklyn Museum's Gallery Shop started the trend and is still a pace-setter in the range and quality of its handicrafts from many countries. It's one of the best anywhere.

The Brooklyn Botanic Garden ♛ ♛ ♛, 1000 Washington Avenue (tel. [718] 622-4433) is a 50-acre oasis that was once the city dump. Peak visiting times are April, when the Japanese cherry trees blossom, and June, when the Cranford Rose Garden is in full bloom. Other times you'll see profusions of magnolias, lilacs, and azaleas. There's also the oldest Children's Garden in the United States and a fragrance garden for the blind.

Best of all, in our view, are the Japanese treasures, some of the finest this side of Honshu. Consider these: a replica of Kyoto's Zen Buddhist Ryoanji Temple Garden ♛ ♛ ♛ with its raked gravel and stones; a 1915 Japanese Garden ♛ ♛ ♛ in the form of a Momoyama period "stroll" garden, complete with pond, *torii* (gate), moon bridge, and Oriental plants; and award-winning bonsai ♛ ♛ ♛ (Japanese miniature trees).

There's a remarkable sculpture garden that features monumental works salvaged from such famous (but now departed) buildings as McKim, Mead & White's Pennsylvania Station. A new conservatory complex is scheduled to open in 1988.

Fin fanciers will want to visit the New York City Aquarium ♛ ♛, West 8th Street and Boardwalk, Coney Island (tel. [718] 266-8500). The Aquarium moved here from Castle Clinton at the southern tip of Manhattan in 1957. Its 22,000 live, watery specimens are displayed in 54 indoor and outdoor exhibits, most popular of which are the shark tank, the African Rift Lake, and sea lion and dolphin shows at feeding times.

Brooklyn also has a Children's Museum ♛ ♛, said to

be the world's first in 1899, at 145 Brooklyn Avenue (tel. [718] 735-4432). Now in a new building, its natural history, science, and art exhibits are all "hands-on," participatory exhibits.

The Bronx

Two world-class attractions in the Bronx, that much-maligned borough, are the Bronx Zoo and the New York Botanical Garden.

The wildest things in New York are to be seen at the Bronx Zoo ♛ ♛ ♛ ♛ ♛ (official name: New York Zoological Park), Bronx Park south of East Fordham Road (tel. 367-1010).

INSIDERS' TIPS

Admission to the Bronx Zoo is free on Tuesdays, Wednesdays, and Thursdays.

Feeding times at the zoo: crocodiles, 2 P.M. Mondays and Thursdays; sea lions, 3 P.M.; lions and other big cats, 3:30 P.M.; penguins, 3:45 P.M. For rainstorms for amphibians and reptiles, 11:30 A.M. and 3 P.M.; thunderstorm in the rain forest at 2 P.M.

This large (225-acre) park has been imaginatively landscaped so that many of its 3,100 wild inhabitants can be seen in "natural" surroundings, not behind bars or in cages (there are exceptions, especially in the older section—the Reptile House, the Bird Houses, others). In the new sections, strategically placed moats protect the animals from unthinking or predatory humans. Seldom have so many exotic creatures (including many endangered and some nearly extinct species) been so visible, accessible and alluring.

Be sure to take the Safari Tour, which transports you via tractor-train or the Bengali Express monorail through "Wild Asia." There is also a Skyfari aerial tramway ride that crosses several sections of the park. These rides are closed in winter.

INSIDERS' TIPS

People don't go to a zoo to look at buildings, but these are well worth your inspection: the 1911 Elephant House (a Byzantine "palace"; note the interior); the three bird houses (1964, 1969, 1972) by Morris Ketchum, Jr.; the replicas of African native dwellings in "The African Plains"; the 1934 art deco bronze gates by sculptor Paul Manship and architect Charles Platt; and the 18th-century Italian fountain.

The Children's Zoo is one of the best. In it, kids can see the "nursery," and actually pet many different harmless animals, ranging from snakes to reindeer.

The other jewel in the Bronx's cultural crown is the New York Botanical Garden 👑 👑 👑 👑 👑, one of the world's leading horticultural resources, located north of Fordham University at Southern Boulevard and Bedford Park Boulevard–Mosholu Parkway (tel. 220-8700). Grounds are open year-round (closed Monday), from dawn to dusk, free. The Botanical Garden is easily reached by Metro-North Harlem line local trains from Grand Central Terminal to the Botanical Garden station. Special tickets include round-trip transportation and admission to the Conservatory.

There's so much for the nature lover to enjoy: Azalea Way, Magnolia Road, the 40-acre Hemlock Forest (300-year-old trees in the city of New York!), Rhododendron Valley, the rock, rose, and herb gardens, and wildflowers of the Native Plant Garden. In the Museum Building there's an herbarium of plant specimens (the nation's largest), a library and a shop selling books, seeds, plants (excellent selection, top quality), and supplies.

INSIDERS' TIPS

Occasionally there are performances of major operas on the grounds (the Metropolitan Opera did *Tosca* on the lawn one year) in midsummer. (For information, tel. 220-8700.)

On the grounds is the Enid A. Haupt Conservatory 👑 👑 👑 👑 👑, a fairyland acre of gardens under a series of soaring (90 feet!) glass domes and galleries, with 11 pavilions, each featuring a specific environment and plants typical of it. You can be in a subtropical rain forest surrounded by banana and palms one minute and in a cactus-studded desert a minute later. The conservatory was built in 1902 (impeccably restored in 1978) in the style of London's Crystal Palace and Kew Gardens' Palm House.

INSIDERS' TIPS

Spring is peak glory time at the Garden, but with the Conservatory's all-weather cover, there are brilliant floral displays year-round.

The Botanical Garden has another treat in its Snuff Mill River Terrace Café, which overlooks the Bronx River. This national landmark building was owned by the Lorillard tobacco family (as was the land) in 1840 and used until the company's factory was moved to Jersey City in 1870. Today you can lunch modestly or have refreshments on the enchanting outdoor terrace adjacent to the stream. (And don't miss the view of the Bronx River gorge from the stone footbridge north of the Mill.)

Staten Island

Staten Island's major cultural attractions include the Jacques Marchais Center of Tibetan Art, the Staten Island Museum at the Staten Island Institute, and Richmondtown Restoration.

The Jacques Marchais Center of Tibetan Arts ♛♛, 338 Lighthouse Avenue, Richmondtown (tel. [718] 987-3478) is unique. It simulates a Tibetan Buddhist monastery and holds the Western Hemisphere's largest collection of Tibetan statues, paintings, musical instruments, and ritual objects.

The monastery-museum is set in terraced gardens that have a lotus pond, stone sculptures, and a view of the lower bay. The collector of all these Tibetan artifacts was an actress who used the Marchais name on stage. When she took on her third husband, a wealthy businessman, her collecting took off. No Buddhist, she never saw Tibet, except through her collection.

The Staten Island Institute is at 75 Stuyvesant Place and Wall Street, St. George (tel. [718] 727-1135), just a short walk from the Staten Island Ferry. The Institute is an active center with a museum whose permanent collection of art 👑👑 ranges widely (African, Asian, pre-Columbian, European, and American) and includes science and history. Its exhibition, film, and nature programs are many and varied.

Richmondtown Restoration Village 👑👑, 302 Center Street NW, Richmondtown (tel. [718] 351-1611) is a collection of buildings of special architectural or historic interest (Court House, general store, oldest elementary schoolhouse in the United States). In July and August there are demonstrations of printing, carpentry, and crafts.

There's also the Snug Harbor Cultural Center, 1000 Richmond Terrace. Once a seamen's retirement home, this old Victorian-*cum*-Greek Revival building is now a visual and performing arts center. Its 80 acres of beautiful parklike grounds contain a "with-it" sculpture garden, where monumental, usually avant-garde, works are displayed.

Queens

Queens's many industrial and bedroom communities—Astoria, Flushing, Forest Hills, St. Albans, Jamaica, Levittown, Long Island City—are just a short subway ride from Manhattan, yet they all have their own separate identities. The borough as a whole is home to 3 out of every 4 New York Jews, some 100,000 Greek-Americans (in Astoria), and sizable colonies of other ethnic groups, including Japanese, Chinese, Koreans, and Hispanics.

A major treat in Queens for modern art lovers is the Isamu Noguchi Garden Museum 👑👑👑, at 32-37 Vernon Boulevard, Long Island City (tel. [718] 204-7088). It's easily reachable by taxi (15 minutes) from Manhattan, or by BMT subway (to Broadway, Long Island City, then walk).

What you'll find is a stroll through the lifework of this prolific Japanese-American sculptor. The highpoint is the serene Japanese stone garden—a triumph of water, stone, space, and trees, juxtaposed with Noguchi sculpture.

The building was his studio, and two floors of it are now divided into 12 galleries, featuring 250 of Noguchi's works, models, designs, and photographs. The range is extraordinary—from portrait busts (George Gershwin, Buckminster Fuller) of 1929 to his spiral marble slide for the 1986 Venice Biennale (which you are invited to try).

PERILS & PITFALLS

The museum is open on a limited, changing schedule: Wednesday and Saturday afternoons from April to November, at this writing. Call ahead to be certain.

Astoria, immediately across the East River from Manhattan, is also Little Athens ♕ ♕, the largest Greek community outside Greece, dating back to the 1890s. Stroll the area—Ditmars Boulevard, Steinway Street, and 31st Street (easily reached from Manhattan via the 59th Street Bridge), and you will find Greek Orthodox churches, *tavernas*, bakeries, shops, and bouzouki music.

The time to visit is Friday or Saturday night, and the places are these: Lefkos Pirgos, 22-85 31st Street (a *kaffenions* or male coffee shop open only Saturday nights to families and accompanied women); Vedeta restaurant, 22-55 31st Street, where a shoulder of lamb rotates on the spit 24 hours a day; Rumeli Taverna, 33-04 Broadway (2 short blocks from the BMT station), with authentic shishkebab, flaky spanakopita (spinach pie), moussaka, and retsina wine; and Grecian Cave, 31-11 Broadway, a huge nightclub featuring top Greek singers, belly dancers, and musicians flown in frequently from Athens.

If you have plenty of time, you might wish to visit the Museum of the Borough of Queens ♛ ♛, located in Flushing Meadow Park. This area was the site of the 1939 and 1964 World's Fairs.

INSIDERS' TIPS

The big annual Greek Festival takes place on a late April or May weekend at the Bohemian Hall, 29-19 24th Avenue, Astoria. For specific dates, call the Federation of Greek Students (tel. [718] 274-3804, evenings).

Long Island

Aptly named, this island is 125 miles long and 20 miles across at its widest point. Its beautiful beaches and outer reaches are accessible by Long Island Rail Road (from Pennsylvania Station, 31st-33rd streets at Seventh Avenue).

INSIDERS' TIPS

Long Island Rail Road goes all out in summer, offering scores of bargain-priced tours that include transportation, meals, and entrance fees to destinations and events all over the Island. For up-to-date information on these, write the LIRR, Jamaica, NY 11435 (tel. [718] 990-7498 or 739-4200), or inquire at LIRR ticket office in Penn Station.

For the tourist who isn't visiting friends or holidaying in the Hamptons or elsewhere, there are several sightseeing stops to lure you to the island.

Fairly close in is Old Bethpage Village Restoration ♛. This collection of 30 buildings, all of them more than a century old, is at Round Swamp Road, Bethpage 11714 (tel. (516) 420–5281). Open Tuesday through Sunday, it constitutes a hamlet where the blacksmith, carpenter, tavernkeeper, craftsmen, and farmers do their mid-19th-century things, authentically.

Along the North Shore are intriguing villages such as Oyster Bay, the whaling town of Cold Spring Harbor, and the museum village, Stony Brook. On the south

shore are the summer playgrounds of Jones Beach and
Fire Island, and the rarefied retreats of the Hamptons.

At Oyster Bay is Sagamore Hill♛ ♛ ♛, Theodore
Roosevelt's 22-room Victorian mansion. It was built in
1885 and is a rambling marvel, as well as a National
Historic Site on Cove Neck Road (tel. [516] 922-4447).

From here, T. R. commuted to his office in New York
City when he was its crusading police commissioner.
The house is crammed with family treasures and tro-
phies from his big-game expeditions and his cowboy
days out West. This is one of those rare houses that
really evokes the man who lived here. In fact, he is
buried in Young's Cemetery nearby, adjacent to the
Theodore Roosevelt Memorial Sanctuary and Trailside
Museum♛, 11 acres of woodlands and self-guided nature trails.

It's obvious why T.R. loved Oyster Bay. It's a delightful town on a splendid protected harbor on Long
Island's North Shore, settled by Dutch traders in 1639.
Now it is a great center of summer sailing, fishing, and
water sports, but it was a Loyalist stronghold during
the Revolution.

It was at the same time headquarters of a rebel spy
ring and of Robert Townsend, Washington's spymaster
in New York City. Townsend is remembered at
Raynham Hall♛, 20 West Main Street (tel. [516] 922-
6808), a farmhouse owned by his father, that is now a
museum. Here you'll learn the tale of how Robert and
his sister Sally helped expose Benedict Arnold's West
Point plot.

Oyster Bay has still another attraction. This one's
for gardeners and flower lovers: Planting Fields
Arboretum♛ ♛ ♛, Planting Field Road (tel. [516] 922-
9200). On a 400-acre wooded estate, there are 160
acres of showcase rhododendrons, azaleas, and other
shrubs, greenhouses of camellias, orchids, and be-
gonias, and a 75-room Elizabethan manor house (once
the home of financier William Robertson Coe), which
stands among handsome landscaped lawns and gardens.

Almost within sight of Roosevelt's Sagamore Hill
home is Cold Spring Harbor♛ ♛, only a few miles east

across the bay. This was once a thriving whaling village whose ships in the mid-19th century sailed the world and enriched many a sea captain and merchant. You'll see their imposing Colonial houses in a walk or drive around town.

It's a charming town, dotted today with attractive boutiques, galleries, antique shops, restaurants, and a Whaling Museum ♛ ♛ (tel. [516] 692-6768) that commemorates the glory days of sail.

Stony Brook ♛ ♛ is another North Shore village on a protected harbor. Its Colonial- and Federal-style houses speak of its early roots. (They were rebuilt in the 1940s by philanthropist Ward Melville.) For visitors, there is a museum consisting of a schoolhouse, a blacksmith shop, a country store, an art museum (with the works of 19th-century artist William Sidney Mount), a grist mill, a carriage museum of horse-drawn vehicles ♛ ♛, and other buildings (tel. [516] 751-0066).

Another great excursion is to Sands Point Park and Preserve ♛ ♛, at Middleneck Road (tel. [516] 883-1612), Port Washington. It includes the former estate of the Guggenheim millionaires, Daniel and Harry, with Tudor-style Hempstead House, Irish-style Castlegould, and the Normandy-style mansion called Falaise. There are nature trails, exhibits, and house tours.

Also handy to Manhattan is Westbury, where garden enthusiasts will find 2 superlative gardens, Old Westbury Gardens ♛ ♛ and Clark Garden ♛ ♛ in the vicinity. The first, on Old Westbury Road in Old Westbury (tel. [516] 333-0048), is the 100-acre former estate of John S. Phipps, a financier and sportsman. The house, built and comfortably furnished in the English country manor style, is enhanced by a series of spectacular English gardens. There are lakes, streams, fountains, a bluebell walk, lilac walk, garden sculpture, temple of Love, pinetum, and a ghost walk. In short, a garden lover's heaven!

Clark Garden, 193 I. U. Willets Road, Albertson (tel. [516] 621-7568), is another former estate, that of Grenville Clark. Affiliated with the Brooklyn Botanic Garden, its 12 acres of splendiferous blooms seem to contain just about every beautiful plant and bulb you'd want to see. The Hunnewell Rose Garden boasts more than 50 All-America specimens, and the property contains streams, pine groves, even a children's garden.

If you want to escape Manhattan's heat and humidity, you can join the throngs heading—especially on weekends—for the sand and surf of Long Island's Atlantic shoreline.

One of the finest beaches (and most crowded on weekends) is Jones Beach State Park, 6½ miles of well-developed facilities on a sand spit off the Long Island coast. It offers both ocean and bay swimming and water sports. Long Island Rail Road trains make the trip directly to Jones Beach frequently each day in summer for low round-trip fares.

Farther east is Fire Island, another sand spit with a decidedly laid-back life-style. The island stretches 32 miles paralleling the Long Island coast. Cars are prohibited; access is by ferry from Bay Shore, Sayville, and Patchogue (which you reach via Long Island Rail Road). For ferry information, call Zee Line, tel. (516) 665-2115; Davis Park Ferry Co., tel. (516) 475-1665; and Fire Island Seashore Ferry Co., tel. (516) 289-8980.

Near the eastern tip of Long Island are the Hamptons: from west to east, Westhampton Beach, Southampton, Bridgehampton, and East Hampton. These are strung out over some 30 miles along the south coast of the Island and are the "in" summer resorts for upwardly mobile Manhattanites (many of them in the performing arts or media) fleeing the city's heat. A list of summer residents reads like a *Who's Who* of current big names in the arts. "Casually elegant" or "elegantly casual" is the prevailing tone. Many of Manhattan's poshest shops have outposts here. And summer season *rentals* range from $20,000 to $200,000 for some of the properties you will see.

Off-season, Easthampton's village green ♛, with its pond, tree-lined streets, and traditional houses, looks like an English country town. You'd never believe it in the frenzy of the red-hot summer scene, what with the foot and road traffic, wall-to-wall art shows, lectures, theater, music, and socializing that go on. Dramatic modern beach houses have added another dimension to the old town.

The summer action circulates around the Guild Hall Museum♛, 158 Main Street, where there are changing art exhibits, lectures, and poetry readings. Its John Drew Theater hosts plays and concerts year-round, but in summer there's the added impetus of 3 plays featuring celebrity actors and directors; jazz and classical concerts with big name artists; and a 3-day film festival, introduced by the film directors. Tel. (516) 324-4050 for details.

Bridgehampton has a Race Circuit on Millstone Road where auto and motorcycle races occur most weekends from May to September (tel. [516] 537-3770). And there's the Bridgehampton Historical Museum♛ on Main Street, in the antiques-furnished Corwith homestead, which dates from 1775. Farm machinery, engines, and a blacksmith shop are on view from June to August, Thursday through Monday from 10 A.M. to 4 P.M. (tel. [516] 537-1088).

INSIDERS' TIPS

Winery tours are offered by several of Long Island's 8 wineries, specifically:

- Bridgehampton Winery, Bridgehampton–Sag Harbor Turnpike, Bridgehampton 11932 (tel. [516] 537-3155). May–September weekends, 11 A.M.–6 P.M.
- Hargrave Vineyard, Alvah's Lane, Box 927, Cutchogue 11935 (tel. [516] 734-5158). June–November, weekends at 2 P.M. by appointment.
- Lenz Vineyards, Main Road, Peconic 11958 (tel. [516] 734-6010). Weekends, 10 A.M.–6 P.M.
- Pindar Vineyards, Main Road, Peconic 11958 (tel. [516] 734-6200). Weekends, 11 A.M.–5 P.M.

In Southampton there's the Parrish Art Museum♛♛, 25 Job's Lane (tel. [516] 283-2118), with a small but agreeable collection that focuses on Oriental art, Renaissance, and 19th- and 20th-century American painting and prints. Outdoor sculpture, an arboretum, and a changing schedule of exhibits and events make this the center of cultural attention in town.

Westhampton Beach thrives as a summer resort and sponsors a well-attended annual Outdoor Art Show the first weekend in August.

INSIDERS' INFORMATION FOR NEW YORK CITY (Area Code 212)

WHERE TO STAY

Carlyle ♛ ♛ ♛ ♛
Madison Ave. at East 76th St., 10021. Tel. 744-1600
2 persons in twin, $200–235
A 35-story building in chic neighborhood. 500 rooms, bar, café (entertainment), elegant restaurant (♛ ♛ ♛). A favorite address for traveling VIPs. Spacious rooms, recently refurbished, marvelous service. The 1812 Suite is splendidly Oriental, preferred by Nancy Reagan and Jackie Onassis.

Helmsley Palace ♛ ♛ ♛ ♛
455 Madison Ave. (between East 50th and 51st Sts.), 10022. Tel. 888-7000 or (800) 221-4892
2 persons in twin, $185–265
Former century-old Villard mansion (reception, lounges, dining and public rooms) is on the National Register of Historic Places. Hotel tower has 963 rooms, Harry's N.Y. bar, café, 3 restaurants. Elegant pampering, spacious rooms, superb views. A few steps from Rockefeller Center, Fifth Ave. and Madison Ave. shops.

Plaza ♛ ♛ ♛ ♛
Fifth Ave. at 59th St., 10019. Tel. (800) 828-3000
2 persons in twin, $200–375
Grande Dame of New York's hotels, with the ambiance of an historic European establishment. 900 rooms, bars, 3 restaurants. Overlooks Central Park. Tea at Palm Court is pure nostalgia. Concierge, large rooms, pampering, gorgeous decor.

Inter-Continental New York ♛ ♛ ♛ ♛
111 East 48th St., 10017. Tel. 755-5900 or (800) 327-0200
2 persons in twin, $180–275

From 1926 as the Barclay, this was a favorite haven for powerful people shunning the spotlight. Recently renovated from top to bottom, it has 691 rooms, bar, La Recolte restaurant (♛ ♛), airport transportation. Quiet elegance, spacious. Excellent location. Well-furnished rooms, excellent service. Concierge.

Omni Berkshire Place ♛ ♛ ♛ ♛
21 East 52nd St., 10022. Tel. 753-5800
2 persons in twin, $190–240
In the Berkshire's earlier life, Rodgers and Hammerstein collaborated on *Oklahoma* and Salvador Dali painted here. 415 rooms, bar, restaurant, atrium lounge. Now renovated, it's one of the most romantic settings in the city, with profusion of trees, plants, fresh flowers. Spacious suites, rooms, and public areas.

Pierre ♛ ♛ ♛ ♛
Fifth Ave. at East 61st St., 10021. Tel. 838-8000
2 persons in twin, $240–330
A New York City tradition, fashionable and convenient location across from Central Park, near shops. 196 antique-laden rooms, bar, café, restaurant, limousine service. Decorously plush, mercifully quiet public areas. A favorite with the international set. Escoffier was once chef here.

Plaza Athenee ♛ ♛ ♛ ♛
37 East 64th St., 10021. Tel. 734-9100 or (800) 255-5843
2 persons in twin, $230–325
17-story building handy to shops. 202 rooms, café, bar, La Regence restaurant (♛ ♛ ♛). Handsome Directoir-style with French antique furnishings, tapestries. Public areas are opulent, similar to its Paris namesake, with vaulted ceilings, a pastoral mural in marble lobby. Now a Trusthouse Forte property.

Stanhope ♛ ♛ ♛ ♛
995 Fifth Ave., 10028. Tel. 288-5800 or (800) 847-8483
2 persons in twin, $225–275
Quietly perfect location for art lovers (across from Metropolitan Museum and Central Park). 118 rooms, bar, restaurant (♛ ♛), tea in Le Salon; sidewalk café (spring to fall), free limo to midtown. Elegantly furnished, quiet, a small-scale bonbon. Helpful staff.

United Nations Plaza ♛ ♛ ♛ ♛
1 UN Plaza (at East 44th St. and First Ave), 10017. Tel.
355-3400 or (800) 228-9000
2 persons in twin, $185–230
Handsome modern building, choice East Side location.
444 rooms, bar, café, restaurant, indoor swimming
pool, tennis court, health club, free A.M. limo service to
Wall St., garment district. Sweeping views of East River
skyline. Minimalist, stylish decor.

Waldorf-Astoria ♛ ♛ ♛ ♛
301 Park Ave. (between East 49th and 50th Sts.),
10022. Tel. 355-3000
2 persons in twin, $175–280 (Luxury-level Waldorf
Towers $300.)
Landmark 1931 art deco hotel, handy for shopping,
sightseeing midtown. 1,400 rooms, bar, café, 3 restaurants. Potentates, presidents, even plain people bed
down here. Quiet, busy, can be impersonal.

Doral Tuscany ♛ ♛ ♛
120 East 39th St., 10016. Tel. 636-1600
2 persons in twin, $165–215
Quiet, conservative hotel in handy midtown location.
133 rooms, bar, restaurant, serving pantries. Marble
baths, refrigerators, extra sinks, VCRs, and exercise
bikes in the large rooms, many extras.

Drake Swissôtel ♛ ♛ ♛
440 Park Ave. (at East 56th St.), 10022. Tel. 421-4900
2 persons in twin, $190–225
A 1926 building, refurbished by Swissair and Nestlé.
634 rooms, piano bar, Lafayette restaurant (♛ ♛ ♛).
Comfortable, well-maintained, with flourishes like
Swiss chocolates in rooms and in huge glass bowl in
lobby.

Golden Tulip Barbizon ♛ ♛ ♛
140 East 63rd St., 10021. Tel. 838-5700
2 persons in twin, $140–185
Formerly the Barbizon Hotel for Women, considerably
renovated. 360 cozy, European-style modern rooms,
bar, 2 restaurants, Olympic-size indoor swimming pool,
health club. Ask about weekend specials.

Grand Hyatt♛♛♛
Park Ave. at East 42nd St., 10017. Tel. 883-1234
2 persons in twin, $185–215
Next to Grand Central Station. 1,407 rooms, bar, 2 restaurants, tennis and health club privileges. Sunny, cheerful greenhouse lounge for drinks, tea. Tip to baseball fans: it's the official hotel for visiting teams. Airport transportation. ("Regency Level" $245, 126 rooms.)

Helmsley Park Lane♛♛♛
36 Central Park South, 10019. Tel. 371-4000
2 persons in twin, $195–255
A 46-story building overlooking Central Park. 640 rooms, bar, restaurant. Pretty park views, comfortable rooms.

Howard♛♛♛
127 East 55 St. (between Lexington and Park Aves.), 10022. Tel. 826-1100 or (800) 221-1074
2 persons in twin, $170–225
Intimate hotel recently completed with modern interiors by Alberto Pinto. 106 rooms (all with marble baths, some with balconies).

Loews Summit♛♛♛
569 Lexington Ave. (at East 51st St.), 10022. Tel. 752-7000 or (800) 223-0888
2 persons in twin, $120–140
20-story hotel in fashionable locale. 766 rooms, bar, café, restaurant, health club, plus 45 luxury-level rooms at $140. Older hotel renovated with style.

Mayfair Regent♛♛♛
610 Park Ave. (at East 65th St.), 10021. Tel. 288-0800 or (800) 545-4000
2 persons in twin, $190–230
Moorish arches, floral displays, European flavor; traditional afternoon teas in palmy lounge. 200 rooms, bar, café, La Cirque restaurant (♛♛♛♛). Numerous perks: bathroom phones, fireplace in some rooms, superb service.

New York Hilton♛♛♛
1335 Ave. of the Americas at 53rd–54th Sts., 10019. Tel. 586-7000
2 persons in twin, $160–205 (Executive suites, $220)

Modern edifice, part of Rockefeller Center complex, well-located between theater and shopping districts. 2,000 rooms, bars, 4 restaurants; Reports of poor desk and telephone service persist.

Nikko Essex House 👑 👑 👑
160 Central Park South, 10019. Tel. 247-0300
2 persons in twin, $195–245
Modernized old building facing Central Park. 715 rooms, piano bar, restaurant; airport, railroad transportation. Compact rooms, but some great Central Park views, attractive public areas.

Novotel 👑 👑 👑
226 West 52nd St., 10019. Tel. 315-0100
2 persons in twin, $135–160
Theater district location. Sleek and modern, with all the expected worldwide chain conveniences. 470 rooms, bar, café, restaurant.

Parker Meridien 👑 👑 👑
118 West 57th St., 10019. Tel. 245-5000 or (800) 442-5917
2 persons in twin, $200–265
Contemporary building, convenient. 700 rooms, bar, café, 2 restaurants including Maurice (👑 👑 👑), heated, glass-enclosed rooftop swimming pool, squash and racquetball courts, health club, outdoor jogging track, and greenhouse. French flair combined with antiques, marble floors. Check the weekend specials.

Regency 👑 👑 👑
540 Park Ave. at East 61st St., 10021. Tel. 759-4100 or (800) 223-5672
2 persons in twin, $190–250
A 21-story building in convenient location. 500 rooms, bar, café, restaurant, health club. Elegant, with antiques and marble interiors, concierge services, extras.

Ritz-Carlton 👑 👑 👑
112 Central Park South, 10019. Tel. 757-1900 or (800) 223-7990
2 persons in twin, $215–285
A 25-story building in handy Central Park locale. 240 rooms, bar, café, restaurant. Understated style, English country decor.

St. Regis-Sheraton♕♕♕
2 East 55th St. at Fifth Ave., 10022. Tel. 753-4500 or
(800) 235-3535
2 persons in twin, $195–280
A 20-story edifice in desirable neighborhood. 525
rooms, bar, café, restaurant. Understated elegance,
many extras, including concierge service. Lovely
rooms.

Sheraton Park Avenue♕♕♕
45 Park Ave. at 37th St., 10016. Tel. 685-7676 or (800)
325-3535.
2 persons in twin, $190–220
European ambiance (Chippendale furniture, flowers,
concierge) in this conveniently located midtown hotel.
150 rooms, restaurant, "jazz bar," and lounge.

Vista International♕♕♕
3 World Trade Center at West and Liberty Sts., 10048.
Tel. 938-9100 or (800) 258-2505
2 persons in twin, $185–255
Modern tower in lower Manhattan with panoramic
views of harbor, Statue of Liberty, boat traffic. 829
rooms, bars, café, 2 restaurants, indoor swimming pool,
health club, airport transportation. Rooms' great water
views compensate for impersonal lobby. Don't miss
American Harvest restaurant (♕♕) for fine regional
food. *The* place to stay in downtown Manhattan.

Westbury♕♕♕
15 East 69th St. at Madison Ave., 10022. Tel. 535-2000
or (800) 223-5672
2 persons in twin, $210–250
Quiet uptown location. 300 rooms, bar, *nouvelle*-style
Polo (♕♕) restaurant. British-owned (Trusthouse
Forte), comfortable, with low-key manner, understated
stylishness. Rooms vary in size and furnishings; look
before you leap.

Beekman Tower♕♕
3 Mitchell Place at First Ave. and 49th St., 10017. Tel.
355-7300
2 persons in twin, $135–145
Handy midtown location. 160 rooms, bar, café, restaurant. Stylish address, great views. Some balconies, private patios. Suites (extra cost) have kitchenettes.

Doral Park Avenue ♛ ♛
70 Park Ave. at 38th St., 10016. Tel. 687-7050
2 persons in twin, $155–165
A 17-story building handy to Grand Central Terminal.
203 rooms, bar, sidewalk café (summer), restaurant,
squash and health club privileges. Understated French
provincial decor.

Dorset ♛ ♛
30 West 54th St., 10019. Tel. 247-7300
2 persons in twin, $147–185
Theater and media people have digs here because it's
convenient to Broadway area. 305 rooms, bar, café.

INSIDERS TIPS

Hotel coffee shops are very expensive for breakfast. You
can slim down your breakfast bills by stepping a half-
block or so away, where you are almost sure to find
fast-food places that make a pitch for business with
inexpensive breakfast specials.

Empire ♛ ♛
44 West 63rd St., 10023. Tel. 265-7400
2 persons in twin, $90–130
Small 11-story hotel in Lincoln Center area. 500 rooms,
café, bar, airport transportation. Nothing fancy, but
good prices for the handy location.

Kitano ♛ ♛
66 Park Ave. at 38th St., 10016. Tel. 685-0022
2 persons in twin, $130–140
High-rise building in handy, quiet location. 96 rooms,
café, Japanese restaurant. Conservative Japanese hotel
with some authentic *tatami* rooms. Midtown location.

Marriott Marquis ♛ ♛
1535 Broadway, 10036. Tel. 398-1900
2 persons in twin, $225–250
New 50-story hotel in Times Square area. 1,877 rooms,
bar, café, restaurant, health club, 46-story atrium.
Handy location, *if* you want to hang around Times
Square. Decor in glitzy Marriott style.

Milford Plaza (Best Western) ♛ ♛
270 West 45th St. at Eighth Ave., 10036. Tel. (800)
221-2690 or, in New York State, (800) 522-6499

2 persons in twin, $100–130

Convenient to theater district and Lincoln Center. 1,310 rooms, 3 restaurants. Huge and noisy (especially lower floors; adjoining rooms). Reserve upper rooms early. Airport transportation.

Sheraton Centre ♛ ♛

811 Seventh Ave., 10019. Tel. 581-1000

2 persons in twin, $130–200

Commercial hotel near Javits Convention Center, handy for business travelers. 1,693 rooms, bars, restaurants. Bustling, noisy lobby. Formerly the Americana.

Warwick ♛ ♛

65 West 54th St., 10019. Tel. 247-2700

2 persons in twin, $150–175

Old 33-story building near Fifth Ave., 500 rooms, bar, café, restaurant. Serviceable, uncharismatic. You're paying for handy location.

Wyndham ♛ ♛

42 West 58th St., 10019. Tel. 753-3500

2 persons in twin, $98–175

A favorite with theater people. 212 rooms, bar, café. Oversized floral motifs on linens, bedcovers, walls. Good maintenance, friendly staff. Negatives: indirect dial phones, no room service.

Algonquin ♛

59 West 44th St., 10036. Tel. 840-6800

2 persons in twin, $120–134

A New York institution, handy to Fifth Ave. and the theater district. 200 rooms, bar, café, restaurant. Rooms small, many odd-shaped. Reports of maintenance problems. Our suggestion: go for a drink, after-theater buffet, and/or memories of hotel's glory days.

Chelsea ♛

222 West 23rd St., 10011. Tel. 243-3700

2 persons in twin: $65–95

Landmark hotel in heart of Chelsea. 350 rooms, El Quijote restaurant (♛). Many artists and writers live here on year-round basis, because of old-fashioned, dowdy coziness, low tariffs, huge studio-size rooms and apartments. Much character, but not for everyone.

Edison ♛

228 West 47th St., 10036. Tel. 840-5000

2 persons in twin, $78–85
This old standby in the theater district is considered a real bargain. 1,000 rooms, bar, café.
Gorham♔
136 West 55th St., 10019. Tel. 245-1800
2 persons in twin, $80–100
Convenience is all in this serviceable hotel. 163 rooms, bar, restaurant. All rooms with kitchenettes, good for long stays or family visits. Simple digs, but a bargain for its location.
Gramercy Park♔
2 Lexington Ave., 10010. Tel. 475-4320
2 persons in twin, $95–100
Unassuming old hotel with grand location overlooking peaceful Gramercy Park. 509 rooms, piano bar, lounge. Nothing fancy, but okay if you want a neighborhood place away from midtown.
Wellington♔
7th Ave. at West 55th St., 10019. Tel. 247-3900
2 persons in twin, $74–105
An old hotel close to theaters, shopping. 700 modest rooms, bar, restaurants. A no-frills "sleeper," popular with foreign artists, performers.
Morgans
237 Madison Ave., 10016. Tel. 686-0300, (800) 334-3408
2 persons in twin, $150–190
A transformed mansion near Morgan Library, Grand Central Terminal. 154 rooms, bar, café. Currently "hot" and hip, but the hype eludes us. No identifying marquee, understated lobby. Stylized Minimalist black/charcoal gray room decor doesn't compensate for impractical sink, bathroom mirror too high to use, doors that don't latch. All vestiges of old mansion are long gone. Rock stars and jet-setters love it anyway.

Queens

Marriott JFK Airport♔ ♔
135–30 140th St., Jamaica 11436. Tel. (718) 659-6000 or (800) 437-7002
2 persons in twin, $130

12-story building near JFK International Airport. 370 rooms, bar, café, restaurant, free airport transport. Does the job between flights.

Marriott La Guardia♛♛
102–05 Ditmars Boulevard, East Elmhurst 11369. Tel. (718) 565-8900
2 persons in twin, $110–170
9-story hotel near La Guardia Airport. 444 rooms, bar, café, restaurant, indoor swimming pool, health club, free airport transportation. Functional, serviceable for airport connections.

Sheraton Inn La Guardia♛
90–10 Grand Central Parkway, East Elmhurst 11369. Tel. (718) 446-4800 or (800) 325-3535
2 persons in twin, $105–160
Located at the end of La Guardia Airport runway. 288 rooms, bar, café, restaurant, swimming pool. Handy to airport, minimal charm.

Long Island

Gurney's Inn, Resort & Spa♛♛♛
Old Montauk Highway, Montauk 11954.
Tel. (516) 668-2345
$110–140 per person, MAP (2 meals)
Famous old resort facing the Atlantic. 125 rooms, restaurant, indoor and outdoor swimming pool, Roman bath, health club, many facilities. Great views, with luxurious 1,000-foot private beach.

WHERE TO EAT

INSIDERS' TIPS

Restaurants near the higher-priced hotels tend to be very pricey, so get away from the high-rent districts if you want to save.

Lutece♛♛♛♛♛
249 East 50th St. Tel. 752-2225
Prix fixe dinner: $55

Time passes (25 years), but chef/owner André Soltner's
classic French magic continues unsurpassed. Perfection all the way. If choices confound, try the *dégustation*
menu. Fine wine selection. Closed Sundays.
Four Seasons 👑 👑 👑 👑 👑
Seagram Building, 99 East 52nd St. Tel. 754-9494
Pre- and post-theater *prix fixe* dinner: $38.50
The mark of a superior restaurant: consistency. Year
after year this elegantly simple restaurant serves its
classic French/*nouvelle* cuisine to heavy-hitters and others in a spacious Philip Johnson interior of leather,
marble, and glass. Notable wine list. Closed Sundays.
Aurora 👑 👑 👑 👑
60 East 49th St. Tel. 692-9292
Average dinner: $40
Aurora as in "dawn"—and the subtle rosy lighting
keeps changing, reminding you of the slow passage of
time. Everything about this restaurant is subtle, from
the exquisite *nouvelle* dishes (Napoleon of salmon, roast
pigeon, etc.) to the expert service and decor. Prices, for
the high quality, are surprisingly moderate by New York
haute cuisine standards. Closed Sundays.
Chantarelle 👑 👑 👑 👑
89 Grand St. (at Greene St.). Tel. 966-6960
Prix fixe 3-course dinner, $58; 4-course dinner, $75
Small is beautiful in this pristine 1-room SoHo temple
of superior New American cooking. Menu changes
often, always superb. Dinner only; closed Sunday, Monday, July, major holidays.
La Grenouille 👑 👑 👑 👑
3 East 52nd St. Tel. 752-1495
Prix fixe 3-course dinner: $62.
Abundance of fresh flowers is a trademark, along with
superb classic French cuisine in small, stylish quarters.
Impressive wine list. Closed Sundays.
La Tulipe 👑 👑 👑 👑
104 West 13th St. Tel. 691-8860
Prix fixe 5-course dinner: $57
An elegantly simple town house is chef/owner Sally
Darr's setting for innovative *nouvelle* creations. Service
can be slow, but the wait's worth it. Superlative des-
serts. Impressive wine list. Closed Mondays.

Le Cirque ♛ ♛ ♛ ♛
58 East 65th St. Tel. 794-9292
Average dinner: $50
A favorite with international luminaries (Princess Margaret or Sophia Loren may be a table away) for classic French dishes, elegant desserts. Cramped quarters in pretty gazebo-like interior. Outstanding wine list. Closed Sundays.

Le Cygne ♛ ♛ ♛ ♛
55 East 54th St. Tel. 759-5941
Prix fixe dinner: $53
The swan *(le cygne)* continues to glide effortlessly along the upper stratum of French *haute cuisine* in *intime* space, with romantic lighting. Closed Sundays and August.

The Quilted Giraffe ♛ ♛ ♛ ♛
55th and Madison at AT&T Arcade. Tel. 593-1221
Prix fixe 4-course dinner: $75; 5-course tasting menu $100
Special-occasion (read "expensive") *nouvelle* American dining in romantic, elegant setting, presided over with a flair by chef Barry Wine. Fine but pricey cellar. Closed Saturdays and Sundays.

Arcadia ♛ ♛ ♛
21 East 62nd St. Tel. 223-2900
Prix fixe 3-course dinner: $55Here's where to find New American cooking at its most inventive. Save room for incredible desserts. Closed Sundays.

Huberts ♛ ♛ ♛
102 East 22nd St. Tel. 673-3711
Average dinner: $40
Attractive dining in Gramercy Park area. Unconventional American fare with Oriental flourishes. Closed Sundays.

Kitcho ♛ ♛ ♛
22 West 46th St. Tel. 575-8880
Average dinner: $50
Longtime favorite with Old Japan hands—with good reason. Some of New York's best Japanese cuisine is served here in typically Japanese dining space, restrained and austere. Closed Saturdays.

INSIDERS' TIPS

To experience a complete Japanese meal, ask for the *omakase*. It will include 7 to 15 traditional items chosen by the chef, for an all-inclusive price (between $50 and $100 per person).

La Côte Basque ♛ ♛ ♛
5 East 55th St. Tel. 688-6525
Prix fixe dinner: $48
Creative French menu, splendid and expensive wine cellar, Old World provincial "timbered" interior. Closed Sundays.

Lafayette ♛ ♛ ♛
65 East 56th St. (in Drake Swissôtel). Tel. 832-1565
Average dinner: $50
French antiques, comfortable decor, French food with flourishes—and you can observe the kitchen through a glass wall if you wish. Closed Saturdays, Sundays.

Le Bernardin ♛ ♛ ♛
155 West 51st St. Tel. 489-1515
Prix fixe dinner: $60
Luxurious space, clublike serenity. Seafood all the way: simple, expert, in unusual variety. Lovely chocolate and caramel desserts. Superior wine list.

Maurice ♛ ♛ ♛
Hotel Parker Meridien, 118 West 57th St. Tel. 245-7788
Prix fixe dinner: $44
French style in somewhat overblown but comfortable surroundings. Leading French chefs visit occasionally.

Montrachet ♛ ♛ ♛
239 West Broadway. Tel. 219-2777
Prix fixe dinner: $29 and $45
Light, expert *Provençale* cooking, limited menu, great desserts. High-ceilinged space in SoHo-TriBeCa locale. Reservations a must, or you'll have a long wait. Well-chosen, affordable wines. Closed Sundays.

Pesca ♛ ♛ ♛
23 East 22nd St. Tel. 533-2293
Average dinner: $35
Spacious dining in old pressed-tin-ceilinged rooms. Imaginatively prepared seafood (memorably spicy fried

calamari) among the best in town. Ingratiating service. Good (affordable) wine list.

Prunelle♛♛♛
18 East 54th St. Tel. 759-6410
Prix fixe dinner: $52
Everything comes together here: elegantly understated decor, seamless service, and—most important—reliable, expert French dishes, served in generous portions. Closed Sundays.

The Sign of the Dove♛♛♛
1110 Third Ave. (at 65th St.). Tel. 861-8080
Prix fixe dinner: $50
New management and menu yield great surprises: robust yet elegant French fare in romantic setting. Service can be slow, food's worth it.

An American Place♛♛
969 Lexington Ave. (at 70th–71st Sts.). Tel. 517-7660
Average dinner: $50
Minimal quarters, maximum taste satisfaction in handsomely presented American regional favorites, standbys, and often exciting combinations. Well-chosen, affordable, all-American wine list. Closed Sundays.

Arizona 206♛♛
206 East 60th St. Tel. 838-0440
Average dinner: $30–35
Whitewashed walls, wood fires, and art transport you to the Southwest. So does the inventive food, casual style. The café's nice too, with a smaller menu, lower prices, panache. Reservations urged. Closed Sundays.

Akbar♛♛
475 Park Ave. (at 57th Street). Tel. 838-1717
Average dinner: $20
Coolly elegant white backdrop for well-spiced northern Indian dishes.

Arqua♛♛
281 Church St. Tel. 334-1888
Average dinner: $30
Stylish Italian food in art deco TriBeCa setting.

Ballroom♛♛
253 West 28th St. Tel. 244-3005
Average dinner: $35
Magnificent long bar (from a 1922 Bronx speakeasy)

makes perfect stage for sausages, cheeses, hams, and dozens of *tapas* (Spanish snacks) that are the *piece de résistance* of this compelling place. Skip the entrées, make a meal of *tapas,* and enjoy the guitar music. Closed Sundays.

Batons ♛ ♛
62 West 11th St. Tel. 473-9510
Average dinner: $35
Eclectic California cuisine—pastas, pizzas, salads, char-grilled meats and fish, lots of choices—in a sophisticated Minimalist setting. Currently a "hot ticket" place to be.

Cabana Carioca ♛ ♛
123 West 45th St. Tel. 581-8088
Average dinner: $25
Authentic, abundant Brazilian fare in exuberant, busy atmosphere. (Opt for downstairs seating, which is more festive.) If *feijoada* (Brazilian national dish—a black bean and meat cassoulet) is featured (always Wednesdays or Saturdays), you're in clover.

PERILS & PITFALLS

Avoid Cabana Carioca II down the street, which is geared to tourist traffic and tastes.

Cafe de Bruxelles ♛ ♛
118 Greenwich Ave. at 13th St. Tel. 206-1830
Average dinner: $32
A lace-curtained bistro with authentic Old World Belgian flair and food. Don't miss sampling the remarkable Belgian beers.

Cafe des Artistes ♛ ♛
1 West 67th St. (off Central Park West). Tel. 877-3500
Average dinner: $40
Romantic, European ambiance with delicious Howard Chandler Christy murals. Food less memorable, but irresistible desserts. Great trysting place.

Cafe Luxembourg ♛ ♛
200 West 70th St. Tel. 873-7411
Average dinner: $35
Rollicking brasserie in Lincoln Center area. Lots of Franco-Italo-American favorites.

Carolina ♛ ♛
355 West 46th St. Tel. 245-0058
Average dinner: $37
If you crave crab cakes, ribs, corn bread, and other down-home delights, this is the place. Grilled and smoked specialties too, not just Southern fare. Theater district central location.

Chelsea Central ♛ ♛
227 Tenth Ave. (between 23rd and 24th Sts.). Tel. 620-0230
Average dinner: $25
Behind a tacky exterior, in the upstairs (not ground floor) dining room of a plain place, you'll find some delicious bistro-type food, mostly grilled in the new American style. Nothing fancy, but done with skill and care.

Coach House ♛ ♛
110 Waverly Place (between Washington Square Park and Ave. of Americas). Tel. 777-0303
Average dinner: $40
When it's good, this old faithful with colonial atmosphere can be very good indeed. Signature American dishes: black bean soup, chicken pie, prime ribs, pecan pie. Closed Mondays, most holidays, and August.

Contrapunto ♛ ♛
200 East 60th St. at Third Ave. Tel. 751-8616
Average dinner: $25
Noisy, frenzied on weekends, but bear with it for moderately priced Italian food: huge pasta (dried and fresh) choices and seafood are stars. No reservations, get there early or late.

Darbar ♛ ♛
44 West 56th St. Tel. 432-7227
Average dinner: $30
High-quality Northern Indian cuisine in elegant, quiet interior. Try *saag paneer* or *saag gosht*.

Gotham Bar & Grill ♛ ♛
East 12th St. at Fifth Ave. and University Place. Tel. 620-4020
Average dinner: $45
Stylish New American specialties in "postmodern" setting—a yuppie magnet. Beautifully presented dishes, but pricey.

Greene Street Cafe ♛ ♛
101 Greene St. Tel. 925-2415
Average dinner: $36
Jazz music and jazzy food to match. A knockout place combines nightclub and good food (a rare duet). Light menu available.

Hatsuhana ♛ ♛
17 East 48th St. Tel. 355-3345
Average dinner: $30
Impersonal, often noisy quarters, but reliable sushi, sashimi, other Japanese dishes. Reservation necessary.

H.S.F. (Hee Sung Feung) ♛ ♛
46 Bowery. Tel. 374-1319
Average meal: $15
A Chinatown favorite for *dim sum*—those steamed and fried Chinese dumplings in variety enough for a complete breakfast, lunch, or brunch. Closes at 4:30 or 5 P.M. An elegant branch is at Second Ave. and 32nd St.

Il Mulino ♛ ♛
86 West 3rd St. Tel. 673-3783
Average dinner: $50
For Northern Italian cooking, this tiny place is a hands-down favorite. The marinated zucchini appetizer served gratis is unforgettable. No wonder Nancy Kissinger and other celebs send for it by limo.

Il Nido ♛ ♛
251 East 53rd St. Tel. 753-8450
Average dinner: $35–40
Handsome Tuscan country inn decor. Some of the best Northern Italian dishes in town. Strong wine list. Closed Sundays.

Inagiku ♛ ♛
Waldorf-Astoria Hotel, 301 Park Ave. between 49th and 50th Sts. Tel. 872-4590
Average dinner: $40
Tasteful but overblown Japanese (Nikko-style) decor; excellent tempura and other Japanese specialties.

Jams ♛ ♛
154 East 79th St. Tel. 772-6800
Average dinner: $30–40
In the vanguard of California cuisine, led by chef/co-

owner Jonathan Waxman. Informal, stylish place with versatile, creative food. Grilled fish are wonderful.

John Clancy's♕♕
181 West 10th St. Tel. 242-7350
Average dinner: $38
Mesquite grilling at its best in this appealing Greenwich Village spot. Also, go with master baker Clancy's mouth-watering desserts. Well-selected, affordable wine list. Dinner only.

La Caravelle♕♕
33 West 55th St. Tel. 586-4252
Prix fixe dinner: $49
Through ups and downs, this bastion of French *haute cuisine* has kept its jet-set loyalists. Now in an up phase, with *nouvelle* infusions, imaginative dishes, premier desserts. Fine wine list. Closed Sundays.

La Gauloise♕♕
502 Ave. of the Americas (between 12th and 13th Sts.). Tel. 691-1363
Prix fixe dinner: $19.50
Consistently reliable French bistro, with homey renderings of old-time favorites, reasonable prices.

Lavin's♕♕
23 West 39th St. Tel. 921-1288
Average dinner: $45–50
A favorite of the rag crowd (Oscar de la Renta may be at the next table). Handsome oak-paneled walls, informal setting, livelier at lunch. Special goodies: mesquite carpaccio, grilled tuna with cilantro pesto, yummy desserts (homemade ice creams, crème brulée, bread pudding). Closed Saturdays and Sundays.

Le Chantilly♕♕
106 East 57th St. Tel. 751-2931
Average dinner: $50
Moving upward from a down phase, with a tempting *nouvelle* menu, better service, revived spirit. Scrumptious desserts.

Le Festival♕♕
134 East 61st St. Tel. 838-7987
Prix fixe dinner: $40
An offshoot of La Côte Basque, with similar Gallic expertise. Restful decor, lively and intriguing food, in-

cluding a notable salmon steak soufflé. Closed Sundays.

Le Perigord♛♛
405 East 52nd St. Tel. 755-6244
Prix fixe dinner: $44–50
Unflappable French cuisine in the classic mode. Closed Sundays.

Menage à Trois♛♛
134 East 48th St. (Lexington Hotel). Tel. 593-8242
Average dinner: $30
Stylish outpost of its London "parent," notable for imaginative creations (especially veggies and seafood), and 8-page grazing menu of mix-and-match appetizers and desserts. Closed Sundays.

Mitsukoshi♛♛
461 Park Ave. (at 57th St.). Tel. 935-6444
Average dinner: $60
Located in basement of Mitsukoshi store. Glittery western decor, but first-rate Japanese food, especially sushi and sashimi. Closed Sundays.

Odeon♛♛
145 West Broadway (at Thomas St.). Tel. 233-0507
Average dinner: $35
Reliable and trendy TriBeCa eatery, known for well-sauced pastas, fish, fowl, meats, yuppies, and artists. Avoid late-evening din and crush.

Orso♛♛
322 West 46th St. Tel. 489-7212
Average dinner: $25
Italian food, trattoria setting, theater neighborhood, reasonable prices for light fare. The pizzas are first-rate.

Oyster Bar♛♛
Lower level, Grand Central Terminal, 42nd St. at Park Ave. Tel. 599-1000
Average dinner: $25
Forget the decibel level (it's stratospheric); you're not here to talk, but to eat some of the freshest seafood in town. Nothing frozen but conversation (take your mother-in-law). Fresh catch of the day and season, simple treatments, many choices. Good California wine list. Closed Saturdays, Sundays.

Palio 👑 👑
Equitable Center, 151 West 51st St. Tel. 245-4850
Pre-theater *prix fixe* dinner: $35
Don't be put off by the garish murals around the entrance bar. In the upstairs dining room, exuberance comes in delicious Northern Italian dishes, including gnocchi, seafood, roast squab. Closed Sundays.

Pamir 👑 👑
1437 Second Ave. (between 74th and 75th Sts.). Tel. 734-3791
Average dinner: $20
Afghan restaurants aren't abundant in New York, but Oriental decor, inexpensive and excellent grilled lamb, and assorted rice dishes make this a winner. Go with a group for sharing and trying new dishes. Closed Mondays.

Primola 👑 👑
1226 Second Ave. (between 64th and 65th Sts.). Tel. 758-1775
Average dinner: $30
Breezy background for wonderful pasta and gnocchi specialties, other Italian dishes, served in abundant portions. Loads of good choices.

Raga 👑 👑
57 West 48th St. Tel. 757-3450
Average dinner: $30
Indian crafts and background music, rare spaciousness, serious Indian food. Our choice for the *best* midtown place for conversation and unhurried meals. Live classical Indian music Monday through Saturday evenings.

Rao's 👑 👑
455 East 114th St. (corner of Pleasant Ave.). Tel. 534-9625
Average dinner: $20
If you crave down-home Italian fare (excellent pasta dishes, soups, shrimp Fra Diavolo) at the quintessential insider's place, head for Rao's (but do so by car or taxi only, as it's remote). A haunt of Woody Allen, Mimi Sheraton, and other natives. Caveat: Rao's is so small (8 tables), be sure to reserve well in advance.

Seryna♛ ♛
11 East 53rd St. Tel. 980-9393
Average dinner: $30–35
This stylish restaurant fulfills several dining needs: it's spacious and quiet, good for a conversational meal; it artfully blends high-quality Japanese dishes with Japanized Western fare in creative ways—proving that East and West *can* meet and dine elegantly (though not cheaply).

Sofi♛ ♛
102 Fifth Ave. (near 15th St.). Tel. 463-8888
Average dinner: $25
A Chelsea delight: high-ceilinged loft is backdrop for simple, elegant New American–style meals. Salads a strong suit. (Same ownership as Lavin's.)

Rosa Mexicano♛ ♛
1063 First Ave. (at 58th St.). Tel. 753-7407
Average dinner: $35
The packed long barroom is Margaritasville North; head for the stuccoed back room for serious Mexican "eats." Winners: guacamole, grilled chicken, fish, carnitas. Reservations essential.

Shezan♛ ♛
8 West 58th St. Tel. 371-1414
Average dinner: $30
Stunning decor, Pakistani and Indian specialties, including tandoori dishes, keep this old-timer on top.

Siam Inn♛ ♛
916 Eighth Ave. (at 54th St.). Tel. 489-5237
Average dinner: $15
Decor a notch above diner belies hot, fresh, and spicy Thai dishes, served in generous portions by friendly waiters.

21♛ ♛
21 West 52nd St. Tel. 582-7200
Average dinner: $50
This longtime watering hole of the rich and powerful, recognized by the jockey statues lined up outside, has been renovated. The big news is that the food is now in the capable hands of 2 chef-superstars, Anne Rosenzweig of Arcadia, and Alain Sailhac, formerly of Le Cirque. Regulars continue to flock here for the status

factor, but now food lovers will find decent, imaginative fare—at 21's usual elevated prices (hamburgers, $36), of course.

Union Square Cafe♛ ♛
21 East 16th St. Tel. 243-4020
Average dinner: $35
Trendy bistro and New American fare in spacious, high-ceilinged setting in publishing neighborhood. Oysters a specialty, also delicious desserts. Thoughtful wine choices. Closed Sundays.

Auntie Yuan♛
1191A First Ave. (at 65th St.). Tel. 744-4040
Average dinner: $40
Atypically modern, sophisticated decor for a Chinese restaurant, with slightly Americanized versions of such classics as Peking duck, orange beef, steamed fish, dumplings.

Barking Fish Cafe♛
705 Eighth Ave. (between 44th and 45th Sts.). Tel. 757-0186
Average dinner: $28
Solid Cajun dishes (great gumbo) in riverboat decor. Sunday brunch a bargain, complete with 3-piece Dixieland band.

Black Sheep♛
344 West 11th St. Tel. 242-1010
Average dinner $16–30
Continental fare attracts locals to this popular Village dining spot, which once was a pool hall frequented by longshoremen.

Blue Nile♛
103 West 77th St. Tel. 580-3232
Average dinner: $20
Subtly spiced Ethiopian dishes eaten communally, using flat bread (in your *right* hand, because Moslems use their left hands only for "unclean" tasks—"custom of the country") rather than utensils. Great as a group experience. Handcraft-decorated setting.

Bombay Palace♛
30 West 52nd St. Tel. 541-7777
Average dinner: $25
Indian decor and Northern Indian cuisine with tandoori

broiling of meats, fish, and fowl. Vegetarian dishes and breads are best. Sunday buffet lunch is a 3-way winner: choices, quantity, price.

Brasserie ♕
100 East 53rd St. Tel. 751-4840
Average dinner: $30
An all-hours, everyday, bustling eatery, close to a Parisienne's heart. Quiches still the best. Great after-theater snackery.

Chez Jacqueline ♕
72 MacDougal St. Tel. 505-0727
Average dinner: $25
You want quiet, tiny, romantic, country French? That's Jacqueline's, tucked into one of the Village's most picturesque streets.

Cinco de Mayo ♕
45 Tudor City Place (between 42nd and 43rd Sts.). Tel. 661-5070
Average dinner: $28
Convivial, lively Mexican eatery near the UN. Inconsistent, but with a commendable black bean soup, *budin de tortilla*, praline soufflé. Closed Sundays.

PERILS & PITFALLS

Anyone who reads the gossip columns across the country knows about Elaine's, 1703 Second Ave. Tel. 534-8103. It's a favorite haunt of Woody Allen and visiting literary and theatrical celebrities. Go if you must, but be forewarned that celebrities are fawned over, the rest of us get short shrift, and everyone gets overpriced, mediocre food. Star-gazers beware!

Elephant & Castle ♕
183 Prince St. Tel. 260-3600. Also 68 Greenwich Ave. Tel. 243-1400
Average dinner: $20
A comforting, non-touristy SoHo café-bar, with an eclectic, interesting light menu—spicy chicken wings, varied omelets, soups, and hamburgers. Nothing fancy, but well done.

Felidia♛
243 East 58th St. Tel. 758-1479
Average dinner: $40
Uneven, but when it's "on mark," here's wonderfully prepared Northern Italian fare: pasta with wild mushrooms, polenta with venison, much more.

Florent's (Restaurant Florent)♛
69 Gansevoort St. (between Washington St. and Ninth Ave.). Tel. 989-5779
Average dinner: $20
Fun, cheap, no-nonsense 1940s diner ambiance, delicious Gallic food. Open late, but taxi to and from. *No credit cards.*

Hakubai♛
Kitano Hotel, 66 Park Ave. Tel. 686-3770
Average dinner: $40
Reliable Japanese specialties, especially sushi choices. Popular with Japanese businessmen (on expense accounts).

Hwa Yuan Szechuan Inn♛
40 East Broadway (between Catherine and Market Sts.). Tel. 966-5534
Average dinner: $20
Avoid the tourist menu, most Cantonese dishes, and "chef's specials"; go with the stoneware casserole stews and diverse appetizers. A Chinatown standby, modest prices.

Indochine♛
430 Lafayette St. (between Astor Place and East 4th St.). Tel. 505-5111
Average dinner: $28
Vietnamese/Cambodian dishes subtly prepared, with appetizers and fish the big palate pleasers. A local artist hang out. *No credit cards.*

La Boîte en Bois♛
75 West 68th St. Tel. 874-2705
Average dinner: $25
A natural for dinner before an evening at Lincoln Center. The restaurant's name means "wooden box," and that's about the size of this small French eatery. Nothing fancy, but decent country-style French fare at affordable prices.

Le Refuge ♛
116 East 82nd St. Tel. 861-4505
Average dinner: $40
Looks like a provincial inn, the menu says so, the kitchen proves it, with French classics. *No credit cards.* Closed Sundays.

Lola ♛
30 West 22nd St. Tel. 675-6700
Average dinner: $25–30
Gorgeous-looking, this high-ceilinged, renovated loft eatery combines Italian, Jamaican, and soul food. If the results are sometimes uneven, sit back and enjoy the ambiance—it's a knockout. And so is proprietress Lola herself.

Maxwell's Plum ♛
1181 First Ave. (at 64th St.). Tel. 628-2100
Average dinner: $35
Theater *cum* dining, courtesy of Hollywood's Warner Leroy, who decorated this zany place. Go to people-watch and drink; food's secondary.

PERILS & PITFALLS

One of the current "in" spots is Mortimer's, 1057 Lexington Ave. Tel. 517-6400. We find it overpriced for its only-fair fare. Unless you want to gape at the local "beautiful people," and don't mind the cost, we'd say skip it and splurge (for better fare) elsewhere.

Pig Heaven ♛
1540 Second Ave. (at 80th St.). Tel. PIO-4333
Average dinner: $18
Unusual all-pig, all-pink decor. Seafood, poultry, and meat dishes, but the emphasis is on pork. Fun place, but Americanized Chinese food.

Quatorze ♛
240 West 14th St. Tel. 206-7006
Average dinner: $40
Bistros are the latest Gotham rage, and this one's a winner for its earthy, unpretentious French food (some hearty Alsatian choices), modest art deco quarters.

Russian Tea Room♛
150 West 57th St. Tel. 265-0947
Prix fixe dinner: $30–40
As the ads say, "slightly to the left of Carnegie Hall."
Longtime standby for blinis, other Russian delicacies,
but it's the celebs who are the *real* draw.

Texarkana♛
64 West 10th St. Tel. 254-5800
Average dinner: $35–40
Suckling pig, barbecued *anything*, Cajun, Tex-Mex, and
Southern treats are what you'll find in this pseudo–New
Orleans courtyard. Dinner only, plus late-night suppers.

Water Club♛
30th St. (at the East River). Tel. 683-3333
Average dinner: $40
Seafood and sea views of the East River from a floating
glass-enclosed barge. If the weather's warm, head for
the open-air, upper-deck bar.

Windows on the World♛
1 World Trade Center, 107th floor. Tel. 939-1111
Prix fixe dinner: $30–34
You're here for the spectacular views of city and harbor,
not the food. Outstanding, famous wine list
(♛ ♛ ♛ ♛ ♛).

   Also in the same area: **Hors d'Oeuvrerie**♛ and
Cellar in the Sky♛ (dinner only). Note the spare-no-
expense opulence of lobby, rest rooms, and telephone
booths.

Yellow Rose Cafe♛
450 Amsterdam Ave. (between 81st and 82nd Sts.).
Tel. 595-8760
Average dinner: $15
Southwestern, Tex-Mex, and Southern cooking (try the
fried chicken, buttermilk biscuits, Texas red chili) are
the styles in a casual luncheonette setting.

NEIGHBORHOOD DINING AND DRINKING

Lincoln Center

For dinner before a Lincoln Center performance, you
have many choices. In the Center itself, there are these

restaurants: Allegro Cafe and Adagio Buffet in Avery Fisher Hall; Fountain Cafe (May through September) in the plaza; Grand Tier Restaurant in the Metropolitan Opera House (opens 2 hours before performances, reservations essential, tel. 799-3400).

Nearby are other options, many serendipitous ones along Columbus Avenue.

Also, there's Tavern on the Green♥, at 67th Street just inside Central Park (tel. 873-3200), which is far better for a drink than for the pricey food, though the setting *is* celebratory, flower-filled, with crystal chandeliers. Try Fiorello's Roman Cafe♥, 1900 Broadway (tel. 595-5330), for pastas and northern Italian fare.

If it's a long, cooling drink in *soigné* circumstances you're after, try Top of the Park in the Gulf & Western building at Columbus Circle, 60th Street and Central Park West (tel. 333-3800). (Stick to liquids, the food is only fair.) You can refresh your tired eyes with views of the park.

Chinatown

Recommending Chinese restaurants isn't easy, as the chefs change almost as fast as an abacus clicks. But among the consistently best of Chinatown's restaurants are Silver Palace♥, 50 Bowery at Canal Street (tel. 964-1204), a sprawling place, always crowded; Phoenix Garden♥♥, 128 Chambers St. (tel. 766-4211), with specialties of roast squab and pepper and salty shrimp; Siu Lam Kung♥♥, 18 Elizabeth Street (between Canal and Bayard streets (tel. 732-0974), serving excellent, inexpensive Cantonese dishes. Nom Wah Tea Parlor, 13 Doyers Street, is Chinatown's oldest and most traditional *dim sum* restaurant.

East Village

Try one of the ethnic spots, such as the Khyber Pass, 34 St. Marks Place, for Afghan food; A Taste of Siam, across from the Second Avenue Theater; Iso, 175 Second Avenue (at 11th Street), for sushi—diagonally across from the "11" Cafe, a Venezuelan restaurant;

and Indochine, across from the Public Theatre on Lafayette.

At 156 Second Avenue is the Second Avenue Deli, a landmark for its great sandwiches, stuffed derma, Hungarian goulash, and kosher goodies. (Note the Hebrew clock by the entrance.)

Among the Indian restaurants on 6th Street you'll find Shah Bagh (the first arrival); Mitali West (very popular); Calcutta (an appealing basement-level eatery); and Passage to India (fanciest of the group). All of them are reasonably priced ($12–20 per meal) and good choices before an evening in one of the East Village's numerous Off-Off-Broadway theaters, cafés, or discos.

Brooklyn

River Cafe ♛ ♛ ♛
1 Water St./Cadman Plaza West. Tel. (718) 522-5200
Prix fixe dinner: $48
Unanimous raves for ravishing views of Manhattan's skyline and Brooklyn Bridge, *and* for original American/ French *nouvelle* dishes (mostly seafood) at this floating restaurant. Good American wine choices.

> ### PERILS & PITFALLS
> Arrive and depart via taxi—the waterfront neighborhood is tough.

Almontaser ♛
218 Court St. Tel. (718) 624-9267
Average dinner: $16
In a Cobble Hill no-frills locale, enjoy Middle Eastern dishes at bargain prices. A neighborhood favorite.

Gage & Tollner ♛
372 Fulton St. (between Smith and Pearl Sts.). Tel. (718) 875-5181
Average dinner: $30. *Prix fixe* lunch: $15.50 Monday–Friday
Gaslights and the Gay Nineties live on in this historic restaurant featuring American standards (since 1879). Ah, nostalgia! Lunch is the best time, steaks and seafoods the best bets.

Moroccan Star ♛
205 Atlantic Ave. Tel. (718) 643-0800
Average dinner: $20
A stellar performer on a street known for reliable Middle Eastern cuisine.

Peter Luger Steakhouse ♛
178 Broadway at Driggs Ave. Tel. (718) 387-7400
Average dinner: $40
Steak, arguably the best in the city, is the reason you're here, not the service (often rude) or the decor (seedy *brauhaus*).

Tripoli ♛
156 Atlantic Ave. Tel. (718) 596-5800
Average dinner: $20–22
Here you'll find delicious Lebanese specialties in an attractive Middle East setting.

Queens

Water's Edge ♛
East River Yacht Club, 44th Drive (at east end of 59th St. Bridge, Long Island City). Tel. (718) 482-0033
Average dinner: $40
Dramatic view of Manhattan from a water-level establishment that specializes in trendy renderings of seafood to piano accompaniment.

Long Island

Zanghi ♛ ♛ ♛
50 Forest Ave., Glen Cove. Tel. (516) 759-0900
Average dinner: $35
Most everything's good, but fresh game and fish are exceptional in this excellent French restaurant. Outstanding wine cellar.

The American Hotel ♛ ♛
Sag Harbor. Tel. (516) 725-3535
Average dinner: $30–35
An eclectic, partially *nouvelle* menu, notable wine cellar, great charm in an 1846 house at the ferry landing. Also guest rooms.

Bobby Van's ♛

Montauk Highway, Bridgehampton. Tel. (516) 537-0590

Average dinner: $20–25

Informal, fun place where the likes of Norman Mailer and other summer visitors hang out, more for the company than the food.

The Bowden Square ♛ ♛

North Sea Road and Bowden Square, Southampton. Tel. (516) 283-2800

Average dinner: $35

Opt for a table on the porch, enjoy the old mansion setting and the stylish New American dishes.

The Grand Cafe ♛ ♛

3 Glen Cove Rd., Glen Cove. Tel. (516) 671-8600

Average dinner: $40

Trendy New American menu, reliable food in stylish habitat.

Homers Oriental ♛ ♛

6600 Jericho Turnpike, Syosset. Tel. (516) 931-1575

Average dinner: $25

If you're not a purist, you'll enjoy the mélange of Chinese and Japanese dishes, prepared with skill, good ingredients, imagination. Attractive modern setting.

Mirabelle ♛ ♛

404 North Country Rd., Saint James. Tel. (516) 584-5999

Average dinner: $30

Inventive French food in comfortable setting. Closed Monday, major holidays and 2 weeks in fall.

SPECIAL PLACES

Open Round-the-Clock

Empire Diner, 210 Tenth Ave. Tel. 243-2736. Reliable, funky. Good food.

Kiev, 117 Second Ave. Tel. 674-4040. Back-to-basic decor, but delicious borscht, mushroom and barley soups, French toast made with challah bread, New York egg creams.

La Brasserie (See 1-crown listings, above.)

Diners of Distinction—a New Craze

Broadway Diner, West 55th St. and Broadway. Tel. 765-0909. A faithful rendition of the 1940s diners some of us remember. No-frills food suggests the same era.

Empire Diner, 210 Tenth Ave. at West 22nd St. Tel. 243-2736. Tiny, trendy, fun—with better-than-diner fare. Good beer selection and a daily "Hedonist Sandwich." Outdoor tables in warm weather.

Exterminator Chili, 305 Church St. Tel. 219-3070. Welcome to the 1950s! Chili's the specialty in this dinerlike offbeat locale.

Restaurant Florent, 69 Gansevoort St. Tel. 989-5779. French-owned, with Gallic-accented fare in old-time diner setting. A brunch hangout for Chelsea artists. Excellent value.

Great Coffee Shops and Cafes

Cafe de la Paix, 50 Central Park S. Never mind all the tourists, enjoy the delightful park views.

Cafe le Figaro, corner of MacDougal and Bleecker Sts. Tel. 677-1100. A neighborhood favorite.

Cafe Reggio, 119 MacDougal St. Open since 1927, a Village landmark.

Caffe Biff', 251 E 84th St. High-tech Italian, with brasserie menu.

Caffe Dante, 79 MacDougal St. Tel. 982-5275. Lively spot, popular for *gelati* and excellent espresso. Outside seating in good weather.

Caffe Primavera, 51 Spring St. Tel 226-0431.

Caffe Roma, 385 Broome St. Tel. 226-8413. Delicious pastry in neighborhood Italian setting.

Caffe Vivaldi, 32 Jones St. Tel. 929-9384. Outside cafe, with variety of coffees, teas, desserts, served on marble tables to classical music.

Silverbird, 505 Columbus Ave. (near 84th St.). Where yuppies congregate for raspberry margaritas and blue-corn chips.

Siracusa, 65 Fourth Ave. Tel. 254-1940. Wines by the glass, light meals, and sensational homemade *gelati* (best in town).

Veselka, 144 Second Ave. (9th St.). Down-home to Ukrainians and others who like good coffee, murals and homey ambiance.

Just Desserts: Special Places to Calm a Raging Sweet Tooth

Ben & Jerry's, 1 Herald Square (at 34th St.). Tel. 564-3992. Also Third Avenue (at 10th St.), 1616 Mac-Donald Ave., Brooklyn. Tel. (718) 336-9755. Some ice cream mavens consider this the *ne plus ultra.*

Caffe Biffi, 251 East 84th St. Tel. 288-6984. Delicious sweets, cakes, and tarts go well with the house espresso, cappuccino, or assorted teas.

Chelsea Foods, 198 Eighth Ave. Tel. 691-3948. Homemade cakes, brownies, and tarts. Light meals, too, in tiny informal setting.

Eclair Pastry, 141 West 72nd St. Tel. 873-7700. Tel. 759-5355. Also take out, Grand Central Station, lower level.

Ferrara Pastries, 195–201 Grand St. Dates from 1892. Great for espresso and ricotta pastry called *fogliatelli.*

Les Delices Guy Pascal, 1231 Madison Ave. (at 89th St.). Tel. 289-5300. Also 939 First Ave. (at 49th St.). Tel. 371-4144. Expert pastries by the baker of the same name, former pastry chef at La Côte Basque. Tiny quarters, mouth-watering tarts and cakes.

Patisserie Lanciani, 275 West 4th St. Tel. 929-0739. Italian coffee shop. Also serves light meals.

Steve's, 145 Second Ave. Also 2891 Broadway, 286 Columbus Ave., and 444 Sixth Ave. Tel. 674-9216. For ice cream fanatics. Fresh and soothing.

Succes La Côte Basque, 1032 Lexington Ave. Tel. 535-3311. Super for coffee and elegant desserts.

For Tea (or Coffee) and Cakes

Agora Boutique Restaurant & Ice Cream Parlor, 1550 Third Ave. (at 87th St.). Tel. 860-3425. Glorious old soda fountain to raise your blood sugar pleasurably.

Algonquin Hotel, Oak Room, West 44th St. Tel. 840-6800. Where Robert Benchley, Dorothy Parker, other literary luminaries once reparteed and *New Yorker* staffers still do.

Boathouse Cafe, in Central Park. Tel. 517-2233. In warm weather, escapists get away from it all at this café on the pond. Bewitching. (Reach it via free trolley pickup at 72nd St. and Fifth Ave. Fun ride.)

Carlyle Hotel, 35 East 76th St. Tel. 744-1600. An oasis for proper tea in The Gallery on Chippendale and velvet banquettes.

Citicorp Atrium, 53rd St. and Lexington Ave. For state-of-the-art, do-it-yourself picnicking. You assemble your tea/snack/lunch/dinner from the surrounding shops (Cafe Buon Giorno, Au Bon Pain, Healthworks!, Nyborg & Nelson), and enjoy it among the trees while browsing through your book.

Columbus, Columbus Ave. and 69th St. Tel. 799-8090. Celebrity-owned, with "beautiful people" patrons.

Helmsley Palace, Gold Room, Madison Ave. and 50th St. Tel. 888-7000. Regal Renaissance setting for thoroughgoing British high tea in what was the music room of the historic Villard Houses. *Prix fixe,* $17.50 per person.

IBM Arcade, East 56th St. at Madison Ave. A circular snack bar for self-serve tea, cider, and croissants among the sunshine, bamboo groves, and seasonal flowers.

Inter-Continental (formerly the Barclay), 111 East 48 St. Tel. 755-5900. Tiffany ceiling, golden birdcage, gilt tables, and flowers with music—stylish ambiance for a memorable tea.

Irish Pavilion, 130 East 57th St. Tel. 759-9040. The place for an Irish coffee pick-me-up.

Les Delices Guy Pascal, 1231 Madison Ave. (at 89th St.). Tel. 289-5300. Pastries from the former pastry chef at La Côte Basque. Also snacks and light lunches, but the sweets say it all.

Mayfair Regent Hotel, Park Ave. (at East 65th St.). Tel. 288-0800. Elegant high tea in the Little Palm Court, served from the cart. Excellent choices.

Mayflower Hotel, 61st St. (at Central Park West). Tel. 265-0060. Here, where Vincent Youmans wrote "Tea for Two," the Conservatory offers tea, cappuccino, espresso, and Viennese pastries.

Museum of Modern Art Garden Cafe, 11 West 53rd St. (requires admission to museum). Tel. 708-9400. One of the modern world's most civilized settings, where sculpture by Rodin, Balzac, Picasso, others, accompany light snacks daily from 11 A.M. to 5 P.M.

Omni Berkshire Place, East 52nd St. at Madison Ave. Tel. 753-5800. Beautifully laid-on traditional afternoon tea poured by hostesses in atrium. Festive at holiday season.

Pierre Hotel, East 61st St. at Fifth Ave. Tel. 838-8000. Splendid, sumptuous setting in the oval Rotunda room for a veddy correct tea.

Plaza Hotel, Fifth Ave. at 59th St. Tel. 759-3000. Does anyone do it better than the famous Palm Court? Complete with candelabra, violins, and fabulous dessert choices.

Sant Ambroeus, 1000 Madison Ave. (between 77th and 78th Sts.). Tel. 570-2211. Luxurious Italian *pasticceria* (a branch of its stylish Milan parent). Paloma Picasso may be at the next table. There are espresso and *gelati* at the stand-up bar. Go for the exhilarating flowery-tented back area.

The Stanhope Hotel, 995 Fifth Ave. Tel. 288-5800. Across from Metropolitan Museum, a prime location for civilized tea, espresso, and people-watching. Outdoors on The Terrace, café-style in warm weather, indoors if not.

The Terrace, West 119th St. at Morningside Drive. Tel. 666-9490. (Closed Sundays and Mondays.) High above Morningside Heights (atop Columbia University's Butler Hall) this flowery, candlelit refuge (not to be

confused with the Stanhope's Terrace listed above)
usually has string music accompaniment to its superb
view of the city. Food plays second fiddle. (Under no
circumstances venture into nearby Morningside Park;
it's unsafe.)

Trump Tower, Fifth Ave. at 57th St. Tel. 371-5030.
Teas (soups, sandwiches) served by Terrace Five restaurant, the "vestpocket" café in a corner of Level 5,
overlooking the waterfall, with a view of the glitter
below . . . and an open terrace for a walkabout and
sunny city view. Tea assortment at $8.50.

INSIDERS' TIPS

Tea and/or snacks are supplied smartly by dispensaries
at major department stores, such as the following:

- **The Cafe** at Lord & Taylor, Fifth Ave. at 39th St.
- **Charleston Gardens** at B. Altman, Fifth Ave. at
  34th St.
- **Le Train Bleu** (copy of a dining car from this famous
  train) at Bloomingdale's, Lexington Ave. at 59th St.

WHERE TO SHOP

Fifth and Madison avenues—Upper East Side

Alfred Dunhill of London, 620 Fifth Ave. (at 50th
St.). Famous tobacconist now carries men's accoutre-
ments and clothing.

Antiquarian Booksellers Center, 50 Rockefeller
Plaza lobby. Rare books on display, yours for a price.

Argosy Bookstore, 116 East 59th St. A town house
stuffed with old books, prints, and maps, rare and of
high quality.

Asprey & Co., 725 Fifth Ave. (at 56th St.) Upscale
gifts, jewelry, precious baubles.

The Athlete's Foot, 16 West 57th St. (and other
locations). Caters to runners, joggers, shoe-wearers.

Banana Republic, 130 East 59th St. Outfits for
safaris or fantasies thereof. Other branches at South St.
Seaport, 87th and Broadway, 6th and Bleecker.

Barnes & Noble, 600 Fifth Ave. (at 48th St.). Tel. 765-0590. Three floors of discounted and remaindered books and recordings. Other branches at Penn Station, Times Square, 105 Fifth Ave. (at 18th St.).

Bijan, 699 Fifth Ave. (at 54th St.). Tel. 758-7500. The ultimate in snobby fashion: no admittance without appointment. Handsome men's and women's clothing, outrageously priced.

Brooks Brothers, 346 Madison Ave. (at 43rd St.). Tel. 682-8800. The original Ivy League look. Now for women & children too.

Cardel Ltd., 615 and 621 Madison Ave. (at 57th St.). Tel. 753-8690. Fine china selection.

Cartier's, 653 Fifth Ave. (at 52nd St.). Tel. 753-0111. Famous for its rocks and metals—in gorgeous settings, of course. Exquisite jewelry and objects.

Caswell-Massey Co. Ltd., 518 Lexington Ave. (at East 48th St.). Tel. 755-2254. Oldest chemists and perfumers in the United States (1752). Vast array of imported toiletries.

Crabtee & Evelyn, 30 East 67th St. Tel. 734-1108. Imported fine toiletries, antique chemist's shop decor. 5 other C&E shops in New York City.

Encore, 1132 Madison Ave. (at 83rd St.). Tel. 879-2850. Designer labels—Yves St. Laurent, etc.—for resale. Virtually new.

F.A.O. Schwarz, G.M. Building, 767 Fifth Ave. (at 58th St.). Tel. 644-9400. The end of the rainbow for children of all ages. Quintessential toy shop. Worth a trip in this new location even if you're not buying.

Gindi, 153 East 57th St. Tel. 753-5630. Great upscale costume jewelry.

Godiva Chocolatier, 701 Fifth Ave. (at 54th St.). Tel. 593-2845. The famous Belgian chocolates, sold by the box or the piece (like gold).

Gotham Book Mart, 41 West 47th St. Tel. 757-0367. Broad literary selection of books (especially poetry) and periodicals.

Gucci, 683 Fifth Ave. (at 54th St.). Tel. 826-2600. Leather in its most beguiling forms as accessories, handbags, shoes, gifts.

Hammacher Schlemmer, 147 East 57th St. Tel. 421-9000. Crammed with "what can this be for?" items and gadgets you never knew existed.

Hans Appenzeller, 820 Madison Ave. (at 67th St.). Tel. 570-0504. The Minimalist look in jewelry. High style.

Hermes Boutique, 11 East 57th St. Tel. 751-3181. Scarves and other delicious French accessories.

Hunting World, 16 East 53rd St. Tel. 755-3400. Equips you for the shoot or safari (you bring the guns).

Isabel Canovas, 743 Madison Ave. (at 63rd St.). Tel. 517-2720. Stylish costume jewelry and accessories.

Jerry Brown Imported Fabrics, 37 West 57th St. Tel. 753-3626. *Couture* fabrics.

Kansai Boutique, 974 Madison Ave. (at 74th St.). Tel. 249-9122. The outré Japanese look in women's clothes.

Kenzo Boutique, 824 Madison Ave. (at 67th St.). Tel. 737-8640. Far-out Japanese designer clothes.

Krön Chocolatier, 884 Madison Ave. (at 70th St.). Tel. 744-3899. Fresh and dried fruit dipped in rich bitter chocolate. Also whole chocolate initials and, for a Freudian kick, body parts (legs, arms, breasts) in chocolate.

The Limited, 691 Madison Ave. (at 62nd St.). Tel. 838-8787. Stylish clothes, affordable prices.

Librairie de France/Libreria Hispanica, 610 Fifth Ave. (at 49th St.). Tel. 581-8810. Large inventory of French and Spanish books.

Loewe Fashion Inc., 711 Madison Ave. (at 61st St.). Tel. 308-7700. Supplest of Spanish leather in coats, handbags, accessories. Also elegant clothes.

Marimekko, 7 West 56th St. Tel. 581-9616. Finnish designer fashion in women's clothes, bedding, bags, accessories.

Mark Cross, 645 Fifth Ave. (between 51st and 52nd Sts.). Tel. 421-3000. Traditional accessories, leather goods; has "women executives" shop.

McGraw-Hill Bookstore, 1221 Ave. of the Americas (at 49th St.). Tel. 512-2000. Specializes in business, technical, and computer books and software.

Mernsmart, 525 Madison Ave. (at East 53rd St.). Tel. 371-9175. Unusual value in men's clothing—bargains for this part of town.

Museum of American Folk Art Shop, 62 West 50th St. Tel. 247-5611. Great variety of interesting naïve wooden sculptures, toys, folk art.

Paul Stuart, Madison Ave. at 45th St. Tel. 682-0320. Very British, upscale men's wear (small women's department), luxurious Italian clothes.

Perugina Chocolates, 636 Lexington Ave. (at East 54th St.). Tel. 688-2490. Superb Italian chocolates. Try *baci* (kisses), chocolate pralines.

D. Porthault, 18 East 69th St. Tel. 688-1660. The ultimate in fine bed linen.

Polo/Ralph Lauren, 867 Madison Ave. (at 69th St.). Tel. 606-2100. Men's designer fashions displayed in beautiful Rhinelander mansion.

Pratesi Linens Inc., 381 Park Ave. (at 54th St.). Tel. 689-3150. Elegant linens.

Record Exchange, 842 Seventh Ave. (at West 54th St.). Tel. 247-3818. For collectors seeking rarities.

The Record Hunter, 507 Fifth Ave. (at 43rd St.). Tel. 697-8970. Big selection of records, good prices.

Rinoldo Maia, 27 East 67th St. Tel. 288-1049. Beautiful variety of plants, fresh flowers, fine arrangements.

INSIDERS' TIPS

Fresh-cut flowers are a New York secret: the less expensive are available on the street and in stalls all over town. Great varieties.

Rizzoli International Bookstore, 31 West 57th St. Tel. 759-2424. Closest thing to a European bookshop—imported books, prints, posters, ambiance.

Ronin Gallery, 605 Madison Ave. (at 56th St.) (2nd fl.). Tel. 688-0188. Contemporary and antique Japanese woodcuts, also excellent ceramics.

Royal Copenhagen Georg Jensen, 683 Madison Ave. (at 60th St.). Tel. 759-6457. Top quality in Danish china, silver.

Saint Laurent Rive Gauche Boutique Femme, 855 Madison Ave. (at 68th St.). Tel. 988-3821. Also for men at 543 Madison. Tel. 371-7912. French designer fashion at its best.

Sam Goody, 666 Third Ave. (at East 43rd St.). Tel. 986-8480. (Also 1290 Ave. of the Americas. Tel. 246-8730.) One of the oldest and largest record and tape stores, with big stereo department.

San Francisco Ship Model Gallery, 1089 Madison Ave. (at 80th St.). Tel. 570-6767. Museum-quality model ships at justifiably elevated prices.

Scribner Book Store, 597 Fifth Ave. (at 49th St.). Tel. 486-4070. Large stock of current books in beautiful landmark setting.

Sherry-Lehmann Inc., 679 Madison Ave., (between East 61st and 62nd Sts.). Tel. 838-7500. Oldest, perhaps finest wine/spirits shop in New York; outstanding selection. Jammed on weekends.

INSIDERS' TIPS

True New Yorkers don't like to pay list prices for *anything,* if they can ferret out places that give **discount prices.** Among the best:

- For men's clothing: **Moe Ginsberg,** 162 Fifth Ave. (at 21st St.). Tel. 982-5254. Especially for shirts.

- For women's clothing: **Loehmann's,** 2467 Jerome Ave., The Bronx. Tel. 295-4100. Also 19 Duryea Place, Brooklyn. Tel. (718) 469-9800. Worth the trip if you want to buy a lot of clothes, great style, designer clothes (without the labels), but best for small sizes). Also **The New Store,** 289 Seventh Ave. (at West 26th St.). Tel. 741-1077.

- For women's shoes (also designer clothing): **S&W,** 26th St. at Seventh Ave. Tel 924-6656.

- **For browsing** (clothing, housewares, miscellany): Canal Street, Hester, Allen, Delancey, and Orchard streets (Lower East Side) are great Sunday-morning experiences, with wall-to-wall shoppers and great bargains in linens, eyeglasses, jewelry, and other items for the discerning. Don't forget to haggle.

Sportsworks, 1046 Madison Ave. (at 78th St.). Tel. 879-4594. Fashions for game playing.

Steuben Glass, 715 Fifth Ave. (at 56th St.). Tel. 752-1441. The name says it all. Premium glassware.

Tiffany & Co., 727 Fifth Ave. (at 57th St.). Tel. 755-8000. The one and only. Fine silver, jewelry, and all good things.

Wittenborn Art Books, 1018 Madison Ave. (at East 77th St.). Tel. 288-1558. Posters, prints, books on art and architecture.

The West Side and Columbus Avenue

Contre-Jour, 190 Columbus Ave. (at 69th St.). Tel. 877-7900. Gadgets you can't live without—now that you've found them.

Fizzazz, 280 Columbus Ave. (at 74th St.). Tel. 580-0881. High-tech sportswear.

Herman's World of Sporting Goods, 135 West 42nd St. Tel. 730-7400. Vast array of sports gear. Also 3 other branches.

The Holding Company, 243 Columbus Ave. (at 72nd St.). Tel. 724-8252. Trendy earrings and clothes.

The Last Wound-up, 290 Columbus Ave. (at 74th St.). Tel. 787-3388. Toys, toys, toys.

Murder, Ink, 271 West 87th St. Tel. 362-8905. The emergency room for tales of detection, blood, and gore.

Ritz Thrift Shop, 107 West 57th St. Tel. 265-4559. For exceptional resale furs.

The Silver Palate, 274 Columbus Ave. (at 73rd St.). Tel. 799-6340. All kinds of great packaged (or bottled) gourmet goodies crammed into tiny storefront space.

Unique Clothing Warehouse, 718 Broadway. Tel. 674-1767. For funky clothes.

67 Wine & Spirits Merchants, 179 Columbus Ave. (at West 68th St.). Tel. 724-6767. A leading resource for bottled delights at bargain prices.

Womanbooks, 201 West 92nd St. Tel. 873-4121. Specializes in books and periodicals about and by women.

Zabar's, 2245 Broadway (at West 80th St.). Tel. 787-2000. *The* place for gourmet foods (also kitchenwares) at remarkably low prices. Expect barely civil treatment in exchange for bargains.

INSIDERS' TIPS

The best shopping for the latest electronic devices at best prices is the 2-block stretch of West 45th Street from Fifth Avenue to Broadway. Showrooms for the major discount chains are: **The Wiz** (12 West 45th, tel. 302-2000), **Crazy Eddies** (25 West 45th, tel. 302-6318), **Newmark & Lewis** (49 West 45th, tel. 391-2690), and **47th St. Photo** (115 West 45th, tel. 398-1410; the original is at 67 West 47th St., upstairs). All of them compete with one another to deliver the lowest prices; all are reputable and offer warranties. (Do your homework and know precisely what you want; clerks in these stores are notoriously brusque.)

Greenwich Village and East Village

Antique Buff, 321½ Bleecker St. All kinds of Victoriana, art nouveau, and art deco *objets*.

Archetype, 411 East 9th St. Tel. 529-5880. Arresting, witting avant-garde furniture, objects.

Astor Wines & Spirits, Corner of Lafayette St. and Astor Place. Tel. 674-7500. Huge supermarket of wines, outstanding selection, good prices.

Back from Guatemala, 306 East 6th St. Tel. 260-7010. Unusual clothes, a few from south of the border, many with Timbuktu label from Morocco and Mali; also Indian and Indonesian crafts, Peruvian masks, exotic jewelry.

Balducci's, 424 Sixth Ave. (at West 9th St.). Tel. 673-2600. A foodie's dream store. One of the greatest gourmet food selections west of Harrod's Food Halls.

Bowl & Board, 9 St. Marks Place. Tel. 673-1724. Bowls, toys, objects, all handcrafted of wood.

Brascomb and Schwab Inc., 148 Second Ave. (at 10th St.). Tel. 777-5363. Vintage clothing from 1920s to 1960s for women and men.

Common Ground, 50 Greenwich Ave. Tel. 989-4178. Superlative American Indian items: silver jewelry and belts, rare baskets, weavings. A super store.

Debris, 417 East 9th St. Secondhand clothing boutique.

Diamond Discount Fabrics, 165 First Ave. (at 11th St.). Tel. 228-8189. Famous for great buys in remnants, all kinds of fabrics.

Golden Disc, 239 Bleecker St. (at Ave. of the Americas). Tel. 255-7899. For the specialist hunting old records.

Lilac Chocolates Inc., 120 Christopher St. Tel. 242-7374. Chocolate delights.

Matt McGhee, 18 Christopher St. Tel. 741-3138. Toys and charming objects.

Oscar Wilde Memorial Bookstore, 15 Christopher St. Tel. 255-8097. Source for gay printed matter.

Paragon Sporting Goods, 867 Broadway (at 18th St). Tel. 255-8036. All sorts of game and camping equipment.

Pierre Deux Fabrics, 369 and 381 Bleecker St. Tel. 243-7740 and 657-4054. Provençal fabrics, clothes, tableware.

Pro Kitchen-Ware, 246 Bleecker St. Tel. 529-7711. Restaurant equipment store, with good-quality china, flatware. Sold by the piece.

St. Marks Bookshop, 13 St. Marks Place. Tel. 260-7853. Big collection of current books; basement specializes in architecture, gay and women's rights, other. 255-8097.

Strand Bookstore, 828 Broadway at 12th St. Tel. 473-1452. The major redoubt of secondhand and remaindered books—by the tens of thousands.

INSIDERS' TIPS

Want a new book cheap? Strand bookstore receives the lastest advance copies from book reviewers, and is famous for selling them even before reviews appear, at a fraction of list price.

Trash & Vaudeville, 4th St. Marks Place. Tel. 982-3590. "Rock 'n' Roll to wear"—fun and funky vintage clothes.

Whitehead & Mangan, 375 Bleecker St. Tel. 242-7815. "Purveyors of fine prints," English and otherwise.

SoHo and TriBeCa

Ad Hoc Softwares, 410 West Broadway. Tel. 925-2652. Linens, curtains, sheets, interesting housewares.

Agnes b, 116–118 Prince St. Tel. 925-4649. "With it" men's and women's sportswear from France.

Antique Boutique, 712 Broadway. Tel. 460-8830. Vintage clothing with panache.

Artwear, 456 West Broadway. Tel. 673-2000. Fanciful jewelry, made by a stable of 45 artisans.

Betsey Johnson, 130 Thompson St. Tel. 420-0169. Clothes with this designer's usual fun flair.

Dean & DeLuca, 121 Prince St. Tel. 254-7774. Gourmet's paradise. Delicacies from the 4 corners of the earth.

D. F. Sanders & Co., 386 West Broadway. Tel. 925-9040. High-tech housewares, great styling.

80 Papers, 510 Broome St. Tel. 431-7720. Exquisite handmade, hand-printed, and marbled papers. Also stationery, cards, gifts.

Ezra Cohen, 307 Grand St. Tel. 925-7800. Elegant linens.

Filippo, 472 West Broadway. Tel. 505-7690. Smart-looking Italian women's clothes, a branch of the Rome store.

The French Connection, 435 West Broadway. Tel. 219-1197. Classic clothes for men and women.

The Gallery of Wearable Art, 480 West Broadway. Tel. 425-5379. Fantasy creations, unusual one-of-a-kind clothes for women.

Grass Roots Gallery de Artes Populares, 131 Spring St. Tel. 431 0144. Sensational folk art, toys, masks from Mexico, Guatemala, South America. Huge collection.

Harriet Love, 412 West Broadway. Tel. 966-2280. Vintage clothes, 1930s memorabilia.

Jacques Carcanagues Inc., 114 Spring St. Tel. 925-8110. 19th-century Turkamen jewelry, Turkish *kilim*, Burmese wood sculpture, Thai jewelry, assorted Asian treasures, old and new.

Miso Clothes Ltd., 416 West Broadway. Tel. 226-4955. Clothes for men and women, toys for kiddies.

Norma Kamali's OMO, 113 Spring St. Tel. 334-9696. Stylish women's clothes.

Reinstein/Ross, Ltd., 122 Prince St. Tel. 226-4513. Original gold jewelry, based on antique themes, using precious stones. Some silver too.

The Second Coming, 72 Greene St. Tel. 431-4424. Vintage department store, with old furniture, clothes, accessories, including James Dean sunglasses ($35). Great fun to browse.

SoHo Emporium, 375 West Broadway. Contains 10 small shops. Only a bit of gold amid lots of glitz and glitter.

Syms, 45 Park Place at West Broadway. Tel. 791-1199. Excellent bargain buys in men's clothing, some women's clothes.

Tower Records, 692 Broadway. Tel. 505-1333. One of the world's largest record and cassette sellers, 24 hours a day, every day. (Has 2 branches.)

Urban Archaeology, 137 Spring St. Tel. 431-6969. Gargoyles, Corinthian capitals, architectural oddments from demolished buildings.

Victoria Falls, 451 Broadway. Tel. 254-2433. Nostalgic clothing, soft, feminine, Edwardian.

Wolfman-Gold & Good Co., 484 Broome St. Tel. 431-1888. Nifty porcelains, baskets, bibelots.

Zona, 97 Greene St. Tel. 925-6750. Lovely shop with unusual home accessories from the American Southwest, Mexico, Europe. Soleri bells; furniture; crafts; housewares.

Zoot, 734 Broadway. Tel. 505-5404. Wacky, wonderful vintage clothes.

Chelsea

Books of Wonder, 132 Seventh Ave. (at West 18th St.). Tel. 989-3270. Noted for its children's books, big collection of Oz books, first editions, and the best of new titles. A small treasure house.

Chelsea Foods, 198 Eighth Ave. (at 18th St.). Tel. 691-3948 (Also at 113 Greenwich Ave. Tel. 929-8830.) Great source of pasta salads, fresh veggies, gourmet foods, with tables for breakfast, light lunches, desserts.

N.Y. Jock, 220 Tenth Ave. (between 22nd and 23rd Sts.). Lively sportswear for men and women.

Pottery Barn, 231 Tenth Ave. (at 25th St.). Tel. 206-8118. Grandaddy of the discount stores for handsome, modern, good-design look in housewares and home furnishings. Still going strong.

Antiques and Auction Houses

A la Vieille Russie, 781 Fifth Ave. (at 59th St.). Tel. 752-1727. Outstanding European jewelry from the 1400s onward, including Fabergé originals. Russian art as well.

American Folk Art Gallery, 19 East 76th St. Tel. 794-9169. Antique quilts, toys, weather vanes, more.

America Hurrah Antiques, 766 Madison Ave. (at 64th St.). Tel. 535-1930. Antique folk art, quilts, tinware, more, much more.

Antiquarium Fine Ancient Arts, 984 Madison Ave. (at 75th St.). Tel. 734-9776. Antiquities, Greek, Egyptian, and beyond—jewelry, objects.

Bernard & S. Dean Levy, 961 Madison Ave. (at East 76th St.). Tel. 628-7088. A 3-generation antique dealer in 18th- and 19th-century American china, silver, furniture.

Christie's, 502 Park Ave. (at East 59th St.). Tel. 546-1000. One of the oldest and largest international auctioneers. (Less costly items are sold at Christie's East, 219 East 67th St. Tel. 570-4141.)

INSIDERS' TIPS

If you're a flea-market hound, stroll down Canal Street any (warm, dry) day; visit Annex Antiques Fair & Outdoor Flea Market, 725 Ave. of the Americas Sundays (April–November); New Essex Street Market, 140 Essex St. (indooors, Friday through Sunday).

Dalva Brothers, 44 East 57th St. Tel. 758-2297. French 18th-century furniture and Sevres china.

Didier Aaron, 32 East 67th St. Tel. 988-5248. This Parisian dealer's eclectic collection includes art deco, Victorian English furniture in town house settings.

Doris Wiener, 1001 Fifth Ave. (at 82nd St.) Tel. 772-8631. Oriental antiques, especially Indian.

Frank Caro, 41 East 57th St. Tel. 753-2166. Classical Oriental, Indian. Fine ceramics, Chinese and Japanese. Old-time dealer.

Fred Leighton, 763 Madison Ave. (at East 66th St.). Tel. 288-1872. Unique estate jewelry, from 1800 onward. Gorgeous stuff.

James Robinson and James II Galleries, 15 East 57th St. Tel. 752-6161. *The* place for antique English silver flatware, jewelry.

Le Cadet de Gascogne, 1021 Lexington Ave. (between East 73rd and 74th Sts.). Tel. 744-5925. A French dealer specializing in Louis XIII–XVI.

Macklowe Gallery, Ltd., 982 Madison Ave. (at East 76th St.). Tel. 288-1124. From Victorian to art deco jewelry, including Lalique and other famous designers.

Manhattan Art & Antiques Center, 1050 Second Ave. (at East 55th St.). Tel. 355-4400. A concatenation of 72 dealers under one roof.

Phillip Colleck of London, 122 East 57th St. Tel. 753-1544. English furniture, accessories.

Phillips, 406 East 79th St. Tel. 570-4830. For art; furniture. Outposts of the London firm.

Ruth Bigel, 743 Madison Ave. (at 63rd St.). Tel. 734-3262. Oriental art, especially noted for Cantonware ceramics.

Sotheby Parke Bernet, 1334 York Ave. (at East 72nd St.). Tel. 472-3400. For art and jewels; tel. 472-4825 for collections (coins, stamps, etc.) and decorative pieces.

INSIDERS' TIPS

Art/antiques lectures are given at both Christie's and Sotheby's, and from September through May, both are open for viewing on Sundays.

Stair & Co., 972 Madison Ave. (at East 74th St.). Tel. 355-7620. New York's oldest and largest English antiques dealer. Fine English furniture.

Thomas K. Woodward, 835 Madison Ave. (at 67th

St.). Tel. 794-9404. American antiques, quilts, hooked rugs.

Vernay & Jussel, 825 Madison Ave. (at 67th St.). Tel. 870-3344. English furniture, clocks.

William Doyle Galleries, 175 East 87th St. Tel. 427-2730. A New York auction house through and through.

INSIDERS' TIPS

The big annual antiques event in New York is the Winter Antiques Show at the Seventh Regiment Armory, Park Ave. at East 67th St., held in late January or early February. Hundreds of dealers, special lectures. A Big Deal. For information, tel. 737-4192.

ART GALLERIES AND DEALERS

Uptown—57th Street, Madison Avenue, Etc.

Acquevella, 18 East 79th St. Tel. 734-6300. For Impressionists.

Allan Frumkin, 50 West 57th St. Tel. 757-6655. New painting and sculpture.

Associated American Artists, 20 West 57th St. Tel. 399-5510. Longtime print gallery with vast international selection of graphic artists. Reasonable prices.

Andre Emmerich, 41 East 57th St. Tel. 752-0124. Pre-Columbian.

Betty Parsons, 24 West 57th St. Tel. 247-7480. Abstract, modern American.

Cordier & Eckstrom, 417 East 75th St. Tel. 988-8857. Contemporary painting and sculpture.

Grace Borgenicht, 724 Fifth Ave. (at 56th St.). Tel. 247-2111. 20th-century American.

Graham, 1014 Madison Ave. (at 76th St.). Tel. 535-5767. City's oldest (1857) commercial gallery, specializes in American art.

Hirschl & Adler, 21 East 70th St. Tel. 535-8810. 19th and 20th centuries.

Kennedy, 40 West 57th St. Tel. 541-9600. Longtime dealer in American art, 18th through 20th centuries.

Knoedler, 19 East 70th St. Tel. 794-0050. Traditional 19th and 20th centuries.

Marlborough, 40 West 57th St. Tel. 541-4900. Large stable of international contemporary artists.

Martha Jackson, 521 West 57th St. Tel. 586-4200. Contemporary.

Merton D. Simpson, 1063 Madison Ave. (at 79th St.). Tel. 988-6290. Wide-ranging African sculpture, other works.

Multiples, 24 West 57th St. Tel. 977-7160. Multiple editions of sculpture, prints by leading international big-name artists. Cheaper than if there were just one copy, but no bargains.

Pace, 32 East 57th St. 421-3292. Contemporary.

Perls, 1016 Madison Ave. (at 76th St.). Tel. 472-3200. Contemporary.

Pierre Matisse, 41 East 57th St. Tel. 355-6269. European contemporary.

Segy, 50 West 57th St. Tel. 355-3859. African.

Sidney Janis, 110 West 57th St. Tel. 586-0110. Leading contemporaries.

Staempfli, 47 East 77th St. Tel. 535-1919. Contemporary Spanish art, others too.

Wally Findlay, 17 East 57th St. Tel. 421-5390. Modern art on the conservative side.

Wildenstein, 19 East 64th St. Tel. 879-0500. American and European masters.

Witkin, 41 East 57th St. Tel. 355-1461. Vintage photographs, some paintings.

Downtown: Greenwich Village, SoHo, and TriBeCa

A.I.R., 63 Crosby St. Tel. 966-0799. Interesting contemporary works.

Beitzel, 113 Greene St. Tel. 219-2863. *Avant* and interesting 1980s art.

J. Camp Associates, 380 West Broadway. Tel. 966-3372. Traditional Asian, African art, objects.

Carolyn Hill, 109 Spring St. Tel. 226-4611. Current works, SoHo artists.

Daniel Newburg, 44 White St. Tel. 219-1885. New artists, cutting-edge work.

Dyansen of SoHo, 122 Spring St. Tel. 226-3384. Sculpture, paintings, graphics.

Exit Art, 578 Broadway. Tel. 966-7745. Contemporary painting, films, poetry, video, performances.

Leo Castelli, 142 Greene St. Tel. 431-6279. A frontrunner in big-name modern paintings and graphics.

Mary Boone, 417 West Broadway. Tel. 431-1818. Here's where it's at, if you're looking for the newest SoHo rage.

O.K. Harris, 383 West Broadway. Tel. 431-3600. 5 huge galleries of leading edge contemporary art, various styles.

Paula Cooper, 155 Wooster St. Tel. 674-0766. The latest in the SoHo scene.

Sonnabend, 420 West Broadway. Tel. 966-6160. Contemporary.

SoHo Center for Visual Artists, 114 Prince St. Tel. 226-1995. Nonprofit exhibitions, sponsored by Aldrich Museum, CT, and Mobile Foundation.

Vorpal, 465 West Broadway. Tel. 777-3939. Late-20th-century and American paintings, prints.

Major Department Stores

INSIDERS' TIPS

Department stores can serve as rest room pit stops when you're out and about the city. Head for the women's or men's clothing department or the store's restaurant/café.

Alexander's, 58th St. at Lexington Ave. The latest fashion in clothing and accessories for men, women, and children—at lower-than-most prices.

B. Altman, Fifth Ave. at 34th St. Attractive shopping for traditional clothing, furnishings, children's wear. Competent service, reliably high quality. No surprises.

Barney's New York, Seventh Ave. at West 17th St. A unique, stylish citadel of men's and women's clothing arranged in boutiques featuring British, American, Italian, Japanese, other designers. Extraordinary range of sizes, prices, in Hollywood setting.

Bergdorf Goodman, 754 Fifth Ave. (at 58th St.). Elegant is the watchword here, where Chanel, Givenchy, Dior, and their peers are featured. High fashion for both men and women. Prices to match.

Bloomingdale's, Lexington Ave. at East 59th St. Showbiz on Lexington—a vertical bazaar of the latest, trendiest clothing, accessories, home furnishings, gourmet foods in highest-voltage settings in modern retailing. Pressurized atmosphere, some uncaring clerks, but a visit is essential to the New York experience.

INSIDERS' TIPS

There are exceptional gourmet food departments—selling a range of cheese, coffee, preserves, patés, baked goods, condiments, and more—in these stores:

- B. Altman. Products of Fortnum & Mason and Paris's Fauchon.
- Bloomingdale's. Petrossian's caviar (sold in a replica of Petrossian's Blvd. Latour-Maubourg Paris store), big bread and pastry selection, pastas, sun-dried tomatoes, and whatever's trendy (and tasty).
- Macy's. The Cellar has an outstanding selection of imported and domestic foodstuffs, British cheeses, etc.

During the year, these stores stage promotions with famous chefs or cookbook authors demonstrating recipes in the store. Check the ads in the daily New York newspapers.

Bonwit Teller, 4 East 57th St. Conservative, dependable, fashionable.

Henri Bendel, 10 West 57th St. A series of attractive boutiques, stores-within-a-store, with high fashion, appealing to chic, affluent trend-setters. For clothing and accessories.

Lord & Taylor, Fifth Ave. at 39th St. Solid, reliable, for conservative clothing, furnishings. No pressure. (Try its Soup Bar on 10th floor.)

Macy's, 151 West 34th St. (at Broadway). Wins Guinness record for size, has mid-range merchandise—clothing, furnishings, linens, toys, housewares. Outposts of P. J. Clarke's uptown tavern and Delices de la Côte Basque patisserie are on premises. Beware distracted clerks.

Saks Fifth Avenue, 611 Fifth Ave. (at 50th St.). Famous for quality and selection in men's, women's, children's clothing, furs, luggage, housewares—and art gallery.

NIGHTLIFE

Bars, Pubs, Cocktail Lounges

INSIDERS' TIPS

Happy Hour? That, if you didn't know, is New Yorkese for a spread of free snacks with your "after 5 P.M." cocktails. Some places specialize in them. Notably generous are **The Cattleman**, 5 East 45th St.; **Raga**, 57 West 48th St.; **Molly Mog's Pub**, 65 East 55th St.; **Teheran**, 45 West 44th St.

Algonquin, 59 West 44th St. Tel. 840-6800. The lobby's the favorite gathering spot for drinks—but get there before the 5:15 crowd.

Dorset Bar, in Dorset Hotel, 30 West 54th St. Tel. 247-3700. Shiny black leather comfort, lively bar, generous Happy Hour canapés

Drake's Drum, 1629 Second Ave. (between East 84th and 85th Sts.). Tel. 988-2826. A post-combat unwinding room for yuppie softball teams. Sawdust floor, jukebox, imported beer and ale.

Fraunces Tavern, Pearl and Broad Sts. Tel. 260-0144. Colonial mementos and flags make an atmospheric setting.

Laurent, 111 East 56th St. Tel. 753-2729. Quiet luxury in a traditional, paneled cocktail lounge.

Manhattan Brewing Company Tap Room, 40–42 Thompson St. Tel. 219-9250. Old brewery offers flavorful beer, pub grub, young congenial crowd nightly.

McSorley's Old Ale House, 15 East 7th St. Tel. 473-9148. Legendary watering hole, bastion of tradition, celebrated in word and song, this authentic Irish saloon resists change (and its devotees thank God for that!). *No credit cards.*

Minetta Tavern, 113 MacDougal St. Tel. 475-3850. This relic of the Village's glory years carries on as a popular watering hole.

Mortimer's (See restaurant listings.)

Old Town Bar, 45 East 18th St. Tel. 473-8874. Sure and the ould booths are comfortable in this vintage Irish bar (seen on "Late Night with David Letterman").

P. J. Clarke's, 915 Third Ave. (at East 55th St.). No tel. Historic, much-loved tavern co-starred with Ray Milland in *The Lost Weekend.* Atmosphere and camaraderie aplenty.

Peculier Pub, 182 West 4th St. Tel. 691-8667. Beer-lover's nirvana, with 2-page list of 250 beers, plus daily specials from around the world. (English Old Peculier Ale is manager's favorite, hence the name.)

Pete's Tavern, 129 East 18th St. Tel. 473-7676. This old O. Henry hangout offers Victorian nostalgia with your libation.

T.G.I. Friday, 1152 First Ave. (at 60th St.). Tel. 832-8512. Where yuppie singles meet and greet.

Top of the Park, Gulf & Western Building, Columbus Circle, 60th St. and Central Park West. Tel. 333-3800. Go for the view of Central Park.

Water Club, 500 East 30th St. at FDR Drive. Tel. 683-3333. Water-level views of river traffic from this floating platform can be spectacular. Arrive and depart by cab.

White Horse Tavern, 567 Hudson. Tel. 243-9260. This unpretentious old-timer (where Dylan Thomas did his antepenultimate drinking) is right out of a Saroyan story.

Wine Bars

(And restaurants where you can try a variety of wines by the glass.)

Cafe Europa and **La Brioche,** 347 East 54th St.

Drake Bar, Drake Hotel, 440 Park Ave. (at East 56th St.).

Grapes, 522 Columbus Ave. (at West 85th St.).

Greene Street, 101 Greene St.

Lavin's, 23 West 39th St.

SoHo Kitchen & Bar, 103 Greene St.

Tastings, 144 West 55th St. (the International Wine Center school)

The Wine Bar, 422 West Broadway

Wine Bistro, Novotel Hotel, 226 West 52nd St.

Cabarets and Nightclubs

Expect a cover charge unless otherwise noted. Many also require a 2-drink minimum.

The Ballroom, 253 West 28th St. (adjoins Ballroom restaurant). Tel. 244-3005. Torch singers, belters, and emotive powerhouses in "comebacks," comedians, and reprises of musical greats. Shows Tuesday–Saturday, 9 P.M.

Broadway Baby, 407 Amsterdam Ave. (at West 79th St.). Tel. 724-6868. Piano bar plus waiters and bartenders singing show tunes. Best after 10 P.M.; jammed weekends. No cover charge.

Caroline's, 332 Eighth Ave. (at West 26th St.). Tel. 924-3499. Comics, mimes, impersonators. Branch at South Street Seaport.

Dangerfield's, 1118 First Ave. (at 58th St.). Tel. 593-1650. Features stand-up comics. Shows Sunday–Thursday, 9:15 P.M.; 2 shows Friday, 3 shows Saturday nights.

Greene Street Cafe, 101 Greene St. Tel. 925-2415. Cabaret sets, revues, satire at one or more of multiple entertainment sites in the building. Fun usually begins at 8 P.M.; some shows on weekends at 1 A.M.

Palsson's, 158 West 72nd St. Tel. 595-7400. Outrageous doings in satirical revues. Shows 8:30 P.M. Tuesday–Thursday, 2 shows nightly Friday and Saturday.

Live Music and Discos

Some of these allow or encourage dancing. Some will probably have disappeared from the scene by the time you arrive in New York (their life cycles are often brief), others may be inexplicably selective (are you hip enough, man?) about whom they allow to enter. Expect a cover charge, possibly a 1- or 2-drink minimum also, unless otherwise noted.

Blue Note, 131 West 3rd St. Tel. 475-8592. A jazz temple. Groups such as Jon Hendricks and Family. 2 shows nightly, 3 on Friday and Saturday; "music charge" plus minimum at tables.

The Baja, 246A Columbus Ave. (at 72nd St.). Tel. 724-8890. Mostly for yuppies and dancing, live music Tuesday. Opens 9:30 P.M.

CBGB, 315 Bowery (at Bleecker St.). Tel. 473-9763. New York's cradle of punk rock. Four bands per night plus matinee on Sunday.

Carlos No. 1 Jazz Supper Club, 432 Ave. of the Americas (between West 9th and 10th Sts.). Tel. 982-3260. Major mainstream jazz groups hold forth here. No cover for diners on Mondays.

China Club, Ltd., 2130 Broadway (at West 75th St.). Tel. 877-1166. Recording company hangout—agents, execs, would-be (and actual) rock stars. Live music during week, disco weekends; from 10 P.M.

Fat Tuesday's, 190 Third Ave. (at 19th St.). Tel. 533-7902. Soloists and small group jazz headliners in shows Tuesday–Thursday at 8 and 10 P.M., plus Friday and Saturday midnight shows. Cover charge.

Freddy's, 308 East 49th St. Tel. 888-1633. Headliners of the 1950s and 1960s often perform here. Tuesday–Thursday at 8:30 and Friday and Saturday at 9 and 11 P.M.

Gregory's Sidewalk Cafe & Jazz Club, 1149 First Ave. (at East 63rd St.). Tel. 371-2220. Mainstream jazz, small combos, and soloists vibrate from 10 P.M. to 3 A.M. most nights, Sundays 5 to 10 P.M. Tiny (35 seats).

Hors D'Oeuvrerie, 1 World Trade Center. Tel. 938-1111. Top-of-the world jazz. Trio from 4 P.M. and nightly from 7:30 P.M. to 12:30 A.M., striking 107th-floor views, canapes. Dance if you wish.

Jazz Center of New York, 380 Lafayette St. (at Great Jones St.). Tel. 505-5660. Concert performances, "loft jazz" by name groups and soloists; 2 shows nightly.

Jimmy Ryan's, 154 West 54th St. No frills, no nonsense, no minimum—just mainstream and Dixieland jazz at this granddaddy of the speakeasies *cum* jazz joints.

King Cole Room, St. Regis-Sheraton, 2 East 55th St. Tel. 872-6140. Candlelit dining, dancing to Bourbon Street Jass (sic) Band Saturday, with *prix fixe* dinner.

Knickerbocker Saloon, 33 University Place (at 9th St.). Tel. 228-8490. Turn-of-century decor provides atmosphere for piano and/or small combos. No cover Sunday and Monday.

Lone Star Cafe, 61 Fifth Ave. (at 13th St.). Tel. 242-1664. Big names in country-western. Music begins 11:30 P.M. Monday–Friday, 7:30 P.M. Saturday and Sunday, terminates 3 or 4 A.M.

Michael's Pub, 211 East 55th St. Tel. 758-2272. Features jazz-pop singers, perennials such as Carmen McRae, emphasis on show tunes, ballads. Shows at 9 and 11 P.M.; closed Sunday.

Nell's, 246 West 14th St. Tel. 675-1567. Hottest of the clubs at this time, capacity 400; dancing downstairs, jazz trio and lounge upstairs. From 10 P.M.

Palladium, 126 East 14th St. Tel. 752-3852. Participate or people-watch. Huge (3,500) capacity.

Saint, 105 Second Ave. Tel. 674-8369. No sign. Great sound-and-light show. Same building as former Fillmore East.

Siberia, 804 Washington St. Tel. 463-8521. New addition to the city's club scene. Live bands and performers.

S.O.B.'s (Sounds of Brazil), 204 Varick St. Tel. 243-4940. Changing groups, disco and dancing to Afro-Latin and other rhythms.

Sweet Basil Jazz Restaurant, 88 Seventh Ave. South. Tel. 242-1785. Mainstream, revivals, and avant-garde.

Tramps, 125 East 15th St. Tel. 777-5077. New and recent groups change almost nightly. *No credit cards.*

INSIDERS' TIPS

Nightclubs seem to have phases. These are popular at this writing (all have cover charges):

- **The Surf Club,** 415 East 91st St. Frowns on jeans, requires jackets.
- **Big Kahuna,** 622 Broadway (near Houston St.)
- **Club A,** 333 East 60th St.
- **Club Broadway,** 2551 Broadway (at West 96th St.). Ladies enter free until 11 P.M. Fridays. Jackets required.
- **Visage,** 610 West 56th St. (west of 11th Ave.)
- **Private Eyes,** 12 West 21st St.
- **Danceteria,** 30 West 21st St. Inexpensive.
- **Limelight,** 660 Ave. of the Americas
- **Heartbreak,** 179 Varick St.
- **Kamikaze,** 531 West 19th St.
- **Area,** 157 Hudson St.
- **The Limbo** Lounge, 647 East 9th St. Inexpensive.

Tunnel, 220 Twelfth Ave. (at West 27th St.). Tel. 714-9886. An 1891 railroad tunnel (capacity 2,500) with red velvet couches, abstract art, and insistent disco beat. From 10 P.M., except Tuesday when it opens at 6 P.M.

Village Gate, 160 Bleecker St. (at Thompson St.). Tel. 475-5120. Another jazz institution, still going with the flow.

Village Vanguard, 178 Seventh Ave. South. Tel. 255-4037. Historic basement showcase for power jazz—old and new. Shows 10 and 11:30 P.M., 1 A.M. *No credit cards.*

West End Cafe, 2911 Broadway (at West 115th St.). Tel. 666-9160. This Columbia University hangout features jazz Tuesday–Sunday from 9 P.M., comedy at other times. Modest minimum.

Zinno, 126 West 13th St. Tel. 924-5182. Single instrumentalists and small groups, contemporary music.

Piano Bars

These are a New York late-hours institution (usually with cover charge or drink minimum).

Backstage, 318 West 45th St. Tel. 489-6100. Music Thursday–Saturday 9 P.M.–1 A.M. Restaurant draws theater people. No cover.

Barbizon, 140 East 63rd St. Tel. 715-6929. Pianists and singers in the Cafe Bar 5–9 P.M., but never on Monday.

Carlyle Hotel, 35 East 76th St. Tel. 744-1600. Long a magnet for piano/cabaret aficionados, Carlyle Cafe features the prince of cabaret singers, Bobby Short. Also has the Bemelmans Bar (with beloved murals by this artist) with jazz pianist Tuesday–Saturday, 9:45 P.M.

Drake Swissôtel, 440 Park Ave. (at East 56th St.). Tel. 421-0900. Tinkling keys 8 P.M.–midnight, Tuesday–Saturday in off-lobby lounge.

Inter Continental Hotel, 111 East 48th St. Tel. 421-0836. On The Terrace there's music Monday–Friday, 7:30 P.M.–12:30 A.M.

Marriott Marquis Hotel, 1535 Broadway (at West 45th St.). Tel. 398-1900. At the Broadway Lounge, the pianist presides Wednesday–Saturday, 10 P.M.–2 A.M.

New York Hilton Hotel, 1335 Ave. of the Americas (at West 53rd St.). Tel. 586-7000. Here you have three shots to find the music you prefer: Mirage room, 5 P.M.–midnight; Hurlingham's, 6–11 P.M.; The Promenade, 3 P.M.–midnight.

Polo Lounge, Westbury Hotel, Madison Ave. at 69th St. Tel. 535-2000. Pianist on duty Tuesday–Saturday, 8 P.M.–midnight.

Ruppert's, 1662 Third Ave. (at East 93rd St.). Tel. 831-1900. Soft lights and suavity, talent changes almost nightly, goes until 3 or 4 A.M. No cover.

BROADWAY THEATER

Older, larger Broadway theaters, where many famous plays and musicals are performed, are concentrated around Broadway north of 42nd Street.

Off- and Off-Off-Broadway theaters are scattered about the city and are categorized by number of seats: Off-Broadway theaters have from 100 to 499 seats; Off-Off-Broadway theaters have fewer than 100 seats.

INSIDERS' TIPS

Deep-discount (50 percent off plus fee) tickets to current Broadway and Off-Broadway plays and musicals are offered the day of the performance at the nonprofit TKTS booths at the following locations:

- Broadway at West 47th St. Tel. 354-5800
- 2 World Trade Center, mezzanine. Tel. 354-5800, 221-0885
- Fulton Mall at De Kalb Ave., Brooklyn. Tel. (718) 625-5015.

Tickets for matinees (curtain at 2 P.M. Wednesdays and Saturdays) go on sale at noon the day of the performance. Tickets for evening performances go on sale at 3 P.M. Show up an hour early in either case. The list of productions for which tickets are available is posted outside the TKTS booths. Have cash or traveler's checks ready—*no credit cards.*

Nowadays, major theaters accept credit cards, so you may call a theater box office and order tickets directly (there's a surcharge). Tickets are also available via Ticketron and Telecharge telephone services (with surcharge).

Listing Broadway theaters would be less useful than current information on what's playing and where. For

that, see *New York* or *The New Yorker* magazine or the
theater pages of *New York Newsday*, the *Village Voice*,
and the *New York Times*—especially the *Times*'s Sunday
"Arts & Leisure" and "Arts & Entertainment Guide"
sections.

INSIDERS' TIPS

Deep-discount vouchers to concerts (sometimes free) and
television shows (always free) and theater (about ⅓
discount on two admissions) are given out by the New
York Convention & Visitors Bureau at 2 Columbus Circle
from 10 A.M. to 5 P.M.

Curtain time is 2 P.M. for matinees, 8 P.M. for evening
performances. There is a trend to matinees on Saturdays and Sundays, with no evening performances on
Sunday or Monday.

INSIDERS' TIPS

FREEBIE: Each summer, Joseph Papp's famed New York
Shakespeare Festival runs from July to Labor Day. The
company performs two plays (not always Shakespeare)
Tuesdays through Sundays at 8 P.M. in the Delacorte
Theatre, Central Park (near West 81st Street, tel 861-
7277). Tickets are distributed at the theater from 6 P.M.
the day of performance, one per person. Arrive in early
afternoon (with reading matter) and expect to wait in
line, because these tickets are coveted.

Off-Broadway and Off-Off-Broadway Theaters

These are usually closed Mondays, and often have
matinees both Friday and Saturday and one performance on Sunday. A selection of the active and consistently most interesting:

Actors Playhouse, 100 Seventh Ave. South. Tel.
691-6226. In addition to professional performances,
presents free Monday evening one-act plays, mono-
logues, scenes in "Actors' Sketchbook" series. Call for
information.

Cherry Lane, 38 Commerce St. (west of Seventh
Ave.). Tel. 989-2020.

Chicago City Limits, 351 East 74th St. Tel. 772-8707.

Equity Library, 103rd St. and Riverside Drive. Tel. 663-2028.

La Mama E.T.C., 74A East 4th St. Tel. 475-7710. One of the leading long-time avant-garde laboratories.

Lucille Lortel, 121 Christopher St. Tel. 924-8782.

Mitzi Newhouse, Lincoln Center, 150 West 65th St. Tel. 787-6868.

Promenade, Broadway at West 76th St. Tel. 580-1313.

Provincetown Playhouse, 133 MacDougal St. Tel. 477-5048, (800) 682-8080.

Public Theater, 425 Lafayette St. Tel. 598-7150. This is the New York Shakespeare Festival's complex of 6 theaters under one roof. Something on the boards almost all the time. At 6 P.M. on the day of the performance, "Quiktix" cut-rate tickets go on sale at lobby (limit, 2 per person).

Quaigh, 108 West 43rd St. (in Hotel Diplomat, 2nd floor). Tel. 382-0618. Specializes in noontime one-acts; bring your lunch, coffee free.

Spanish Repertory Theatre, 138 East 27th St. Tel. 889-2850. Dance, music, comedy, drama by companies direct from Spain or Latin American countries. In Spanish.

Sullivan Street Playhouse, 181 Sullivan St. Tel. 674-3838.

Comedy Showcases

Catch a Rising Star, 77th St. at First Ave. Tel. 794-1906.

Comedy Cellar, 117 MacDougal St. Tel. 254-3630.

Comedy U., 55 Grand St. Tel. 431-4022.

First Amendment, 2 Bond St. Tel. 473-1472.

Good Times, 449 Third Ave. (at 31st St.). Tel. 686-4250.

Improvisation, 358 West 44th St. Tel. 765-8268.

Mostly Magic, 53 Carmine St. Tel. 924-1472.

Stand-up New York, 236 West 78th St. Tel. 595-0850.

Film, Video

For movie aficionados we list here theaters that regularly schedule unusual or important films—revivals, festivals, *auteur* films, etc. Call to find out what's playing.

American Museum of the Moving Image, 34–31 35th St., Astoria, Queens. Tel. (718) 784-4520. Mixed bag of oldies, goodies, silents, significant, slight.

Collective for Living Cinema, 41 White St. Tel. 925-2111. Heavy stuff, for serious film buffs.

Donnell Library, 20 West 53rd St. Tel. 621-0618. Free daytime showings at this New York Public Library branch.

Film at the Public, 425 Lafayette St. Tel. 598-7150.

Film Forum 2, 57 Watts St., west of Ave. of the Americas. Tel. 431-1590.

Japan Society, 333 East 47th St. Tel. 752-3015. Often screens retrospectives of great Japanese directors or festivals on specific themes.

Lincoln Center. Write Film Society of Lincoln Center, 140 West 65th St. 10023. Tel. 877-1800.

Millennium Film Workshop, 66 East 4th St. Tel. 673-0090. Avant-garde and experimental filmmakers showcase.

Museum of Broadcasting, see New York with Plenty of Time, "Museums of Special Interest."

Museum of Modern Art, 11 West 53rd St. Tel. 708-9490. Significant, historically important films from all quarters of the globe.

Whitney Museum of American Art, 75th St. at Madison Ave. Tel. 570-0537. American films, many from waaaaay back.

Regency, 67th St. at Broadway. Tel. 724-3700.

Thalia SoHo, 15 Vandam St. west of Ave. of the Americas. Tel. 675-0498.

Theater 80, 80 St. Marks Pl. Tel. 254-7400.

Music and Dance

Check listings in the media or call *On Stage Hotline* at 587-1111.

INSIDERS' TIPS

Half-price tickets to dance, opera, and concerts are sold at a nonprofit ticket booth in Bryant Park, Avenue of the Americas between 40th and 42nd streets, behind the New York Public Library. Open Tuesday through Saturday from noon to 2 P.M. and 3 to 7 P.M.; opens an hour earlier Wednesday and Saturday, has Sunday hours from noon to 6 P.M. Closed Monday. Tel. 382-2323. Cash or traveler's checks only.

Asia Society, 70th St. at Park Ave. Tel. 288-6400. Outstanding artists from Asian nations in a jewel of a theater.

Carnegie Hall, 881 Seventh Ave. (at 57th St.) 10019. Tel. 247-7800. Exquisitely renovated, this is one of the world's premier concert halls on every count—especially acoustics.

City Center Theater, 131 West 55th St. Tel. 246-8989. This cavernous Arabic hall has a varied menu of excellent music and dance. Beware acrophobia in second balcony and avoid dead sound areas directly beneath balconies.

Joyce Theater, 175 Eighth Ave. Tel. 242-0800. Dance is the main attraction here.

Juilliard School of Music, 155 West 65th St. at Lincoln Center Plaza. Tel. 799-5000. Frequent concerts and recitals at this outstanding training institution.

INSIDERS' TIPS

Want to hear tomorrow's musical stars today—for free? Check the Juilliard School of Music, Lincoln Center Plaza, for upcoming recitals. Tel. 799-5000.

Lincoln Center, 140 West 65th St. at Broadway (between Columbus and Amsterdam Aves.). Tel. 877-2011. Includes the following theaters:

- **Alice Tully Hall,** tel. 362-1911. For chamber works.
- **Avery Fisher Hall,** tel. 874-2424. Home of the New York Philharmonic.
- **Library Museum of the Performing Arts,** tel. 870-1630. For *free* recitals and special presentations weekdays at 4 P.M. and Saturdays at 2:30 P.M.

- **Metropolitan Opera House,** tel. 362-6000. Home of the Met.
- **New York State Theater,** tel 870-5570. Visiting national dance and folk groups usually appear here.

Metropolitan Museum (Grace Rainey Rogers Auditorium), 82nd St. at Fifth Ave. Tel. 570-3949.

92nd Street Y, 92nd St. at Lexington Ave. Tel. 427-4410. Fields a lively menu of music and dance.

Town Hall, 123 West 44th St. Tel. 840-2824. For concerts, recitals, chamber and small groups.

Music and Dance in Other Boroughs

Brooklyn Academy of Music, 30 Lafayette Ave., Brooklyn. Tel. (718) 636-4100. BAM, as it is affectionately known, fields a world-class roster of dance and musical offerings.

Brooklyn Center for the Performing Arts, Nostrand Ave. at Ave. H, Brooklyn College. Tel. (718) 434-1900.

Bargemusic Concerts, Fulton Ferry Landing, Brooklyn. Tel. (718) 624-4061. The Manhattan skyline provides an unforgettable backdrop.

Concerts of Pop, Folk, Jazz, and Rock

Check the latest listings in the media.

INSIDERS' TIPS

Every summer there is a major jazz festival (once called Newport, recently the JVC Jazz Festival) that draws top talent from around the world. Some concerts are outdoors and free. Check with New York Convention & Visitors Bureau, 2 Columbus Circle 10019. Tel. 360-1333.

Citicorp Atrium, 53rd St. at Lexington Ave. Usually noon or 5:30 P.M., free.

South Street Seaport Pier 17 Pavilion at East River and Fulton St. Different group(s) every day, free.

Weill Recital Hall, Carnegie Hall, Seventh Ave. at 57th St. Tel. 247-7800.

Spectacles and "Performance Art"

Call to confirm dates, times.

Danspace at St. Mark's Church, Second Ave. at East 10th St. Tel. 674-8112. Experimental, works in progress. Far out.

Darinka, 118 East 1st St. Tel. 598-0157. Experimental, emphasis on music. Far out.

P.S. 122 (Performance Space 122), 150 First Ave. (at 9th St.). Tel. 477-5288. Experimental, works in progress. Far out.

Radio City Music Hall, Ave. of the Americas at West 50th St. Tel. 757-3100. Home of the Rockettes and extravaganzas at Easter, Christmas, and otherwise. Classics, traditional, far in.

Gambling

The games you find in Las Vegas and foreign resorts (roulette, baccarat, blackjack, craps) are illegal in New York State. The big (legal) thrills in gambling here are the New York State Lottery (chances sold at grocery, drug, and news stores) and betting on the horses. You can play the ponies at the track or in *Off-Track Betting* parlors. For the OTB office nearest you, tel. 704-5451.

USEFUL ADDRESSES AND TELEPHONE NUMBERS (ALL AREA CODE 212 UNLESS OTHERWISE NOTED)

Emergency Telephone Numbers

911 (or 0)	Police, fire, ambulance
577-0111	Consumer complaints, New York City Consumer Affairs Dept.
533-6200	Consumer complaints, Better Business Bureau

577-7777	Crime Victims' Hotline
679-3966	Dental Emergency Service (of Dental Society of NY)
(718) 238-2100	Doctors on Call (24 hours, all boroughs)
566-0972	Mayor's Office of the Handicapped, 52 Chambers St., New York City
582-1462	New York County Medical Society
755-2266	Kaufman's Pharmacy, 24 hour, Lexington Ave. at East 50th St.
247-1538	Windsor Pharmacy, 8 A.M.–midnight, Ave. of the Americas at West 58th St.
764-7667	Poison Control Center
239-2533	Police car tow center
732-7706	Rape Help Line

Useful Information

264-4462	Federal Information Center
971-7176	General Post Office, 8th Ave. at West 33rd St (8 A.M.–midnight).
625-6200	Lost property
755-4100	New York City parks and special events (mostly free)
999-1111	New York City Report (daily events, recorded)
962-7111	Telegrams (to send them via Western Union)
976-1616	Time
976-1212	Weather, local New York metropolitan area
394-5561	Weather, national

Travel Information

(800) AIR-RIDE (247-7433)	For advice on best and/or cheapest routes to city airports.

736-4545	Amtrak, Penn Station
697-3374	East Side Airlines Terminal, Carey bus
895-1695	East Side Heliport
656-4520	JFK International Airport
476-5000	La Guardia Airport
(718) 739-4200	Long Island RR, Penn Station
(201) 961-2000	Newark International Airport
397-8222	New York Convention & Visitors Bureau, 2 Columbus Circle, Central Park West and 59th St.
(718) 330-1234	Subway and bus information (New York Transit Authority)
564-8484	Port Authority Bus Terminal, Eighth Ave. at West 41st St.
747-0930	Taxi and Limousine Commission (to report a problem with a taxi)
999-1234	Traffic report on highways, bridges, tunnels

LOWER HUDSON VALLEY, WESTCHESTER, AND ROCKLAND COUNTIES

A day, a weekend, or even a week along the Hudson River introduces you to one of the most intriguing, historic, and scenic areas in the state, where there is much to do and see—some of the most important homes in the United States, battlefields, country inns, wineries, art galleries, and a plethora of antiques shops. And all of it is easily accessible from New York City.

The best way to go is by car, although with limited time you might take a one-day Dayliner boat cruise, via the Hudson River Day Line (see New York with Plenty of Time).

By car, you can drive north almost to Hudson on the east side of the river, cross the bridge to Catskill, and loop back south to the city. There are 5 bridges that cross the Hudson, so you can hopscotch back and forth as whim or time dictates (there are tolls eastbound, but not westbound).

The 309-mile-long Hudson, since the day when Henry Hudson sailed up it in 1609, has always attracted Europeans. Traders used it to transport goods from New York to Albany, and prosperous Dutch and later English and American settlers built their mansions on hilltops above its swirling waters.

THE LOWER HUDSON

To begin your Hudson journey, take I-87 north, then I-287 west to Tarrytown, where you get on to NY-9 north. Tarrytown has 5 sites of special interest. Primary, in our view, is Sunnyside ♛ ♛ ♛, West Sunny-side Lane (tel. [914] 631-8200).

This was the home of America's first internationally acclaimed writer, Washington Irving, who in 1835 bought what was then a simple Dutch farmhouse. Over the years he made many changes and additions, and the house today is almost as Irving left it.

Irving called the house his "snuggery," and its numerous turrets, chimneys, gables, and stairstep roof give it enormous character. Inside, the many little rooms are full of Irving's own belongings, including his desk, piano, and furniture. You'll see Irving's shaving kit, flute, pipes, and walking sticks, and his cloak hanging from a peg as if he has just returned from a walk. (If you're lucky, you may even meet "Irving." On weekends, a male tour guide dons the cloak and Irving *persona.*) Rarely does a house evoke its owner so vividly.

Contrasting with the hominess of Sunnyside is the 1840 Gothic Revival mansion of Lyndhurst ♛ ♛ ♛, 635 South Broadway (tel. [914] 631-0046). This formal estate on 67 acres was built for Philip K. Paulding, mayor of New York, then enlarged for a later owner, Wall Street financier Jay Gould, one of the richest of the robber barons. It's a splendid example inside and out of affluent late Victorian taste.

Also in Tarrytown on Route 9 is the Old Dutch Church of Sleepy Hollow ♛, which has been restored to its 1697 Dutch shape. In the adjacent Sleepy Hollow Cemetery, Irving, Andrew Carnegie, and other luminaries are buried. Just being there might evoke images of Ichabod Crane and the Headless Horseman.

Farther north on NY-9 is Philipsburg Manor ♛ ♛, whose origins go back to 1680 when it was the property of a prosperous Dutchman, Frederick Philipse.

The solid fieldstone manor house looks much as it did in the early 18th century, and the old water-powered grist mill is operating again. As you stroll through the garden, past the ducks on the millpond, you get a sense of what farm life was like then.

A final Tarrytown sight is the Union Church of Pocantico Hills ♛ ♛, Route 448 (tel. [914] 631-8200).

In this modest country church you may be surpised to find 9 luminous stained-glass windows by Marc Chagall, depicting Old Testament prophets, and a rose window by Henri Matisse. What are the works of these famous artists doing in such an out-of-the-way place? It helps to know that the Rockefeller estate is nearby at Pocantico Hills. In fact, the Matisse window was a memorial to Abby Aldrich Rockefeller.

Next along the way north is the Van Cortlandt Manor ♛ ♛, just off NY-9 in Croton-on-Hudson. The house and its beautiful 18th-century gardens, "long walk," and outbuildings reflect the style and taste of a prosperous Colonial Dutch-English family, who owned the 80,000-acre property for 260 years.

INSIDERS' TIPS

The Van Cortlandt Manor, Philipsburg Manor, and Sunnyside are all part of Sleepy Hollow Restorations. It is a big saving to buy a single admission to all three sites.

Your next stop as you wend your way north might be at one of our favorite Hudson mansions, Boscobel ♛ ♛ ♛, 4 miles north of Garrison on Route 9D (tel. [914] 265-3638). This elegant Robert Adams–style Federal house, with its Palladian window and unusual wood swag frame, was built in 1804 by States Morris Dyckman. It sits on the crest of a hill with particularly fine river views. (The name Boscobel derives from the Italian *bosco bello*, "beautiful woods.")

In a 45-minute tour, you will enjoy Boscobel's many architectural delights and fine early 19th-century furniture. You'll also hear how Boscobel was literally saved from demolition and moved to its present glorious site.

The tour ends with lemonade and cookies. But allow yourself time to savor the splendid hilltop views (you can see West Point across the way), and to wander along walks lined with potted oleanders, through the well-planned rose garden with 300 species, past weeping cherry and hemlock trees and apple orchards. In the gift shop you can buy Baldwins, Ravensteins, Northern Spys and other apples grown in the orchards.

Just a few miles up 9D is Cold Spring, a delightful river town whose Victorian buildings now shelter antiques and craft shops—a great browsing stop.

At Beacon, there's another house worth your attention: the Madame Brett Homestead♛♛, Van Nydeck Avenue (tel. [914] 831-6533). Dutch in style (1709), its furnishings reflect the taste of 7 generations of a single family, with most of the original furnishings intact.

INSIDERS' TIPS

A "sleeper" is Manitoga♛♛, also in Garrison—80 acres of wild and planned nature trails, waterfalls, streams, and woodlands that the owner, the late designer Russel Wright, created out of an abandoned stone quarry. You can wander the grounds on your own, but if you want a guided tour (that includes Wright's house, Dragon Rock), you need a reservation (tel. [914] 424-3812).

On leaving Beacon, take NY-52E to Fishkill, where there are two 18th-century churches, a block apart on Route 52: the Trinity Episcopal♛, which served as a hospital for American forces in the Revolution, and the more interesting Dutch Reformed Church♛ (now called First Reformed).

The latter has fortresslike, 3-foot-thick walls and was the scene of some derring-do during the same war. It seems an American counterspy (one of our first), Enoch Crosby, was among a group of Loyalists captured by American troops. He was put into the church fortress with the other prisoners, but then, in order to set him free and preserve his double identity, he was allowed to "escape" through an unlocked window. Crosby was believed to be the inspiration for James Fenimore Cooper's novel *The Spy*.

Poughkeepsie, as the largest city (population 29,757) along the Hudson between New York and Albany, has several worthy attractions. Locust Grove♛, South Road (tel. [914] 454-4500), was the home of Samuel F. B. Morse, artist and inventor of the telegraph. It is now open to view, with 19th-century furniture, antiques, china, and paintings (Morse was an accomplished portraitist). The 1847 Italianate Revival mansion has a commanding view of the Hudson.

Poughkeepsie is also the home of Vassar College, the first all-women's college in the United States (founded in 1861 by a local brewer, Matthew Vassar). Since the late 1960s it has been co-ed.

Enter Gothic Taylor Gate on Raymond Avenue for a drive through the campus, where you'll have a *précis* of architectural styles, from Gothic and Romanesque right up to the contemporary work of Marcel Breuer. Drop by the Vassar Art Gallery ♛ ♛, which has a choice collection of Oriental ceramics and jade and 20th-century American paintings.

Hyde Park is just 5 miles north on NY-9. Here you'll find the boyhood home of Franklin D. Roosevelt ♛ ♛ ♛, which has been kept as comfortably modest as it was during the last years of our 32nd President's life in the 1940s (if you can call 50 rooms and 9 baths modest).

The large, shuttered Georgian house was nothing more than a frame farmhouse in 1826. Roosevelt's father bought it in 1867, and major additions and renovations were made in 1915. Like so many Hudson mansions, this one too has a commanding overview of the river. Unlike some of the others, it is unpretentious and feels "lived in." FDR's mother, Sara Delano, was an awesome figure in his (and his wife's) life, and her formidable presence is still felt here. The house suffered a fire several years ago, but has been restored.

The FDR Library adjoins the house, and nearby in the rose garden are the simple graves of both FDR and his wife Eleanor. A shuttle bus takes visitors from the parking lot 2 miles to Val-Kill, Eleanor's country home from 1925 until her death in 1962.

INSIDERS' TIPS

The CIA (Culinary Institute of America), one of the best cooking schools in the country, is located in Hyde Park and has three restaurants open to the public. For lunch or dinner at either of the fancier twosome, you must reserve *well*—sometimes weeks—in advance. (See Insiders' Information at the end of this chapter.)

Five miles up NY-9 is the Vanderbilt Mansion♛♛♛, a prime example of the late 19th-century Beaux Arts style. The 5-story, Renaissance-style house was built in 1898 as an enlarged copy of the Petit Trianon for Frederick W. Vanderbilt (grandson of the Commodore) by the popular architectural firm of McKim, Mead & White.

Its 54 rooms are funished so opulently (at a cost of $1.5 million in 1898) that one is reminded anew of the meaning of the term "Gilded Age." Seeing the two Hyde Park houses in tandem is a study in contrasts: the Vanderbilt mansion imposing and formal, the FDR house casual and countrified.

Nearby is the little stone St. James Episcopal Church, in whose 1844 English Gothic interior generations of Roosevelts, Vanderbilts, and Livingstons worshiped.

A few miles north, at Staatsburg, is another classic Hudson house, the Mills Mansion♛♛♛ in Mills-Norrie State Park. The property is aged. It belonged first, in 1792, to Morgan Lewis, the third governor of New York. His original house gave way in 1832 to a Greek Revival one. Later, in 1895, when the property was inherited by Ruth Livingston Mills (whose husband Ogden later was Herbert Hoover's Secretary of the Treasury), it was remodeled and enlarged to French Renaissance proportions by McKim, Mead & White. The architects hired a Parisian firm to do the interiors, and the effects are dazzlingly rococo in Louis XV and XVI styles.

No expense was spared. There are 14 bathrooms, 25 fireplaces, a 50-foot long, 30-foot-wide dining room with marble floors and walls, an oak-paneled library the same size as the dining room, Flemish tapestries, mammoth Chinese celadon bowls, Japanese bronze vases, gilded plasterwork, and cabinets still stocked with Vichy water from the 1930s. In its heyday, maintenance of the house and its 198 acres required a staff of 24 in the house, 120 on the grounds. Those were the days.

Six miles north is Rhinebeck, whose roots date back to 1686. Today it is a tourist mecca, with bookstores, country stores, and craft shops. But the town's most famous attraction—and a delightful one it is—is the Old Rhinebeck Aerodrome♛♛ on Stone Church Road (tel. 758-8610). If you're visiting any Saturday or Sunday afternoon from May 15 through October, you'll know you're getting close by the traffic, the crowds, and the noises overhead, signifying that the air show is going on.

You'll see mock "dogfights" staged between vintage World War I aircraft. Before and after the air show (which begins at 2:30 P.M. and lasts 90 minutes), you can have a barnstorming ride in an open-cockpit 1929 biplane. Even when there's no air show in progress, you can visit the Air Museum, which is chock-full of more than 50 World War I and older pioneer aircraft. Among the prizes are a 1909 Bleriot, the Curtiss Pusher Model D, Fokkers, a Sopwith Snipe, a Siemens-Schuckert D-III, and a Pitcairn Mailplane.

Rhinebeck's older landmark is the Beekman Arms♛♛, whose doors first opened in 1766. It has been called America's oldest continuously operating inn, and low overhead beams, uneven floorboards, age-burnished wood, and hooked rugs all add to the vintage image.

Lafayette once stayed in room 21. Aaron Burr had a confrontation with another guest in the dining room in 1813, and William Jennings Bryan once spoke to a political gathering from a second-story window. Benjamin Harrison, FDR, Gore Vidal, Norman Mailer, Paul Newman, and Brooke Shields have graced the premises at various times.

PERILS & PITFALLS

Charming as the Beekman Arms is, food is not its strong suit. Have a drink, then move on elsewhere for a meal (preferably the CIA).

Less than 10 miles north of Rhinebeck you'll come to Clermont♛♛, on NY-9G, just 4 miles south of Germantown. Clermont was the ancestral home of Chancellor Robert R. Livingston, one of the five men elected to draft the Declaration of Independence. (Livingston was father-in-law to Robert Fulton and helped him in the development of his steamboat, named, not surprisingly, the *Clermont.*) You can wander the lovely grounds, picnic, and hike nature trails year-round, but the mansion itself is open only from late May to October, Wednesday through Sunday. (For information on hours, tel. [518] 537-4240).

Less than 15 miles farther north is Olana♕♕♕, one of the great houses of the Hudson River valley. This was the home of Hudson River painter Frederick E. Church. It looms above the river on a hilltop like the palace of an Oriental potentate, with towers and turrets, loggias and open Arabic archways, reminiscent of the Alhambra.

In his fantasies, that may very well be what Church had in mind. His friend and mentor Thomas Cole introduced him to the Hudson River valley in 1844. By the time he was ready to build Olana in 1872, Church had traveled extensively abroad, and knew the kind of location and house he wanted. He even designed the landscape to make his fantasy complete.

Virtually every room was created to capitalize on the sweeping views of river and lake below. In the house interior, Church indulged all his romantic notions and those of his period, when things Arabic or Persian were the rage. Oriental carpets, draperies, low-slung, elaborately carved Indian chairs, mother-of-pearl-inlaid tables, Oriental artifacts, delicate fretted and arched windows and doorways, repetitive stenciling around doorways, all reflect this obsession with the Islamic Middle East and with complexity of designs and color. Even the name Olana has Eastern origins: it is a Latin corruption of the Arabic *Al'ana*, "Our Place on High."

It is the house of an artist, and because it remained in Church's family until acquired as a New York State Historic Site, it is just as Church lived in it, as he loved it and as he wanted it to be. As a reflection of a very specific artistic sensibility (that also reflects a period in history), Olana is unique.

The house now is open to the public on guided tours from late May until late October (tel. [518] 828-0135 for hours and precise dates). You may reserve your tour ahead of time; the 45-minute tours are limited to 12 people at a time to preserve the house.

The 250-acre grounds are open year-round, from 8 A.M. to sunset. And they are glorious, with towering pines, birch and dogwoods, as the road winds through beautiful orchards, past a lake, up to the turreted 5-story stone-and-brick house and its magical overview of the Hudson. Church once wrote a friend, "I think it better to reside on a mountain which overlooks the world than to be a mere creeping thing trying to see it as a mass of details. From an eminence you take in the beauties only." That pretty much encapsulates what he accomplished with Olana.

Just 5 miles north of Olana is the old town of Hudson. Its long ribbon of a Main Street has been restored, and many of the old brick Federal row houses are quite handsome. The residential area melts into the commercial section, where the storefronts dating from the 1920s and 1930s are so much of a piece that one can understand why so many scenes of the movie *Ironweed* (about Albany in the 1930s) were filmed here.

NY-9 north brings you next to Kinderhook, one of the most charming of the river towns, with numerous Colonial, Victorian, and Gothic Victorian houses along quiet, tree-shaded streets. Martin Van Buren, the eighth U.S. President, was born here, and a marker on Hudson Street notes his birth site in December 5, 1782. His retirement home, called Lindenwald♛, is just 2 miles south on Route 9H—a plain but comely cream-colored brick Federalist house with cocoa trim, set back from the road on 13 acres. From mid-June to September, from 9 A.M. to 5 P.M., the 36-room house is open to view.

A companion piece to the Martin Van Buren Homestead is the 1737 red brick Luykas Van Alen House♛, nearer to town on the same road. According to tradition, Katrina Van Tassel (immortalized by Washington Irving) lived here. The house, even today, looks straight out of a Dutch painting. Fittingly, it is now a museum of 18th-century Dutch artifacts and culture.

Just a few miles farther north is Old Chatham♛♛, where the 18th-and-19th-century sect of Shakers—officially known as the United Society of Believers in

Christ's Second Appearing (no wonder the name was shortened)—established one of their first American settlements in 1774. The hardworking communal sect prospered for decades, but eventually died out because of internal dissent, strict rules of celibacy, and other problems.

What remains today at Old Chatham is an exemplary Shaker Museum 👑 👑 👑 on Shaker Museum Road, along with 7 outbuildings—an herb house (moved from a Connecticut Shaker community), a museum shop, and a Shaker reference library. The museum provides a wonderful look at the 200-year history of an unusual, inventive sect that created remarkable furniture, household objects, and crafts by hand, leaving a legacy of fine craftsmanship that is admired and avidly sought today.

Shaker productivity is evident in the medicine room, seed department, kitchen with all its implements, wash shop, cooperage/wheelwright shop, meeting room, and ministry dining room, all of them full of objects created by and in some cases invented by the Shakers. The museum is open daily from 10 A.M. to 5 P.M. May 1 through October 31 (tel. [518] 794-9100).

INSIDERS' TIPS

The musuem shop sells well-made reproductions of Shaker furniture. Also, the Shaker Museum Antiques and Arts Festival is held on the first Saturday in August. For collectors, it's a time to browse the offerings of 175 or more dealers' wares from New England and mid-Atlantic states. Music, foods, and exhibits are part of the scene. For specific dates this year, tel. (518) 794-9100.

THE WEST SIDE

Now take I-90 across the Rip Van Winkle Bridge to Catskill, on the west side of the river. As its name suggests, the town is a springboard to the Catskill Mountains. This is also the area in which Irving set his story about the man who slept for 20 years, dozing off when King George III ruled the country, awakening to learn about President Washington.

Catskill was home to Thomas Cole, an English painter who discovered his concept of the American wilderness in the Catskills and settled in the nearest little village to paint it. Cole influenced others through the haunting beauty of his Catskill Mountain scenes, and was the founder of what has been labeled the Hudson River school of painting. His plain clapboard house ♛, 218 Spring Street (tel. [518] 943-6533), is open to visitors Wednesday through Saturday, 10 A.M. to 5 P.M., Sunday 1 to 5 P.M. in the summer, and by appointment other times of the year.

A brief detour north on NY-385 takes you through Athens, an old river town still graced with many handsome houses. About 7 miles farther north is Coxsackie. The Bronck Museum ♛ ♛ here, on Pieter Bronck Road, is a collection of early Dutch houses (1663–1738) on property owned by Pieter Bronck (brother of Jonah, whose vast "bouwerie," his 500-acre holdings in New York City, became the Bronx).

Among the numerous old Dutch buildings, you'll see a 13-sided barn. The houses and their furnishings provide a fascinating glimpse of early Dutch life. Open summers only (tel. [518] 731-8862).

Just 10 miles west of Catskill is the Catskill Game Farm ♛, an enjoyable outing if you have children along. Here you may see as many as 2,000 animals, some wild but semi-tamed and feedable, including deer, llamas, and antelope. There are also rare creatures such as prehistoric Przewalski horses from Mongolia, a pair of South African white rhinos, and a pair of Burmese takin (a cross between goats and antelopes, the only ones in the United States).

En route from Catskill south to Kingston, antiquers like to roam the village of Saugerties for buys.

The Quarryman's Museum and Opus 40, 7480 Fite Road (tel. [914] 246-3400), are unique. The first is a collection of quarry and other worker and artisan tools, well arranged in a museum setting. Opus 40 is the lifelong endeavor of sculptor Harvey Fite, who spent almost 40 years creating a monumental bluestone sculpture that rises eerily from an abandoned quarry—and covers more than 6 acres.

Kingston is a lovely little pre-Revolution town, settled in 1653 by the Dutch. The first meeting of the state
senate was held here, and the state's first constitution
was adopted here in 1777. Later that year, John
Vaughan, a British general, "wantonly set fire to the
town in reprisal for the Revolutionary activities that
occurred there." Vaughan saw Kingston differently, of
course. In his words, "[Kingston] being a nursery for
almost every villain in the country, I judged it necessary
. . . to reduce the place to ashes."

Kingston recovered, and much of the historic area is
well restored, beginning with the Senate House ♛ ♛
itself, a sturdy stone structure of 1676 built in the
Dutch style. Notice the irregular bull's-eye glass in the
doors (the guide explains that the glass was put in the
doors for added light, because windows were taxed),
and some of the original Delft fireplace tiles are back in
place.

INSIDERS' TIPS

A guided walking tour of the historic 8-block
Stockade ♛ area can be arranged by the Kingston Visitor's Center, 7 Albany Avenue (tel. [914] 338-5100), or
by writing Friends of Historic Kingston, U.P.O. 3763,
Kingston, NY 12401. At the Visitor's Center, you can
pick up a pamphlet with map that helps you make a
self-guided walking tour of this fascinating section of
town, chockablock with interesting houses.

Restoration along Rondout Creek, the inlet from the
Hudson, has made Kingston's waterfront a special delight. The recently refurbished Hudson River Maritime
Center, 1 Rondout Landing, has daily boat tours of the
1912 Kingston Light, one of 5 lighthouses left on the
river. A Trolley Museum of New York is nearby at 89
East Strand.

Inland on I-87 is New Paltz, which we have included
in our Catskills chapter, but it is easily visited as you
swoop south along the Hudson.

Following NY-9W southward, you reach Newburgh.
The 1750 Jonathan Hasbrouck house ♛ ♛, 84 Liberty
Street (tel. [914] 562-1195), served as Washington's

headquarters for more than 16 months (1782–83) at the war's end. It's a typical Dutch fieldstone house furnished as Washington (and Martha, who lived here with him) kept it. It was here that Washington rejected attempts to turn the new nation into a monarchy. A small museum is nearby on the grounds.

INSIDERS' TIPS

Consider a bit of winery-hopping. Among the wineries that welcome visitors for tours and tastings are the Hudson Valley Winery in Highland (with great river views); Windsor Vineyards, Cottage Vineyards, and Benmarl Wine Company, all in Marlboro; and, inland, Baldwin Vineyards at Pine Bush.

Brotherhood Winery, Washingtonville, is America's oldest winery, founded by 18th-century monks. A tour includes a visit to the ancient underground cellar where the wine is aged in handmade wooden casks. There are tastings, and a cheerful picnic site is on the grounds. Most of the wineries charge a parking fee (about $2), but the tastings are usually free.

Five miles south, at Vails Gate, is the New Windsor Cantonment♛, site of the last encampment of the Continental Army. During the summer, drills and demonstrations in full Revolutionary War uniform are staged and are free to the public.

Just east of Vails Gate is Knox's Headquarters♛, Forge Hill Road (tel. [914] 561-5498). The sturdy 18th-century stone house belonged to the Ellison family. During the Revolutionary War they shared their home with Generals Henry Knox and Horatio Gates and other American officers. A visit gives you a glimpse of what this military occupation of a private household must have been like.

The Hudson twists and turns dramatically along the next stretch of NY-9W south, making for some beautiful vistas between Newburgh and West Point. Art aficionados will surely want to stop at Storm King State Park, Mountainville, to visit Storm King Art Center♛ ♛ ♛, a 200-acre sculpture park with some 130 permanent works by Mark Di Suvero, David Smith, Alex Liberman, and others, and a museum containing the Lipman Collection of sculpture from the Whitney Museum of Art. Storm King is only open from May 31 to October 31, daily (except Tuesday) from noon to 5:30 P.M.

Military and/or history buffs have more treats in store in the next few miles south. First there's West Point♛ ♛ ♛, where you can tour the U.S. Military Academy. You may find the Cadet Chapel, restored Fort Putnam, Trophy Point, and the West Point Museum of greatest interest. The museum has the largest military collection in the Western Hemisphere. River views from West Point are superlative.

INSIDERS' TIPS

The Cadet Review takes place before every home football game in the fall, and at certain other times as well. If you want to see it, check in advance at the Public Affairs Office, Building 600, U.S. Military Academy, West Point 10996 (tel. [914] 938-3507).

The other military "special" is Stony Point♛ ♛, about 20 miles south on NY-9W. (You'll pass through Bear Mountain State Park♛ ♛ en route, and may want to pause to stroll the nature trail, visit the zoo, or just enjoy the spectacular river views at Jones Point.)

This is the locale of an important Revolutionary War battle. At midnight, July 15–16, 1779, General "Mad" Anthony Wayne stormed British fortifications and secured control of the river for the Continental Army, thus eliminating any further threat to Washington's forces. You can visit the museum to bone up on the story of the battle, then walk the battle sites, earthworks, and hiking trails.

A few miles south, in Nyack, you'll discover the Hopper House Art Center, 82 North Broadway. This is where realist painter Edward Hopper was born in 1882, but don't expect to see much of Hopper left except a few posters and postcards. The house features monthly exhibits of other local artists' work. Nyack is a gentrified little village of gingerbread houses, with enough antique and craft shops to keep even the most dedicated shopper busy for hours.

Below Nyack a few miles is the venerable town of Tappan♛, where Major John André was imprisoned in 1755 in the '76 House (which was a tavern at the time and is now a restaurant) and later hanged in 1780 on André Hill. André had expected to "be shot like an officer and a gentleman." The monument on André Hill was erected in 1879 by Cyrus Field, and has been subject to numerous attacks (twice with explosives) by chauvinistic vandals.

Also in Tappan is the De Windt House (1700)♛, Rockland County's oldest house. It was Washington's headquarters 5 different times betwen 1780 and 1783. Legend has it that during the period when André was tried and hanged, Washington closed the shutters and never left his room.

WESTCHESTER COUNTY

Throughout time, Westchester has been a region of evolutions that began when 13 Indian tribes shared its woods and Henry Hudson sailed up the river to start the European colonization process. John James Audubon found the area still pretty much a forest primeval in the early 19th century, but the coming of the railroad in 1844 and subsequent settlers—farmers and wealthy escapees from New York playing country gentlemen— ended that; by the 1880s, the county was 80 percent cleared.

Only later did residents recognize the beauty of a tree-sheltered environment. Today the county's 450-square-mile area—bordered by the Hudson River on the west and Long Island Sound on the east, stretching north to Cortland, Yorktown, and North Salem, and south to Pelham, Mount Vernon, and New Rochelle—is once again 80 percent wooded.

It's probably no accident that the cocktail was first created in Westchester, the archetypal suburb, that platform or paddle tennis—a favorite winter sport of East Coast executives—was invented here, and that the first American golf game was played in the center of what we now know as Yonkers.

Following the Hudson takes you along Westchester's west side. Two highways make parallel routes through the county's east side. I-95 is the fast coastal road that takes you quickly from New York City northeast to Providence and Boston. More scenic is the Hutchinson River Parkway (nicknamed "the Hutch"), which winds its way north from the Bronx to the Connecticut line (where it changes its name to the Merritt Parkway).

PERILS & PITFALLS

Westchester's third parallel road is the venerable Boston Post Road, or just the Post Road (or US-1), as it is called these days. This modernized ribbon of highway winds from New York all the way northeast to Boston, as it did 200 years ago. But then stagecoaches left New York 3 times a week, and the journey took six 19-hour days. Forget the romance of the name; today the Post Road is a clogged stop-and-go bottleneck of traffic lights and commercial (and often tacky) strips—to be avoided whenever possible.

Many Westchester towns that are bustling modern suburbs today have ancient origins and their share of history. Rye was founded in 1600, Mamaroneck and Port Chester in 1650. An important Revolutionary War battle took place in White Plains, which the Algonquin Indians knew as *Qua-rop-pas*, or White Marshes, and which many executives now call corporate headquarters.

You can still see (and visit) Tom Paine's Cottage ♛, 20 Sicard, in New Rochelle. John Jay, the first Chief Justice of the U.S. Supreme Court, is buried in Rye, and you can visit his family homestead near Katonah.

Westchester's east side makes a pleasant half-day, whole day, or weekend excursion from New York City—about a 30-to-40-minute drive. There are comfortable hotels, good restaurants, and enough sights and activities to keep you hopping. Distances are short between towns.

Among the major sights is the John Jay Homestead ♛ on NY-22 (tel. [914] 232-5651), between

Katonah and Bedford. Jay built the comfortable frame house in 1800 and spent the last 29 years of his life here. The house has been called "Mount Vernon North," which is a sizable overstatement.

Katonah has two other attractions. In the village center is the Katonah Gallery👑 (attached to the old public library), 28 Bedford Road. It features top-notch art exhibits, which often travel elsewhere in the country. The gallery also shows (and sells) the work of area artists (tel. [914] 232-9555).

Outside town is the Caramoor Center for Music and the Arts👑👑, Girdle Ridge Road, a wondrous wooded sanctuary. On the grounds, an imposing Italianate villa, built in the 1930s, is the setting for a series of summer concerts in which leading chamber groups perform in a graceful, open Spanish courtyard.

Many concert-goers come early and picnic on the beautifully maintained lawn. It is also possible at times to tour the house; many of the rooms were brought intact from European palaces, and there are lavish objects and art, from Chinese porcelains to Renaissance furniture, paintings, and sculpture (tel. [914] 232-5053).

Another focal point for a visit should be SUNY (State University of New York) at Anderson Hill Road in Purchase. On the tree-shaded campus you'll find the Neuberger Museum👑👑, with an extensive collection of African art and 20th-century painting and sculpture. The campus is studded with contemporary sculpture by name artists. It is the site, also, of the multifaceted Pepsico Summerfare, a festival of the arts.

The SUNY campus is on Anderson Hill Road, Purchase, reached from Exit 28 on the Hutchinson River Parkway.

Across Anderson Hill Road you'll find Pepsico Sculpture Gardens👑👑👑 on the grounds of Pepsico Corporation. The gardens are open without charge to the public, and people are free to wander from one major work of art to another, along paths marked by groves of rare trees and shrubs. There are dozens of modern works scattered throughout the grounds, among them major works by Alexander Calder, George

Segal, Louise Nevelson, and others. It is possible to spend half a day here, enjoying the sculpture, the vistas, and the plantings.

INSIDERS' TIPS

Pepsico Summerfare, held mid-July to early August at the Performing Arts Center of SUNY, is a bang-up cultural festival, with dozens of sparkling, innovative events rarely duplicated in such intensity elsewhere. Every day features truly spectacular events: opera, concert, theater, dance with major companies and stars. Call (914) 253-5900 for upcoming dates, schedule, and prices.

In North Salem there's another treat: the Hammond Museum with its Oriental Stroll Gardens, off June Road (tel. [914] 669-5135). The museum features changing exhibits, but it's the tranquil gardens that are the draw: an array of Oriental trees and flowers, highlighted by Japanese stone and cast-iron lanterns, around a scenic pond.

INSIDERS' INFORMATION FOR THE HUDSON VALLEY AREA

Amenia
(Dutchess County; Area Code 914)

Hotel
Troutbeck ♛ ♛ ♛ ♛
Leedsville Rd., P.O. Box 26, 12601 Tel. 373-8581
2 persons in double, $250–400 (includes 3 meals, open bar)
Historic 1920s English-style manor, secluded 422-acre property with wildlife preserve and lake. 31 rooms, bar, restaurant (♛ ♛) with New American specialties; 2 swimming pools, tennis courts, library. Fulfill your fantasies about being Lord or Lady Gotrocks. Antiques, wood-burning fireplaces, morning newspaper, many extra touches, friendly staff. Meals served from Friday dinner through Sunday brunch only; reservations essential.

Brewster
(Putnam County; Area Code 914)

Restaurant
The Arch ♛ ♛ ♛
Route 22. Tel. 279-5011
Prix fixe dinner: $40
Old stucco hilltop house with glassed-in, fieldstone-walled porch, 2 other cozy dining rooms. Beautifully maintained, expertly run, top-notch French menu and matching wine list. Chef-owner George Seitz knows what he's about.

Canaan
(Columbia County; Area Code 518)

Hotel
The Inn at the Shaker Mill Farm ♛ ♛
Cherry Lane, off Route 22. Tel. 794-9345
2 persons in double, $70 (includes breakfast)
Old house conveniently near Shaker sights. 18 rooms plus 2 suites with fireplaces, no TV or room phones; sauna, sun room overlooking waterfall; restaurant (♛) known for abundance; swimming in Queechy Lake; horses. A great weekend-away-from-it-all choice, options nearby: skiing, ice skating, cross-country trails.

Carmel
(Putnam County; Area Code 914)

Restaurant
Dreamwold ♛
Gypsy Trail Rd., Route 301. Tel. 225-3500
Average dinner, $28
This Tudor-style country house overlooks a lake. You can have drinks on the patio and dine inside on standards (steak, scampi, cannelloni, lobster). Closed Mondays and Tuesdays.

Catskill
(Greene County; Area Code 518)

Restaurant
La Rive ♛ ♛
Old King's Rd. (County 47), 7 miles west. Tel. 943-4888
Average dinner: $25
French-accented menu in charming old farmhouse.
Chef-owned favorite. Closed Mondays, also from
November to April.

Central Valley
(Orange County; Area Code 914)

Restaurant
Gasho of Japan ♛
Route 32. Tel. 928-2277
Average dinner: $30
The draw here is not the Japanese steak house (stan-
dard), but the authentic farmhouse transported from
Japan, with Japanese garden setting.

Cold Spring
(Putnam County; Area Code 914)

Hotel
Hudson House ♛ ♛ ♛
2 Main St., 10516. Tel. 265-9355
2 persons in twin, $60–75 (includes continental break-
fast)
Restored old clapboard house (1832) facing river in
town center. 14 rooms, no TV or room phones; bar,
restaurant, bike rentals. Furnished with antiques, folk
art, homey, witty, and original touches by owner Mary
Pat Bevis, former New York City ballet dancer. A warm,
welcoming delight of an inn. Closed January.
Restaurant
Plumbush ♛ ♛
Route 9D. Tel. 265-3904
Prix fixe dinner: $27.50
Try the fresh trout, veal, other continental specialties,
and home-baked goodies in this comfortable "hideaway." Dine outdoors in clement weather, listen to live

piano Saturday evenings. Closed Tuesdays, also Mondays in winter.

Shopping

Cold Spring Antique Center, 91 Main St. 12 dealers under one roof, lots of variety. Open daily.

River Cruises

Ring Maritime, Inc., c/o Hudson House, 2 Main St. Luxurious cruises for 6 to 8 aboard traditional 32-foot ketch; 2-hour, half-day, or full day or overnight cruises May through October.

Dover Plains
(Dutchess County; Area Code 914)

Hotel

Old Drovers Inn♛ ♛

Old Post Road at Route 22, 12522. Tel. 832-9311

2 persons in twin, $100–120

Delightful time-worn clapboard 1750 house in wooded setting. 3 rooms, private baths, no TV or room phones; bar and excellent restaurant (♛ ♛) with imaginative menu. Beautifully furnished with sleigh beds, antiques, woodburning fireplaces, restful getaway for weekenders. Closed Tuesdays and Wednesdays, also 3 weeks in December.

Fishkill
(Dutchess County; Area Code 914)

Theater

Cecilwood Playhouse, Route 52. Tel. 897-9620. Summer theater specializing in Broadway hits and big-name performers.

Garrison
(Putnam County; Area Code 914)

Hotel

The Bird and Bottle♛ ♛ ♛

Nelson's Corners, Route 9, 10524. Tel. 424-3000

2 persons in twin, $100

1761 house on 5 wooded acres with stream. 4 rooms

(all with fireplace), bar, restaurant (♛♛). A favorite weekend getaway spot for city dwellers. Cozy, low-ceilinged dining rooms with fireplaces, exposed beams. Outside terrace dining amid flowering trees. Closed Mondays and Tuesdays, mid-November to April.

Garrison's Landing
(Putnam County; Area Code 914)

Hotel
Golden Eagle Inn♛♛
Garrison's Landing, 10524. Tel. 424-3067
2 persons in twin: $90 (includes continental breakfast)
An imposing 3-story brick houselike inn faces West Point across the Hudson. 5 rooms (2 with shared bath), no TV or room phones; café. Serving wayfarers since 1840 (seen in the film *Hello, Dolly*). Comfortable, individualized rooms, terrace overlooking river, great views. Closed January to March.

Granite Springs
(Westchester County; Area Code 914)

Restaurant
Maxime's♛♛♛
Old Tomahawk Rd., Junction Route 118. Tel. 248-7200
Prix fixe dinner: $45
Country elegance with fireplace, polished service, classic French menu, special occasion dining. Sizable wine cellar. Closed Mondays and Tuesdays.

Hartsdale
(Westchester County; Area Code 914)

Restaurant
Auberge Argenteuil♛♛♛
42 Healy Ave. Tel. 948-0597
Average dinner: $25
A favorite with knowledgeable Westchesterites for its Gallic flair, French Empire decor. Quail in cream with grapes is just one of many succulent specialties.

High Falls
(Ulster County; Area Code 914)

Hotel
Captain Schoonmaker's 1760 Stone House♛ ♛
Route 213, 12440. Tel. 687-7946
2 persons in double, $55–65 (includes continental breakfast)
Historic 1760 stone house near canal. 12 rooms (shared baths), no room phones, elaborate breakfast served on request, no other meals. Well-restored, some rooms with fireplaces, all with antiques. Friendly management.

Restaurant
DePuy Canal House Tavern♛ ♛ ♛ ♛
Route 213. Tel. 687-7700
Prix fixe 3-course dinner: $38; 7-course $48
Charming as this 1797 stone house is, with 8 cozy dining rooms, fireplaces, exposed beam ceilings, fresh flowers, antiques, and exquisite tableware, it's the food that stars here. Under chef-owner John Novi's direction, everything's homemade and imaginative perfection: smoked sausages, Dijon rabbit, duck breast schnitzel with orange-tomato curry, bluefish with oyster sauce. Dinner only, Thursday to Sunday; closed mid-February to April 1.

Hillsdale
(Columbia County; Area Code 518)

Hotel
Swiss Hutte♛ ♛
Route 23, 12529. Tel. 325-3333
2 persons in twin, $195 (MAP, includes 2 meals)
Comfortable lodge/motel adjacent to Catamount ski area. 21 rooms, 1 suite (with fireplace), bar, café, restaurant (♛ ♛), heated swimming pool, tennis, golf privileges. Comfortable vacation choice. Many rooms with balconies or private patios. Restaurant with alpine theme, fireplace coziness, continental specialties.

Restaurant
L'Hostelrie Bressane♛ ♛ ♛
P.O. Box 387, Routes 22 and 23. Tel. 325-3412

Average dinner: $50
Easily the most memorable cooking in the area.
Meticulous French food and style make this crisply
perfect little inn a delight. 1783 house has 6 lovely
guest rooms (4 with shared baths), at $65–$85 per
double (including continental breakfast). Closed Mondays and Tuesdays and March through April.

Shopping

Rodgers Book Barn, Rodman Rd. Tel. 325-3610.
Rare, old, and out-of-print books in a voluminous barn.
Call for directions; it's hard to find.

White Birch Farm, Gingras Rd., off Route 22. Tel.
325-3527. Homemade *chèvres* cheeses, made with garlic, basil, chives, and other herbs.

Hudson
(Columbia County; Area Code 518)

Restaurants
Charleston ♛ ♛
517 Warren St. Tel. 828-4990
Average dinner: $20–25
New American style and skills in a pleasingly facelifted
storefront, main thoroughfare locale. Try the smoked
duck or Hoisin chicken.
Bucci's ♛
517 Warren St. Tel. 828-4990
Average dinner: $22
Longtime (since 1933) local favorite for its homey Ita-
lian specialties.

Shopping

Warren St., the town's main thoroughfare, is dotted
with interesting antiques shops. Among them: **Town-
house Antiques** (306), **Bobbie's Flea Market** (510),
Watnot Shop (525), **Hudson Antiques Center** (536),
The Irish Princess (612). Nearby: **The English Antiques Centre,** Union and South 4th St.

INSIDERS' TIPS

Available at the Columbia County Chamber of Commerce, 729 Columbia St., tel. 828-4417, is a handy and
free "Guide to Antiques Dealers and Auction Houses."

Hyde Park (Dutchess County; Area Code 914)

Restaurants
American Bounty♛♛ **and Escoffier Room**♛♛♛
Culinary Institute of America, North Rd., Route 9. Tel. 471-6608 or 452-9600
Average dinner: American Bounty $15; Escoffier Room $36
Proving ground for future chefs, these two CIA (Culinary Institute of America) restaurants in old Jesuit College building offer full service, professional meals. As you'd guess, American Bounty features a wide range of regional dishes; Escoffier Room is classic French all the way. Advance reservations a must.

Shopping
Hyde Park Antiques Center, 184 Albany Post Rd. (Route 9). Tel. 229-8200. Offerings of 28 antiques dealers in roomlike settings. Antique clothing, furniture, accessories, collectibles. Open daily, 10 A.M.–5 P.M.

Katonah (Westchester County; Area Code 914)

Theater and Concerts
Caramoor Center for Music and the Arts♛♛♛, Girdle Drive. Tel. 232-5035. Spanish courtyard of estate on 117 acres is enchanting scene for chamber music concerts, opera, dance, children's theater. Summer only.

Kinderhook (Columbia County; Area Code 518)

Restaurant
Carolina House♛
Broad St. Tel. 758-1669
Average dinner: $25–30
Old-fashioned Southern cooking (fried chicken, Chesapeake crab cakes) in front of a warming fire in a log cabin.
Kirk's Country Cuisine & Bakery♛
1 Broad St., Route 9. Tel. 758-7247

Average lunch: $5
Home-cooked soups, salads, sandwiches, great breads, and mouth-watering desserts make this a dandy, informal lunch stop. The cheesecake, cranberry crunch, bear claws, and giant cookies are show-stoppers.

The Old Dutch Inn♛
Route 9 on the Village Square. Tel. 758-1676
Average dinner: $15
Standard home-style cooking in old clapboard house converted to restaurant. Popular tavern attached.

Kingston
(Ulster County; Area Code 914)

Restaurants
Schneller's♛♛
61 John St. Tel. 331-9800
Average dinner, $20
Dishes are familiar, but treatments are imaginative—Mexican-style steak, with salsa; mussel tureen, tournedos with artichokes, clams with barbecue sauce. Closed Sunday through Tuesday.

Hillside Manor♛
Route 32. Tel. 331-1386
Average dinner $19
This citadel of northern Italian cookery boasts 75 entrées, including homemade pastas, veal and seafood, authentic cappuccino.

Theater
Ulster Performing Arts Center, 601 Broadway. Tel. 331-1012. An ornate 1927 theater where major concerts are held and Broadway touring companies appear.

Millbrook
(Dutchess County; Area Code 914)

Hotel
Cottonwood Inn♛
Route 44, 12545. Tel. 677-3919
2 persons in double, $45–65
A rambling 1790 house, recently restored. 14 rooms, no room phones. Welcome B&B-type simplicity, privacy.

Restaurant
Paolucci's ♛
Route 44. Tel. 677-9774
Average dinner: $20
Abundant northern Italian food in pleasant, informal setting, glassed-in porch. Good value. Closed Monday.

Shopping
MAM (Millbrook Antiques Mall), Franklin Ave. Tel. 677-9311. Some 24 antiques dealers, variety of goods.

Millbrook Antiques Center, Franklin Ave. Tel. 677-3921. Collections of more than 40 antiques dealers represented. Enormous selection. Open Monday, Thursday, Saturday, 11 A.M.–5 P.M., Sunday 1–5 P.M.

Millerton
(Dutchess County; Area Code 914)

Shopping
McArthur's Smokehouse, Route 44. Known throughout New York and Connecticut for its delicious home-smoked sausages, meats, poultry, and game.

Mount Kisco
(Westchester County; Area Code 914)

Hotel
The Kittle House ♛
Route 117, 10549. Tel. 666-8044
2 persons in double, $75
A two-century-old country inn on 7 acres near New York City. 17 rooms, bar, restaurant ♛ ♛, lounge (live entertainment weekends). Large, comfortable rooms, some with walk-in closets. Better known as a restaurant for New American cuisine, old-time ambiance.

New Lebanon
(Columbia County; Area Code 518)

Restaurant
Shuji's ♛
Junction Routes 20 and 22. Tel. 794-8383

Average dinner: $25
A touch of sushi and Japan in Governor Samuel Tilden's 19th-century manor house. Closed mid-November to mid-March.

Theater

The Theater Barn, P.O. Box 390, 12125. Tel. 794-8989. Professional musicals and plays presented year-round (6 in summer, 2 in October–November, 2 in January–February).

North Salem
(Westchester County; Area Code 914)

Restaurant

Auberge Maxime ♕ ♕ ♕

Ridgefield Rd. Tel. 669-5450

Prix fixe dinner: $41

A longtime area favorite for its elegant French cuisine. Duck is a specialty here. Closed Wednesdays, Thanksgiving, Christmas Eve.

Old Chatham
(Columbia County; Area Code 518)

Hotel

Locust Tree House ♕

P.O. Box 31, 12136. Tel. 794-8651

2 persons in double, $50 (includes breakfast)

A large Colonial in town center. 4 rooms. Comfortable, antiques-filled rooms make this B&B a find, handy to Shaker sights. Closed January–March.

Patterson
(Putnam County; Area Code 914)

Restaurant

L'Auberge Bretonne ♕ ♕ ♕

North on Route 22. Tel. 878-7882

Average dinner: $25

French flair, style, with specific Brittany accent in dishes and decor. Closed Wednesdays, and Christmas, also 1 week in mid-April.

Port Chester
(Westchester County; Area Code 914)

Restaurant
Angsavanee ♛ ♛ ♛
163 North Main St. Tel. 937-2727
Average dinner: $25–30
Northern Italian cuisine with an elegant flair, including
pasta (angel hair Bolognese), scampi, chicken, and
veal, in spite of the exotic name. Closed Mondays.

Poughkeepsie
(Dutchess County; Area Code 914)

Restaurants
Treasure Chest ♛ ♛
568 South Rd. Tel. 462-4545
Average dinner: $20
Ambiance outstars cuisine, with exposed beams, fire-
places, vintage (1741) house. Go with rack of lamb,
chateaubriand.
Christos ♛
155 Wilbur Blvd. Tel. 471-3400
Average dinner: $20
Scenic McCann golf course locale, dependable con-
tinental dishes.
Mill House ♛
289 Mill St. (Routes 44-55 west). Tel. 471-1166
Average meal: $15
Reliable continental cuisine in attractive 1830 land-
mark house. Moderate prices.
Noah's Ark Antique Bar and Eatery ♛
135 Mill St. Tel. 454-9296
Average dinner: $15
Casual, old-fashioned backdrop for light menu of
quiche, salads, desserts. A late-night favorite with
younger crowd.
Vassar College Alumnae House ♛
College and Raymond Aves. Tel. 485-3700
Average dinner: $15
Lighthearted American fare served in pleasant dining
room or cozy pub. A collegiate (and faculty) hangout,
it's most fun for brunch, lunch, or snack. Modest prices.

Sweet tooth? Try Vassar Angel, Devil, or Gremlin (desserts). Selection of 50 beers in pub. Open daily, 7:30 A.M.–midnight.

Bars, Pubs, Etc.

Kimlin Cider Mill♕, Cedar Ave., off Route 376. Rustic, old-fashioned cider mill has been a Vassar hangout for generations. Delicious fresh cider, homemade cookies, and donuts are specialties.

Theaters

Bardavon, 35 Market St. Tel. 473-2072. National and regional performances of opera, dance, music, and theater in restored 1869 opera house (New York's oldest).

Mid-Hudson Civic Center, Civic Center Plaza. Tel. 485-5800. Huge hall hosts stage shows and concerts.

Cruises

Riverboat Tours, 310 Mill St., 12601. Tel. 473-5211. Hudson cruises aboard enclosed double-deck paddle wheeler. Sightseeing, dinner, and brunch cruises available.

Purdys
(Westchester County; Area Code 914)

Restaurants

The Box Tree♕♕♕

Route 684. Tel. 277-3677

Average dinner: $35–40

Authentic 1775 farmhouse (the Purdy Homestead), 3 small dining rooms (2 with woodburning fireplaces) provide romantic ambiance to match menu. For a *real* romantic splurge, rent 3-room suite upstairs ($260 including breakfast and butler service) for the night.

Red Hook
(Dutchess County; Area Code 914)

Hotel

The Red Hook Inn♕

31 South Broadway, 12571. Tel. 758-8445

2 persons in double, $65 (including full breakfast)

A shuttered Colonial house-turned-inn on village's main

street. 5 rooms, no TV or room phones; taproom-bar, restaurant. Nothing fancy here, but comfortable rooms, simply furnished, in old-fashioned village.

Rhinebeck
(Dutchess County; Area Code 914)

Hotel
Beekman Arms ♛ ♛
Route 9 at Beekman Square, 12572. Tel. 876-7077
2 persons in twin, $50–84
In-town historic 1766 clapboard inn. 60 rooms, bar, restaurant. Long on charm and history, sometimes short on service.

Restaurant
Chez Marcel ♛ ♛
Route 9. Tel. 876-8189
Average dinner: $17
French menu favorites—coquilles St. Jacques, veal Cordon Bleu, etc.—in pleasant setting. CIA-graduate chef. Closed Mondays, also January 1 and Christmas.

Shopping
Dutchess Valley Antique Gallery, NY-9. Tel. 876-2121. Full range of antiques—furniture, accessories, jewelry, silver, prints. Open daily 10 A.M.–5:30 P.M.

La Melangerie, 38 Montgomery St., NY-9. Tel. 876-4986. A gallimaufry of antiques, toiletries, plants, gourmet items. Coffee or tea served while you browse.

Old Gristmill Antiques Center, NY-9. Tel. 876-6818. 18th- and 19th-century antiques—glass, china, jewelry, furniture—featured by 5 dealers.

Theater
Upstate Films Theatre, 26 Montgomery St. Tel. 876-2515. Year-round showcase for the best American and foreign films, also children's films, lecture series, and chamber music concerts.

Cruises
Shearwater Cruises and Sailing School, Inc., RD 2, Box 329, 12572. Tel. 876-7350. Crew aboard 28-foot

sailboat, take scenic tour, or learn to sail. May–October.

Rye (Westchester County; Area Code 914)

Restaurant
La Panetiere♕♕♕
530 Milton Rd., 10580. Tel. 967-8140
Average dinner, $34–47
Relaxed setting, superb modern French cuisine, done with panache. Among Westchester's very best.

South Salem (Westchester County; Area Code 914)

Restaurant
Rene Chardain♕♕
NY-123. Tel. 533-6200
Average dinner: $35–40
Classic French cooking by a master, in beautiful stone mansion on 10-acre wooded estate. Formal tone, handsome decor in 2 small dining rooms. Special-occasion dining. Fine wine list. 2 seatings (7 and 9 P M). Dinner only. Closed Sunday and Monday.

Stephentown (Rensselaer County; Area Code 518)

Hotel
Millhof Inn♕
NY-43, 12168. Tel. 733-5606
2 persons in double, $70–95 (includes continental breakfast and afternoon tea)
Bavarian-style chalet with fireplaces. 12 rooms, no smoking, telephones, or TV in rooms; swimming pool, brook, lounge, garden. Handy for Shaker Village sightseeing. A comfortable, tiny treasure. Closed April and early May, reopens last week in May.

Stormville (Dutchess County; Area Code 914)

Restaurant
Harralds♛ ♛
Route 52. Tel. 878-6595
Prix fixe dinner: $50
Romantic setting (candlelight, classical music), French food, and *flawless* service. Special splurge experience.

Tarrytown (Westchester County; Area Code 914)

Hotel
Marriott Westchester♛ ♛ ♛
670 White Plains Rd. (exit 1 off I-287), 10591. Tel. 631-2200
2 persons in twin, $150
Modern, 10-story hotel handy to various transportation points. 444 rooms, bar, restaurants, indoor-outdoor swimming pool, health club. Well-equipped chain hotel. Some rooms with balconies facing pool.

West Point (Orange County; Area Code 914)

Hotel
Hotel Thayer♛ ♛
U.S. Military Academy grounds, 10996. Tel. 446-4731
2 persons in twin, $60
Landmark hotel just inside South Gate of West Point (your innkeeper: Uncle Sam). 210 rooms, bar, restaurant, terrace (nice for drinks in summer). Great views overlooking Hudson.

White Plains (Westchester County; Area Code 914)

Hotels
Arrowwood of Westchester♛ ♛ ♛
Anderson Hill Rd., Rye Brook. Tel. 939-5500
2 persons in twin, $160–310
5-story resort hotel. 276 rooms, bar, restaurants

(Mallards ♛ ♛ for *nouvelle* French/American), indoor-outdoor pool, tennis, 9-hole golf, health club, bicycles. For sports and recreation, name it, it's probably here. Some rooms with fireplace, balcony, private patio. Many amenities. Handy to corporate Westchester.

Rye Town Hilton ♛ ♛ ♛
699 Westchester Ave., Rye Brook 10573. Tel. 939-6300
2 persons in twin, $120–160
Modern hotel complex, handy to highways. 450 rooms, bar, restaurant, indoor-outdoor pools, sauna, tennis, golf privileges. Resort facilities for business travelers.

Holiday Inn–Crowne Plaza ♛ ♛
66 Hale Ave. Tel. 682-0050
2 persons in twin, $126–152
Top-of-the-line Holiday Inn accommodations. 404 rooms, indoor pool, tennis, golf, health club privileges, bar, restaurant, dancing.

La Reserve ♛ ♛
5 Barker Ave. Tel. 761-7700; outside New York, (800) 431-2906
2 persons in twin, $160–185 (includes continental breakfast)
15-story hotel in city center. 142 suites, bar, café, restaurant, health club, concierge. Convenient to business, but quiet, with many luxury touches. A comfortable small hotel.

Stouffer Westchester ♛ ♛
80 West Red Oak Lane, 10604. Tel. 694-5400
2 persons in twin, $99–149 (includes breakfast Monday through Friday, daily newspaper)
8-story building. 306 rooms, bar, café, restaurant, indoor swimming pool, tennis court (lighted, enclosed in winter), exercise room, concierge. Some rooms with balcony, private patio. Many amenities.

Restaurant

Bengal Tiger ♛
140 East Post Rd. Tel. 948-5191
Average dinner: $25
A cozy, longtime favorite for reliable northern Indian dishes.

THE CATSKILLS

The Indians called the region Onteora ("land of the sky"). The Dutch came along and renamed it Kaatskill, or Wildcat Creek, after the many wildcats who then roamed the forests and mountains. Readers of Washington Irving have forever locked it in mind as the place where Rip Van Winkle slept for 20 years.

Credit for the Catskills' longtime popularity as a resort-*cum*-wilderness region probably should go to a clutch of 19th-century artists and writers who were the first to romanticize the area: Irving, James Fenimore Cooper, the poet William Cullen Bryant, and the painter Thomas Cole.

Irving wrote, "To me [the Catskills] have ever been the fairy region of the Hudson." Irving first saw the Catskills in 1800 on an initial voyage up the river, and the mountains had "the most witching effect" on his boyish imagination.

The Catskills also captivated Cooper, who used them to symbolize the American Wilderness. In *The Pioneers* (1823), the first of his Leatherstocking novels, someone asks the hero what he can see when he reaches a particular mountaintop. "Creation," says Leatherstocking. "The river is in sight for seventy miles, looking like a curled shaving under my feet. . . . I saw the hills in the Hampshire grants, the Highlands of the river, and all that God had done, or man could do, far as eye could reach."

New Englander Bryant called the Catskills "a region singular for its romantic beauty," and together with his friend, the Englishman Thomas Cole, explored "every cleft and crevice" of the mountains. Cole's paintings of the Catskills' chasms, cascades, forests, and river over-

THE CATSKILLS

ALBANY

88

9W

9

Coxsackie

23

23

Catskill

9G

87

9

Rhinebeck

Poughkeepsie

55

84

Beacon

Hudson River

TACONIC STATE PKWY

NEW YORK STATE THRUWAY

Newburgh

West Point

9

NEW JERSEY

87

9W

oneonta

88

23

Stamford

Grand Gorge

Prattsville

Lexington

23A

23A

Hunter

28

10

Delhi

Delaware River

42

Hunter Mtn

214

Shandaken

Saugerties

212

Woodstock

28

West Branch

ulton

28

28

ownsville

30

Pepacton Reservoir

Ashokan Reservoir

17

— To ancock

Neversink Reservoir

Rondout Reservoir

Kingston

209

26

Liberty

42

55

55A

Ulster Lake

Mohonk Lake

New Paltz

52

52

Woodridge

Ellenville

299

55

Cragsmoor

Marlboro

Monticello

17

Wolf Lake

Wurtsboro

52

55

Lebanon Lake

42

209

97

Middletown

Port Jervis

84

Delaware River

PANIA

PENNSYLVANIA

0   10   20   30 Miles

views were imbued with such a mysterious romanticism that other painters flocked to the area to discover and paint it themselves.

Where artists paved the way, tourists followed suit. In more recent times, the Catskills have evoked another image, not that of nostalgia for the lost wilderness, but the place to go for a good time. To generations of New Yorkers, the southern Catskills have been synonymous with Playland, a vacation area of large and small resorts (some 20,000 accommodations available), with terrain and climate conducive to skiing and snowmobiling in winter, swimming, fishing, and hiking in summer, and recreation anytime, year-round.

To New Yorkers, the Catskills also evoke memories of the "Borscht Belt," the resort proving grounds where beginning comedians of the 1930s through the 1950s honed their jokes and skills at Grossingers, the Concord, and other famous resorts. Phil Silvers, Buddy Hackett, and the late Danny Kaye are among many who went on to fortune and fame elsewhere.

Catskill State Park, which encircles the Catskill Mountains, covers some 688,660 acres (272,000 of which are state-owned, the rest protected) in Greene, Ulster, Sullivan, and Delaware counties, extending from a few miles west of the Hudson River at Kingston, stretching north and inland from the town of Catskill, west as far as East Branch near the northeast Pennsylvania border, south just above Liberty and Ellenville.

The park encompasses many villages, resorts, farms, and fishing and hunting clubs, as well as 8 campgrounds. But it is also a protected wildlife area, with more than 200 miles of wooded, marked hiking trails, where you'll see deer, foxes, raccoons, and other wild creatures and can reel in trout and other fish in the mountain streams.

The Catskill Mountains themselves (all 2 million acres of them, stretching across 6 counties) are usually considered part of the Appalachian range, but they differ from the rest of the range significantly in geological formation. Characterized not by long ridges, but by groupings of flat-topped mountains (once as high as the

Rockies), they are separated from each other by narrow, precipitous valleys, punctuated by steep brooks and cataracts.

But when people refer to the Catskills, they usually mean more than the mountains or the well-preserved, forested park per se. They're talking about the entire vacationland spawned by the mountains and forested park. Monticello, Ellenville, Wurtsboro, Liberty—all are Catskill towns, focal points of recreation in the area.

More for the vacationer than for the dedicated tourist, the Catskills encourage leisurely pursuits: a day spent hiking, swimming, hang gliding, fishing a quiet stream (there are 2,227 miles of trout streams in the area), golfing, or antiquing along Route 17.

The Catskills are richer in sports and activities than in sightseeing and historic monuments. For that reason, you'll find this chapter a brief one that points you in the right direction, with a *précis* of the sights available, but leaves the rest to you. Catskill pleasure comes in doing it *your* way, at your own speed, as quickly or as leisurely as you may wish.

Reaching the Catskills is a cinch. From Albany, travel south on I-87 to Exit 21 near Catskill village, then head west on NY-23. Binghamton is another entry point from the west or from Pennsylvania traveling east on NY-17.

But for the purposes of outlining tour possibilities, we'll begin from New York City, as so many vacationers do, on NY-17 north, passing through Goshen and Wurtsboro, with the option of a side drive to Ellenville, then northwest to Monticello, Liberty, and Livingston Manor, We'll pick up NY-30 east to Margaretville, where we'll enter the park again on NY-28 east, following it through Shandaken, Phoenicia, Mount Tremper, and Woodstock. Then it's back via Kingston on I-87 south, stopping at New Paltz on the way.

We've arbitrarily included the towns west of I-87 in this chapter, those east of it in our Lower Hudson Valley chapter.

From New York City you can follow I-87 north, cross

the Hudson on the Tappan Zee Bridge, and continue north to Monroe, where you'll pick up US-6 and NY-17 heading northwest.

INSIDERS' TIPS

The towns along the west side of the Hudson River are contiguous with the Catskills, so you may want to weave in and out of some of these historically interesting towns during your Catskills visit. See the chapter on the Lower Hudson Valley.

An interesting detour, if you're architecture-minded, is off I-87 at exit 15 to Route 17 north to Tuxedo, for a quick drive through Tuxedo Park♕ ♕. Here on some 13,000 acres are multi-turreted mansions and estates of some of America's 19th-century millionaires, reminiscent of the opulence of Newport, Rhode Island.

Pierre Lorillard IV, of the tobacco Lorillards, fenced in 4,000 acres in 1885 as a hunting preserve, then turned it into housing for the rich and famous, selling off tracts to his prominent friends. It was one of the first such planned communities.

At the Tuxedo Club's first Spring Ball in 1896, the formal dinner jacket with tails clipped was first worn; from it the name *tuxedo* evolved. The entire community, still considered Billionaires' Row, is on the National Register of Historic Places.

INSIDERS' TIPS

From the first weekend of August to the next-to-last in September there's an annual Renaissance Festival at Sterling Forest, Tuxedo—with knights on horseback, jousts, jugglers, mimes, and Shakespeare's plays. A delightful time to schedule a visit.

Off US-6 at Monroe is Museum Village of Orange County♕, a 19th-century hamlet consisting of 35 typical buildings of the time. A few are authentic—a log cabin and cider mill, for instance. The rest are replicas of rural southern New York State buildings of the period, though many were re-created using old timbers, bricks, and stones. The country flavor exists especially on weekends, when there are craft demonstrations, the smithy is hammering, and the village is rife with special events.

In Goshen is Historic Track♛, Park Place, one of the world's oldest harness racetracks, dating back to 1838. You can visit the old barn and blacksmith shop. Grand Circuit racing and the New York Sire Stakes take place here in early June. During the rest of the summer, antiques and craft fairs, concerts and special events are typical fare. Goshen is also home to the Hall of Fame Trotter Museum, 240 Main Street.

On NY-17, Wurtsboro, snuggled into the valley with the Catskills framed in the distance, is a prime vacation target in summer. The cottages and cabins on lakes west of town were the locale of the old Broadway show *Having a Wonderful Time,* and Wurtsboro is still a popular jumping-off place for Catskill holidays. The town, a historic marker proclaims, was named "in honor of Maurice Wurts of the Delaware & Hudson Canal Company, which had a mercantile business here for a short period in 1828."

INSIDERS' TIPS

At Wurtsboro Airport, you can soar over the magnificent mountainscape in a sailplane. The pilot does all the work; you just admire the views as you glide, motorless, for a 15-to-20-minute ride. For information, call Wurtsboro Flight Service, (914) 888-9923.

A detour on NY-209 northeast to Ellenville will take you through Phillipsport with its old Greek Revival houses, and then bring you, via a scenic mountaintop drive to Cragsmoor, to Ice Caves Mountain♛, one of the area's most unusual natural sights.

Ice caves with underground rivers, connected by a nature trail, lead past dramatic rock formations to Sam's Point, a 2,225-foot-high cliff offering views into 5 states.

THE HEART OF THE CATSKILLS

It's 11 miles north of Wurtsboro to Monticello, the heart of the Catskills resort region, with facilities ranging from big resort hotels like the Concord and Kutsher's Country Club to motels, cabins, cottages, campgrounds, and B&Bs.

The area is replete with lakes, trout streams, summer theaters, nightclubs, children's camps, and enough recreation options to keep you busy through your entire vacation. There are 18 golf courses in the area, all open to the public. If all else fails, there's the Monticello Raceway with harness racing, and the Holiday Mountain ski area 3 miles east off NY-17.

PERILS & PITFALLS

Although Grossinger's (600 rooms), Kutsher's (375 rooms), and the Concord (1,250 rooms) are almost synonymous in many people's minds with Catskill resorts, we find them disappointing: too big, impersonal, mass-trafficked, and jammed with tour groups to include in our hotel listings. Be forewarned.

For a scenically rewarding day trip from Monticello, we'd recommend making a loop west on NY-17B almost to Callicoon on the Pennsylvania border, turning north perhaps to North Branch for a refresher stop at the old North Branch Cider Mill, then back along the state line from Callicoon south on NY-97. The narrow, winding road alongside the surging Delaware River from Narrowsburg to Minisink Ford is truly invigorating.

At Narrowsburg you might pause long enough to visit old Fort Delaware♕, now an open-air museum depicting the life of the pioneers who settled this Upper Delaware River valley in 1754. It's open daily from July to Labor Day, weekends from Memorial Day to mid-June.

This is whitewater canoe, raft, and kayak country, also a favorite spot for hunters and fishermen. The Delaware boasts at least 12 species of fish. At Minisink Ford, site of a Revolutionary War skirmish, is the

Roebling Suspension Bridge ♛, held by 6 columns with cables looped over them. The oldest spun-wire cable suspension bridge in the United States, it was an early experiment (1848) by the same John A. Roebling who later built the Brooklyn Bridge.

You can walk or cycle (but not drive) over this historic bridge. Then walk up the hill to the Minisink Battlefield Memorial Park ♛, where colonial militiamen fought a grim battle with the British and their Indian allies. The park offers great overviews of the river and the twisting drives.

A few miles north on NY-55, past stands of oaks and pines, is the Eldred Preserve, a remarkable enclave of more than 1,200 acres, 3 ponds, and an additional 600 or so acres for hunting white-tailed deer. The "camp" was bought in the 1970s by the Precision Valve Corporation of Yonkers to preserve trout fishing, and it has expanded considerably since then.

You don't have to hunt or fish to enjoy Eldred Preserve. The restaurant on the grounds offers fresh trout prepared any of a dozen ways (or they'll cook to order any that you catch).

Back on NY 97 again, the roller-coaster drive southeast continues, until you take a left-hand turn north on NY-42 (just before Sparrow Bush) and head back to Monticello, then on 17 north to Liberty.

Antiques browsers will enjoy the drive along Route 17 from Liberty to Hurleyville, Livingston Manor, and Roscoe. It's dotted with antiques shops and warehouses.

INSIDERS' TIPS

A free pamphlet, "Antiques, a Treasure Hunter's Guide to Ulster County," is available from the Antiques Dealers Association of Ulster County, Box 246, Hurley 12443.

THE CENTRAL CATSKILLS

Margaretville, Arkville, and Fleischmanns all cater to vacationers heading into the central Catskills along

NY-28. This is a scenic drive through steep, piney mountainsides, opening to narrow valleys crossed with mountain streams.

Keystone to the area is Shandaken. Its Iroquois name means "rapid waters," an accurate description, as wild and raging Esopus Creek (great for trout fishing and tubing) flows past at the doorstep. The Esopus White Water Canoe and Kayak Slalom an uninhibited annual race, is usually held the first weekend of June.

Nearby is Slide Mountain, the Catskills' highest peak, at 4,204 feet. Shandaken is also ski country, with Belleayre Mountain and Highmount Ski Center just 8 miles to the west on NY-28.

North on NY-214 brings you to Hunter Mountain, where you (and hordes of others) can ski from November through April on 44 different slopes and trails. In summer you can enjoy a ride in the Skyride, the longest, highest chair lift in the Catskills (3,200 feet above sea level) with great mountain-and-valley views.

Like much of the Catskills, Hunter knows no seasonal restraints—it's lovely in summer, too. There is a seemingly nonstop series of festivals (German Alps, Country Music, Italian, Celtic—7 in all), and an annual Antique Auto Show that winds up the tourist season early in September.

PERILS & PITFALLS

Despite an abundance of facilities, Hunter on winter weekends can be clogged with lines. If you don't want long waits at the ski lifts, plan a midweek visit.

Routes NY-23 and 23A encircle still other mountains—Blackhead, Cave, Tower, Black Dome—as well as such scenic "draws" as Devils Tombstone, North Lake, and Haines Falls. You'll pass through Palenville on NY-23A. This, during the Gilded Age, was *the* art colony of the Catskills. It was described even in 1897 as "a famous gathering place for landscape artists, as the wildness of the ravines and the massive projecting rocks above you . . . afford an endless variety of subjects for their pencils."

It was also believed to be the "little village of great antiquity" that was the home "at the foot of these fairy mountains" of the legendary Rip Van Winkle. His creator, Washington Irving, never confirmed this, leaving readers to speculate.

If you head south on NY-32, then west on NY-212, you'll reach Woodstock, which is often a high point of a Catskill adventure for visitors prone to sightseeing. (The more athletically inclined often have other reference points for a vacation.)

"Woodstock Nation," the flower children of the 1960s who gave us the famous Woodstock Music Festival in 1969 (though the concerts themselves were not held in the town of Woodstock, but in White Lake, miles away) may be long gone, but Woodstock's longtime reputation as a bohemian art colony lingers on. This image goes back to 1902, when an Englishman, Radcliffe Whitehead, settled in and launched a craft community.

It's no wonder he was attracted to the town, what with its prime Catskills location, its clear fresh air and scenic vistas, and the attractiveness of the vintage Colonial houses in the village center.

PERILS & PITFALLS

Woodstock's calm is hard to find in midsummer, when the town is a beehive of tourist activity. This presents a dilemma: to see it at its prettiest and most tranquil, you'll want to go off-season, ATBS (any time but summer). But if you want to enjoy the excitement, you'll put up with the crowds and join the fun of summer, when the Woodstock Playhouse is in session and the Maverick Concerts (July and August) are scheduled. In other words, summer is Woodstock at its best *and* worst. Your choice.

The Art Students' League of New York established a summer school soon after, and in 1916 the Maverick Summer Music Concerts (oldest chamber concerts series in the United States) were begun by Hervey White. Since then, artists of all kinds (performing and video artists, actors, dancers, and singers, as well as those in the fine arts) come and go freely, considering

Woodstock their summer or year-round home base, savoring the laid-back tranquility of the delightful little town (population 2,280). The painter George Bellows called Woodstock home until his death in 1929.

Woodstock is a browser's paradise, both for shoppers and for those interested in art. Drop by the Woodstock Artists Association and its neighbor, the Guild of Craftsmen, for news of current happenings. For handcrafts and all kinds of trendy boutiques and art galleries (as well as the requisite clunky gift shops), look along Mill Hill Road and, beyond the green, on Tinker.

As you drive north on Rock City Road (from the green), there are still more galleries. But the prize of the drive is the view from the fire tower's Overlook Trail on Mead Mountain.

INSIDERS' TIPS

For a stunning view of fall foliage, climb to the top of Overlook Mountain. Then, to fill the needs of inner man and woman, check out the gorgeous-looking and even better-tasting apples at the many roadside fruit and vegetable stands along Route 28.

As you head south from Woodstock on NY-375 to NY-28 southeast toward Kingston (see the chapter on the Lower Hudson Valley), you might take a scenic detour west on NY-28 to 28A around the crescent-shaped Ashokan Reservoir. In fall, this is a spectacular foliage drive, but it's beautiful anytime, with the interplay of water, mountains, and woods.

Back on NY-28 heading southeast, you can pick up I-87 south to New Paltz (which could just as easily be part of our Lower Hudson chapter), architecturally and historically one of the most intriguing towns in the area. It was settled in 1678 by French Huguenot refugees, many of whose descendants still live in the vicinity.

Among the special sights are the original Huguenot stone houses ♛ ♛ with peaked roofs (vintage 1692–1712) along Huguenot Street, one of America's oldest streets. A single $5 ticket admits you to 6 authentically furnished (with family antiques) houses and a restored 1717 French stone church, all open Memorial Day weekend through September.

Of special interest, if you're pressed for time, is the Jean Hasbrouck House ♛ ♛, in medieval Flemish style, with its steeply gabled fireplace, great beehive chimney, kitchen where cockfights were once held, and even a secret room to hide in if Indians threatened.

South of town 4 miles on NY-32 is Locust Lawn ♛, a 12-room mansion built by Colonel Jacob Hasbrouck in 1814. The property also contains a Farm Museum, a smokehouse, the 1738 Terwilliger Homestead, and a bird sanctuary.

INSIDERS' TIPS

An annual Art & Craft Fair, a high-quality juried show with 200 or more artist-craftsmen, is held in the Ulster County Fairgrounds, New Paltz, in late May, usually Memorial Day weekend. For details, tel. (914) 679-8087.

For all the up-to-date recreational facilities available in the Catskills, the sometimes glitzy tourist attractions, and the hordes descending on the area for fun and frolic, it is still possible to find vast wooded and rugged areas of the Catskills as Cooper and Irving knew them. In fact, when there's thunder in the mountains, one can almost imagine it to be the sound of little men playing ninepins, as in Rip Van Winkle's fantasy.

INSIDERS' INFORMATION FOR THE CATSKILLS

Eldred (Sullivan County; Area Code 914)

Hotel
Eldred Preserve ♛ ♛
Route 55, 12732. Tel. 557-8316
2 persons in double, $55
Chalet-like lodge-motel surrounded by pond and woods

(often deer sightings). 20 rooms, bar, swimming pool, tennis, boating, hiking trails, excellent restaurant (👑👑), with specialties including fresh trout prepared 12 different ways, hasenpfeffer, prime ribs, and Wiener schnitzel. An away-from-it-all delight. Closed Tuesdays September through June, also Christmas and January.

Ellenville
(Ulster County; Area Code 914)

Theater
Shadowland Theater, 157 Canal St. Tel. 647-5511. Cooperative Artists, a New York City professional company in residence, performs May through November in 67-year-old art deco theater.

Mt. Tremper
(Ulster County; Area Code 914)

Hotel
Mt. Tremper Inn👑👑
NY-212 and Wittenberg Rd., P.O. Box 51, 12457. Tel. 688-9938
2 persons in double, $55–85
An 1850 Victorian house in the heart of the ski area. 12 rooms, only two *with* baths. Comfortable B&B retreat after skiing or sightseeing. Handy to Woodstock, Hunter Mountain, and Esopus Creek.

Neversink
(Sullivan County; Area Code 914)

Hotel
New Age Health Farm
Neversink 12765. Tel. 985-7601 or (800) NU-AGE-4-U
2 persons in twin, $79–86 per person (includes program and meals; weekly rates available)
Clapboard farmhouse in woodsy setting. Note: This isn't a hotel, but a *spa* with a supervised diet, weight-and-exercise program, massage, beauty and health care, swimming pool. Restful place for those with specific needs.

New Paltz
(Ulster County; Area Code 914)

Hotel

Mohonk Mountain House 👑 👑 👑

Lake Mohonk 12561. Tel. 255-1000

2 persons in twin, $139–270 (AP, all meals included)

A historic, rambling, old-fashioned resort hotel set in a 5,000-acre nature preserve on Shawangunk Mountain. 300 rooms, bar, fine restaurant (👑 👑), lake swimming, tennis, 9-hole golf course, horseback riding, carriage rides, skating, and winter sports. Many private balconies, fireplaces, amenities, and a rugged, secluded landscape. A real family vacation spot.

Restaurants

DuBois Fort 👑

81 Huguenot St. Tel. 255-1771

Average dinner: $15

The star here is the 1705 Colonial house full of antiques, mementos, and a menu featuring old American favorites, such as pot roast.

Locust Tree Inn 👑 👑

215 Huguenot St. Tel. 255-7888

Average dinner: $17–26

Old standards (veal Oscar, for instance) competently done and served in a pleasant setting. Closed Mondays.

Cruises

Hudson River Cruises, 524 N. Ohioville Rd., 12561. Tel. 255-6515. Sails aboard MV *Rip Van Winkle* from Kingston to West Point. Daily from June 23 to Labor Day, Sundays May 4 through October.

North Branch (Sullivan County;
Area Code 914)

Shopping

North Branch Cider Mill, Route 123. Tel. 482-4823. A good stop for cold, refreshing sweet or hard cider, apples, produce in season, and assorted baskets. Closed January–March.

Palenville
(Greene County; Area Code 518)

Theater
Interarts—A World's Fair of the Arts, Woodstock Ave. Tel. 678-9021. Home to all kinds of performing arts: dance, plays, music, puppeteers, mimes.

Roscoe
(Sullivan County; Area Code 607)

Restaurant
Antrim Lodge♛
Highland Ave. Tel. 498-4191
Average dinner: $16–30
A rustic setting, complete with wood fire in old stone fireplace, makes a cozy backdrop for standard American fare. Also accommodations.

Round Top
(Greene County; Area Code 518)

Hotel
Winter Clove Inn♛ ♛
Winter Clove Rd., P.O. Box 67, 12473. Tel. 622-3267
2 persons in twin, $104 incl. all meals
Old-fashioned, 3-story resort hotel at edge of woods. 35 rooms (plus 15 in cottages), no TV or room phones; restaurant, café, 9-hole golf course, 2 swimming pools (indoor and outdoor), tennis courts, putting green, bowling, game room. Something for everyone here, plus natural attractions all around. Same family ownership since 1850.

Shandaken
(Ulster County; Area Code 914)

Hotel
Shandaken Inn♛ ♛
Golf Course Rd., NY-28, 12480. Tel. 688-5100
2 persons in double, $150 incl. breakfast and dinner
An 1880 vine-covered stone dairy barn converted to an inn in a country setting. 12 rooms, no TV or room phones, swimming pool, tennis court. Personalized

rooms (one with large fireplace), antiques. Idiosyncratic schedule—open only weekends, with advance reservations mandatory. Closed weekdays, also April and November.

Restaurant

Auberge des 4 Saisons ♕ ♕

Route 42. Tel. 688-2223

Average dinner: $17–27

A-frame chalet-like setting, serving French dishes. Cheerful, friendly, family-owned, rustic. Closed April and May and 2 weeks in November.

Tannersville
(Greene County; Area Code 518)

Hotel

Greene Mountain View Inn ♕

Church and South Main streets, 2 blocks off NY-23A, 12485. Tel. 589-5511

2 persons in twin, $45–48 with continental breakfast. Straightforward ski lodge–type inn near the Hunter Mountain slopes. 22 rooms, bar, dining room, TV, but no room phones. All-you-can-eat buffets (Tuesday, Friday, Saturday) popular with skiers. So is the casual atmosphere.

Restaurant

Chateau Belleview ♕

Route 23A. Tel. 589-5525

Average dinner: $20

Gallic-American pleasures—sweetbreads à la crème, stuffed pheasant, seafood Bretonne—combined with a Catskills view. Dinner only. Closed mid-May, also mid-October.

Windham
(Greene County; Area Code 518)

Hotel

Windham Arms ♕

Route 23, 12496. Tel. 734-3000

2 persons in twin, $45–70

Comfortable motel in ski area. 70 rooms, bar, café,

restaurant (♛), tennis, golf privileges. Many amenities, comfortable rooms, some with balconies, good value.

Restaurant

La Griglia ♛ ♛
Route 296. Tel. 734-4499
Average dinner: $20–25
A find for its fine rendering of northern Italian specialties (try the *osso bucco* or game in season). Closed Mondays (also Tuesdays, September through June).

Woodstock
(Ulster County; Area Code 914)

Hotel

The Tokalon B&B ♛ ♛
Route 375, West Hurley, 12498-0963. Tel. 679-5360
2 persons in double, $50–65 (incl. full breakfast)
An old frame house on a tree-shaded, 7-acre property. 5 rooms, no TV or room phones, lounge, library. An exceptional B&B, with many antiques, books, stereo, cozy fireplace, family warmth and friendly ambiance. Expertly kept and run.

Restaurants

Deanie's Towne Tavern ♛
Junction NY 212. Tel. 679-6508
Average dinner: $20
Attractive 1863 house sets stage for homemade soups and desserts, char-broiled swordfish steak, chicken Florentine, prime ribs. Closed Tuesdays.

Little Bear ♛
Route 212, Bearsville (outside Woodstock). Tel. 679-9497
Average dinner: $20–25
In a gussied-up old barn on a pretty stream you can order any of 93 Chinese dishes, plus the specials of the day. Enchanting views, especially in snow.

Theaters and Concert Halls

Byrdcliffe Theatre, P.O. Box 1166, 12498. Tel. 679-2100. Home to River Arts Repertory Company, professional group staging classics and world premieres of new plays. June–September.

Maverick Concerts, P.O. Box 102, 12498. Tel. 679-7969. One of America's oldest chamber music series, featuring big and new names. Sundays, July and August.

Woodstock Chamber Orchestra, P.O. Box 711, 12498. Tel. 679-7558. Chamber orchestra performs at St. John's Catholic Church, West Hurley, October–June.

Woodstock Playhouse, P.O. Box 396, 12498. Tel. 679-2436. Oldest continuously operating summer theater in New York State, presents plays, dance programs, and films.

Wurtsboro
(Sullivan County; Area Code 914)

Shopping

Canal Towne Emporium, Sullivan and Hudson Sts. Tel. 888-2100. A country store since 1845, full of nostalgia, antiques, reproductions.

ALBANY, SARATOGA, AND LEATHERSTOCKING COUNTRY

New York City dwellers consider their city the center of the universe, but for the inhabitants of the rest of the state, Albany is looked to as the focus of the action.

After all, as the state capital, it is where laws are passed (or fail to pass), and where decisions are made that affect the lives of the 17,558,072 state residents. Yet for all of that, Albany for many years was not the most exciting place to visit. Readers of novelist William Kennedy's books—*Ironweed, Legs, Billy Phelan's Greatest Game*—have a picture of what Albany was like in the not-too-distant past.

During Nelson A. Rockefeller's years as governor (1959–73), he cleared 98 downtown acres and began a building program that has substantially changed Albany's core and its image. The Empire State Plaza, praised by some for revitalizing the city, vilified by others for its vast stretches of impersonal, institutional architecture, stands now as the symbol and centerpiece of the revitalized city center. You, as a visitor, can judge it for yourself.

Logistically, Albany is of interest to a visitor because it is a springboard to key areas of the state. If you want to visit and vacation in the Adirondacks, you can fly into Albany, rent a car, and head north. Albany also can be a takeoff point for exploration of the Catskills and the Leatherstocking region. Visitors who want to eschew New York City can begin a circuit of the Hudson River from Albany, looping south and then north again.

Yet the area within shouting distance of the capital has much of interest in itself. In this chapter, we will look at the major attractions of the tri-city Albany-Troy-Schenectady area, Saratoga Springs to its immediate north, and the central part of the state between Albany and Syracuse that has been dubbed Leatherstocking Country.

ALBANY

Albanians, as capital residents call themselves, are justifiably proud of their city's revitalized look. The fulcrum of downtown rejuvenation is the Empire State Plaza, an 11-building complex that combines state government offices with a whole range of cultural and convention facilities.

Join a free tour at the Visitors Assistance Office (11 A.M., 1 P.M.., 3 P.M., tel. 474-2418). This leads you to various Plaza sights, past the "Egg" (the Empire State Institute for the Performing Arts building, shaped like a concrete egg on pedestals), a host of dramatic contemporary sculpture, and splendid wide-angle views of the city skyline. Take a ride up to the 42nd floor of the Corning Tower Observation Deck for a spectacular view of the city, the Hudson River, and the surrounding countryside.

The most impressive aspect of the Plaza is the scope of the New York State Modern Art Collection👑👑👑, one of the most unusual state-owned art collections in the country. You'll see among the outdoor sculptures an Alexander Calder black stabile in a pool, a weathered teak Stonehenge-like *Labyrinth* by François Stahly, and works by Toni Smith, Louise Nevelson, and Isamu Noguchi. Then stroll along the indoor Concourse to see tapestries by Ellsworth Kelly, Robert Motherwell, and Adolf Gottlieb, paintings by Franz Kline, Richard Anuszkiewicz, James Brooks, Clyfford Still, Mark Rothko, Grace Hartigan, and dozens of others.

The collection is virtually a catalog of big-name American artists of the 1960s. We won't assess Rockefeller's record as governor, but he was an art collector of stature himself, and did a remarkable job in assembling the state's outstanding collection.

Also of major touristic interest in downtown Albany is the State Capitol👑👑👑, which anchors the

Empire State Plaza esplanade. The massive red Scottish sandstone building, which resembles a monumental French château, took three sets of architects, $25 million (twice as much as the U.S. Capitol in Washington, D.C.), and 32 years to complete. The famous architect H. H. Richardson began the project, but died before its completion, and his partner declined to finish the job. That task fell to Isaac Perry.

INSIDERS' TIPS

One-hour free tours of the Capitol leave from the entrance lobby from 9 A.M. to 4 P.M. daily, and are extremely illuminating.

The Capitol is laden with symbolism. For instance, the 77 steps leading up to the entrance represent the year (1777) when the first legislature met in Kingston. Among many highlights, note the lavishly ostentatious Senate Chamber, a great, highly polished rose marble-walled room decorated with gold leaf and red Spanish leather chairs.

You will enjoy the "Evolutionary" sandstone staircase, which sports 4 floors of intricate carvings showing animal evolution from clam to camel. The handsomely appointed Senate Lobby and the hallway lined with former governors' portraits are pure pomp-on-parade. (Only former Governor Hugh Carey's picture is missing.) In the Governor's Chamber, the guide will point out the brass doorknob in one mahogany-paneled wall. This opened the door to an elevator (long gone) used to transport then-Governor Franklin Roosevelt in his wheelchair up to the room.

While in the Empire State Plaza, allow time for the New York State Museum ♛ ♛ ♛ in the Cultural Education Center (tel. 518-474-5877). Admission is free, and the museum is divided into 3 main sections, each of which is absorbing: "New York City—The Metropolis"; "The Adirondacks—Wilderness"; and "Upstate."

What makes the displays so compelling is the variety of visual effects used: life-size dioramas, gigantic photo murals, sound effects, and historic objects ranging from

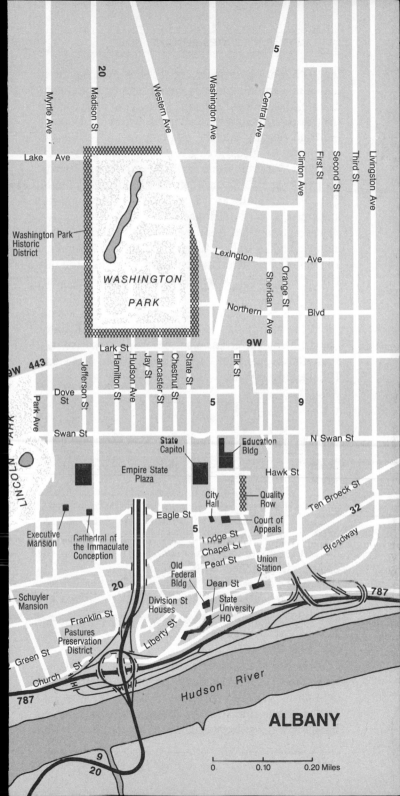

ALBANY

the 19th-century utensils and lifelike mannequins in authentic garb in a diorama called "Dining at Delmonico's" to a real 1940s "A Train" subway car once used on the 8th Avenue Express (complete with soundtrack of the train rushing into the station).

Among the visual treats are a detailed Ellis Island immigrant arrival scene, a 1920s classroom (transplanted from P.S. 52 on Ellery St., Brooklyn), a Fulton Fish Market stall, and a wilderness campsite (with loons crying in the distance).

The museum has a number of other special, changing exhibits, as well as a video theater, an Orientation Theater, and an attractive museum shop full of nature and history books about New York, toys and home accessories.

A block away from the Plaza to the west is a renovated neighborhood, Robinson Square on Hamilton Street. There you'll find upscale shops, galleries, and restaurants, many of them ensconced in handsome 19th-century brownstones.

INSIDERS' TIPS

If you want to tour the public areas of the Governor's Mansion, 138 Eagle Street, it's possible Thursday afternoon by reservation only. Call ahead to Visitors Services, (518) 474-2418.

The Albany Institute of History and Art♛ ♛, 125 Washington Avenue, is the state's oldest museum, and it has a variety of crowd-pleasers. Just a block from the Capitol, it's packed with antique (18th- and 19th-century) furniture, silver, ceramics, and other artifacts from the Mohawk–Upper Hudson area, as well as a fine collection of Hudson Valley paintings and sculpture. The Institute is open daily except Mondays. (For hours, tel. [518] 463-4478.

From the city's modern skyline, you might not realize its early Dutch beginnings. Henry Hudson reached here on his *Half Moon* voyage in 1609. The area was settled soon afterward by Dutchmen and later by Danes, Germans, Norwegians, and Scots. The present name came from the Duke of Kent and Albany, after the British took charge in 1664.

Dutch reminders still exist, however. One such is the Schuyler Mansion♛♛, 32 Catherine Street, the 1761 home of Philip Schuyler. He was a famous general of the Revolutionary War, a delegate to Philadelphia for the signing of the Declaration of Independence, and a New York State senator. His solid red brick Georgian manor has been well restored, with attention to the architectural details of the original building. Inside, the sparse furnishings are of the period, though few belonged to the family (some very fine pieces, nonetheless).

The house has many historic associations. Schuyler, though Dutch, sided with the Revolution, unlike many of the Dutch landed gentry in the state. Alexander Hamilton married Schuyler's daughter in the house, and George Washington was godfather to another Schuyler daughter. Many years later, in 1858, after the Schuylers were long gone, President Millard Fillmore was married in the drawing room to the then-owner of the house.

Two other houses of historic interest are Cherry Hill♛♛ and Arbour Hill♛♛. The first, at 523½ South Pearl Street (tel. [518] 434-4791), was the 1787 home of Philip Van Rensselaer. It was lived in by 5 generations of the family (until 1963), with all the accumulated family furnishings that such a long tenure entails. In short, the house is a mine of 18th- and 19th-century decorating and personal details.

Arbour Hill, a.k.a. Ten Broeck Mansion, at 9 Ten Broeck Place (tel. [518] 436-9826), was built by General Abraham Ten Broeck in 1798 and is replete with period furnishings. Its herb garden and beautiful lawns are especially nice in summer.

Albany is as rich in fine churches as in houses. St. Peter's Episcopal Church♛, State and Lodge streets, is considered a superior example of French Gothic style. Note the splendid stained-glass windows. Among its treasures are a Paul Revere silver baptismal bowl and pitcher (1775) and a silver communion service from England's Queen Anne (1712).

In the Gothic Revival–style Catholic Cathedral of the Immaculate Conception ♛, Eagle Street and Madison Avenue, you'll see some more fine stained glass and a carved pulpit. High points of the Episcopal Cathedral of All Saints ♛, South Swan Street near Washington Avenue, are carved 17th-century Belgian choir stalls, stone carvings, mosaics, and stained glass.

INSIDERS' TIPS

Anytime is visiting time in Albany, of course, but choicest may be during the 3-day Tulip Festival in early May. Kickoff (or wash-off) is the scrubbing down of State Street by women in Dutch costumes. Festivities include a tulip show at St. Peter's Church, a city-wide tulip competition, a Tulip Queen coronation, a *Kinderkermis* (children's fair), and a *Pinksterfest,* an arts-crafts-food-music-dance-theater street fair.

NEAR ALBANY

Just across the Hudson from Albany is Rensselaer, another early (1631) Dutch settlement. Its notable tourist attraction today is Fort Crailo ♛ ♛, Riverside Avenue, just one and a half blocks south of US-9/20. Built as a fortified home for the Van Rensselaer family in 1705, the Dutch Colonial house now serves as a free showcase—a museum, in fact—of Dutch culture throughout the Hudson Valley, with exhibits, slide show, and guided tours.

Less than 5 miles north of Albany is Troy, home of RPI (Rensselaer Polytechnic Institute), Russell Sage College, and the richly Victorian Troy Savings Bank Music Hall ♛, lodged in a lavish Italian Renaissance building.

Schenectady, northwest of Albany 10 miles via I-90, is usually a surprise and a delight to tourists. "With a name that hard to pronounce," one local resident said, "you wouldn't expect to find such a pretty town."

She's right. It isn't just the campus of Union College ♛ ♛ ♛, which is a visual treat. It was the first planned campus in the United States, and its original 1812–14 buildings were designed by the French architect Joseph Jacques Ramée. Dominating the campus is the dark stone Nott Memorial, the hemisphere's only building with a sixteen-sided dome. For a campus tour that includes beautiful Jackson's Gardens (with 27 acres of assorted perennials, annuals, and a maze), tel. (518) 370-6000.

All of Schenectady is a harvest of handsome Victorian and period houses, such as the 130 built around 1900 in the residential area called G.E. Plot, between Wendell Avenue and Lennox. (That's where General Electric executives built their homes.)

But the real focal point for a visit should be the Stockade♕♕♕, a downtown area 3½ by 4 blocks long, 2½ by 3 blocks wide, chockablock with some 66 historic homes and churches. The houses are still lived in and were built between 1700 and 1850. Most of the churches are along Front, Union, and North Church streets and Washington Avenue.

INSIDERS' TIPS

For a 90-minute walking tour of the Stockade contact the Schenectady County Historical Society, 32 Washington Avenue (tel. [518] 374-0263). The Society also offers a free pamphlet outlining a self-guided tour. Next door to the Historical Society is the YMCA (whose rest rooms come in handy if you're on a walking tour).

Among the houses you'll pass is the Governor Yates House♕, 17 Front Street, a white brick dwelling with hunter-green shutters, which dates back to 1760.

INSIDERS' TIPS

On the last Saturday of September the "Stockade Walkabout" takes place, when 3 historic churches, 6 houses, and a garden are open to the public on a special one-day tour (10 A.M.–5 P.M.).

The Hendrick Brouwer House♕ (c. 1700), 14 North Church Street, may be the city's oldest house still standing, a strong example of the sturdy, unadorned shelters built by early settlers.

Especially rich in architectural details (fine pilasters, semicircular transom, oval sunburst, English-style medallion) is the Jeremiah DeGraaf House♛ (1790), 25–27 Front Street.

SARATOGA

"The rich have always had five seasons," someone once wrote, "Winter, spring, summer, Saratoga, and fall."

This seems incontrovertible in August, when owners of thoroughbreds arrive *en entourage* at Saratoga Springs, along with racing fans from all over the country, to watch some 2,000 of the best racehorses compete in daily trials.

In fact, Saratoga's "season" nowadays spans 3 full months, June through August, and differs dramatically from the first two months to the third.

In June and July the emphasis is cultural, with a calendar crammed with plays, concerts, and ballets at the Saratoga Performing Arts Center (SPAC). The huge, partly open-air amphitheater and arts complex is ensconced in the bucolic, peaceful woods of 2,000-acre Saratoga Spa State Park. A high point for many visitors is early July, when the New York City Ballet Company is in residence, putting its best feet forward.

From the end of July through mid-August, Saratoga is home to the Philadelphia Orchestra, with numerous performances scheduled at SPAC. The New York City Opera, the Newport Jazz Festival, SPAC's Little Theatre productions, and the Twilight Chamber Series are just a few of the other lively features at SPAC.

INSIDERS' TIPS

For a current performance schedule, write SPAC, Saratoga Springs 12065 (tel. [518] 584-9330; in season, [518] 587-3333).

New to Saratoga (in 1986) is the National Museum of Dance, located in the former Washington Bathhouse, a

1909 National Historic Landmark at the edge of Saratoga Spa State Park. Changing exhibits of costumes, photography, and dance history are the highlights.

For August visitors, the scene quickly shifts (at least by day) to the Saratoga Race Track♛♛ on Union Avenue (tel. [518] 584-6200). The mood in town becomes exuberant, even feverish.

This is the season of horsy balls, slews of private parties and galas, a celebrated horse auction, parades, polo matches, and one of racing's prized events, the Travers Stakes. Saratoga's reputation as the "graveyard of favorites"—because both Man o' War and Secretariat lost here—adds to the track's mystique. Even for the casual tourist, August bursts with color, excitement, and pageantry.

PERILS & PITFALLS

August's popularity and Saratoga's limited number of hotel rooms means you should book months and months ahead if you want to find a place to stay during this ultra-popular month, when Saratoga's 25,000 population triples—and hotel rates double.

Fans of harness racing are quick to point out that flat-track racing isn't the only game in town. Saratoga Raceway harness racing, at Nelson Avenue, is great fun even for the novice to watch and has its own coterie of enthusiasts. Billed as "the fastest half-mile track in the U.S.", *its* season runs Thursday through Saturday evenings from early January to mid-March, then daily (except Sundays) from early May to mid-November (tel. [518] 584-2110).

INSIDERS' TIPS

Dinner at the track is an enjoyable (and moderately priced) experience in a 4-tiered, second-floor dining room with large picture-window visibility of the track and races-in-progress. If harness racing is new and confusing to you, look for the "Ask Me" girls in green outfits. Their job is to explain the races and betting system.

The rest of the year, Saratoga reverts to being a somewhat sleepy little college town (home of Skidmore College) and art colony (Yaddo), where selected artists and writers work and create in the privacy of a 500-acre estate. (The grounds are open to the public, and the rose gardens are beautiful all summer long.) Trivia tidbit: Edgar Allan Poe supposedly wrote "The Raven" here—*before* the property became Yaddo.

Saratoga has a long and fascinating history, from the time that Iroquois Indians discovered the healthful qualities of the area's bubbly mineral springs. By the end of the American Revolution, George Washington not only had sipped the waters, but had tried in vain to buy the land.

By the 1830s, Saratoga Springs was "Queen of the Spas," and everybody who was anybody made the trek to "take the waters." In 1861 gambling was introduced, followed two years later by horse racing. Saratoga soon became *the* great Victorian resort of the East.

In her novel *Saratoga Trunk*, Edna Ferber evoked the raffish flavor of Saratoga of that time. "July and August there's nothing like it in the whole country. Races every day, gambling, millionaires and pickpockets and sporting people and respectable family folks and politicians and famous theater actors and actresses, you'll find them all at Saratoga."

Since then, Saratoga has been off and running. And dancing, singing and concertizing.

If you're an architecture buff, Saratoga is a feast for the eye. As you drive along the town's spacious boulevards, you can almost visualize the horse-drawn carriages clop-clopping along in their heyday. North Broadway♛, with its wide lawns shielding Italianate, Colonial and Gothic Revival, Queen Anne, and fish-scale Victorian houses, is especially beautiful.

PERILS & PITFALLS

While Saratoga is at its liveliest in August, it's also when restaurant lines are longest, hotels are jammed, and local tempers are sometimes frayed. If you want a more laid-back visit (and don't care about the horses and peak events), aim for June–July or September–October.

The big orange brick building on the corner of Broadway and Greenfield was once owned by a U.S. senator who rented it to Diamond Jim Brady, who in turn lent it to Lillian Russell. She lives in Saratoga legend for having ridden through town on a gold-plated bicycle with handlebars initialed with emeralds and diamonds. Jim, no slouch in the conspicuous-consumption department, supposedly carried satchels of diamonds, handy for making deals with his millionaire railroad buddies.

Drive or stroll Circular Street and the streets around the old Skidmore campus, off North Broadway, with their wealth of Victorian and Greek Revival houses.

INSIDERS' TIPS

For a first-time overview, take a 2-hour Saratoga Circuit Tour, 417 Broadway (tel. [518] 587-3656).

As small and contained as the town is, it boasts 397 historic buildings in its inner historic district. Your minibus tour will yield local lore, history and gossip, as well as bird's-eye views of the major sights. You may learn, for instance, that Napoleon's brother, Joseph, once tried to buy the Yaddo land; which racing dynasties own which estates along North Broadway; and that the potato chip was a Saratoga creation, first known as the "Saratoga chip."

Racing fans will want to visit the National Museum of Thoroughbred Racing♕, Union Avenue and Ludlow Street, to see all the racing memorabilia and films (shown weekday mornings during the racing season). But even if you're not a racing maven, you'll enjoy viewing the pristinely kept grounds, trimmed lawns, paddocks, wooden grandstands, brilliant flower borders bursting with petunias and geraniums, and old-fashioned cast-iron fountains of the 118-year-old Saratoga Race Track♕ ♕. It's the oldest and most beautiful in the country.

Sipping the waters can be done at springs all over town, though Saratoga's original 150 springs have now trickled down to a mere 25. (There's even a mineral spring inside the Saratoga Knitting Mills on High Spring Avenue.)

INSIDERS' TIPS

During August, you can have an early buffet breakfast at the track, while watching the horses being exercised at full gallop. Breakfast is served from 6:30 A.M. Arrive early to get an upstairs table with a good overview of the track. And be sure to sample a Saratoga melon, unique to this place and time.

When visitors took their spas more seriously, the minerals found in the many different springs were credited with specific restorative powers (digestive, cardiac, arthritis, etc). The mineral taste in many of the springs is so strong and disagreeable we have to believe that anything that tastes that bad must be doing some good.

INSIDERS' TIPS

If you want a massage after your soak in the mineral waters of the Roosevelt Baths (the only remaining spa left in Saratoga Spa State Park), you have to make a reservation months in advance (April–May) for a bath and massage ($9 plus tip) in the peak month of August. A bath alone ($4) doesn't require such advance booking.

Another Saratoga sight is the Canfield Casino♕ in Congress Park on Broadway in the center of town. The 25-acre park and its Italian gardens are a beautifully manicured and restful place for strolling. They are dotted with lawn sculpture by Daniel Chester French and Bertel Thorvaldsen and lagoons full of gliding swans and geese.

The now-defunct 1870 casino preserves the high-stakes gaming rooms of the casino's heyday and contains two museums: the Saratoga Springs Museum, layered with Saratoga history and mementos, and the Walworth Memorial Museum♕, which traces in fascinating soap-opera fashion the ill-starred lives of a prominent local family.

Allow some time in this grand old resort to sample the many good restaurants in town (see Insiders' Information at the end of this chapter) and browse among the many attractive boutiques, art galleries and antiques shops along Broadway.

Outside of town, northeast on NY-29 to NY-32 and US-4, is the Saratoga National Historical Park♛♛, site of two major encounters of the Revolutionary War, the first on September 19, the second on October 7, 1777. General Horatio Gates's forces—with the help of a daring rally by Benedict Arnold—defeated the British Army under General John Burgoyne.

Strategically important, the battles are considered the turning point of the war because they kept the British from capturing the Hudson Valley and splitting New England from the rest of the colonies, and catapulted France into entering the war on the colonists' side.

History buffs love the 10-mile, self-guided drive through the area, with 10 stops for interpretive exhibits. The battlefield and main sections of the site are located in Stillwater, near the west bank of the Hudson. Also, there is an informative Visitor Center and Museum (with an excellent 20-minute film, "Checkmate on the Hudson," narrated by Burgess Meredith, that explains the battle).

Don't forget the General Philip Schuyler House, on Route 4 nearby. This 18th-century structure was the home of the patriot who, among many other achievements, was in command of northern Revolutionary forces (later replaced by Gates), and was a founder of Saratoga. This particular house replaced one that General Burgoyne dined and slept in, then torched.

LEATHERSTOCKING COUNTRY

If you drive west and northwest from Albany, gear yourself for shunpiking. That's the best way to enjoy the villages, rising hills, and sweeping valley views of Leatherstocking Country, the area made famous by James Fenimore Cooper in his *Leatherstocking Tales* and other books. (Leatherstocking, by the way, referred to the leather leggings early settlers wore as protection against the scruffy underbrush in this as-yet-untamed terrain.)

You can approach the area from the southwest, via Binghamton, if you prefer, but for the purpose of this chapter, we recommend heading southwest from Albany. Either will do.

Worth a stop, if not for lunch, at least for snapshots, is Rensselaerville, on Route 85, 25 miles or so southwest of Albany. This is a storybook village of spired white churches and imposing clapboard houses tucked into tree-dotted hillsides. No wonder the TV humorist Andy Rooney has chosen the village as his "escape hatch."

Schoharie, to the north, is another picture-pretty village—one of the oldest in this part of the state, with many original buildings intact or being restored. Have a look at the Schoharie Museum of the Iroquois Indian ♥ (tel. [518] 295-8553 for hours), with historic exhibits *and* contemporary craft works.

See also the Old Stone Fort Museum Complex ♥ ♥ (tel. [518] 295-7192), a 1772 Dutch Reformed church, reinforced as a fortress during the Revolutionary War. Using the steeple as a lookout and gunport, colonist sharpshooters successfully held off 800 British and Indian attackers.

Ten miles north of Schoharie are the Howe Caverns ♥, which constitute one of the major tourist attractions of the area. A tour of the caverns, which were discovered in 1842 by a farmer named Lester Howe, takes 70 minutes and costs $7 for adults and youngsters 13 and above, $3.50 for children 7 to 12 years old.

PERILS & PITFALLS

The caverns aren't the place for anyone with a handicap or a walking problem. An elevator takes you 56 feet below ground, and then you have a 1¼-mile hike up and down steps and around curves, and a quarter-mile underground boat ride that involves some agile maneuvering to get into and out of the flatboat.

Some 35 miles northwest are Jordanville and the Holy Trinity Monastery ♛ ♛. If you visit on a clear day, the monastery's golden onion domes and spires gleam in the sunlight. The monastery is home to 40 Russian Orthodox monks and a religious community of 100 or so.

At prescribed hours (during services), outsiders may visit the church, whose walls and ceiling are covered with Byzantine-style religious frescoes, as marvelous as Orthodox icons, of the saints and of Christ's life. If you can peek into the monks' refectory, you'll be treated to additional ornamented walls.

The centerpiece of Leatherstocking Country is Cooperstown ♛ ♛ ♛ ♛, 12 miles or so south via US-20 via NY-80.

In this era of overdevelopment and commercialization, it is a joy to see a town that seems relatively unchanged in the 10 years since our last visit. This is unusual anywhere these days, but Cooperstown isn't just any little mid-state village. This town of 2,340 on the southern edge of Lake Otsego boasts 3 major attractions: the National Baseball Hall of Fame (which attracts some 250,000 visitors a year), the Farmers' Museum, and Fenimore House.

Despite this, the town's many Victorian houses remain intact, the space around the placid lake is wooded and devoid of overbuilding, resorts, or industry, and the town's main street is free of neon signs, plastic façades, and offensive fast-food outlets.

A local family deserves the credit for Cooperstown's preservation. The Edward Clark family (heirs to a Singer sewing machine fortune) have been major Cooperstown benefactors, encouraging others to follow in their path. The area may not look as it did when George Washington first saw it in 1783, or when Judge William Cooper (James Fenimore Cooper's father) founded it 3 years later, but it's refreshingly quiet and bucolic, considering the passage of more than 200 years.

Abner Doubleday, a local boy who supposedly invented (in 1839) the game of baseball as we know it, probably played on grassy fields very similar to those that exist in the 5-block-long town today.

The major Cooperstown attraction is the National Baseball Hall of Fame♕♕♕, a modest-looking brick building on Main Street. Inside the 3-story structure is all you'll ever want to know about our national pastime's history. If you last visited before 1981, you'll be surprised at the changes.

Multimedia techniques have been used to highlight exhibits and create a sense of excitement. This is no bone-dry display of balls and bats behind glass. On the contrary, one room is a cacophony of ballpark sounds and photo blow-ups that re-create the feeling of Being There.

Another room boasts IBM computer-based displays in which you can select any of the more than 1,200 men enshrined in the Hall of Fame and ask the computer to display his statistics, highlights of his career, and see movie or TV clips of his actual performances.

In other rooms you can see the evolution of the baseball uniform, team by team; a history of black baseball players; "Great Moments in Baseball"; many artifacts and the actual lockers of Babe Ruth and other giants; a massive collection of baseball cards; and an exhibit about baseball today.

Then, of course, there's the Hall of Fame Gallery, where you'll see plaques, displayed in colonnaded alcoves, of every single member (this mausoleumlike room is the only "downer" in the place). In short, there's something for everyone—old fans, young fans, current fans, even non-fans.

INSIDERS' TIPS

Tickets for the popular Hall of Fame Game (played between American and National League teams, following the induction of new members into the Hall of Fame) are sold—and often sold out—in March. The game is played in midsummer. For ticket information, write *early* to Hall of Fame, Public Relations Dept., P.O. Box 590, Cooperstown 13326.

A separate building in the rear, the National Baseball Library, features special exhibits and baseball films. The library faces Cooper Park, a grassy lawn with a bronze statue of James Fenimore Cooper in the middle. This is the site of the original Cooper house, which burned to the ground in the late 18th century. Beyond is Doubleday Field, where the annual Hall of Fame Game is played each summer.

Cooperstown's two other major attractions are just 1 mile north of town, facing each other on Route 80. They are the Farmers' Museum and Village Crossroads♔♔ and Fenimore House♔♔♔. Both were established through the largesse of the Clark family.

INSIDERS' TIPS

Ask about combination tickets, available for all 3 major attractions: $9 for adults, $3 for children.

The Farmers' Museum and Village Crossroads has been compared to Old Sturbridge Village in Massachusetts. The museum is ensconced in a huge stone barn and creamery, so large and solidly built that it was locally dubbed the "cow palace." It makes a spacious exhibit hall for a museum of 19th-century farm life.

Village Crossroads consists of 11 wood and field-stone structures, dating from 1785 to 1830, collected from a radius of 100 miles around Cooperstown. Houses, barns, steepled church, country store, temperance tavern, and offices are grouped as they were in real life around a pastoral village green, where photogenic sheep gambol freely all day long.

INSIDERS' TIPS

A weekend program, offered during winter, called "Day in the Life," permits a maximum of 8 people of all ages to spend a day from 10 A.M. to 6 P.M. participating in the old-fashioned chores of the farm village—from smoking meat to farming to fireplace cooking—for a $20 fee. It's a delightful *family* adventure.

This museum village functions as a working community. There are no guided tours marching in lockstep, no craft demonstrations per se. You can watch the artisans working in various buildings, ask questions as the spirit moves you, and even participate in the jobs if you wish—milking cows, feeding poultry, making brooms, and cooking. Crafts made in the village are sold in the general store.

The handsome red brick, colonnaded Fenimore House across the road was originally the home of Edward Clark, but now houses the New York State Historical Association. The house is beautifully furnished with antiques, and functions as a "stage" for a first-rate collection of American folk art, with frequently changed exhibits—a must-see for anyone who cares about 18th- and 19th-century naïve paintings, weather vanes, quilts, sculptures, and other artifacts. All items are cleverly displayed, with informative captions and explanatory materials.

INSIDERS' TIPS

While you're at the Fenimore House, ask for a free brochure of the New York State Historical Association, which outlines a self-guided walking tour of some of the historic homes in town.

Both the Fenimore House and the Farmers' Museum are open daily from 9 A.M. to 6 P.M., May 1 through October 31. (For winter hours, tel. [607] 547-2533).

Now a fourth Cooperstown attraction is up and running. It's the Alice Busch Opera Theater, a new (1987) open-sided showcase for the popular local Glimmerglass Opera Company. (See Insiders' Information at the end of this chapter.)

INSIDERS' TIPS

A do-it-the-easy-way tour of Cooperstown is possible through Historic Cooperstown Tours, a 1-hour limousine drive through town with taped and live talks en route (tel. [607] 547-9085 or 547-5134).

North of Cooperstown, as you head back to Route 20 west, is Springfield Center, where antique shops square off and face each other along Route 80.

Further exploration of Leatherstocking Country might bring you to the delightful college town of Hamilton, where Colgate University is located. North of US-20 on NY-12B is Deansboro, home of a unique, hands-on Musical Museum♛, in which you are encouraged to squeeze, push, prod, and play assorted instruments to your heart's content.

Back on US-20 to the west is Cazenovia, a town beautifully situated on a lake of the same name. The lake was originally called *Ho-wah-ge-neh* (Lake Where Yellow Perch Swim) by the Indians. When John Linklaen, a Dutchman working for the Holland Land Company, settled the area in 1793, he renamed it after the general manager of his company, Theophile Cazenove.

Three inns, antiques shops, many 19th-century homes, and an old-fashioned main street make this a pleasant overnight stop., An added incentive is misty, tumultuous Chittenango Falls♛, 4 miles north on NY-13, a scenic picnic-and-nature-trail stop. A drive along the east side of Lake Cazenovia is another exhilarating visual delight.

So is Lorenzo♛, a handsome red brick Georgian mansion facing the lake, off NY-13 (tel. [315] 655-3200). For admirers of antiques and of the continuity of history, Lorenzo is fascinating. The house was in a single family's possession from 1806, when John Linklaen built it, until 1968.

The original furnishings, mosting dating from the 1850s, reflect the changing decorating trends of Victorian times. As the guide explains, the house represents "accumulation, not *collection*, over a century and a half."

Continuing west on US-20, you'll come to the Finger Lakes area. But that's another story—and chapter.

Instead, you might get on I-90 and loop back east through Rome and Utica. A major sight in Rome is Fort Stanwix♛♛, a restored 18th-century fortress, smack in the center of town, at 112 East Park Street (tel. [315] 336-2090/2092). From a distance, the walls seem low and minimal and the prospect uninviting. Persevere.

Inside the massive earth-and-wood walls are some surprises. The fort is run by the National Park Service, and staffers in period costumes present a you-are-there version of a dramatic year (1778) in the old fort's history. Built by the British in 1758, the fort was later taken over by Revolutionary forces who were outnumbered, but withstood a British siege in 1777.

Throughout the year, special events are staged on the grounds, such as a Memorial Day encampment of 18th–20th-century "soldiers." Also in Rome, along the old Erie Canal, is the Erie Canal Village ♛, 5789 New London Road. On the bank of the Erie Canal an 1840s village has been re-created, with houses that were moved here from sites within 50 miles of Rome. The village is open mid-May through September (tel. [315] 337-3999).

Six miles east of Rome is the Oriskany Battlefield, site of one of the bloodiest battles of the Revolution in 1777. In what is now a peaceful meadow, British and Indian forces ambushed 800 Mohawk Valley militiamen. There are paths through pastures and woods and descriptive signs, should you want to take a self-guided tour.

Utica, 12 miles southeast on NY-49, has a number of attractions for the intrepid traveler: cruises along the Erie Canal, a stunning art museum, a Victorian mansion, a hands-on Children's museum, a zoo, and, for the inveterate shopper, a sizable factory outlet center, with more than 40 outlets installed in an old factory. You can even take a free tour of an old-time brewery.

A highpoint, for us, is the Munson-Williams-Proctor Institute ♛ ♛ ♛, a spacious concrete contemporary building, designed by Philip Johnson, housing a top-drawer collection of 18th- to 20th-century works of art, with several splendid Hudson River school paintings by Thomas Cole.

Note the black sculpture *(Three Arches)* by Alexander Calder outside the front door, and, just inside the entrance, a finely sculpted wooden-winged man by Leonard Baskin, along with works by Henry Moore, Marino Marini, and Gaston Lachaise. Paintings by Jackson Pollock, Frank Stella, and Andy Warhol, among others, can be found on the second floor. A surprising touch: to the right of the entrance is a playroom for young children, complete with bright, well-made toys to keep them busy.

Behind the Institute (and associated with it) is Fountain Elms ♛ ♛, a remarkably well preserved Victorian mansion, whose rooms exude period accuracy. The details are letter-perfect. Both buildings are open year-round.

At the F. X. Matt Brewery, Court and Varick streets (tel. [315] 732-0022), you can have a free 45-minute tour through an old building where Victorian antiques blend with up-to-date brewing equipment. At the tour's end, a short trolley ride brings you back to the Victorian-decorated tavern (complete with stained-glass swinging doors and an old-time, steel disc music-player), where you can sample 2 home-grown brews (or a root beer if you prefer).

I-90 east leads you quickly back the 55 miles to the Schenectady-Albany area, unless you want to make a stop—and we'd recommend it to art lovers—at Canajoharie to see the collection of Winslow Homer paintings and other oils and watercolors by Sargent, Whistler, Inness, Stuart, and the Wyeths at the Library and Art Gallery ♛ ♛, 2 Erie Boulevard (tel. [518] 673-2314).

Other Canajoharie attractions include Fork Klock ♛, which contains a restored farmhouse, Indian trading post, schoolhouse, blacksmith shop, and other buildings; and Fort Plain Museum, on the site of a 1780s fort, with a collection of local artifacts and memorabilia.

Canajoharie's name derives from an Indian word that means "washed pot," a reference to a large "pothole" in the Canajoharie Creek Gorge ♛ ♛, whose dramatic 45-foot waterfall can be seen from Wintergreen Park nearby. (Another reason for making the Canajoharie stop.)

Back on I-90, you might, if you're a glove maven, wheel off at Exit 28 and head north up NY-30A less than 5 miles to Gloversville, which is very likely the glove capital of the world. There are more discount stores than you can shake a mitt at.

Just 5 miles southeast is Schoharie Crossing, where you can view the guardlock and canal bed of the original Erie Canal. This is a pleasant spot for picnicking on the banks of the Mohawk River, watching boats drift by on today's Barge Canal, or hiking (some prefer biking) along the towpath, which is marked with signs telling the canal's history.

Then it's back to I-90 and Albany.

INSIDERS' INFORMATION FOR ALBANY, SARATOGA, AND LEATHERSTOCKING AREA

Albany
(Albany County; Area Code 518)

Hotels

Albany Hilton 👑👑👑
Ten Eyck Plaza, State and Lodge Sts., 12207. Tel. 462-6611
2 persons in twin, $109–129
Modern 15-story edifice in handy city-center location. 387 rooms, bar, nightclub, 2 restaurants, indoor swimming pool, full big-hotel amenities, fine views of cathedral and Capitol.

Albany Marriott 👑👑👑
189 Wolf Rd., 12205. Tel. 458-8444
2 persons in twin, $111
Large, modern brick high-rise near airport. 302 rooms, bar, nightclub, 2 restaurants, 2 heated pools, health club. Popular with locals for special events. Attractive lobby, subtler decor than many in this chain.

Desmond Americana 👑👑👑
660 Albany-Shaker Rd., 12211. Tel. 869-8100
2 persons in double, $100–140
Large, inviting 4-story brick-and-clapboard complex, designed to look like an Early American village, off I-87. 340 rooms and suites, bar, 2 restaurants (Scrimshaw 👑👑 for seafood), 2 pools (indoor and outdoor), health club, saunas, billiards and game room.

Mansion Hill Inn 👑
115 Philip St., 12202. Tel. 434-2313/465-2038
2 persons in suite, $85 (including full breakfast)
Restored downtown building near Capitol. 2 large suites only, with kitchen and living room. This cozy

B&B's adjoining restaurant serves dinner and is a favorite local breakfast stop. Nothing fancy, but homey and agreeable, with comfortable refurbished rooms.

Restaurants

La Serre ♛ ♛

14 Green St. Tel. 463-6056

Average dinner: $30

Albany at its most elegant. Dining with grace, fine service, an Italian/French-accented menu featuring veal Normande or Français, duckling au poivre, rack of spring lamb, lobster ravioli.

L'Auberge ♛ ♛

351 Broadway. Tel. 465-1111

Formal French dining with flair: Dover sole, *Magret de canard* among the specialties.

Sitar ♛ ♛

1929 Central Ave., Colonie. Tel. 456-6670

Average dinner: $25

Authoritatively prepared Indian specialties, including tandoori dishes—but if you've a penchant for the incendiary, you'll have to request it.

Truffles ♛ ♛

Albany Hilton, State and Lodge Sts. Tel. 462-6611, ext. 210

Average dinner: $30

Elegant French menu, but if you're in town Friday night, come for the blockbuster lobster and seafood buffet (all you can eat for $24.95), accompanied by live jazz.

Yono's ♛ ♛

Robinson Square. Tel. 436-7747

Average dinner: $20

Authentic Indonesian dishes (and European classics) served on 3 floors of an old town house (plus garden in summertime) with stylish flair. Try Chef Yono's *satay, ikan pepes* (baby salmon stuffed with seafood, wrapped in banana leaves), and *ayam Bandung* (chicken breast with shallots, ginger, coconut milk, and chili peppers). Save room for his wife Donna's prize-winning chocolate rendezvous cake ♛ ♛ ♛ ♛ and other luscious desserts.

Cafe Capriccio ♥
49 Grand St. Tel. 465-0439
Average dinner: $20–25
Northern Italian (pastas, lamb) is the theme here, with a few Hispanic numbers such as paella Valenciana, classical guitarist performs Thursday evenings.

China Pavilion ♥
256 Old Wolf Rd., Latham. Tel. 869-4624
Average dinner, $20
Quality Chinese restaurants are hard to come by, but count on this one for reliable Hunan and Sichuan specialties. Attractive setting.

Hiro's ♥
1933 Central Ave., Colonie. Tel. 456-1180
Average dinner: $25
If you hunger for sushi, tempura, and other Japanese favorites, here's your Albany answer. Reservations essential.

Jack's Oyster House ♥
42 State St. Tel. 465-8854
Average dinner: $25–30
A longtime standby with Albanians, reliable for steaks, and of course oysters and other seafood.

Yates Street ♥
492 Yates St. Tel. 438-2012
Average dinner: $25
A favorite of Albanian cognoscenti—with reason. Known for its *nouvelle* American food, impeccably presented.

Shopping

The Oriental Line, 295 Hamilton St., Robinson Square. Exquisite Oriental antiques, custom-designed jewelry, frequently changing exhibits.

The Rice Gallery, Albany Institute of History and Art, 135 Washington Ave. Tel. 463-4478. High-quality handcrafts and art for sale, special shows periodically. Open 11 A.M.–3 P.M., Tuesday–Saturday.

Stuyvesant Plaza, Western Ave. and Fuller Rd. An upscale shopping complex of 62 stores and restaurants. **The Cheese Connection** (deli, gourmet goodies, box lunches), **Crabtree & Evelyn** (English soaps and toiletries), **Dandelion Green** (fun clothes, dancewear and footwear) are just a few of the terrific shops here.

Theaters

Cohoes Music Hall, P.O. Box 586, Cohoes 12047. Tel. 235-7969. Live musical theater, professional company. Old and new musicals.

Empire State Institute for the Performing Arts, Empire State Plaza, P.O. Box 2088, 12223. Tel. 474–3518. Snazzy showcase for plays and musicals by resident professional company, also music, dance guest artists. Open September–May.

Palace Theater, 19 Clinton Ave. Tel. 465-4663/4755. This 3,000-seat movie "palace" is Albany Symphony Orchestra's home, also hosts guest performances. Open September–May.

Cambridge
(Washington County; Area Code 518)

Shopping

New Skete Farms, off Route 67, east of town. Tel. 677-3928. Russian Orthodox monastery gift shop sells the monks' homemade products: smoked chickens, hams, sausage, bacon, cheddar cheese spreads, maple syrup, hand-painted icons, and traditional Easter eggs, as well as delicious cheesecakes made by nuns who live nearby.

Cazenovia
(Madison County; Area Code 315)

Hotels

Brewster Inn ♛ ♛ ♛
Box 507, US-20 near junction with NY-13, on south shore of Lake Cazenovia 13035. Tel. 655-9232
2 persons in double, $50–120
Imposing Victorian mansion facing lake. 8 rooms, bar, restaurant ♛ ♛, tennis courts, boating and water sports. A beautiful house, built for a John D. Rockefeller partner. Charming, spacious rooms, some with Jacuzzis, all with unique antiques, handmade quilts, great originality.

Linklaen House♛♛
P.O. Box 36, 79 Albany St., 13035. Tel. 655-3461
2 persons in double, $50–70; in twin, $80
Delightful 1835 hostelry on main street of town. 24 rooms, a bed-sitting room, restaurant, lounge. As close to an English inn as you'll find in the United States, with elegant afternoon tea from 3 to 5 P.M. daily, Sunday brunch from 10 A.M. to 3 P.M. Antique furnishings, relaxed, friendly ambiance. The inn's eggs Benedict are famous.

Brae Loch Inn♛
5 Albany St., 13035. Tel. 655-3431
2 persons in twin, $65–125 (incl. continental breakfast)
Chalet-style building in central village location. 12 rooms, delightful pub, restaurant (with kilted waitresses). You'll either love this ornately decorated Victorian retreat or find its heavy Scots accent too *twee* for words.

Cherry Valley
(Otsego County; Area Code 607)

Restaurant
Tryon Inn♛
124 Main St. Tel. 264-9301
Average dinner: $21
More than 4½ acres of parklike lawns with towering maples, an antiques-filled inn featuring reliable prime rib, steak, seafood specialties. Try the open-air dining terrace in warm weather. 12 guest rooms also available in a separate building on the grounds.

Cooperstown
(Otsego County; Area Code 607)

Hotels
Otesaga♛♛♛♛
Lake St. on Route 80, 13326. Tel. 547-9931
2 persons in twin, $81–87 (MAP—includes 2 meals daily)
Enormous Georgian resort hotel on Lake Otesaga, within walking distance of town. 125 rooms, 11 parlor suites, Hawkeye Bar (with 1894 cherrywood bar), Glim-

merglass Lounge, café, restaurant, heated pool, health
club, tennis courts, lake swimming, boating, and fishing, 18-hole golf course adjacent. An impeccably maintained, well-run resort where dressiness is the mode.
Seasonal.

Cooper Motor Inn♛ ♛
Chestnut St., 13326. Tel. 547-2567
2 persons in twin, $80–90 (incl. continental breakfast)
Handsome brick Colonial house on wooded grounds in
village center. 22 rooms with TV, comfortable public
rooms, antique furnishings. Owned by Otesaga Hotel,
the name "motor inn" is misleading. This is a bona fide
in-town inn, not a motel.

Inn at Cooperstown♛ ♛
16 Chestnut St., 13326. Tel. 547-5756
2 persons in twin, $68 (incl. continental breakfast)
Beautifully restored Victorian house one block from
Main Street. 17 rooms, no TV or room phones; lounge
with TV. Open porch with rockers. Rooms are comfortable, roomy, staff extremely cheerful and helpful.

Tunnecliff Inn♛ ♛
34–36 Pioneer St., 13326. Tel. 547-9611
2 persons in twin, $58–68
An 1802 house just off Main Street. 17 rooms, no TV,
"The Pit" pub (popular lunch and evening hangout),
restaurant (with New American cuisine menu). A local
landmark, Tunnecliff has new ownership and a much-
needed facelift. Simply furnished rooms, convenient
central location.

Restaurant

Cross Roads Inn♛
4 miles outside town at Fly Creek
Average dinner: $20–25
Competently prepared roasted duck with raspberry
sauce, chicken breast stuffed with Brie, and other
nouvelle favorites.

Shopping

Homescapes, Main St. Out-of-the-ordinary Americana home accessories and furniture.

Gallery 53/Smithy Gallery, 55 Pioneer St. Tel. 547-
8671. Both art galleries share space in historic 1786
stone edifice (town's oldest) built by William Cooper.

Frequently changing shows of local, regional, and SoHo artists, all works for sale. In Smithy, look for mid-summer show with baseball theme, many performing-art shows. Open summers.

Theaters

Alice Busch Opera Theater, NY-80 (8 miles north of town), P.O. Box 191, 13326. Tel. 547-5704. Professional Glimmerglass Opera productions in English, late June through August, in brand-new, open-sided opera house.

Cooperstown Theatre Festival, NY-80 (7 miles north), P.O. Box 851, 13326. Tel. 547-2335. Professional resident company performs comedies, dramas, musicals with New York casts. Tuesday–Sunday, July–August.

Hamilton
(Madison County; Area Code 315)

Hotel

Colgate Inn ♛ ♛

Payne St., On-the-Green, 13346. Tel. 824-2300

2 persons in twin, $60 (incl. continental breakfast, newspaper)

A 1925 Dutch Colonial house at one end of village green. 46 rooms, Tap Room, Salmagundi Restaurant (♛), golf, tennis, swimming pool, ski tow. Hitchcock furniture, antiques give inn a comfortable 19th-century air.

Ilion
(Herkimer County; Area Code 315)

Hotel

Chesham Place ♛ ♛ ♛

317 West Main St., 13357. Tel. 894-3552

2 persons in double, $35–40 (incl. large continental breakfast)

1872 Italianate Victorian house on a wooded hilltop

above the main street. 2 rooms, TV in hallway "lounge." This B&B is a "sleeper," both literally and figuratively. Owners Ann and Bob Dreizler have decorated with authentic Victorian antiques, exceptional flair. Great comfort, privacy, congeniality, and taste, as well as helpful info on places to see and dine at in the area.

Restaurant
The Whiffletree ♛ ♛
345 East Main St. Tel. 895-7440
Average dinner: $15–18
Another Ilion "sleeper." From the outside, this looks like a run-of-the-roadside motel (it *is* a motel, too). Four attractive lower-level dining rooms face old canal and showcase delicious dishes, such as shrimp and mushrooms in sherry butter; *plaki* (reflecting owner's Greek background)—superb halibut baked with raisins, garlic, spinach, tomatoes, onions, and white wine; mouthwatering chocolate-chip pie. Live music.

Shopping
The Finding Shoppe, 632 East Main St. Tel. 823-3173. Antiques, country furniture, primitives, collectibles. Open 9 A.M.–5 P.M. daily.

Leonardsville
(Madison County; Area Code 315)

Restaurant
The Horned Dorset ♛ ♛ ♛
Main St., NY-8, 13364. Tel. 855-7898
Average dinner: $30
This is the kind of dining discovery every food maven craves: excellent cooking with freshest ingredients in which everything works. A former community meeting house tastefully furnished with Victoriana sets the stage for beef bourguignonne, lamb in a Madeira-juniper sauce, other delights. Menu changes often. Also 2 rooms, 2 suites available next door in an Italianate villa overlaid on a Federal foundation.

Little Falls
(Herkimer County; Area Code 315)

Restaurants
Canal Side Inn ♛ ♛
395 South Ann St. Tel. 823-1170
Average dinner: $17–20
A small, stylish establishment with French accent, knowledgeable service, and *nouvelle* food (duckling with mandarin oranges and curaçao, coquilles in lemon butter), appreciative local clientele.
Beardslee Manor ♛
NY-5, 13365. Tel. 823-9870
Average dinner: $20
Victorian-era "Irish castle" doesn't overshadow competent continental fare. Family place.

Rensselaer
(Rensselaer County; Area Code 518)

Hotel
Tibbetts House Inn ♛
100 Columbia Turnpike (NY-9 and NY-20), 12144. Tel. 472-1348
2 persons in twin, $36
Old farmhouse close to Albany. 5 rooms, *shared baths,* no TV or room phones. Longtime guest house with antiques, braided rugs, quilts, large grounds.

Rensselaerville
(Albany County; Area Code 518)

Restaurant
Palmer House Cafe ♛
2105 Main St. Tel. 797-3449
Average dinner: $18
An unpretentious eatery inside a neoclassical building in village center. Homemade soups, pastas, salads, creative entrées (*cassoulet Toulousain,* veal scallopini with balsamic vinegar and hazelnuts), yummy desserts. A sleeper. Closed Tuesdays.

Rome
(Oneida County; Area Code 315)

Hotel
Paul Revere Motor Lodge and Conference Center♛
Turin Rd., Route 26, 13440. Tel. 336-1776
2 persons in twin, $36–45
Motel snuggled into wooded landmark property at the edge of town. 75 rooms, bar, The Beeches restaurant (♛), up the hill in former mansion, swimming pool. Wooded setting, motel decor, but peacefully private and quiet at night.

Restaurant
The Savoy♛ ♛
255 East Dominick St. Tel. 339-3166
Average dinner: $8.50–10
Pat Destito's homey, old-fashioned eatery is an obligatory stop for all campaigning politicians (national or statewide) and other visiting celebrities. Famous for its local color, Italian home cooking (homemade pastas), gargantuan servings, Depression-era prices, Pat's hospitality, and a room-long bar the likes of which they don't make anymore.

Shopping
Revereware Factory Outlet, Liberty Plaza. New store with attractive displays of discounted Revere cookware. Excellent prices.

Saratoga Springs
(Saratoga County; Area Code 518)

Hotels
Adelphi♛ ♛ ♛
365 Broadway, 12866. Tel. 587-4688
2 persons in twin, $65–125 (August rates: $120–250)
A 3-story 1877 building on the main thoroughfare. 24 rooms and suites, bar, café, courtyard, Saratoga Club restaurant (open only July and August). A museum of Victoriana, eloquently evokes another era. Even the elevator has damask-covered walls. Closed November through April.

Gideon Putnam ♛ ♛ ♛
Saratoga Spa State Park, 12866. Tel. 584-3000
2 persons in twin, $78–99. (August rates: $260, AP with 3 meals.)
132 rooms, bar, restaurant, swimming pool, health club. A Saratoga classic, beautiful park location, amenities. Spacious rooms, bustling atmosphere.

Ramada Renaissance ♛ ♛ ♛
534 Broadway, 12866. Tel. 584-4000 or (800) 242-6232
2 persons in twin, $65–75 (August rates: $160)
Red brick high-rise hotel on main street. 190 rooms, bar, restaurant, indoor swimming pool, tennis. Newcomer to town, with all amenities, convenient to shops, restaurants. Ramada's top-of-the-line.

Restaurants

Chez Pierre ♛ ♛
NY-9, Gansevoort. Tel. 793-3350
Average dinner: $25
Peaceful country setting. Family-run auberge-like eatery with French flair, specialties like veal Oscar, sole Marguery.

Court Bistro ♛ ♛
60 Court St. Tel. 584-6009
Average dinner: $20–25
A converted storefront now sports mirror-lined walls, *fin de siècle* style, contemporary menu that changes often, expertly cooked fare. Live entertainment Saturday night. Alfresco breakfast is a warm-weather delight.

The Elms ♛ ♛
NY-9, Malta. Tel. 587-2277
Average dinner: $25
A family-run Italian restaurant noted for its suberb veal and homemade pasta dishes (like fusilli in a Gorgonzola-walnut sauce). Don't skip the luscious Italian desserts.

Union Coach House ♛ ♛
139 Union Ave. Tel. 584-6440
Average dinner: $25
Substantial American/continental fare in handsome house metamorphosed from a smithy/carriage shop/

boardinghouse/hotel. Chicken Baltimore and pork chops Barnstable are standouts. Convenient to track. Closed Sundays and Mondays, also January.

Hattie's Chicken Shack ♛
45 Phila St. Tel. 584-4790
Average dinner: $10
Mrs. Hattie Moseley's little storefront eatery has been a Saratoga institution since 1938. Plain, no-nonsense American fare is Hattie's forte (at bargain prices). Her batterless fried chicken is a must.

Manna Inn ♛
19 Phila St. Tel. 587-7770
Average dinner: $20
Try the stuffed leg of lamb, seafood, or pasta specialties in this pleasing Italian-accented establishment.

Ye Olde Wishing Well ♛
NY-9, Gansevoort. Tel. 584-7640
Average dinner: $20–25
Combine a vintage (1823) farmhouse, solid American fare such as roast duckling, prime ribs, and fresh seafood, and live entertainment, and you've got the picture.

Bars, Cafés, and Sundries

Ben and Jerry's Ice Cream Shop, Phila and Putnam Sts. From a former gas station emerges a delicious assortment of ice cream cones and sundaes.

Bruegger's Bagel Bakery, Broadway. Read the morning newspapers hung from poles, Viennese coffeehouse style, while breakfasting on cinnamon raisin, whole wheat, or other bagel choices.

Olde Bryan Inn, 123 Maple St. Tel. 587-2990. Cozy tavern with 3 fireplaces, 1773 building. Popular with Skidmore students for light snacks, lunches, salads, Buffalo wings, etc.

Pehl's Bake Shoppe and Cafe, Broadway. Tel. 587-8900. A cheerful early-morning choice for strawberry-filled crepes and other breakfast delights, light lunches, and after-theater snacks. Open till midnight.

Trade Winds, 51 South Broadway. Tel. 584-3500. Pub atmosphere, generous portions, American/continental fare.

Shopping

Design Works/Contemporary Crafts, Lower Level, 480 Broadway. Tel. 584-0987. Wide range of the newest and best in modern American handcrafts.

Museum Antiques & Art of Saratoga Springs (MAASS), 153 Regent Street. Tel. 584-0107. 30 dealers display their wares—marvelous Victoriana, toys, dolls, games, other antiques, literally thousands of treasures—in a series of rooms in an old house.

Saratoga Art Gallery, 465 Broadway. Tel. 587-7580. Graphics and prints by artists from Appel to Wyeth. Also custom framing.

Theater

Saratoga Performing Arts Center (SPAC), 12866. Tel. 587-3330. July–August performances of New York City Ballet, Philadelphia Orchestra in wooded, indoor/outdoor amphitheater.

Schenectady
(Schenectady County; Area Code 518)

Restaurants

Luigi's ♛ ♛
1125 Barrett St. Tel. 382-9044
Average dinner: $20
Reliable Italian dishes in congenial setting.

The Ritz ♛ ♛
1725 Van Vranken Ave., 12308. Tel. 381-9426
Average dinner: $20
Stained-glass foyer, mirrored walls, dishes such as chicken *chausseur,* shrimp Dijonaise, and gingered veal are scene-stealers in this quiet French chef-owned establishment. Ambrosial desserts, especially marzipan torte, Mexican chocolate mousse.

Truc's Orient Express ♛ ♛
450 State St. Tel. 346-1940
Average dinner: $20
A Vietnamese eatery with creative flair in menu and decor. A family enterprise with branches in Hartford, Ct., and West Stockbridge, Mass. Try the 5-spiced

chicken, singing chicken, crispy fried whole fish, or happy pancake.

The Van Dyck ♛ ♛
237 Union St. Tel. 374-2406
Average dinner: $25
The place to hang out if you like live jazz—it's on deck weekends. Standard American dishes like pot roast, steak, seafood. Pleasant dining in rear garden on clement evenings.

Shopping
The Gallery, Schenectady Museum and Planetarium, Nott Terrace Heights. Tel. 382-7890. Top-notch handcrafts—pottery, silver, weaving, woodwork—*juried* before being admitted for sale.

Tea, Morning/Afternoon
The Sweet Tooth, Upper Union St. Cheerful tearoom aptly named for scrumptious desserts. Also lunch and brunch.

Theater
Proctor's, 432 State St. Tel. 382-3884. A 1926 movie and vaudeville theater lovingly restored to its vintage grandeur. An amazing organ (dubbed "Goldie") does everything but high kicks. Theater features classic productions, Shakespeare, revivals, ballet, vaudeville, music groups, sharing traveling talent circuit with Washington's Kennedy Center and Carnegie Hall.

Springfield Center
(Otsego County; Area Code 315)

Shopping
Bobbi von Dehmlein at The Cherry, Lake Rd. NY-80, near Cooperstown. Tel. 858-0232. Lots of antiques and collectibles. Victorian ice cream parlor in the rear.

Country Memories Gift Shop, Lake Rd., NY-80, near Cooperstown. Tel. 858-2691. Old-fashioned country store, toys, baskets, antiques, cheese, some food. Also B&B, with 2 huge, comfortably furnished suites upstairs ($50).

Troy
(Rensselaer County; Area Code 518)

Restaurant
River Street Cafe ♛
492 River St. Tel. 273-2740
Average dinner: $18
Informal setting for some spirited New American renderings—Dover sole in hazelnut butter, scallops in Pernod, and the like.

INSIDERS' TIPS

Favorite nibbles among upstaters are Freihofer cookies, an Albany specialty widely available in Troy and elsewhere. Their chocolate chip cookies are so delicious you'd guess they were homemade.

Theater
Troy Savings Bank Music Hall, 33 Second St. Tel. 273-0038. Classical and jazz performances in top floor of an 1870 bank. Superb acoustics.

Cruises
Cape Islander Cruises, Riverfront Park. Tel. 274-2545. Afternoon, moonlight dinner, brunch cruises, charters. May 1–October 31.

Utica
(Oneida County; Area Code 315)

Restaurants
The Metro ♛ ♛
606 Huntington St. Tel. 733-4130
Average dinner: $22–25
Located in an old corner bank building, near the F. X. Matt Brewery. Inside, it's art deco cool, with a menu that highlights chicken Veronique, shrimp scampi, swordfish *en papillote.* Live jazz Friday and Saturday nights.
The Trackside Tavern ♛
Baggs Square. Tel. 797-1200
Average dinner: $15–18
Fin de siècle decor, yuppie clientele, seafood and pasta

emphasis at dinner, lively lunch and snack menu (winners: barbecued ham on rye, crabmeat broiler).

Snacks and Sundries

The Columbia Garden Cafe, corner of Columbia and State Sts. Attractive spot for pizzas and other light dishes.

Pubs

F. X. Matt Brewery, Court and Varick Sts. Tel. 732-0022. Brewery tours where Utica Club beer is made, with chance to sample beer in 1888 Victorian tavern.

Mayo Gate, Columbia St. An Irish pub.

Shopping

Bass Shoe Factory Outlet, NY-12 south, Barnesveld. Well-displayed, wide selection of Bass shoes for men and women at big reductions.

Charles Town, 311 Turner St. Tel. 724-9848. Good buys in dozens of name brands (such as Ann Klein, Bass, London Fog, Calvin Klein, Adidas, Perry Ellis, Hush Puppies, Austin Hill), 25-to-70-percent discounts, in old factory building.

PERILS & PITFALLS

Check carefully before you buy, as some items have serious flaws and irregularities.

THE NORTH AND THE ADIRONDACKS

Few countries in the world—let alone provinces—can afford to set aside 5.7 million acres as parkland and nearly half of that as wilderness area. That is what New York has done in its Adirondack Park, established in 1892, to protect and preserve some of the most glorious forested mountain and lake terrain in North America.

This is an area in which you can enjoy nature to the fullest, whether as an activist (skiing, snowmobiling, skating, sailing, fishing, canoeing, rafting, hunting, hiking, camping, mountain climbing) or as a spectator searching for beauty in unspoiled vistas and native flora and fauna.

INSIDERS' TIPS

Look for wild natives: osprey, blue heron, loon, white-tailed deer, beaver, otter, muskrat, porcupine, raccoon, fox, mink, black bear.

In prehistoric times the Algonquin Indians reportedly held sway here. After Europeans arrived, explorers, trappers, and settlers used the valleys of the St. Lawrence and the Hudson, and Lakes Champlain and George, as thoroughfares. So did opposing armies in the wars involving French, British, Indians, and Americans. In the 19th century, baronial retreats and rustic resorts proliferated in the outback. Today, many Adirondack areas are noted for their resorts and outdoor sports.

For the visitor interested in doing rather than viewing, see Insiders' Information listings at the end of this chapter.

For the sightseer, we suggest the following itineraries:

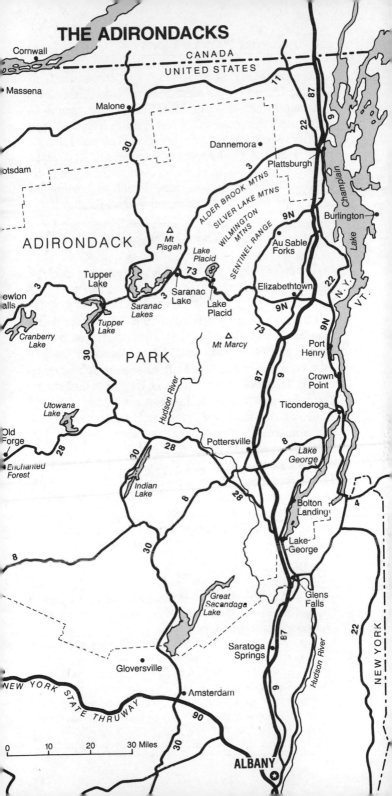

THE ADIRONDACKS

Cornwall

Massena

CANADA
UNITED STATES

Malone

11

87

Dannemora

otsdam

30

3

Plattsburgh

22

9

ALDER BROOK MTNS

SILVER LAKE MTNS

WILMINGTON MTNS

9N

Burlington

ADIRONDACK

△ Mt Pisgah

Lake Placid

SENTINEL RANGE

Au Sable Forks

Lake Champlain

Tupper Lake

73

9

ewton alls

3

Saranac Lakes

Saranac Lake

Elizabethtown

N.Y.

22

9N

VT.

3

Tupper Lake

Lake Placid

9N

Cranberry Lake

30

PARK

△ Mt Marcy

73

Port Henry

87

9

Crown Point

Hudson River

Utowana Lake

Ticonderoga

Old Forge

28

28

Pottersville

8

Lake George

Enchanted Forest

30

8

Indian Lake

28

Bolton Landing

4

8

Lake George

Great Sacandaga Lake

Glens Falls

30

87

22

NEW YORK

Saratoga Springs

9

Hudson River

Gloversville

Amsterdam

NEW YORK STATE THRUWAY

90

30

0   10   20   30 Miles

ALBANY

One route begins at Albany and drives north to Ausable Chasm on the west bank of Lake Champlain, then southwest to Lake Placid, and loops south to Amsterdam. A second route drives north from Syracuse to Alexandria Bay in the heart of Thousand Island country on the St. Lawrence Seaway, east to Tupper Lake, and loops south to Rome. Both include generous helpings of the gorgeous lake, forest, and mountain terrain for which the Adirondacks are so famous.

PERILS & PITFALLS

Check your fuel. In the Adirondacks, gas stations are fewer and farther apart, and they often close at dinnertime.

I-87 from Albany arrives in the Adirondack Park area at Glens Falls. This town was destroyed by the British in 1780, rebuilt in 1788 by American Colonel John Glen as a mill site, and flourished as a lumbering center. That boomtown period is long past, and today Glens Falls is known for its resort activities.

Yet amid a surfeit of commercial enterprises (rides and amusement park-type attractions), you'll find a different category: The Hyde Collection ♛ ♛ ♛, a gem of a small museum, at 161 Warren St. (tel. [518] 792-1761). Its treasure trove consists of works by artists ranging from Botticelli, Raphael, Rubens, and Turner to Degas, Picasso, and Matisse, displayed in the collectors' Italian Renaissance–style house, a treat in itself.

INSIDERS' TIPS

The Lake George Opera Festival, from mid-July to mid-August, features a repertory company plus name performers who perform English-language operas in the Queensbury Festival Auditorium. Unique are the 2-hour Opera-on-the-Lake Cruises in July and August, with singers doing excerpts from famous operas, operettas, and musicals. Departures are from Lake George Steel Pier Sundays at 7:30 P.M. Reservations for both: Lake George Opera Festival, P.O. Box 425, Glens Falls 12801 (tel. [518] 793-6642).

If your Walter Mitty fantasy is to go hot-air ballooning, this may be the place for it, for the views from the sky are spectacular. Adirondack Balloon Flights take off daily at sunrise and sunset from Howard Johnson's, I-87 exit 19 (tel. [518] 793-6342). Popular in winter are the lighted cross-country ski trails in Crandall Park.

Lake George, which boosters call "America's Lake Como," begins 5 miles north of Glens Falls and continues for 32 miles. With blue waters surrounded by mountains and tufted with 225 islands, it is an understandably popular summertime resort area, heavily trafficked and commercially exploited. There is a fine overlook from Prospect Mountain directly west of Lake George Village.

PERILS & PITFALLS

Beautiful as the lake itself is, there are some spots where you can't see the lake for the signs and ticky-tacky attractions. Be forewarned.

From the village of Lake George, NY-9N follows the shoreline 39 miles to Ticonderoga. En route, at Bolton Landing, you will pass the majestic old (1883) Sagamore hotel, restored magnificently in 1985 on its island (see Insiders' Information), and well worth a visit.

INSIDERS' TIPS

White-water rafting is increasingly popular, and Indian Lake is a center for it, reachable from Lake George Village northwest via US-9 and NY-28. There's a 5-hour white-water raft trip from Indian Lake to North Creek. Best times are early April through May and in September.

On a narrow neck of land between Lakes George and Champlain is perched Fort Ticonderoga, which effectively commanded the north-south route from the time the French built it (as Fort Carillon) in 1755 until British General Burgoyne burned it to the ground in 1777.

The faithfully restored (to the French design)

fort♛♛♛ is now an impressive museum. It offers guided tours, fife and drum music, and military demonstrations in July and August.

PERILS & PITFALLS

The Adirondacks are black fly country. The season is early May to mid-June, and the flies are more plentiful the farther you penetrate the backwoods areas. Be sure to use insect repellents with DEET, or Avon Skin-So-Soft (which New York State Black Fly Research Station staffers swear foils the flies—for reasons unknown).

From Ticonderoga, NY-9N and NY-22 continue along the bank of Lake Champlain 58 miles north to Ausable Chasm♛♛♛, a natural marvel formed by the dynamic action of the energetic Ausable River during centuries of erosion. The French named the river after its sandy *(au sable)* delta in Lake Champlain. The river was once famous for its salmon, which were mercilessly speared out of existence by 1830. Its 1½ miles of rapids, cliffs up to 200 feet high, flume, and pools are both thrilling and awe-inspiring. Here you can enjoy a walking tour and an exciting boat ride that shoots two sets of rapids and a whirlpool.

INSIDERS' TIPS

The Adirondack region is famous hiking country, offering spectacular views from well-marked trails. Be smart: take sturdy walking/hiking shoes and clothing and light rain gear with you.

The 1799 Kent-Delord House Museum♛ (tel. [518] 561-1035) was occupied by British officers in 1814 until the Redcoats were defeated on land and lake that year. Here you'll find furnishings of three generations of Delords.

Following NY-9N and NY-86 18 miles southwest brings you to Wilmington. Continuing southwest on NY-86, this route takes you through High Falls Gorge♛♛♛, which the fierce Ausable River has slashed through the granite of 4,868-foot Whiteface Mountain. Well-marked paths enable you to walk through the most exciting parts of this sensational valley. The Ausable in this stretch is "special trophy water" for trout fishermen, like Mount Kilimanjaro to mountain climbers.

INSIDERS' TIPS

A side trip to Plattsburgh, just 15 miles north of Ausable Chasm on I-87, brings you to the northland's major industrial and resort town. Located on Lake Champlain, it boasts the State University College of Arts and Sciences, with its concerts, craft fairs, and cultural activities. On campus are the Rockwell Kent Gallery♛ (tel. [518] 564-2288), and Myers Fine Arts Gallery♛ (tel. [518] 564-2288).

It's only 17 miles from Wilmington to famed Lake Placid, site of the 1932 and 1980 Winter Olympics. Nestled between Lake Placid and Mirror Lake, the resort village is—because of its excellent modern facilities—a major winter destination for Eastern U.S. winter sports buffs. (The 70- and 90-meter ski jumps are used with plastic mats when the snow goes.)

INSIDERS' TIPS

Boat excursions on Lake Champlain are a scenic delight. MV *Juniper* leaves from Dock Street from mid-May to September, with special moonlight sails Friday and Saturday (tel. [518] 561-8970).

Nearby are the rare bobsled and luge runs at Mount Van Hoevenberg Recreation Area. Alpine Olympic events took place at Whiteface Mountain, 8 miles to the north. (There are superb views from the top, and weekly science lectures at the State University's Atmospheric Science Research Center near the road.)

Summer visitors enjoy ice skating in the Olympic arena where the American hockey team won its upset victory in 1980, as well as water sports, golf, tennis, boat trips on the lakes, horseback riding, and hiking. Look in also at the Lake Placid Center for Music, Drama and Art, which has concerts, classes, and exhibits.

INSIDERS' TIPS

For the craft-minded, a fair called Something in the Woods Arts and Crafts Festival is held in Wilmington the third week in August every year. For information, contact Mountain Artists of New York, P.O. Box 152, Wilmington 12997.

If you are a maple syrup enthusiast (despite propaganda to the contrary from a New England neighbor, New York State is the largest maple syrup producer) you'll find the latest if not the last word on this addictive sweet at the Uihlein-Cornell Sugar House on Bear Cub Road (tel. [518] 523-9337). It goes full blast in late March and April during sap-boiling time, but is open other seasons as well.

INSIDERS' TIPS

More crafts: North Country Crafts Center in the Lake Placid Center for the Arts, Saranac Ave., Lake Placid (tel. [518] 523-2062).

Less than 10 miles farther west on NY-86 is Saranac Lake, famous for its annual Winter Carnival and Ice Palace Festival. For information about these, call the Saranac Lake Chamber of Commerce, 30 Main St., 12983 (tel. [518] 891-1990).

You may wish to see the State Fish Hatchery in operation. It's off Forest Home Road and can be visited any time of year.

And if you want to see how the wealthy lived it up when they were playing rustic, stop in at Topridge ♛ ♛. This Saranac Lake mountain retreat of heiress Marjorie Merriweather Post now belongs to New York State and is open to visitors. It dates back to the 1920s and originally consisted of 65 buildings, which required a staff of 85 to keep in tip-top woodsy shape. One building was made to resemble a Russian dacha, because Marjorie's husband had been U.S. Ambassador to the USSR (tel. [518] 327-3131).

The cottage ♛ where Robert Louis Stevenson repaired for treatment of his tuberculosis in 1887 can be visited at 11 Stevenson Lane (tel. [518] 891-4480). No winter sports enthusiast, Stevenson sailed for Tahiti as soon as the ice melted in 1888.

From Saranac Lake it is 17 miles west to Tupper Lake via NY-3. Once an old logging center, this is now a major ski area in winter (for Big Tupper Ski Area information, tel. [518] 359-3651). Mountain climbing is paramount in summer, as are boating and fishing on 40 miles of navigable waters. Annual canoe races are held the second weekend in June.

INSIDERS' TIPS

John Brown's farm♛, which the Abolitionist bought 10 years before he was executed for his raid at Harpers Ferry, is 2 miles south on NY-73 and on John Brown Road. There's a restored farmhouse and monument at his gravesite. Ten of his followers were also buried here.

Going south on NY-30, it is 33 miles to Blue Mountain Lake. In addition to the summit of Blue Mountain (3,800 feet) with its eagle's-view observation tower, the area is noted for the highly praised Adirondack Museum♛♛ (tel. [518] 352-7311). It's a mile north of town on NY-30—a cluster of 20 buildings displaying regional history exhibits, boats, vehicles, and paintings. In July and August there are week-long demonstrations of such Adirondack specialties as snowshoe, canvas canoe, pack basket, and rustic furniture making. A major exhibition of rustic furniture was featured here in 1987; the curator is an expert in this craft.

INSIDERS' TIPS

If you want to visit craft shops during your Adirondack trip, consult the brochure listing them. It's available from Ms. Martha Strodel, 14 Alden Ave., Warrensburg, NY 12885.

As you reach the post office, you will note the Adirondack Lakes Center for the Arts next door. Depending on the time of your visit, you're likely to find a film showing, concert, art and/or craft workshops or *kaffee-*

klatsch in session. There are daily activities during July and August, and weekdays only the rest of the year (tel. [518] 352-7715).

From Blue Mountain Lake it's a continually fascinating panorama of mountain-lake-forest scenery (brilliant when the leaves turn) for the 96-mile drive south on NY-30 to the intersection with I-90 at Amsterdam.

A WESTERN ITINERARY

Our second itinerary departs from Syracuse via I-81 north 70 miles to Watertown. (Here the annual Jefferson County Fair is held the last week in July.) The terrain becomes even more interesting for the next 24 miles to Fishers Landing, where a 50-year-old international toll bridge crosses the St. Lawrence River to Wellesley Island and then to Canada. (There's a commercial "Waterfun Village" amusement park at the bridge entrance.)

INSIDERS' TIPS

The St. Lawrence offers some of the finest freshwater game fishing to be found. It's famous for bass and muskellunge (the largest muskie ever caught was 1 ounce less than 60 pounds, landed in 1957). Boats and tackle are available at almost every stop along the St. Lawrence.

The route along the St. Lawrence is an easy 97 miles via NY-12 and NY-37 all the way to Rooseveltown, where the international bridge crosses to Cornwall, Ontario. Just beyond are the massive Eisenhower Locks that make it possible for oceangoing ships to travel to the Great Lakes.

Four miles northeast on NY-12 is Alexandria Bay, the resort center and key town for access to the Thousand Islands. (If you want to be picky, there are really 1,800.) There's an observation tower nearly 400 feet tall for views of the islands. It's open from mid-May to mid-October (tel. [613] 659-2335).

At Clayton, 11 miles west of Alexandria Bay, boat

lovers will want to visit the Thousand Islands Shipyard Museum♛, where historic boats and nautical history displays are on exhibit. It's at 750 Mary St., Clayton 13624 (tel. [315] 686-4104). Admission includes antique (1902) boat ride.

INSIDERS' TIPS

Love's labors lost: A poignant sight nearby is Boldt's Castle, seen on boat tours. Begun in 1900 by wealthy hotelier George Boldt (Waldorf-Astoria and others) for his wife Louise, it was to have been 120 rooms, 11 buildings on a heart-shaped island. When Louise died in 1904, Boldt abandoned the project and never set foot there again. It's now preserved by the Thousand Island Bridge Commission.

Return to Watertown and take NY-3 east past Fort Drum Military Reservation. You will find Natural Bridge Caverns, where a subterranean Indian River boat ride and natural history spiel are offered. Continue into Adirondack State Park at Fine, and onward to Tupper Lake. Drive south on NY-30 to Blue Mountain Lake and turn west on NY-28 to Raquette (French for "snow-shoe") Lake.

INSIDERS' TIPS

A boat cruise through the islands can be exciting. There are ever-changing vistas of islands, tidy resorts, rustic cabins, manicured yards and houses—and oceangoing ships! At least three boat companies book day trips through the Thousand Islands: Paul Boat Line, 4 Church St., Alexandria Bay 13607 (tel. [315] 482-9511); Uncle Sam Boat Tours, James St., Alexandria Bay 13607 (tel. [315] 482-2611); 1000 Islands Seaway Cruises, Clayton 13624 (tel. [315] 686-4104).

Opulent rusticity—that's what you'll find if you visit Camp Sagamore♛♛ (not related to the Sagamore Hotel), 4 miles south of Raquette Lake, off NY-28, at Sagamore Road. It was built by auto pioneer and millionaire William Durant in 1897, bought by Alfred Vanderbilt in 1901, and is now a 27-building National

Historic Site open to daily mouth-agape, 2-hour tours from June 28 to mid-October, with a brief hiatus August 24–28.

Just 12 miles west of Raquette Lake on NY-28 is tiny Old Forge. It's a popular outdoor action center. In winter, it is a snowmobile mecca, and in summer, canoeing enthusiasts begin here on excursions through the Fulton chain of lakes ending in Saranac Lake.

For sports information:

- about skiing—Ski Information Center, (315) 369-6983 or 369-3225
- about canoeing—New York Department of Environmental Conservation, Albany 12233
- about rafting—Adirondack River Outfitters, Box 649, Old Forge 13420 (tel. [315] 369-3536 or 788-1311)
- about lake cruises—Old Forge Lake Cruise, P.O. Box 72, Old Forge 13420 (tel. [315] 369-6473)

Old Forge has a Community Arts Center where activities include arts, crafts, film showings, classes (tel. [315] 369-6411)

Continue south on NY-28 and NY-12 to Utica and the intersection with I-90.

INSIDERS' INFORMATION FOR THE NORTH AND THE ADIRONDACKS

Alexandria Bay (Jefferson County; Area Code 315)

Hotels
Bonnie Castle ♛ ♛
Holland St., Box 219, 13607. Tel. 432-4511
2 persons in twin, $90–135 mid-May to Labor Day; lower rates off-season
Riverbank location offers a maximun of fine views of the St. Lawrence. 100 rooms, bar, café, outdoor pool, tennis, golf privileges, dancing, entertainment; no elevator. Many rooms have super outlooks.

Thousand Islands Club♛♛
R.D. 1, Box 340W, 13607. Tel. 482-2551
2 persons in twin, $68–108 mid-May to mid-September
Prime location overlooking river. 118 rooms, bar, café, swimming pool, tennis, golf, boating, entertainment, no elevator. Attractive property. Closed mid-September to mid-May.

Blue Mountain Lake
(Hamilton County; Area Code 518)

Hotels
The Hedges on Blue Mountain Lake♛♛
Hedges Rd., Blue Mountain Lake, 12812. Tel. 352-7325
2 persons in twin, $48–54 with 2 meals
Log-and-stone lodges and cottages on 12 lakefront acres. 28 rooms (half in lodges, half in cottages), no TV or room phones; dining room (notable Saturday-night buffet), tennis, lounge, library. Once owned by caretaker of nearby Vanderbilt estate, now a comfortable rustic inn with nice extras: picnic lunches for hikers or canoeists, bedtime hot chocolate and sweets, complimentary beverages all day long. Closed mid-October to late June. *No credit cards.*

Hemlock Hall♛♛
P.O. Box 114, 12812. Tel. 352-7706
2 persons in twin, $75–104 with 2 meals
A rustic 1895 country inn on the lake. 24 rooms (each different, all but 3 with private bath), no TV or room phones; bar, restaurant (with solid American fare), tennis, water sports, boating. Also cottages, some with terraces, kitchenette, fireplaces. Comfortable family-type place. Closed mid-October to mid-May. *No credit cards.*

Theater
Adirondack Lakes Center for the Arts, P.O. Box 101, NY-28, 12812. Tel. 352-7715. A visual and performing arts center, with traditional and classical music concerts, plays, films, and craft workshops.

Bolton Landing
(Warren County; Area Code 518)

Hotel
Sagamore ♛ ♛ ♛
P.O. Box 450, Sagamore Rd., 12814. Tel. 644-9400 or 358-3585
2 persons in twin, $214–360 with 2 meals, 4-night minimum May–October; lower rest of year
Old-time Lake George luxury resort, splendidly refurbished, on private island. 130 rooms, 100 suites, bar, 4 restaurants, indoor swimming pool, tennis, championship golf course. You name it, it's here: horse-drawn carriages, children's program, beach, boating and water sports, winter sports, racquetball, health club, dancing.
Restaurant
Trillium ♛ ♛
(at Sagamore resort)
Average dinner: $33
Elegant dining with string ensemble and Victorian background, plus lake vistas.

Chestertown
(Warren County; Area Code 518)

Hotels
The Balsam House ♛ ♛ ♛
Potterbrook Rd., Friends Lake 12817. Tel. 494-2828
2 persons in double, twin, $75–95
An old-fashioned (1865) clapboard house overlooking pristine 3½-mile-long lake. 20 rooms, no TV, some phones, bar, café, sophisticated French restaurant (♛ ♛), tennis, beach, boating, water sports. Classical music serenades you at breakfast.
Friends Lake Inn ♛ ♛
Friends Lake Rd., 12817. Tel. 494-4751
2 persons in double, $100 with 3 meals
An 1860s inn on the lake. 14 rooms (7 with private bath), bar, popular restaurant (♛ ♛), lake sports. Nicely restored old inn, furnished with antiques, features aerobics, golf, canoeing, hayrides, skating parties, hikes, local arts and crafts.

Glens Falls
(Saratoga County; Area Code 518)

Hotel
Queensbury Hotel♕ ♕
88 Ridge St., 12801. Tel. 792-1121
2 persons in room, $79–109, depending on season
Large hotel (143 rooms) with indoor pool, Garden on the Park restuarant (♕ ♕), health club, and bar, this independent competes successfully with the chain motel/hotels.

Theater
Queensbury Festival Auditorium, 13 South St., P.O. Box 425, 12801. Tel. 793-3866. Home for the professional productions of the Lake George Opera Festival, musicals, operettas, theater, opera cruises on Lake George. Open mid-July to mid-August.

Lake George
(Warren County; Area Code 518)

Hotel
Roaring Brook Ranch & Tennis Resort♕ ♕
Luzerne Rd., Lake George (NY-9N, 1 mile west of I-87 exit 21) 12845. Tel. 668-5767
2 persons in twin, $118–134 during high season, July through Labor Day; lower in September–October and January–June
Resort with lakeside vistas. 142 rooms, 3 swimming pools, tennis, golf, saunas, beach and water sports, horseback riding, skiing, snowmobiling. Full vacation facilities. Closed November–December, March–April.

Restaurant
Montcalm South♕ ♕
US-9 at I-87, P.O. Box 1914, 12845. Tel. 793-6601
Average dinner: $14–38
Traditional favorites on continental menu, roast, grilled veal, chicken, lamb, seafood; home-baked goods. Closed Thanksgiving, Christmas, New Year's Day.

Lake Placid
(Essex County; Area Code 518)

Hotels
Hilton♛ ♛ ♛
1 Mirror Lake Dr., 12946. Tel. 523-4411, (800) 462-1083
2 persons in twin, $76–100, June through October, lower off-season
Five-story property on water. 178 rooms, bar, café, restaurant (♛ ♛), 4 swimming pools, beach and boating activities. Superb lake views, many amenities.
Mirror Lake Inn♛ ♛ ♛
35 Mirror Lake Dr., 12946. Tel. 523-2544
2 persons in twin, $56–116
A rambling Colonial house on hillside overlooking lake. 100 rooms (including beach cottages), bar, handsome restaurant (♛ ♛) (with delicious home-style cooking), heated swimming pool, tennis courts, health club, private beach with water sports (including windsurfing, sailing). Afternoon tea, other amenities. Penthouse terrace rooms have cathedral ceilings, private balconies, exceptional vistas. Closed April to late June, mid-October to mid-December.
Whiteface Resort Golf & Country Club♛ ♛
Whiteface Inn Rd., 12946. Tel. 523-3872
2 persons in twin, $75–110
Lakeside cabins and cottages with fireplaces, heated swimming pool, tennis, golf, playground and pool for children.

Restaurants
Frederick's♛ ♛
Signal Hill. Tel. 523-2310
Average dinner: $24
Look for classical French treatments, *tournedos Rossini*, other continental dishes, seafood, cherries jubilee, sorbets, while enjoying lake views.
Interlaken Restaurant♛ ♛
15 Interlaken Ave. Tel. 523-4411
Average dinner: $22
Pleasing European atmosphere, emphasizing Swiss and French specialties (duck à l'orange, steak au poivre).

Theater
Lake Placid Center for the Arts, Saranac Ave. Tel.
523-2512. Year-round performances in music, dance,
theater, as well as films, art exhibits.

North Creek
(Warren County; Area Code 518)

Hotel
Garnet Hill Lodge ♛ ♛
13th Lake Rd., North River 12856. Tel. 251-2821
2 persons in twin, $89–105 with 2 meals
This luxurious but rustic log lodge overlooks the lake.
26 rooms, birch buildings separate, all with lake and/or
mountain views; restaurant, fireplace. Resort boating
facilities (canoeing, sailing, fishing), water sports, tennis, winter sports, nature trails.

Saranac Lake
(Franklin County; Area Code 518)

Hotels
The Point ♛ ♛ ♛ ♛
c/o Edward Carter, Upper Saranac Lake 12983. Tel.
891-5674
2 persons in twin, $300–375 (AP, includes all meals)
A 1930s rusticated log "camp" of 9 buildings built on
the lake for William A. Rockefeller (which he dubbed
Camp Wonundra). 8 rooms, no TV or room telephones;
bar, restaurant (♛ ♛ ♛), water sports, boating, fishing, ski equipment. Rough it like a millionaire, surrounded by *knotless* pine paneling, trophy heads, baronial ceiling in the main Long House lodge, massive
fireplaces (in most guest rooms), rustic "twig" furniture
in simple decor with luxury facilities. Expect gourmet
meals, breakfast in bed, afternoon tea, open bar, and
dressing for cocktails and dinner. Total privacy, security. A rare experience.

Hotel Saranac of Paul Smith's College♛
101 Main St., 12983. Tel. 891-2200
2 persons in twin, $48–54, mid-June to mid-October;
off-season rates lower
A 1927 hotel with an Italian *palazzo* foyer. 92 rooms,
bar, bakery, restaurant (♛) where college students
train, golf. Oversize beds, various extras.
   Theater
   Pendragon Theatre, 148 River St., 12983. Tel. 891-
1854. Regional theater productions throughout the
year.

Westport
(Essex County; Area Code 518)

   Hotel
Inn on the Library Lawn♛ ♛
Main and Washington Sts., P.O. Box 381, 12993. Tel.
962-8666
2 persons in twin, $60 (incl. full breakfast), May–
October, lower rates rest of year
Waterside inn on Lake Champlain. 20 rooms, 2 cottages, bar, tennis, golf, beach. No lunch or dinner
served except in winter. Rooms furnished with antiques.
   Theater
   Depot Theatre, Westport Train depot (c/o C. Bucha-
nan, 12993). Tel. 962-4449. For well-regarded summer
theater, musicals, recitals, performed in a 19th-century
train station, with art exhibits in the lobby.

Wilmington
(Essex County; Area Code 518)

   Restaurant
Hungry Trout♛
On NY-86, 2 miles southwest of Wilmington. Tel. 946-
2217
Average dinner: $23
Antique furnishings and Whiteface Mountain views en-
hance fresh seafood, steaks, home-baked goods.

Travel Information

North Country Bed & Breakfast Reservation Service, The Barn, P.O. Box 286, Lake Placid 12946. Tel. (518) 523-3739. This agency has a register of B&B homes, lodges, and inns throughout the Adirondack area. Accommodations range from clean but minimal to quite luxurious, with comparatively modest prices.

Adirondack North Country Ass'n, P.O. Box 148, Lake Placid 12946. Tel. (518) 523-9820.

New York State Department of Environmental Conservation, 50 Wolf Rd., Albany 12233. Tel. 457-5400. For general information about hunting, fishing seasons and licenses.

New York State Department of Commerce, P.O. Box 992, Latham 12110. Send for these free Adirondacks leaflets: *Camping Guide; Upstate Travel Guide; Vacation Planner; Skiing and Winter Sports; Winter Events; Learn to Ski.* Specify title. The Adirondacks Regional Tourism Office is at 90 Main St., Lake Placid 12945. Tel. (518) 523-2412.

THE FINGER LAKES AND SYRACUSE

Our itinerary in the Finger Lakes region begins in Syracuse and ends in Rochester (you can reverse it) with a loop around lakes Cayuga and Seneca, including Ithaca, Watkins Glen, Geneva, and Canandaigua (about 160 miles). An optional side trip to Elmira and Corning might include Hammondsport and Keuka Lake (add 100 miles).

South of Lake Ontario, between the cities of Syracuse and Rochester, is the Finger Lakes region of New York. This 9,000-square-mile area, with its 600 miles of shoreline and 11 glacial lakes, is blessed with topography, climate, and produce similar to parts of France, Bavaria, and Austria.

Its limpid lakes, verdant vineyards, and American wineries attract 7 million visitors a year. They find, in addition to the Moselle-like vineyards and hills of the wine region, country roads with Amish buggies, historic houses and baronial castles, plus such delights as old-fashioned home cooking and hand-packed ice cream, roadside stands selling home-grown strawberries, apples, corn, and squash. Fortunately, the attractions are plentiful and so widely distributed that visitors seldom bunch up uncomfortably or overuse the facilities available.

The region's impressive beauty spots—its narrow, incredibly deep (up to 600 feet) finger-shaped lakes, and its hills and waterfalls and fertile valleys—are the result of Ice Age glacier action. This was the homeland of Hiawatha, the Cayuga, Onondaga, and Seneca Indians, members of the powerful Iroquois Confederacy.

Jesuit missionaries were the first Europeans to see the area, and soon spread the word of forests and hills teeming with wild turkey, deer, and other game. This brought settlers, some of whom applied their knowledge of wine production to the verdant land. By the early 1800s the combination of favorable terrain, soil, and growing conditions yielded exceedingly pleasant wines. (At a Paris wine tasting more than a century ago, a New York wine won top honors.)

SYRACUSE

Our circuit begins in Syracuse, a city of 170,000, approximately in the middle of the state. It blossomed after the Erie Canal reached it in the 1820s and has been a thriving center of industry, agriculture, and education ever since.

For the visitor, Syracuse offers the Everson Museum of Art♛ ♛, 401 Harrison Street (tel. [315] 474-6064). Lodged in an I. M. Pei building (with excellent exhibition space), it has frequently changing exhibits and a wide-ranging permanent collection of contemporary American ceramics♛ ♛. Special visual treats: a Tiffany window ("New Jerusalem") from a Unitarian Church, and a reclining bronze sculpture by Henry Moore near the outside entrance.

Syracuse's Burnet Park Zoo♛ ♛, South Wilbur Avenue, 13204 (tel. [315] 478-8516, is newly reorganized and fun because its open-to-view animal areas are designed so the animals are visible even in cold weather. Excellent, lively teaching labels and saucy, "trivia-type" questions keep visitors involved and curious. There are 36 acres of walks past elephant, antelope, and other domains.

INSIDERS' TIPS

The Burger King on the zoo grounds is supposedly the only nonprofit one (by design) in the world. Proceeds from its fast snacks go to the zoo.

History buffs may wish to look at the Erie Canal Museum♛, 315 East Water Street (tel. [315] 471-

0593), where a real canal boat houses exhibits of historical events in the only surviving "weighlock," where tolls were collected.

Ethnically, Syracuse is diverse and therefore celebrates appropriately with an Irish Fest (May), German Day and Greek Festival (June), Bavarian Festival and Scottish Games (August) and Oktoberfests (September). In the heart of the Irish section on Tipperary Hill is the nation's only upside-down traffic light (Irish green on top, forever). Here too, as a place for a whistle-wetting stop, is the remarkable Coleman's Authentic Irish Pub♕♕ (see Insiders' Information at the end of this chapter).

For sheer beauty, few activities match the annual Hot Air Balloon Festival at Jamesville Beach Park each June (tel. [315] 470-1343). *The* major event of the year is the Great New York State Fair♕♕, Fairgrounds, State Fair Blvd., 13209 (tel. [315] 487-7711). This popular festivity brings masses from all over New York State for 10 days of exhibiting, gawking, eating, and sheer enjoyment, beginning the end of August, culminating with Labor Day.

INSIDERS' TIPS

Our routing takes you via direct highways from one major site or town to the next. We strongly recommend that you check your map and take back roads whenever possible, if you have time—they're far more scenic and this is lovely country where, depending on the season, you'll find family roadside fruit stands and orchards where you can pick your own apples.

THE FINGER LAKES

To get to the Finger Lakes, leave Syracuse and drive 18 miles west on NY-175 to Skaneateles (scan-e-at'-a-luss), a graceful old town hugging the northern end of Lake Skaneateles. A leisurely drive along its streets that parallel the shore will show you grand Victorian mansions and gorgeous lake vistas. A stop at the

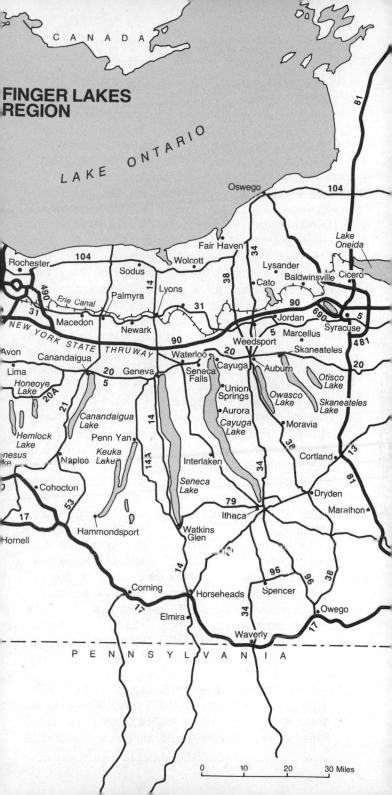

historic 180-year-old Sherwood Inn♛♛♛ will revive flagging spirits.

If you have the time, you can actually book a brief boat cruise on the lake or a lengthy one on the Erie Canal with the Mid-Lakes Navigation Company, P.O. Box 61-M, Skaneateles 13152 (tel. [315] 685-5722).

Follow US-20 west from Skaneateles 7 miles to Auburn, another 19th-century town, but with more bustle than many in this area, busier than its population of 33,000 suggests. A fascinating stop here, especially for history and/or Civil War buffs, is at the home of William H. Seward, President Lincoln's Secretary of State, who also was a founder of the Republican Party and responsible for the Alaska purchase. The house is located at 33 South Street (tel. [315] 252-1283).

The lavish two-story mansion♛♛♛ was the first brick house ever built in Auburn (1816). Brigham Young worked on it as a 15-year-old laborer. What makes the house so intriguing, aside from its considerable historical memorabilia, is that it represents the changing taste of a single affluent 19th-century family. Everything is original; the Sewards were the only family who ever lived here. In the 30 rooms (with 15 fireplaces), you'll see 100 years of gowns (from 1820 to 1920), gilded furniture, an 1825 Federal-style piano, and more than 10,000 books. Five U.S. Presidents were guests here (John Quincy Adams, Martin Van Buren, Ulysses Grant, Andrew Johnson, and William McKinley).

An exceptionally lively guided tour reveals that while Seward was in the U.S. Senate, his Quaker wife was hiding fugitive slaves in the back of the house.

Not far away, at 180 South Street, an unpretentious farmhouse is the Harriet Tubman home♛ (shown by appointment only; tel. [315] 253-2621). It was here that Ms. Tubman brought more than 300 runaway slaves as a safe stop on their Underground Railroad journey to freedom in Canada.

Seneca Falls is some 18 miles farther west on US-20. Here, at 116 Fall Street, is the U.S. Park Service Visitor Center♛ of the Women's Rights National Historical Park (tel. [315] 568-2991). Currently, the Visitor Center has exhibits and a slide program about the women's suffrage reformers who were active here. The plan is to acquire local sites of significance—but at present the Wesleyan chapel where the suffragists convened in 1848 is now the Seneca Falls Laundromat! The restored Elizabeth Cady Stanton home ♛, at 32 Washington Street, can be visited.

Seneca Falls is at the northern tip of Lake Cayuga, one of the most beautiful of the Finger Lakes, with many vineyards on its banks. The lakes have ideal microclimates for growing grapes of the types found in Europe's finest wine regions. The glacial soil drainage and sloping hillsides for air drainage are key factors in the favorable results growers achieve in these vineyards.

INSIDERS' TIPS

Winter sports hereabouts include pond ice skating and cross-country skiing. Plane's, for instance, has 200 acres for skiing plus a pond for skating, weekends through March.

Literature describing the many features is available from Cayuga Wine Trail, RD 2, Box 273, Ovid, NY 14521.

WINE TRAILS

We suggest that you see for yourself by driving south on NY-89 and enjoying one of the delightful Finger Lakes "wine trails." Along the west bank of Lake Cayuga, strung out along Route 89, are nine wineries that welcome visitors and offer tours and tastings (listed from north to south):

- Lakeshore Winery, 5132 NY-89, Romulus 14541. Tel. (315) 549-8461.
- Fleur de Bois, 5196 NY-89, Romulus 14541. Tel. (315) 549-7647.
- Knapp Vineyards, 2770 County Road 128, Romulus 14541. Tel. (315) 568-2142.

- Swedish Hill Vineyard, RD 2, Box 295, Romulus 14541 (on NY-414 parallel to NY-89). Tel. (315) 549-9326.
- Lakeshore Winery, 5132 NY-89, Romulus 14541. Tel. (315) 549-8461.
- Plane's Cayuga Vineyards, RD 2, Box 273, Ovid 14521. Tel. (607) 869-5158.
- Hosmer, RD 2, Box 264, NY-89, Ovid 14521. Tel (607) 869-5585.
- Lucas Vineyards, RD 2, County Road 150, Interlaken 14847. Tel (607) 532-4825.
- Americana Vineyards Estate Winery, RD 1, Box 58, Interlaken 14847. Tel. (607) 387-6801.

All these wineries grow at least some vinifera grapes and produce wines such as Riesling, Cabernet Sauvignon, Chardonnay, and Gewurtztraminer.

INSIDERS' TIPS

Superb is the word for the late-harvest Ravat dessert wines. Be sure to try them. (The Gewurtztraminers, Chardonnays, and Johannisberg Rieslings are often outstanding as well.) Fresh grape juice is available at each winery for nonalcoholic refreshment.

The lakeside is ideal for dining alfresco and picnicking. Some of the wineries offer box lunches and modest snacks on grounds or decks overlooking the lake. There are also pleasant feeding stops such as Bodine Farms Fruit Stand (for picnicking), Deerhead Inn (for lunch buffet), and O'Malley's Log Cabin on the Lake restaurant. Another point of interest is the Misty Meadow Hog Farm, 2828 Vineyard Road, Romulus 14541 (tel. [315] 549-8839), a working pig farm that offers unique guided tours and meals.

INSIDERS' TIPS

Bibliophiles please note—Ithaca may be the town for you. It has more than 20 bookstores.

One of the most spectacular natural waterfalls (a straight drop of 215 feet) in the nation is in beautiful

Taughannock Falls State Park♛ ♛, just off Route 89 near Trumansburg. It's also a great place for swimming, hiking, picnicking, and lazing about.

Just 8 miles farther south on NY-89 is Ithaca, home of Ithaca College and Cornell University.

Cornell offers several attractions. The modern Herbert Johnson Museum of Art♛ ♛ (tel. [607] 256-6464) has a permanent collection, strong in Asian art, and special exhibitions.

Gardeners and flower lovers will want to visit Cornell Plantations♛ ♛ ♛, 1 Plantations Road, Ithaca 14850 (tel. [607] 256-3020). You can roam some 2,600 acres, abundant with lake, creek, ponds, an arboretum, gardens of herbs, peonies, wildflowers, rhododendrons, and annuals. Also vegetables, grain crops—and poisonous plants. Picnicking is permitted.

INSIDERS' TIPS

There's fine dining in and around Ithaca. Highly recommended are L'Auberge du Cochon Rouge♛ ♛, Taughannock Farms Inn♛ ♛ and Turback's♛ ♛. See listings in Insiders' Information.

Cornell's ornithology laboratory will appeal to bird lovers. The library and observation room are open daily (tel. [607] 255-5056), and the Lyman K. Stuart Observatory♛ ♛ offers 4 miles of trails in Sapsucker Woods (open at all times).

INSIDERS' TIPS

There is a summer series of classical music concerts Monday evenings at 8:15 in Cornell's Statler Auditorium. Tickets are available at the auditorium box office before the performance, or at Summer Session Office, B-12, Ives Hall, Cornell University, Ithaca 14850.

At this point you may decide to head directly west to Watkins Glen on NY-79, or you may opt for a side trip to Elmira and Corning, returning to Watkins Glen.

A Side Trip

Follow NY-13 and NY-14 southwest to Elmira, where you may visit the collection of Mark Twain memorabilia in Elmira College's Cowles Hall. Highlights: the taproom♕ where Twain enjoyed bending an elbow (in the Gannett Tripp Learning Center) and the study♕♕ where he reportedly wrote parts of *Tom Sawyer* and *Huckleberry Finn* while visiting his in-laws.

The study is built like a Mississippi riverboat pilot house. Twain and his wife, Olivia Langdon (whose family lived in Elmira), and three children are buried at Woodlawn National Cemetery in town.

Elmira has a notable art collection in the Arnot Art Museum♕♕, 235 Lake Street (tel. [607] 734-3697). Here, in an 1833 mansion with a new wing, are displayed European paintings of the 17th to 19th centuries.

This area is famous as a sailplane and soaring center. Harris Hill Gliderport, RD 1, 14903 (tel. [607] 734-3128), has been the site of the national championships since 1930. The annual competitions are held at the field for two weeks in July, and the National Soaring Museum♕♕ is here, offering a tour, gliders, exhibits, and a film.

To experience the thrill of soaring, you can take a sailplane ride at the Harris Hill Gliderport or Schweizer Soaring School, Chemung County Airport, between Elmira and Corning (tel. [607] 739-3821). The season is limited to May 1 through Columbus Day, and advance reservations are recommended at Schweizer; at Harris Hill, however, it's first come, first served—so get there early.

It's about 15 miles from Elmira to Corning via NY-352 and NY-17. It was here that Thomas Edison's light bulbs were first produced. Today a major feature is the Corning Glass Center♕♕♕, Corning 14831 (tel. [607] 974-8271).

This modern, glass-walled (what else?) museum displays 20,000 glass objects from prehistoric to contemporary times and has many push-button exhibits and demonstrations. The real kick is watching the gaffer (glass craftsman) blow red-hot molten glass into the beautiful shapes that become Steuben crystal.

INSIDERS' TIPS

A London double-decker bus takes visitors from the Center to other attractions in town.

Also to be seen in Corning is the Rockwell Museum♔♔, Cedar Street and NY-17, 14830 (tel. [607] 937-5386), with the largest collection of Western American art in the East. You'll see works by such well-known artists as Catlin, Remington, and Russell, along with antique toys, glass, and Western artifacts.

From Corning it's an easy 20-mile drive to Watkins Glen via NY-414. The town has a superb location at the southern tip of Seneca Lake and, though a bit dowdy, has a splendid lakefront and several notable attractions.

The town's name derives from the gorge♔♔ that begins beyond Main Street and extends 1½ miles west. You can follow the walkway and view the 19 waterfalls plus grottoes and cascades within the canyon. On the high ground above is the Watkins Glen State Park, with excellent views of the lake, picnic and camping facilities, and an Olympic-size pool.

After dark, a sound and laser-light show called "Timespell" can be seen (for a fee) in the gorge, telling the geological story of how all this happened.

Perhaps the town is most famous for the annual Watkins Glen International road races. Professional drivers compete in events (New York 500, Camel Continental, etc.) from June through October. Information is available from Watkins Glen International, P.O. Box 500, 14891 (tel. [607] 974-7162 or 535-2406).

From Watkins Glen you can take boat cruises during summer on Capt. Bill's Lake Ride. The hour-long scenic cruises leave from 10 A.M. to 8 P.M. daily (tel. [607] 535-4541), and sail 5 miles north along one shore, cross over, and return along the other bank, giving restful, splendid views of vineyards and farms.

At Watkins Glen you are well situated to follow

another "wine trail" north along the shores of Seneca Lake. There are 5 wineries on the east bank and 4 on the west bank open to visitors—and if you have time you can do them all.

INSIDERS' TIPS

A Seneca Lake wine trail map and information are available from Seneca Lake Winery Association, P.O. Box 91, Hector 14841.

Here are the open-to-view wineries on the east bank, as you follow NY-414 and NY-96A north to Geneva:

- Rolling Vineyards Farm Winery, Hector 14841 (tel. [607] 546-9302).
- Chateau Lafayette Reneau, Box 87, Hector 14841 (tel. [607] 546-2062).
- Wickham Vineyards, 1 Wine Place, Hector 14841 (tel. [607] 546-8415).
- Hazlitt 1852 Vineyards, P.O. Box 53, Hector 14841 (tel. [607] 546-5812).
- Wagner Vineyards, Lodi 14860 (tel. [607] 582-6450).

INSIDERS' TIPS

If you have time for only one stop, make it Wagner's. This is the big producer in the area, at more than 40,000 gallons a year, and turns out some remarkably appealing wines. (Notable are its Johannisberg Rieslings, '84 Chardonnay Reserve, and '84 Seyval Blanc.) The Wagner winery is in a unique octagonal building and nearby is a festive striped-tent, open-air restaurant, the Ginny Lee Cafe (for salads and light meals, with grape juice or wine), which overlooks the vineyards and the lake.

HAMMONDSPORT AND AREA

There's an alternate route to Canandaigua, via Hammondsport, where you may visit the Taylor Great Western–Gold Seal Winery Visitor Center ♛ ♛, Hammondsport 14840 (tel. [607] 569-2111). In this 1860 winery, whose clumsy name is the result of mergers in the industry, you can take the tour, see a film in a gargantuan cast converted into a theater, view the displays, and taste the product. At various times there are concerts in the local park sponsored by Taylor, which is the behemoth of wine producers in New York.

There's more to Hammondsport than Taylor Wine, however. There's the Glenn Curtiss Museum♔, Main and Lake streets (tel. [607] 569-2160). Aviation pioneer Curtiss's early aircraft, plus other planes, cars, and memorabilia, are on display.

Also on or near Keuka Lake are four other wineries that welcome visitors and offer tastings. To the northeast:

■ McGregor Vineyard, 5503 Dutch St., Dundee 14837 (tel. [607] 292-3678).

To the west:

■ DeMay Wine Cellars, County Road 88, Hammondsport 14840 (tel. [607] 569-2040).

To the north:

■ Cana Vineyards, RD 2, Box 358, Hammondsport 14840 (tel. [607] 569-2737).

■ Finger Lakes Wine Cellars, 4021 Italy Hill Road, Branchport 14418 (tel. [607] 595-2812.

INSIDERS' TIPS

Still another delightful alternative for you: If you take the bucolic NY-53 from Hammondsport to Naples (22 miles), you may visit John Jacob Widmer's Wine Cellars, NY-21 (tel. [716] 374-6311). Begun here in 1888, it's one of the state's largest and offers daily tours and tastings. From here you can rejoin the tour by driving 23 miles north on NY-245 to Flint and then east 7 miles to Geneva.

Back to our original route, proceeding along the west bank of Seneca Lake via Route 14, you will arrive at Geneva, a handsome 19th-century small town situated at the northern end of the lake. Its South Main Street is a contender for "most beautiful street in America," with many fine old trees and buildings. Also visually delicious are Rose Hill Mansion, NY-96A, a Greek Revival gem above Seneca Lake, and the campuses of Hobart and William Smith colleges.

INSIDERS' TIPS

Two uniquely attractive hostelries beckon, if you are interested in luxurious lakeshore inns. They are both on Seneca Lake's northwest shore: Belhurst Castle ♛ ♛ ♛ ♛, built in the 1880s, and Geneva on the Lake ♛ ♛ ♛ ♛. For details, see Insiders' Information below. If you'd like an attractive B&B, write the Finger Lakes Bed & Breakfast Association for their brochure, map, and information, P.O. Box 6576, Ithaca 14851.

It is a mere 16 miles west on US-20 to the resort town of Canandaigua, at the apex of the lake of that name. Here, at the Finger Lakes Performing Arts Center, the annual Finger Lakes Music Festival ♛ ♛ ♛ is held every July and August. It features the Rochester Philharmonic Orchestra in pop and classical concerts, along with various headliners.

The major attraction in the area (other than the lake) is Sonnenberg Gardens and Mansion ♛ ♛ ♛. It's off NY-21 north in Canandaigua 14424 (tel. [716] 924-5420). The 50-acre Victorian mansion and estate have nine formal gardens (Japanese and Italian among them), pools, waterfalls, and walks. The Canandaigua Wine Company has a tasting room on the premises where you wind up your tour. There also are light snacks and desserts available in the Garden Cafe.

It's 28 miles from Canandaigua to central Rochester via NY-332, I-90, and I-490.

Rochester is described in the next chapter.

INSIDERS' TIPS

They're off! Thoroughbred racing fans may want to see the ponies in action at the Finger Lakes Race Track. It's 1 mile south of I-90 Exit 44, between Manchester and Victor, and the action extends from the last week in April through Veterans Day in November. Tel. (716) 924-3232.

INSIDERS' INFORMATION FOR THE FINGER LAKES AND SYRACUSE

Aurora
(Cayuga County; Area Code 315)

Restaurant
Aurora Inn♛ ♛
Main St. (NY-90), Aurora. Tel. 364-8842
Average dinner: $13–22
Established in 1833, this old-timer has been lovingly restored, and presents a traditional American menu to be enjoyed while watching sunsets on Cayuga Lake. Closed December–March.

Canandaigua
(Ontario County; Area Code 716)

Theater
Finger Lakes Center for the Performing Arts, East Lake Road, 14424. Tel. 454-7091. An indoor/outdoor theater overlooking Lake Canandaigua, where the Rochester Philharmonic plays on summer evenings.

Corning
(Steuben County; Area code 607)

Hotels
Corning Hilton Inn♛ ♛
Denison Parkway East, 14830. Tel. (800) 445-8667 or 962-5000
2 persons in twin, $67–95
Contemporary motel. 180 rooms, bar, café, Garden Court restaurant(♛ ♛), indoor swimming pool, adjacent (winter) ice rink. Comfortable overnight stop.
Rosewood Inn♛ ♛
134 East First St., 14830. Tel. 962-3253
2 persons in twin, $55–70 (incl. continental breakfast)
A 3-story Tudor cottage in convenient in-town location. 6 rooms (4 with private baths), no TV or room phones. Friendly ambiance in historic old house, furnished with charming Corning memorabilia.

Shopping
The Corning Store, 114 Pine St. Tel. 974-4343.
Great selection of Corning glass products.
Theater
Corning Summer Theatre, Corning Glass Center,
P.O. Box 51, Corning 14830. Tel. 936-4634. Presentations of Broadway shows, July through Labor Day.

Elmira
(Chemung County; Area Code 607)

Theater
Samuel Clemens Performing Arts Center. Tel.
734-8191. Elmira has a year-round program of theater,
dance, and classical and pop concerts. Phone for schedule and information.

Geneva
(Ontario County; Area Code 315)

Hotels
Belhurst Castle ♛ ♛ ♛ ♛
Lochland Rd. and US-20, Geneva 14456. Tel. 789-7190
2 persons in twin, $80–110
A 3-story Victorian Romanesque castle (1885) on Seneca Lake. 12 rooms, bar, restaurant ♛, sauna, golf privileges, no elevator. Former speakeasy (circa 1926), became an opulent inn in 1975. Imposingly furnished with antiques, medieval armor, stained glass, other baronial necessities. Try for a turreted room (no elevator) for lordly view of the lake and 25-acre domain.
Geneva on the Lake ♛ ♛ ♛ ♛
1001 Lochland Rd., 14456. Tel. (315) 789-7190
2 persons in suite, $107–222 (incl. continental breakfast)
3-story Italian Renaissance villa-style resort hotel directly on lake. 29 suites (with kitchens), bar, swimming pool, tennis, water sports, sailing, golf privileges, no elevator. Posh pampering with wine, fresh fruit, and flowers in rooms. Some rooms have fireplaces, king-size beds, private patios. Antiques and precious *objets* abound. Dinner served only Friday and Sunday nights. Closed November to April.

Ithaca
(Tompkins County; Area Code 607)

Restaurants

L'Auberge du Cochon Rouge♔♔
NY-96B (1152 Danby Rd.), Ithaca. Tel. 273-3464
Average dinner: $21–41
An 1828 farmhouse on a duck pond is the setting for
French treatments of fish, poultry, meats (not limited to
pork), and pastries.

Turback's ♔♔
919 Elmira Rd. (NY-13), Ithaca. Tel. 272-6484
Average dinner: $23
This 11-gabled 1850 Victorian mansion is lively and fun
whether you eat in the "library," upstairs "bedroom," or
main dining room. Menu features all–New York ingredients (garlic festival day, it's garlic all the way),
and has the state's best New York wine list. The
welcoming bar is worthy of a visit, too.

Theater

Hanger Theatre, Cass Park. Tel. 273-2432. One of
the state's best summer theaters, with productions
from mid-June to August, nightly except Mondays.

Restaurant

Ginny Lee Cafe♔
NY-414, Lodi. Tel. 582-6450
Average lunch (no dinners): $4–14; open mid-May to
mid-October, 11 A.M.–4 P.M.; Sunday, 10 A.M.–4:30 P.M.
Under a festive striped tent you lunch on hasty-tasty
food (turkey crepes, leek and potato soup, Brie and
compote), relax and enjoy the appealing wines of Wagner Vineyards while overlooking Seneca Lake, the vines
and winery.

Skaneateles
(Onondaga County; Area Code 315)

Hotel

Sherwood Inn♔♔♔
26 Genesee St., 13152. Tel. 685-3405
2 persons in twin, $65 (incl. continental breakfast)
A large 180-year-old clapboard house facing the lake in
town center. 16 rooms, no TV or room phones, wood-

paneled taproom-bar, congenial restaurant(♛♛) with *nouvelle*-style dishes, fine wine list. Former stagecoach tavern, now an engaging inn. Beautifully renovated, comfortable period-style rooms, with antiques, some four-poster canopy beds, cozy lounge areas. Open front-porch dining is especially agreeable in summer. A welcoming place.

Restaurant
Krebs♛
53 West Genesee St., US-20. Tel. 685-5714
Average dinner: $25
A local mainstay for solid American fare—prime ribs, lobster Newburg, etc. Old frame house cozily decorated with Early Americana. Popular for Sunday brunch. Closed November–April.

Syracuse
(Onondaga County; Area code 315)

Hotels
The Hilton at Syracuse Square ♛♛♛
500 South Warren St., 13202. Tel. 471-7300, (800) 462-1083
2 persons in twin, $60–90
A modern 15-story tower hotel in center of city. 200 rooms, adjacent parking garage, café, bar, restaurant, tennis and golf privileges, health club privileges. Large rooms, attractively furnished. Shares spacious refurbished lobby with Hotel Syracuse (see below).
The Hotel Syracuse ♛♛♛
500 South Warren St., 13202. Tel. 422-5121, (800) 963-1498 (in New York State)
2 persons in twin, $35–76
Large 60-year-old downtown hotel recently rejuvenated. 500 rooms, free adjacent parking garage, café, bar, restaurant, tennis, golf and health club privileges. Shared management with Hilton (see above) provides impressive lobby, many services.

Pub
Coleman's Authentic Irish Pub,   100 South Lowell Ave. Tel. 478-9584
Enter this Victorian fantasy pub in the Tipperary Hill

district via regular or (if you can) tiny Leprechaun's Door. Imported Irish windows (stained- and frosted-glass), fabrics, fixtures, and music, plus elaborate dark wood bar make Coleman's the most Gaelic of outposts. Live Irish music on weekends.

Shopping

Syracuse China Factory Outlet Store, State Fair Blvd. Tel. 455-5818. Excellent values in the china, table accessories, and kitchenwares produced by this well-known company.

Theaters

Landmark Theatre, 326 South Salina St. Tel. 475-7980. A 1928 orgiastic Persian fantasy lobby and interior sets off year-round schedule of concerts, plays, classic movies.

Syracuse Stage, 820 East Genesee St. Tel. 423-3275. Professional theater in six productions per year (October–May).

Travel Information

Finger Lakes Association, 309 Lake St., Penn Yan 14527. Tel. (315) 536-7488.

THE WEST

New York's second and third largest cities (Buffalo, 360,000; Rochester, 250,000) are in its western precincts, on Lakes Ontario and Erie. Foremost among numerous attractions of the area is one whose fame has overshadowed all others: Niagara Falls.

Yet the riches of this area far transcend falling waters alone. Here you'll find everything needed for a memorable holiday: first-rate art and architecture, a plethora of top-flight museums, music and theater, historic sites, preservations and re-creations. Add to that good restaurants, comfortable and diverse lodgings, and world-class wineries. Then there are the sports possibilities: swimming, sailing, and water sports in the Great Lakes, white-water rafting, championship fishing contests, skiing, skating, and snow sports.

Distances here are not great, and roads are good and well marked. We recommend an itinerary that starts at Rochester and ends in Buffalo (or vice versa), with appropriate side-trip excursions to explore other appealing areas. (Rochester is 1 hour by air from New York City, 7 hours by Amtrak train.)

ROCHESTER

In the first quarter of the 19th century, Rochester grew and flourished as "The Flour Capital of the United States." Then came George Eastman's Kodak works and Xerox's original factories. Evidence of the wealth generated here in the past can be seen in the mansions on East Avenue, a parade of architectural styles that range from Greek Revival through Gothic, Italianate, Tudor, and Georgian. (For contrast, there's the simplicity of the 1800 Federal-style Stone-Tolan farmhouse♛ at 2370 East Avenue.)

A prime destination for visitors from all over the world is the International Museum of Photography♛♛ at George Eastman House, 900 East Avenue (tel. [716] 271-3361). The ground floor of the 50-room, 1905 house that Eastman built for himself and his mother is shown on free tours. (He built the house as two separate entities, with 13 baths and 9 fireplaces.) Note the magnificent organ in the solarium. It was played each morning as a "wake-up call" for George.

In the gallery rooms are displayed rare pictures from the Museum's 500,000-print collection, which shows photography's development as an art, featuring works of famous photographers. In the Dryden Theater, selections from the collection of 5,000 motion pictures are presented Tuesday through Friday at 8 P.M. for $3 admission. A film buff can luck into some rare, seldom-seen footage.

PERILS & PITFALLS

Don't expect to see the house as George lived in it. It is sparsely furnished. After his death in 1932, the house was donated to the University of Rochester. One of the U of R officials who lived here didn't care for the furniture and piled it on the sidewalk to get rid of it. Now, with plans afoot to build a separate addition for the museum, efforts are being made to find the original furnishings and restore the house as a bona fide Eastman home.

Photography buffs may also want to join a free tour of the Eastman Kodak plant♛, Kodak Park, 200 Ridge Road West at NY-104 (tel. [716] 722-2465).

Rochester's commercial underpinnings and prosperity have given the city a broad cultural base. You'll discover this for yourself at the recently expanded Memorial Art Gallery♛♛♛♛ of the University of Rochester, 490 University Avenue (tel. [716] 275-3081). Its outstanding collection is especially deep in 19th- and 20th-century American art; you'll see works ranging from early naïve folk art through Thomas Cole and other Hudson River school painters, to George Bellows, John Sloan, and Milton Avery, sculpture by Frederick Remington, David Smith, Isamu Noguchi, and Alexander Calder, right into the 1980s. But there is really something choice for everybody: Asian art, 12th-to-19th-century European paintings, African, Oceanic, and American Indian works.

INSIDERS' TIPS

Newly opened is the terrific Gallery Cafe (operated by Edwards Restaurant ♛ ♛ ♛) which serves lunch, tea, and dinner. Unusual quality for a museum café.

Also notable is the Museum's Gallery Shop, with exemplary, often *avant* handcrafts.

A real Rochester "sleeper" is an astonishing collection of Americana from 1820 to 1940, theatrically displayed in the Margaret Woodbury Strong Museum ♛ ♛ ♛ ♛, 1 Manhattan Square (tel. [716] 454-7639 [recorded info] or 423-0746).

Unique and frequently changing exhibits focus on how the Industrial Revolution changed American life. They're fascinating, witty, and illuminating, on subjects such as "Male and Female Beauty," "A Century of Childhood," and "Palmer Cox's *Brownies*." It's mind-boggling to think that one person collected these thousands of objects, ranging from gimcracks to priceless Oriental sculpture. Margaret's father was one of Eastman's earliest associates, so money and storage space were no problems.

You'll find here the largest museum-owned doll collection in the world, but that's just a tiny hint of what's in store. Allow a half-day to see this marvelous place properly. The new building and exhibitions are imaginative. And the museum shop is outstanding for toys and gifts.

Rochester has numerous historic sites to share with visitors. (For assistance or information on historic Rochester, contact the Landmark Society, 130 Spring Street, tel. [716] 546-7029.) One of these is the upper falls of the Genesee River, which powered those 19th-century grist mills. The falls are best viewed from the Pont de Rennes bridge—right downtown—an amazing sight. While here, walk to the Romanesque City Hall ♛ ♛, which has an exhilarating, sunlit atrium. (The old county building has an excellent, elegant restaurant, Chapel's ♛ ♛ ♛ ♛ in what used to be the basement jail). Note the fine art deco Times Square building nearby, with its "Wings of Progress" sculpture on top. Susan B. Anthony's modest little red brick home ♛, where she lived for 40 years, can be visited at 17 Madison Street.

For an enjoyable walk past attractive recycled buildings of lesser pretensions, stroll through the gentrified Alexander and Park Avenue districts, where boutiques, eateries, craft shops, and galleries have blossomed, turning the area into a veritable Restaurant Row. Also of note is the Corn Hill area, newly rejuvenated, now a prime residential section. (Buffalo Bill Cody once lived in the neighborhood.)

INSIDERS' TIPS

For an ethnic, trendy, and/or inexpensive meal, there are literally dozens of good choices on Alexander Street and Park Avenue. To cite a few: Aladdin's (Lebanese), Charlie's Frog Pond (egg dishes, fabulous desserts), Giorgio's (Italian), Hogan's Hideaway (homemade soups, sandwiches), J. Wellington's Waterworks (wings, pizza, salads), Le Bistro (French/Dutch/Indonesian).

Rochester is considered a horticultural center, noted for its many outstanding parks and gardens. Its Lilac Festival in May is a 2-week-long gala of parades and music events at Highland Park, Mt. Hope Avenue, South Goodman Street, or Highland Avenue, one of the most glorious gardens in the city.

A pioneer in the city's botanical development was a 19th-century German horticulturist, George Ellwanger. With his partner, he assembled 500 species of lilacs and many other flowers on some 650 acres. You can see what's left of his garden at 625 Mt. Hope Avenue (tel. [716] 546-7029). Other gardens of note: Harris Moran

Seed Co. Flower Trails, 3670 Buffalo Road (tel. [716] 594-9411); and Maplewood Rose Garden on Park Avenue from Lake Avenue to St. Paul Street.

Rochester is also known as a Music City. The Eastman School of Music, the Hochstein Music School (where there are free lunchtime concerts), and the Rochester Philharmonic are here, and almost daily throughout the year there are recitals and concerts in the afternoons and evenings. In addition, there are citywide festivals during which there is a concentrated outpouring of music (Lilac Festival, Oktoberfest).

INSIDERS' TIPS

For information about concerts, recitals and opera by Eastman Schoolers, tel. (716) 275-3111; for tickets, tel. (716) 275-3500. For symphonic concerts, tel. (716) 454-7091. For live entertainment, the most complete listing of performers, performances, and venues is in the free biweekly *Freetime* guide available at hotel counters. The "Visitor FunFone" number is (716) 546-6810.

Rochester is by no means all culture, no play. Fishing in Lake Ontario for record muskies, trout, salmon, and other fish is popular and easy from Rochester. Among the sport fishing specialists are Ringneck Charters (tel. [716] 482-3431), and Ubiquitous Charters (tel. [716] 248-5192).

INSIDERS' TIPS

Team sports: The Rochester Red Wings AAA baseball team plays at Silver Stadium (tel. [716] 467-3000); the Rochester Americans hockey club skates at War Memorial (tel. [716] 454-5335).

Side Trips

About 28 miles southwest of central Rochester via I-490 west, to NY-19 south to NY-5 east is Genesee Country Village and Museum ♣ ♣, Flint Hill Road, Mumford 14414 (tel. [716] 538-6822. This is a 55-building assemblage of authentic 19th-century buildings, with activities, demonstrations, and tour guides in appropriate costumes, where the blacksmith, potter, tinsmith, basket maker, and printer do their things. There's a small working farm, gallery of sporting and wildlife art, country store, and carriage barn. Special events are scheduled, including an Independence Day celebration and an Old Time Fiddlers' Fair in late August.

INSIDERS' TIPS

Try a dining excursion to Richardson's Canal House of 1818 ♛ ♛ ♛, part of the 1821 terminus of the Erie Canal at Bushnell's Basin canal boat turnaround. This cluster of early-19th-century buildings also includes Oliver Loud's 1814 Stagecoach Inn ♛ ♛, an authentic hostelry recently restored and open again as an overnight stop. (Reach Bushnell's Basin via I-490 12 miles east of downtown Rochester.)

From Rochester to Niagara Falls, the "Seaway Trail" takes the Lake Ontario State Parkway and NY-18 along the lake. You'll be passing fruit farms on one side, the lake on the other. The fast route is via NY-31 or NY-104 west, directly to downtown Niagara Falls.

INSIDERS' TIPS

On your way, there's a public beach at Charlotte and another at Hamlin State Park.

Truly impressive is the Genesee Gorge ♛ ♛ ♛ ♛ in Letchworth State Park ♛ ♛ just 35 miles southwest of Rochester via I-390 to Mount Morris, the northern entrance to the 18-mile-long park. The river has routed out valleys nearly 600 feet deep, with cliffs similar to those at the Grand Canyon. Within the park, the river tumbles over three waterfalls, one of them more than 100 feet high. (The Senecas believed the beauty of the Middle Falls caused the sun to stop in wonder at midday.) The Genesee is one of the few rivers that flows *north*. Its beginnings are on a small farm in Pennsylvania.

Also to be seen is a small Museum of Pioneer and

Indian Life that features Indian artifacts and the fascinating story of Mary Jemison, the "white woman of the Genesee." She was captured by Indians as a child, had two Indian husbands, 8 children, and her own "reservation" where the park now is. Her fence-enclosed grave is located near the 18th-century log Seneca Council House. The life of William P. Letchworth, the benevolent Quaker harness maker whose obsession was to save this land from spoliation, is illustrated as well.

INSIDERS' TIPS

Wine buffs may wish to visit Rochester's own Casa Larga Vineyards & Winery, 2287 Turk Hill Road, Fairport (tel. [716] 223-4210). The Rieslings and Cabernets are excellent and so is the view, from the highest point in Monroe County.

Letchworth Park offers breathtaking views, back-to-nature tranquility, 100 small streams, and gorgeous foliage as the oak, hickory, maple, beech, poplar, and dogwood turn color. The park is popular with campers, but for greater comfort between scenery watches, consider Glen Iris, a comfortable inn (also a good lunch stop) ensconced in Letchworth's home. Views from the inn of Middle Falls are among the best you'll have. In summer, there's often a rainbow over it.

Thrilling white-water rafting is possible at the park from April to October, from Adventure Calls, Inc., 20 Ellicott Ave., Batavia 14020 (tel. [716] 343-4710), at $20 per person.

PERILS & PITFALLS

Foliage time is so popular here, you'll need reservations at Glen Iris months in advance. (See Insiders' Information for address and phone.)

NIAGARA FALLS

The focus of this city of 75,000 is its natural spectacle, the falls. If you haven't been here in years, you'll be pleased to find that much of the commercial tawdriness of the past has been replaced on the American side with attractive, well-maintained modern buildings and an uncluttered park.

> **PERILS & PITFALLS**
>
> Parking can be a problem. Head for the well-marked municipal lots and park your car early. Distances are short and it's easy to get about on foot.

To see the falls, your best alternatives are these:
- **Maid of the Mist**♛♛♛♛, a 20-minute boat trip past the American Falls and into the mouth of the Canadian (Horseshoe) Falls. Breathtaking, beautiful, awe-inspiring—since 1843 the quintessential way to see the Falls. You reach the boat landing from Prospect Point Park via elevator, and buy boat tickets at the bottom. Once you are aboard, hooded slickers are provided (and needed) as protection against the spray. The boat ride can be chilly, even in summer. Best to wear a sweater or jacket, kerchief and sneakers. Tel. (716) 284-4233.

  The *Maid of the Mist* name stems from the legend of an Indian chief's daughter sent over the falls in a canoe with gifts to propitiate the Thunder God living behind the curtain of water. The god reached out and saved her.
- **Observation Tower**♛♛, Prospect Point Park, rises 282 feet from bottom of gorge, overlooks American Falls; elevators descend to base of cliff (where you board *Maid of the Mist* boats) for a close-up view.
- **Niagara Viewmobile**♛♛ tourist "train" makes a 40-minute circuit of major sites, including Prospect Point, Cave of the Winds, and Goat Island. You can stop and re-board. (Fare: adults $2, seniors $1.50, children $1.)
- **Helicopter flights** over the falls are provided by Rainbow Helicopter, 454 Main St., 14303 (tel. [716]

285-0492); and Heussler Air Service, 9900 Porter Rd., 14304 (tel. [716] 282-6964).

■ **Cave of the Winds** ♕ ♕. Via wooden walkways you walk in the gorge between American and Canadian falls at the base of the falls. Rain slickers are provided. Access is from elevator on Goat Island. Call ahead about time and availability of this one. Tel. (716) 285-3641 or 282-8979. Adults $3, seniors and children 12 or younger, $2.50.

For close-ups on foot, you will do best at Prospect Point Park and Goat Island, between Cave of the Winds and Terrapin Point.

On the Canadian side there are dozens of "attractions," but the best one is free—and in our opinion, *the* best on either side of the water. It's the splendid overlook ♕ ♕ ♕ of the entire Canadian Falls, Goat Island, and American Falls panorama from Victoria Park, which is immediately southwest of the Rainbow International Bridge, at the cliff's edge. Someone should give Eye Pollution citations to Kodak and Minolta for their enormous signs on the Canadian side that desecrate the natural beauty of the falls and surroundings. For shame!

INSIDERS' TIPS

There are several commercial observation towers offering prime falls views, but for a smashing view from the Canadian side, try cocktails or tea at the rooftop restaurant in the Sheraton Hotel.

Other U.S. Niagara Falls attractions to consider are these:

Adjoining Prospect Point Park, the shiny new metal office tower is Occidental Chemical's, whose Lobby Gallery presents free exhibits arranged by the Niagara Council of the Arts. There is a "skywalk" from this building to the Rainbow Centre shopping mall, which contains more than 60 shops and restaurants and a parking garage. This adjoins the enormous, 7-story, triangular Wintergarden atrium ♕, filled with tropical plants, birds, and greenery on multiple levels. It is open all year, free, and is a pleasant place to rest.

Near the Wintergarden, at 25 Rainbow Mall, is the Native American Indian Museum, in the shape of a huge turtle (Indian legend said the world was carried on a turtle's back.) Call for exhibits, programs, hours, prices. (We found it inexplicably closed when we tried to visit, though its signs said it was open.) Tel. (716) 284-2427.

Side Trips

Outside Niagara Falls are two features of extraordinary interest. One is Artpark♛ ♛, a 200-acre park 7 miles north of the falls on the R. Moses Parkway in the small town of Lewiston. During the summer this place jumps with concerts, theater, opera, dance, jazz, and artists, craftsmen, and performers doing their things. There are also mammoth, especially commissioned sculptures adorning the grassy hillsides. Park admission is free, but there's a charge for parking, another for theater and events. Tel. (716) 754-9001 or 754-3377.

The second feature is the historic and handsome Old Fort Niagara♛ ♛ ♛, 14 miles north of the falls on the R. Moses Parkway. One of the best of such historic forts to be found anywhere, this one has its original 18th century stone buildings, ramparts, and parapets with excellent displays and costumed "soldiers" and civilians showing how they lived. There are drills, demonstrations, and reenactments, and the setting is beautiful. Tel. (716) 745-7611.

A delightful diversion, especially in warm, sunny weather, is an excursion into Canada from Lewiston via the toll bridge (50¢ for car and driver, 10¢ for each additional passenger—you can pay in either Canadian or U.S. money).

On the Canadian side, drive north 7½ miles on the Niagara Parkway, which borders the river and is lined with tidy farms and roadside fruit stands, to Niagara-on-the-Lake♛ ♛ ♛, a picturebook Victorian village. Queen Street, the main thoroughfare through town, is almost too picture-perfect to be real. For luncheon, high tea, or simply a cooling drink, try the Queens Royal Lounge♛ of the 1864 Prince of Wales Hotel♛ ♛. It's a

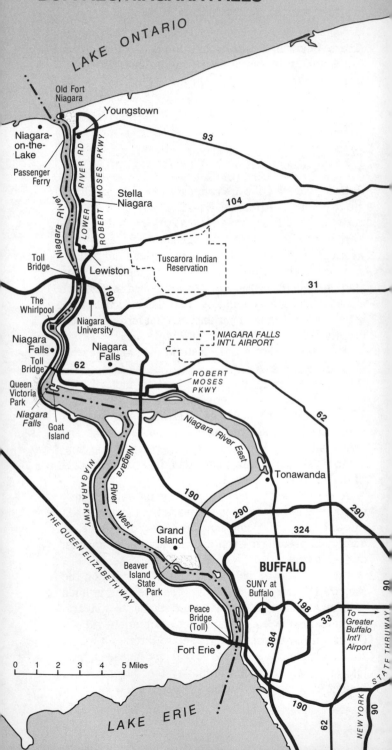

BUFFALO/NIAGARA FALLS

LAKE ONTARIO

Old Fort Niagara

Youngstown

93

Niagara-on-the-Lake

Passenger Ferry

LOWER RIVER RD

ROBERT MOSES PKWY

Stella Niagara

104

Niagara River

Tuscarora Indian Reservation

Toll Bridge

Lewiston

190

31

The Whirlpool

Niagara University

NIAGARA FALLS INT'L AIRPORT

Niagara Falls

Niagara Falls

Toll Bridge

62

ROBERT MOSES PKWY

62

Queen Victoria Park

Niagara Falls

Goat Island

Niagara River East

Niagara River West

NIAGARA PKWY

Tonawanda

190

190

290

290

324

THE QUEEN ELIZABETH WAY

Grand Island

Beaver Island State Park

BUFFALO

SUNY at Buffalo

198

33

To Greater Buffalo Int'l Airport

Peace Bridge (Toll)

Fort Erie

384

90

0 1 2 3 4 5 Miles

NEW YORK

STATE THRUWAY

190

62

LAKE ERIE

proper British pub, serving a generous *prix fixe* buffet and à la carte light lunch selections with Canadian beers on tap.

PERILS & PITFALLS

Canadian money may look the same as U.S. currency, but it's worth about 35 percent less. Forgetful Americans often pay in U.S. currency and blithely accept Canadian money in change without receiving the benefit of the exchange differential. Use your credit card rather than cash in Canada (you'll get the accurate exchange rate when the paperwork is processed). Otherwise, exchange dollars for Canadian money at a bank on the U.S. side before you cross over. Or use your calculator to figure what your U.S./Canadian change should be.

From Niagara Falls, Buffalo is easily reached via I-190, which crosses Grand Island. The drive takes from 20 minutes to an hour, depending on time of day and traffic.

BUFFALO

This city is not all snow and chicken wings—though it has plenty of both.

INSIDERS' TIPS

Famous Buffalo Chicken Wings, those spicy-battered, deep-fried bird limbs, originated at Frank & Teresa's Anchor Bar, 1047 Main Street, late one night by default (improvisation to feed a hungry crowd). They're widely available, but natives insist Anchor's wings are best and spiciest. They come in 3 styles: mild, medium, and incendiary.

Today, New York's second city is surging back from the decline of waning heavy industry. It is an open, airy (often windy) town with a handsome waterfront and some architectural gems, along with splendid museums, theater, music, and sports.

Of special interest, if you respond to architectural

genius, are the city's grand stone churches, with façades, towers, and steeples reflecting European originals. Other architectural delights include Louis Sullivan's 1895 Guaranty Building at 30 Church Street, H. H. Richardson's State Hospital complex, and Buffalo City Hall, a 28-story art deco prize completed in 1931 (try the sweeping view from the top, free, from 9 A.M. to 3:30 P.M. weekdays) at 65 Niagara Street. A bronze sculpture of Grover Cleveland in front reminds you that he was mayor here before becoming President of the United States. A William McKinley monument is another reminder: he was assassinated in Buffalo (though not on this spot) in 1901.

Also notable are Stanford White's Butler Hall♔, 672 Delaware Avenue, and Pratt House♔, 690 Delaware Ave. Frank Lloyd Wright built 5 houses in Buffalo. Most accessible, perhaps, is the 1904 D. D. Martin House♔, 125 Jewett Parkway. By all means, visit the Metro stations♔ of the city's new Niagara Frontier Transportation Authority: Sleekly functional, they feature bold contemporary art.

Art lovers will make the Albright-Knox Art Gallery♔♔♔ their top destination. It is at 1285 Elmwood Avenue (tel. [716] 882-8700). World-renowned for its contemporary art collection, the Albright also has important Impressionist and Post-Impressionist works and fine examples of Cubism, Surrealism, and other 20th-century trends. In short, works by everyone from Gauguin to Giacometti, Lautrec to Lichtenstein, Renoir to Rauschenberg, Van Gogh to Warhol.

PERILS & PITFALLS

If you're driving, keep in mind that the Albright-Knox parking lot demands exact change to be fed into its mechanical maw as you enter. This is a pain and a hazard for the unknowing. Have your 75¢ handy.

Unusual among such institutions is Buffalo's Museum of Science♔♔, Humboldt Parkway (tel. [716] 896-5200). From the outside it looks like many a science museum, but several exhibits inside are unique:

the "Insect World" exhibit (where you go eyeball-to-eyeball with giant butterflies); and "Dinosaurs and Co." The museum also has first-rate exhibits of animals, minerals, and Indian life, and a large, in-depth collection of Japanese and Chinese ceramics and bronzes and Polynesian artifacts.

Famed watercolor artist Charles Burchfield's works can be seen at the Burchfield Art Center♛♛, 1300 Elmwood Avenue (tel. [716] 878-6012). And if you're a fan of Louis Comfort Tiffany, you'll find his windows in Trinity Cathedral♛ on Delaware Avenue.

Another Buffalo treasure is Max Abramowitz's striking Temple Beth Zion♛♛ with its stunning interior and stained-glass "Creation" and "Hallelujah" windows♛♛♛ and Ten Commandment pillars♛ by Ben Shahn. It's at 805 Delaware Avenue (tel. [716] 886-7150), and can be seen by request if you call at the rear door of the complex.

Nearby, at 641 Delaware Avenue, is the imposing Greek Revival Wilcox mansion♛ in which Theodore Roosevelt was sworn in as President after McKinley's assassination. It has memorabilia about T.R., the Pan American Exposition, and the attack on McKinley. Much of the furniture that was here at the time has been returned, so you have an approximation of the house as Teddy saw it (tel. [716] 884-0330).

Delaware Avenue is a prestigious address in Buffalo. F. Scott Fitzgerald lived nearby in the re-gentrified Allentown neighborhood when he was a prep school student at Miss Nardon's Academy. In addition to appealing shops, boutiques, galleries, and eateries, there are open-air events here. Call Allentown Association, 234 Allen Street, 14201 (tel. [716] 881-1024), for information about walking tours.

INSIDERS' TIPS

While you're in the market, try a *kümmelweck,* a Buffalo original. It's a light roll with caraway seeds and salt on top, delicious when filled (typically) with roast beef.

Another stop might be at the Broadway Market, in the heart of Buffalo's old Polish section. This big indoor market is busy and of interest anytime (but don't expect bargain prices) for the variety of ethnic foods it displays. The high point of the year is Holy Week, when all the local food mavens arrive to buy butter molded into lamb shapes, as well as lamb cakes and other Polish Easter specialties.

On the Lake Erie waterfront is Buffalo's Naval and Servicemen's Park♛, where you can visit a World War II U.S. Navy destroyer, a missile cruiser, a PT boat, and a museum. It's at the foot of Main Street and is open daily from April to November. From the park you have a wide-angle view of the Buffalo skyline.

INSIDERS' TIPS

You can tour Buffalo's waterfront in a horse-drawn carriage. Call Buffalo & Erie County Historical Society (tel. [716] 873-9644) or Smoke Creek Carriages (tel. [716] 824-2838) for current prices and availability.

Sports are big in Buffalo. The Buffalo Bills NFL football team plays in Orchard Park (tel. [716] 649-0015); the Buffalo Sabres hockey team plays in Buffalo Memorial Auditorium (tel. [716] 856-3111); and the Buffalo Bisons AAA baseball team plays at War Memorial Stadium (tel. [716] 852-2131).

INSIDERS' TIPS

Skiing, anyone? There are 20 ski areas within 90 miles of Buffalo, the closest only a 45-minute drive from the center of the city.

Side Trip

East Aurora, 13 miles southeast of Buffalo via NY-78/NY-16, is a pleasant small town in which you'll see the charming clapboard cottage♛ that 13th U.S. President Millard Fillmore built for his bride in 1825. It's at 24 Shearer Avenue (tel. [716] 652-1252), and is furnished in 1820s antiques, some of them Fillmore's. (Fillmore may be all but forgotten elsewhere, but he's still appreciated in this area. After he left the presidency, he retired to Buffalo and was so civic-minded that he helped establish many local institutions that are much used and appreciated today. So beware, no jokes about Fillmore in Buffalo, please.)

Within walking distance is the National Historic Landmark Roycroft Campus♛, South Grove Street (tel. [716] 655-0571), with 14 buildings made by followers of Elbert Hubbard (a holistic philosopher and design pioneer who went down with the *Lusitania*).

The rustic Roycroft Inn♛, with its Gothic windows and sturdy wooden Roycroft furniture and woodwork, is open; craftsmen, craft shops, and businesses occupy the other buildings. Roycroft (which stands for "royal craft") was a popular arts and crafts movement in the late 1880s, taking inspiration from the William Morris craft movement in England. Followers believe that Hubbard influenced Frank Lloyd Wright in his back-to-nature approach, a reaction against the Industrial Revolution.

Side Trip

Chautauqua Institution well warrants a visit. It began in 1874 as a 2-week summer training ground for Methodist Sunday school teachers and quickly became a nationwide 19th-century movement featuring education, lectures, and learning.

Its 856 acres on a 20-mile-long lake are embellished with dozens of attractive Victorian buildings and the gigantic 1881 Athenaeum Hotel♛ ♛ ♛. Neither cars nor alcohol are allowed, but there are plenty of porches, rockers, flags, and the best of lake activities, plus golf and tennis.

You could be one of 9,000 students during the annual 9-week summer session, studying a multitude of offerings in a health-and-religion-oriented regimen. Nondenominational Sunday services attract overflow attendance, as do superstar dance, music, and theater performances. (See Insiders' Information at the end of this chapter for details.) Chautauqua Institution is 70 miles southwest of Buffalo via I-90 to NY-394 south at Westfield.

This southwestern part of New York is one of the world's major grape and wine-producing areas. The county has more vineyards than California's Napa and Sonoma counties combined. It's probably no accident that in the small town of Fredonia the Women's Christian Temperance Union was founded in 1873 and nearby Charles Welch established his Concord grape juice company ("God did not mean the grape to be fermented!" he believed) to counter the use of grapes in wine.

There are 8 wineries in the "Lake Erie District," and 5 of them welcome visitors:

- *Chadwick Bay Wine Co.*, 1001 NY-60, Fredonia 14063. Tel. (716) 672-5000.
- *Johnson Estate Wines*, West Main Road, P.O. Box 52, Westfield 14787. Tel. (716) 326-2191.
- *Merritt Estate Winery*, 2264 King Road, Forestville 14062. Tel. (716) 965-4800.
- *Schloss Doepken Winery*, East Main Road, RD 2, Ripley 14775. Tel. (716) 326-3636. Tours by appointment.
- *Woodbury Vineyards*, South Roberts Road, Dunkirk 14048. Tel. (716) 679-1708.

INSIDERS' TIPS

This is also important antiques country. There are two dozen antiques dealers on the "Route 16 Corridor" southeast of Buffalo, and Westfield, on I-90 west of Buffalo, is a major center for antiques shopping.

INSIDERS' INFORMATION FOR THE WEST

Buffalo
(Erie County; Area Code 716)

Hotels
Buffalo Hilton at the Waterfront ♛ ♛ ♛
120 Church St., 14202. Tel. 845-5100
2 persons in twin, $68–96
Multilevel modern hotel facing Lake Erie. 500 rooms, 2 bars, 3 cafés, restaurant with atrium dining, indoor swimming pool, health club, indoor tennis, racquetball,

squash, saunas. All-purpose comfort, attractive lake-front location.

Hyatt Regency Buffalo ♛ ♛ ♛
2 Fountain Plaza, 14202. Tel. 856-1234
2 persons in twin, $105–120
A landmark office building, converted to modern hotel next to the Convention Center and theater district. 400 rooms, bar, café, restaurant ♛ ♛, indoor swimming pool, health club, tennis and golf privileges. Vast, airy atrium with waterfall, live piano music; center of what's happening downtown.

Ramada Renaissance ♛ ♛ ♛
4243 Genesee St., 14225. Tel. (800) 272-6232; 634-2300
2 persons in twin, $ 87–107
Remodeled modern hotel across from Buffalo International Airport entrance. 300 rooms, bar, 2 cafés, restaurant, indoor swimming pool, health club. Comfortable lobby, lively bar, convenient location for car trips around the area.

Hotel Lenox ♛
140 North St., 14201. Tel. 884-1700
2 persons in twin, $48
A refurbished apartment hotel in residential neighborhood. 154 rooms, bar, restaurant. This is something of a "sleeper," clean, comfortable, and modestly priced for its handy in-town location.

Restaurants

E.B. Greens ♛ ♛
2 Fountain Plaza (in Hyatt Regency Buffalo Hotel). Tel. (800) 228-9000; 856-1234
Average dinner: $30
Seafood and open-hearth cooking, Continental menu with *nouvelle* accent, dressy and special. Sunday brunch is a winner here.

Asa Ransom House ♛ ♛
10529 Main St., Clarence Hollow (exit 48A off I-90). Tel. 759-2315
Average dinner: $20
Silversmith Asa Ransom's house dates back to 1801, its life as a tavern to 1853. Two dining rooms brimming with character, antiques, and cozy fireplaces, cheerful

waitresses in 19th-century costumes, homey American specialties served in abundance, at modest prices, all add up to a memorable dining experience for the whole family. Excellent New York State wines available. Closed Fridays and Saturdays (Seventh Day Adventist-owned). Also 4 attractive guest rooms available.

(Frank & Teresa's) Anchor Bar♛
1047 Main St. at High St. Tel. 886-8920
Average dinner: $12.50
From this simple, no-frills neighborhood hangout, Buffalo Barbecued Chicken Wings soared to fame. They still fly high in flavor here.

Cabaret

Tralfamadore Cafe, 100 Theater Pl. (next to Shea's). Tel. 854-1415. Nationally known performers, rock, pop, jazz; comedy every Wednesday.

Theaters

Center Theatre, 681 Main St. Tel. 847-6461 or 831-3742. Showcase for State University of New York at Buffalo's theater and dance department. Performances October to December and February to May.

Kleinhans Music Hall, 370 Pennsylvania St. Tel. 888-5000. Buffalo Philharmonic Orchestra performs regular classical and pop concert series in this Saarinen-designed building with great acoustics.

Shea's Buffalo Center for the Performing Arts, 646 Main Street. Tel. 847-1410. A resuscitated, lavish 1926 movie palace, now the cultural focus of the city, featuring first-rate offerings of all types.

Studio Arena Theater, 710 Main St. Tel. 856-5650. Plays, musicals, specials, and classic films. Season is May to October.

INSIDERS' TIPS

Check *ARTSline* (tel. 847-1444) for round-the-clock hotline of information about music and art events in the area. Also *Buffalo News*'s "Friday Gusto Magazine" for entertainment schedule of the week.

Travel Information

Greater Buffalo Chamber of Commerce, 107 Delaware Ave., 14202. Tel. 852-7100.

Chautauqua
(Chautauqua County: Area Code 716)

Hotel

Athenaeum Hotel♛ ♛ ♛

Janes & South Terrace Aves., Chautauqua 14722. Tel.
(800) 862-1881; in New York State, (800) 821-1881
2 persons in twin, $179 (AP, includes 3 bountiful meals
daily)

An 1881 high-Victorian resort hotel (totally modernized) with lake view. 160 rooms, no TV or room
phones; bar, café, restaurant (♛) (set meal, 2 desserts), tennis, golf, boating. A National Historic site
originally electrified by Thomas Edison, son-in-law of
Chautauqua's founder. Open from late June to late August only.

Restaurant

The White Inn♛ ♛

52 East Main St., Fredonia. Tel. 672-2103
Average dinner: $21
Handsome Victorian interior in venerable hostelry,
featuring contemporary American cuisine by Culinary
Institute of America-graduate chef.

Theater

Chautauqua Institution, Box 1095, Chautauqua
14722. Tel. 357-6200. Each 9-week summer season
offers 21 concerts, operas, dance, jazz programs. Tickets by day, week, or season.

Letchworth Park, Castile (cast-aisle)
(Wyoming County; Area Code 716)

Hotel

Glen Iris Inn♛ ♛

Letchworth State Park, Castile 14427. Tel. 493-2622
2 persons in twin, $42
Pleasant 19th-century house-turned-inn in peaceful
park setting. 20 rooms, bar, café, restaurant♛ ♛, park
facilities, swimming pool, hiking trails. Furnished in
Victorian style, antiques, fine woodwork. Many rooms
have views of stately falls. Rooms are named after trees
in the park: Linden, Cherry, Birch, etc. Open April to
October.

Niagara-on-the-Lake, Canada
(Ontario, Area Code 416)

Hotel

Prince of Wales ♛ ♛

6 Picton St., Niagara-on-the-Lake, Ontario, Canada LOS
1J0. Tel. (800) 263-2452 or (416) 468-3246
2 persons in twin, $63–71
Large brick hotel on village main street. 104 rooms,
pub-like bar, restaurant ♛, lounges, indoor swimming
pool, platform tennis, golf privileges, health club. This
1864 charmer in the English mode is thoroughly up-to-
date in amenities, curb's-eye view of museum-quality
Victorian town.

Theater

Shaw Festival, P.O. Box 774, Niagara-on-the-Lake,
Ontario, Canada LOS 1J0. Tel. (416) 468-2172. Outstanding professional productions of plays by George
Bernard Shaw and others, staged from end of April to
mid-October.

Niagara Falls
(Erie County; Area Code 716)

Shopping

Factory Outlet Mall, 1900 Military Rd., Niagara
Falls 14304. Tel. 773-1797. Canadians flock to the
more than 70 factory outlets here for savings (in spite
of their 70¢ dollars) on famous brands such as Polo/
Ralph Lauren, Bass, Royal Doulton, Van Heusen.

Rainbow Centre Shopping Mall, Rainbow Blvd.
North, Niagara Falls, 14303. Tel. 285-9758. One block
from the falls, air conditioned, free parking, dozens of
shops, department store, restaurant, lounge.

Music

Artpark, Lewiston. Tel. 745-3377 or 754-9001.
Musicals, opera, concerts, jazz, dance by professionals,
performed late June through August.

Information

Niagara Falls Convention & Visitors Bureau, 345
Third St., 14303. Tel. 285-2400. For maps, brochures.
24-hour recorded events info: 278-8112.

Rochester
(Monroe County; Area Code 716)

Hotels

Strathallan♛♛♛♛

550 East Ave., 14607. Tel. 461-5010

2 persons in twin, $65–95

1980 small hotel on millionaire/museum row. 151 rooms (all with kitchenette), rooftop bar, elegant restaurant (♛♛), sauna, solarium, library. Handsome privately owned hotel, popular with business/university visitors, handy to most major city sights. *Chinois* decor in stylish lounge. Note gorgeous antique French reception desk. Concierge, helpful staff. Antique limo does airport shuttle service. Jazz several nights a week in rooftop lounge.

Rochester Hilton♛♛♛

175 Jefferson Rd., 14623. Tel. 475-1910

2 persons in twin, $75–99

Modern 4-story building, next to Rochester Institute of Technology. 170 rooms, bar, restaurant, indoor swimming pool. All the amenities you'd expect from this chain, including luxury-level rooms ($99) with complimentary newspaper, breakfast, bar.

Rose Mansion & Gardens♛♛♛

625 Mt. Hope Ave., 14620. Tel. 546-5426

2 persons in double, $79–89 (incl. continental breakfast)

An 1867 garden-encircled brick-stucco mansion (former home of horticulturist George Ellwanger), handy to downtown. 8 rooms (named after roses), no TV or room phones, beautiful garden. Delightful country inn in the city, friendly young owners, immaculate housekeeping, handsome Victorian salon, beautifully decorated rooms. Ask for "Carrousel"—spacious room with working fireplace.

Oliver Loud's Stagecoach Inn♛♛

1474 Marsh Rd., Bushnell's Basin, Pittsford 14534. Tel. 248-5200

2 persons in double, $115 (incl. continental breakfast)

Authentic clapboard 1814 2-story house located in Rochester suburb. 8 rooms, no TV or room phones, lounge, old-fashioned porch facing canal. Historic old tavern relocated and impeccably restored. Antiques, four-poster canopy beds. Part of Richardson's Canal House Village. Continental breakfast served in picnic basket to each room.

Restaurants

Chapel's (cha-pells') ♛ ♛ ♛ ♛
30 West Broad St. Tel. 232-2300
Average dinner: $31
Simply superb French *nouvelle* cooking in several intimate, exposed-brick dining quarters (a former jail)—"The Duck Room" is especially appealing. Chef-owner Greg Broman's *cuisine du marché* is exquisite, imaginative, everything fresh: sole soufflé, *escalopes* of veal with lemon and mango, veal sweetbread pasta with white truffles. Mouth-watering desserts, fine New York wines.

Edwards ♛ ♛ ♛
1 Academy Pl. Tel. 423-0140
Average dinner: $30–40. Closed Sundays
Stylish dining in Edwardian aura, in transformed basement of historic 1873 Gothic Revival school building. Grilled chicken breast and chestnuts in Calvados sauce, venison medallions in Zinfandel wine are among the select menu choices. Outstanding wine list.

Richardson's Canal House ♛ ♛ ♛
1474 Marsh Rd., Pittsford 14534. Tel. 248-5000
Prix fixe 5-course dinner: $25.
Authentic Federal atmosphere, numerous cozy dining rooms (including several private alcoves for *au deux* dining—nicknamed "Sin Bins" by staff), in 1818 Erie Canal tavern. Food thoroughly modern, with expert New American renderings (duckling with apricot/strawberry glaze, beef tenderloin with leek Hollandaise). Lunch buffet and *prix fixe* dinner bargains. Choice wine list includes winning New York selections.

Strathallan ♛ ♛
550 East Ave. Tel. 461-5010
Average dinner: $31
Handsome decor, contemporary menu with regional/seasonal specialties. Excellent Caesar salad prepared tableside. Good wine selection.

Daisy Flour Mill♨
1880 Blossom Rd., 14625. Tel. 381-1880
Average dinner: $24
Atmospheric, with a capital *A*, is this rustic restaurant in an 1848 mill building. You dine amid massive machinery on regional treatments of beef, poultry, seafood.

Jazzberry's♨
715 Munroe Ave., 14620. Tel. 244-5040
Ethnic and vegetarian selections. Good choice for Sunday brunch, snack, or light meal in rejuvenated 1900s firehouse. Excellent beer list. Jazz and name entertainers. Closed Mondays.

Oven Door Bakery & Soupçon
Locust Grove, Bushnell's Basin, Pittsford. Tel. 248-5749
Modest soup and sandwich spot across from Richardson's Canal House. Delicious baked goods at bakery. Good choice for breakfast or light lunch. Closed Mondays.

INSIDERS' TIPS

If you crave something ethnic, trendy, or inexpensive, head for Park Ave. and Alexander St., dubbed Restaurant Row, with dozens of shops and eateries.

Pubs

Blades, 1290 University Ave. Tel. 442-6979. A popular watering hole in *fin de siècle* saw-blade factory, with outdoor patio. Great bar, inside and out. Good raw bar too.

California Brew House, 402 West Ridge Rd. Tel. 621-1480. Largest beer selection in town. (Locals will tell you Rochester is the largest consumer of imported beer of any city its size in the United States.)

Cheers, 293 Alexander St. Tel. 262-4710. Great for snacks and pre-dinner gatherings. Free hot and cold buffet from 5 to 9 P.M. nightly.

Hattie's, Strathallan Hotel, 550 East Ave. Tel. 461-5010. A delightful top-floor lounge/bar with twinkly nighttime city views. Fireplace and decor create comfortable living room ambiance. Jazz for listening and dancing.

Lloyd's, 289 Alexander St. Tel. 546-2211. English pub look, with fireplace and second-floor balcony. Outdoor patio, too. A popular local hangout. Jazz upstairs.

Oswald's Hof-Brau Haus, 406 Lyell Ave. Tel. 254-9660. Bill Oswald's Old World *Gasthaus* specializes in *bier,* Bavarian cooking, and *musik.* More than 50 varieties of imported and domestic beers. (Oktoberfest is the *utmost.*)

Shopping

Village Gate Square, 274 N. Goodman St. (near U of Rochester). Old printing factory converted to indoor/outdoor shopping complex. Dozens of individual shops: clothes, jewelry, crafts, antiques.

Theaters and Concert Halls

Dryden Theater, 900 East Ave. (on Eastman House grounds). Tel. 271-3361, ext. 213. Call for information about film series (from silent classics to avant-garde and foreign works).

Eastman Theatre & Kilbourn Hall, Eastman School of Music, Gibbs and East Main Sts. Tel. 275-3111. Daily concerts by students at this famous school, at little or no charge: classical, opera, jazz. Call for information.

GeVa Theatre, 75 Woodbury Blvd. at South Clinton Ave. Tel. 232-1363. Equity repertory company presents 8 productions a year in historic building.

Travel and Recreation Information

Visitors Information Center, 120 East Main St., Rochester 14604. Tel. 546-3070.

FunFone Recorded (Rochester) Events Listing Tel. 546-6810.

INDEX